THE INDOCHINA CHRONICLES

Travels in Laos, Cambodia and Vietnam

PHIL KARBER

Times Editions
Marshall Cavendish

Author: Phil Karber
Cover picture: Eric and Hoa Herter

Published by Marshall Cavendish Editions
An imprint of Marshall Cavendish International
1 New Industrial Road, Singapore 536196

Other Marshall Cavendish Offices:

Marshall Cavendish Ltd. 119 Wardour Street, London W1F OUW, UK • Marshall Cavendish Corporation. 99 White Plains Road, Tarrytown NY 10591-9001, USA • Marshall Cavendish Beijing. D31A, Huatingjiayuan, No. 6, Beisihuanzhonglu, Chaoyang District, Beijing, The People's Republic of China, 100029 • Marshall Cavendish International (Thailand) Co Ltd. 253 Asoke, 12th Flr, Sukhumvit 21 Road, Klongtoey Nua, Wattana, Bangkok 10110, Thailand • Marshall Cavendish (Malaysia) Sdn Bhd, Times Subang, Lot 46, Subang Hi-Tech Industrial Park, Batu Tiga, 40000 Shah Alam, Selangor Darul Ehsan, Malaysia

Marshall Cavendish is a trademark of Times Publishing Limited

National Library Board (Singapore) Cataloguing in Publication Data

Karber, Phil, 1951.
      The Indochina Chronicles : travels in Laos, Cambodia and Vietnam / Phil Karber.
– Singapore : Times Editions-Marshall Cavendish, c2005.

      p. cm. Includes bibliographical references and index.
      ISBN : 981-261-036-7

1. Karber, Phil, 1951 — Travel – Indochina. 2. Indochina – Description and travel. I. Title.

      DS535
      915.9 — dc21   SLS2005032410

Printed in Singapore by Utopia Press Pte Ltd

To Joyce, Joellen,

Maggie and Parker

My sense is that cultures and individuals are subtler than their governments and actually are the only way we can make bridges between them. Governments are rooted in their ideologies and survive by keeping up the sense of "us" versus "them." They have to have a keen sense of enmity; whereas many individuals don't have that. So that's one reason I've become a great advocate of travel, especially for Americans. I think it's dangerous in a global world to screen ourselves from realities.

—Pico Iyer, travel writer, A Sense of Place.

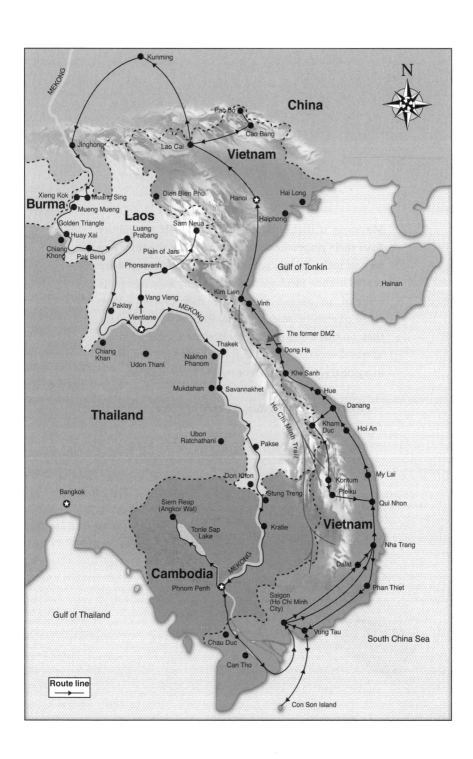

Contents

Prologue

The war in Indochina first touched me and my hometown of Fort Smith, Arkansas, in 1966, my sophomore year of high school. During a pep rally one Friday morning, the head football coach walked onto the field to present one of the team's outstanding former linemen, Charlie Belue, five years my senior. Until the coach said his name, no one recognized him. He was a shadow of his former robustness, after having taken just one wrong step in Vietnam, onto a landmine.

Old Belue didn't take the mike for a speech. He never was much of a talker, but that day his presence spoke volumes. Hobbling on crutches, he put his weight onto his right leg and new orthotic foot, with the left leg of his jeans folded back at the knee. The students applauded thunderously. He seemed embarrassed, though, by all this attention. I was transfixed, blanking out the cheers around me, my pulse racing in empathetic terror. If the war could do that to Old Belue, a natural born fighter, then we were all in for a heap of trouble.

Over the next two years I began to sense that I too would likely be sent to Vietnam. It was otherwise the happiest time of my life there in Fort Smith, a blue-collar town of 50,000 at the foothills of the Ozark Mountains, along the bluffs and banks of the Arkansas River. There were beautiful estates mixed with Babbit-style neighborhoods, sylvan hillsides and stream-fed valleys. Rodeo arenas, well-groomed baseball parks and football stadiums were hallowed ground, lighting up the nights with the magic of the Maji's North Star. White church steeples fenced the horizons. With Cleaver-family conformity, the Karbers took pride in our prim slice of America.

The widening Arkansas River slips around the city in a light brown noose, cinched firmly with middle-America morals, and knotted loosely on the outer banks with old outlaw enclaves with names like Tenkiller and Shady Grove. Long ago known as "Hell on the Border," Fort Smith was famous for its "hanging judge," Isaac Parker. In the latter part of the 19th century, Judge

Parker sent 79 outlaws to the gallows, thus a determined runner-up to Robespierre's guillotine notches a century before. The judge's whitewashed gallows are now enshrined as Fort Smith's main historical attraction, located just off Garrison Avenue, the frontier business district where five brothels operated openly throughout my rite-of-passage years.

About five miles from Fort Smith was a World War II army base, Fort Chaffee, where my father John Karber Jr. spent weekends training as a pilot in the Arkansas National Guard. He wore a uniform 30 years, both in the Guard and during World War II. He had a day job as County Agent—the local Mr. Green Acres.

On parade day at the end of the Guard's summer training in the stifling heat of August, Governor Faubus would drive up from Little Rock, join the flag rank officers in the shaded reviewing stand, and fan his fedora while inspecting the troops as they marched to Sousa. Owing our livelihood to Roosevelt's New Deal, my mother and father would line their five boys up in stair-step formation to shake hands with the defiant segregationist governor, himself a Democrat.

One of my first jobs was shining boots at 50 cents a pop for my dad's officer friends during summer camp starting in 1960. After a few years of that easy money and several other summer jobs, I was a civilian KP (kitchen patrol) at Fort Chaffee, a job that paid $1.70 an hour for washing crusty pots and pans and peeling potatoes 12 hours a day, six days a week. It sounds like penance, but by all accounts at the time I had landed a plum job.

During those years, my passions were less for work, study and sports, and more for fast cars, whiskey and fast girls. My indulgences soon caught the attention of local police and school officials. Although I had been kicked out of school several times, and thrown in jail more often than that, my rebelliousness caught fire in 1968.

That same epochal year, rebellion and turbulence seemed to be sweeping all of America, even the planet's far reaches. On January 23rd the USS Pueblo was captured by North Korean gunboats, a stunning escalation of the Cold War. A week later the Tet offensive swept South Vietnam. Many American bases were nearly overrun. The evening news broadcast play-byplay glimpses of fighting in the streets of Saigon and Hue. The body bags piled up. Militarily the Viet Cong and North Vietnamese lost heavily—up to 100,000 killed—but politically they may have won the war during those weeks following Tet.

I had many friends in Vietnam at the time, some I knew to be in heavy combat—in alien places like Pleiku and I Corps. By the end of March, with the feverish fighting of Tet ongoing, U.S. President Johnson announced he would not seek re-election. He was a man defeated by his own dilemma; the demons of Hanoi and Ho Chi Minh had consumed him personally and politically.

Only a few days later, on April 4th, Dr. Martin Luther King was assassinated on a balcony of the Lorraine Motel in Memphis, Tennessee. With the country already riven by race riots, Dr. King—the voice of reason, of Ghandi-esque passive resistance—had disappeared in a single puff of focused hatred. The streets of urban America quaked for weeks, while race riots spread to over 130 cities.

The all-white Fort Smith School Board held out to the bitter end on desegregation, and had only partly integrated by the time I'd entered high school. They couldn't bring themselves to give Dr. King the same remembrance accorded President Kennedy a few years before, voting only to allow the blacks to leave school to watch the funeral. I walked off campus that day anyway, and was kicked out of school for my act of disobedience. I did, however, see part of the funeral. Senator Robert Kennedy delivered a healing eulogy.

Only a month and a half later, I was en route to my early morning summer job as a civilian KP at Fort Chaffee. The car radio was all news...Robert Kennedy had been shot the night before and died in the early morning hours. It was a somber, tiring day. Although Kennedy had run on an anti-war platform, even the GIs hung their heads.

By mid-August my KP gig was up, and I collected my last paycheck of $70 early one Friday evening. After a typical weekend evening of good-ole-boy fun, around midnight I went home and threw a pile of clothes into the middle of my bed sheet, tied it in a knot, and slunked out my bedroom window like a cat burglar stealing my own freedom. Three friends were waiting outside in a white Ford Fairlane. Within minutes the car swung over the Oklahoma bridge and before daylight we were on Route 66 pointed in the direction of California.

It was our first trip to the ocean, and practically my first trip out of Arkansas. When we stopped to refuel in Albuquerque the next evening, I mailed my father a postcard telling him of my plans. We pushed on through Arizona, popping NoDoz to stay awake, suffering through the desert heat. VW vans of hippies passed us waving the peace sign all the way to Santa Monica.

We spent our first evening there prowling Sunset Boulevard, the world of Kookie Burns and 77 *Sunset Strip*, or so we thought. The neon lights and cacophony of music, cars and people were simply surreal. Apparently, we made an impression as well. The guys we encountered—all with long hair, scraggly beards, wild-eyes—jeered at the four of us, in our buttoned-down Gant shirts, khaki slacks, penny loafers. The chicks snickered, calling us the "Bobsy Twins."

Irritated by the cute remarks, we huddled, deciding to blend in better by checking out the "head" shops. The wild-eyed guys and gals all seemed to like incense, so we bought a double handful of strawberry and banana flavor, retreating to our white Fairlane. For what must have been an hour we sat chugging beers and sniffing the joss. In the rear-view mirror, we checked our pupils for that wild, dilated look.

Upon our return to Fort Smith the local newspaper ran a feature story on our adventure: "California Dreamers" or some such headline, but it left out many of the sordid details of our sojourn, like the brothels of Tijuana.

Back in the Midwest at the Democratic National Convention in Chicago, social unrest and national disunity dominated prime time television. Outside the Hilton Hotel where the convention was held, the Illinois National Guard cordoned the streets around Chicago's Lincoln Park with bayonets; their intimidation was real.

Mayor Daley's police bludgeoned yippies and hippies and college preppies who dared protest the Vietnam War. When the tear gas cleared, Senator

Hubert Humphrey had been nominated among a divided Democratic field—the anti-war factions of Eugene McCarthy and the late Robert Kennedy. Out of that turbulent convention, Mayor Daley became America's poster boy for police brutality. The Chicago Seven—Abbie Hoffman, Jerry Rubin and Tom Hayden to name a few—rose to the national stage as folk heroes after being indicted for crossing state lines to incite a riot. Hubert Humphrey, tainted by the Johnson years of deceit over Vietnam, lost the election to Nixon by a narrow margin, and till this day, the fragmented Democratic Party has never returned to their pre-1968 glory.

As for my slant on Chicago, I had been schooled to believe that communist authoritarianism was the greatest threat to the freedoms of mankind. The Chicago police had bludgeoned those freedoms; they had blurred the lines between democracy and totalitarianism. As for overzealous cops, I had had plenty of experience with them back in Fort Smith.

October rolled around. I left a party one night with a good friend to reload on beer and whiskey. We pulled out of the liquor store and hadn't gone 100 yards when the blue lights of bad luck spun behind us. I was already on probation for a handful of misdemeanor arrests, mostly for possession of alcohol, and I had only recently spent four days in jail. So this time I made a dash for it, ignoring the cop's warning shots fired into the night air. I dodged arrest for a few days. After landing back in jail, the judge gave me a choice between serious jail time or joining the military. On Halloween, I turned 17, old enough to enlist in the army, my father's branch of the service.

The Beatles' *White Album* came out in November: "Back in the U.S.S.R.," and "Happiness is a Warm Gun." I partied through several days of that month, with a friend I had known since we were pre-school tykes, Jackie Gilker. We argued which cult of masculinity was tougher, the army or the marines, the branch his dad had served in World War II. It would have been filial impiety for Jackie to join anything but the marines. So he did.

The same month, another good friend, Carl Bates, was home on leave from the army before his year's tour in Vietnam. Playing poker together one night, I told him I was on my way to the army. Next morning, Carl accompanied me to the recruiter's office and cosigned my enlistment papers. The army, in return, gave him an extra week's leave. What did I want to be in the army, the recruiter asked. Not comfortable with wanting to be anything in the army, I turned to Carl for advice. He asked if I could type, which indeed I could. "Well, become a clerk like me," he said. So I did.

Around the same time another friend returned on leave after spending the last year as an infantryman with the First Air Cavalry in Vietnam. Tuck Freeman had been in the thick of it in the Tet Offensive of 1968. Outwardly, he appeared the same—sandy locks of thick, curly hair, downy-faced good looks, and a hipster swagger. But he had changed. He spoke "Namese"—*bukku, di di* motherfucker, gooks, Charlie, search and destroy. He even favored the laid-back jargon of my black friends: "Hey man. Dude. That's cool."

One Saturday night that fall we doubled-dated to a school boy fraternity dance. My date and I danced to ditties by the Boxtops, The Kingsmen, and Mitch Ryder and the Detroit Wheels. But Tuck danced all night by himself, playing an imaginary guitar—removed from the scene as if a stranger in town.

Later at his place Tuck and I sipped on a pint of cheap bourbon and chain-smoked cigarettes. From his dresser drawer, he took out his ribbons—two purple hearts and a silver star. Then he showed me pictures of four dead "gooks," two of them with slit throats. They had been captured and tried to escape. Tuck had chased down one of the young men and sliced his throat with his bayonet. Then he took the pictures.

Tuck's stories left an impression I could not easily shake off the next morning. As we gorged on one of his mama's famous country breakfasts—ham, eggs, biscuits and gravy—I kept looking into his face for a twitch, some sign of derangement. Instead, as his mama pampered her youngest son, he seemed like the same average American boy I had met on the basketball court a few years before. I went on to church that morning, and Tuck left for Fort Hood. He was excited about seeing his Nam buddies again. The night before, he'd confided that he and his friends had packed their duffel bags with some heroin. It was waiting for them at Fort Hood.

After that evening, I found the mental geography of Vietnam disorienting. Tuck's postwar self was not of the heroic cool personified in my favorite westerns and war movies. Tuck had been dancing with ghosts and bloody ghouls. He had lost his youthful innocence, leapfrogged into the seen-it-all heaviness of an old man. I would meet more like him as the months and years passed.

I joined the green machine on December 10th, 1968. Within weeks of basic training at Fort Polk, Louisiana, I had learned the same words Tuck knew to describe the Vietnamese—"chinks, dinks, zips and gooks." In my training unit was a small squad of pro football players—Jim Beirne, Roy Hopkins and Larry Carwell—Houston Oilers all. It seemed unfair that those prime physical specimens—seemingly possessed with courage—had found their way into the Texas National Guard, in the off-season no less, and would be taking a pass on the war in Indochina. They were accompanied by an elite group of educated white guys who had found their own connections with the local draft boards and National Guard units. The rest of us—90 percent of the company—were lower class, mostly black. Or like me, they were guys who had failed to use their middle-class connections.

The blacks were a platoon of in-your-face rage. They were angry to the bone at whites—and not at the Red Hordes of Vietnam. Muhammad Ali (nee Cassius Clay) spoke for them when he declared, "Ain't no Viet Cong ever called me nigger."

Near the end of basic training and after a long day at the rifle range, I was mustered into formation together with several black draftees, many from inner Detroit. Like a work gang, we boarded a bus that took us to "Tiger Camp," the dreaded infantry-training center, where we were offloaded and ordered into an empty World War II era barracks. Bleary eyed, we spent the next two hours taking the G.E.D. exam (the high school equivalency test).

That was my high school graduating class. My "yearbook" pictures from basic training featured me half-showing a peace sign, only months after my wide-eyed sojourn to California. My travel boots were just getting some traction; Indochina was echoing in the distance.

Before that summer's end, Jackie Gilker and Carl Bates returned from Vietnam in body bags. Tuck Freeman, however, met a different fate. I saw him a few years ago for lunch, about the time he turned 50. I had a hamburger. He threw back three beers, plus 20 milligrams of valium. The local police had just charged Tuck for attempted manslaughter after he turned a butcher knife on an acquaintance while in a drunken rage. Tuck's face was grizzled; his teeth traced in green, like algae on worn limestone. His eyes were hollow, hardly visible under the weight of his lids. Not a peekaboo from his former self. Tuck's 1968 tour in Vietnam had no tidy ending.

Introduction

One Friday night in the spring of 2002, I set out from my residence in Hanoi's French Quarter together with an English friend to begin a 4,000 mile journey. We cabbed through the raucous cavalcade of motorcycles and beeping taxis on Tran Hung Dao Street, the tree-lined boulevard-approach to the Hanoi railway station, *Ga Hanoi*. The street was named for the Vietnamese commander-in-chief who repelled the 13th-century Mongol invasion dispatched by the great one himself, Kublai Khan. Tran Hung Dao and many other semi-mythical warriors from Vietnam's heroic past are honored in every city with prominent streets bearing their names. The nation revels in its long history of resistance to invading foreign powers.

Stepping out of the taxi at the French-built station into a souk's snare, we were surrounded by money changers, postcard boys and a string of frail market ladies under palm-leaf hats, yoked for life by shoulder poles carried like crucifixes for the peasant caste.

From here, we would travel the roads, rivers and rails of the former French and now communist Indochina—Vietnam, Laos and Cambodia. Having lived in Hanoi for four years up to that point, my circumstances—as an American veteran and insatiable traveler living in the bosom of the former beast—struck me as a calling to canvass postwar Indochina.

Three decades after the war, its aftershocks still convulse through my generation, and it remains a tar-baby in American politics. In the paddies of Indochina, far from American preoccupations, the war quite literally continues to detonate. Although I had succeeded in pushing the war aside within my own life, living in Hanoi I came to recognize how greatly it still shapes everyday life in Southeast Asia.

My destination would be the route itself. Unlike other trips to exotic places, this trip would be one where my memories would shape my impressions, and my own aging would be juxtaposed against an area I helped devastate. My fellow traveler was Simon Redington, a London artist and friend who lives seasonally in Hanoi. Simon was nine years old in 1968 and eating "baked beans on toast during tea time" when he first viewed the rat-a-tat-tat geography of Vietnam on television news.

Raised in a well-known London theatrical family, Simon attended art school at the University of London. After completing his degree, he continued to paint while tuning into Punk Rock music and squatting in nearly derelict housing on the south side of the city. He financed his artistic pursuits by working variously as a hospital porter, dustman, street sweeper, and art therapist in a psychiatric hospital, before becoming a social worker dealing with the homeless. Through it all, he became a kind of anthropologist of the urban jungle. "The duty of the artist is to live the artist's life," he is fond of saying.

In the early 1990s, he was creating powerful etchings of London's downtrodden, set against the ironic backdrop of the moribund institutions charged with their care, in which he had worked. By 1996, a foggy montage of unrequited loves and his own dark artistic creations in the London East End led him to seek clarity and refuge in Hanoi.

The first half of our journey would, with a couple of detours, follow the Mekong River, the lifeblood for much of Indochina and a watershed still fresh with the stain of war. We would descend from Yunnan—China's southernmost province, through which the river passes—to Vietnam's Mekong Delta, a region known in ancient times as Funan. Most of Indochina's diverse ethnic groups have made part or all of the same journey, filtering down from India or China through the Mekong River Basin, endowing the region with its cultural sustenance. The last half of our Indochinese wander would be from Saigon (Ho Chi Minh City) to Hanoi, the axis of war remembered by most Americans.

After a night of sleep during the train's climb toward China, we were jolted into dawn in Vietnam's northern border city of Lao Cai, razed by the Chinese in 1979 as payback for Vietnam's military incursion into Cambodia.

Simon dashed outside for a cigarette and some fresh air, almost in the same breath. Facing another 24 hours on the train to Kunming, the capital of Yunnan Province, he gave a young market girl selling baguettes three dollars and sent her after a bottle of *ruou thuoc*, Vietnamese rice whiskey.

She returned in a few minutes feigning high drama by concealing the liter bottle of bourbon-tinged solution and floating detritus from the view of two policemen standing nearby. It was a vain attempt to avoid giving them a cut of her early morning windfall.

As we crossed the river to Hekou, the Chinese side of the border, a wacky tour guide, speaking snatches of six languages, stuck his head in our compartment offering his services in each flavor. Meanwhile, the Chinese immigration police were attempting to extort $20 from a young American couple two cabins down. Such common scam proceeds dwarf their salaries. They stopped by our cabin, pointed to the Antarctica stamp in my passport from a Brazilian research station and guffawed in Chinese.

Taking advantage of a three-hour layover, we walked the banks of the Red River, the breadbasket of northern Vietnam. With its source in China, the river eventually courses through Hanoi and out to the South China Sea. Antiquated bicycles, fashioned out of industrial-strength iron with attached carts, shuttled their brimming loads through the streets of Hekou. In the market, men in olive drab pith helmets and women in conical hats mingled with huddles of hill people in traditional raiments of homespun indigo hemp crowned in headdresses of tartan towels. Along the central market street, stir-crazed hedgehogs and coiled cobras were confined in metal cages next to aquariums of Red River catfish. Buckets of eels and croaking frogs were set amid a blaze of fruits, vegetables and spices. The busy street was bracketed by several wild game restaurants fronted by braziers with open fires and tandoori-style ovens. Hawkers offered hedgehog and cobra, two of Hekou's hottest dishes.

Many of the animals and animal parts leaving Vietnam—bear's gallbladder, anteater's tail, tiger bones, turtles and various snakes—cross the border at Lao Cai, supplying the raw materials for traditional medicines and aphrodisiacs for Chinese men.

By late afternoon the train coursed along a dizzying aerie that tumbled into a jagged gorge. The river was a distant ribbon of *café au lait*, whipped into a white froth at times, pouring through the narrow ravine. Curved rice paddies rose from the lofty valley walls like steps for a giant climbing to the heavens. The manicured symmetry of vegetable plots bore the fingerprint of the human hand. It was the *crachin* season, the time when foggy skies shroud the region in an atmospheric malaise.

I joined Simon in the dining car. A cook in greasy kitchen whites donned a paper toque, wearing it in a stylish tilt. He chopped up beef gristle and greens, while a cigarette drooped from his mouth. The ash fell where he stood.

The windows were open, the air crisp and liberating as the train climbed on through hill tribe hamlets opportunistically anchored to the upper slopes. Hearing the approach of the train, swarms of shirtless men emerged from tents—*corvee* laborers, caterwauling like inmates on visitor's day. The hardiest of women defied gravity along the abrupt slopes, dressed in flashy headdresses, leggings, culottes and vests: doll-like props on the vast mountainous backdrop. We ate from tin trays filled with squares of vegetables and rice, feasting on our TV dinners tuned to the dreamy landscape scrolling by.

At dawn's break we arrived in Kunming, where the ancient hill tribe markets, rusticated Buddhist temples and the medieval wooden city, are hidden like fossils beneath the aggressive skyward advance of modern monoliths: towering trade centers, department stores, supermarkets and superhighways. Having skipped the Industrial Revolution in favor of Mao and the Cultural Revolution, China is now making up for lost time, purging the past in favor of *fazhun*, or development, which is the motto of modern China. Their ancient history of cultural development and massive public works programs—the Grand Canal, the Great Wall, the Forbidden City—makes them once again believe in themselves as celestial heirs to the Middle Kingdom. Although this fluorescence of *fazhun* shadows Indochina, throughout our southerly journey, we would not see any place so modern as Kunming.

We hired a car and driver at the local Holiday Inn, and throttled onto a six-lane national highway, or *guadao*, that unfurled itself in fairway fashion through mountainous terrain in the direction of Jinghong. In only six years, China's 1,800 miles of dual carriageways have become 12,000 miles. We raced along until the road dwindled to one lane, forcing us to adjust our estimated arrival time in Jinghong from six hours to 12 hours.

Loosely rooted villages grew along the steep ridges of the Ailao Shan mountains. With an archway of Chinese characters, each village gate opened into a scrofulous gathering of brick huts with thatch or russet-tile roofs, their front doors hung in bulbous lanterns like last year's Christmas ornaments. Cocks of paddy straw, fodder for the domestic animals, were wrapped around bamboo masts and held aloft on stilts. Men congregated in front of shops to smoke from cannon-size bamboo water pipes, exhaling clouds of tobacco smoke. One proud man walked down the middle of the road displaying a fresh-caught cobra over six feet in length, beaming as if he'd won a lottery.

Around the larger villages and cities, such as Yuanjiang and Mojiang, which were once known as "brigades" during Mao's Cultural Revolution, towering smokestacks rose above white-tile buildings, glazed in smoky-blue.

Many of the near-perpendicular hillsides were corduroyed in government tea plantations. The glossy, green-leafed camellia bushes were first grown here almost exclusively for Chinese consumption. But in the 17th century, the British took such a liking to it that the import of tea caused a substantial trade imbalance. This fiscal dilemma prompted the British East India Company to force the sale of foreign opium on the Chinese peasantry, a misguided policy with an enduring legacy.

To the east of Simao, as the valley narrowed, we twined upward through the twilight of mature conifers, paced by carbon-spewing cargo trucks, all uniformly painted in cerulean blue, grumbling their way uphill.

Suddenly the sky darkened. Gale-force winds ripped through the river divide, tossing trees into the road before us like matchsticks. The roofs flew off several houses. Rain gushed headlong as if unleashed by a broken dam. We watched as a loaded sleeper-bus slid from the road and came to rest in a 30-degree lean against a rock wall. Bedding and few clothes were scattered around the skeletal remains of several huts. Suddenly the angry sky turned calm. We had witnessed a spring tornado. Yet as the hill people instantly began reconstituting their huts and returned to the slushy mud of their paddies, I imagined them singing "my country, my country, is where the rain falls."

An hour later we were passing along a boulevard-like road wicketed with white-painted trees. Vendors stacked watermelons in perfect pyramids the size of huts. "All the tea in China" was illustrated in an ocean of hilltops planted in tea. Darkness fell by the time we reached Jinghong, announced by the smoky pink and blue glow of the modernist tower surmounting the new bridge over the Mekong River—the lifeblood for much of Indochina and the perfect compass for much of our journey.

Although most of our planet was mapped long ago, the source of the Mekong was not pinpointed until 1994, when French adventurer Michel Peissel found it bubbling out of a rocky hillside at an altitude of 16,318 feet, in Rupsa-la Pass in eastern Tibet. From there, the rivulet courses 2,697 miles to its bountiful dispersion in the Mekong Delta of Vietnam and out into the South China Sea.

In the middle years of the 19th century, the Mekong region attracted the imperialist ambitions of France—a response to Russia and England's grab for land in Central Asia, the "Great Game." The French were lured by commercial prospects and by a rationalized calling to tame the "savages" of the lower Mekong through a policy of *mission civilsatrice*—all similar in time and spirit to Queen Victoria's Pax Britannia.

Seeking to chart a navigable trade route to China, France dispatched Doudart de Lagree on a fact-finding mission up the Mekong in 1866, traveling via gunboat, barge, elephant, horse and palanquin. Two years later, after a series of setbacks, Lagree perished of tropical diseases and liver tumors near Kunming. Meanwhile, the remaining members of the expedition led by Francis Garnier arrived at Dali, a walled Muslim enclave on the shores of Lake Erhai in Yunnan. Receiving news of Lagree's death, and under threat of violence by the Sultan of Dali to depart the region, Garnier decided to halt the beleaguered expedition and return to Vietnam. Yet this French project managed to accurately map approximately 1,700 miles of the Mekong and its environs, provided landscape engravings of the catchment area, and recorded insights into the anthropology of the river's boundary states.

France's subsequent gunboat diplomacy—an integral component of the nation's *mission civilsatrice*—helped it colonize Vietnam, Cambodia and Laos by the end of the 19th century, making the middle and lower Mekong a *de facto* French conduit. It would be almost a century before the middle-to-lower boundary countries of the Mekong regained a phase of relative peace, stability and independence.

The Mekong's long journey unveils painterly landscapes, rich histories, and countless cultures. Many of the river's inhabitants have ancient forgotten roots in the Middle Kingdom, having fled from the hegemonic Chinese centuries ago. The myriad peoples of the Mekong—Bai, Dai, Shan, Lao-lum, Thais, Khmers, Chams, Viets and many others—all cultivate wet rice and have domesticated the water buffalo.

Buddhism is the most pervasive religion along the Mekong, from the Mahayana school that holds sway in Tibet, to Theravadism in Indochina. Never far away is the crescent moon that rises above Islam's mosques or the holy cross of Christianity perched atop old French missionary churches. The sacred *lingam* of Siva pops up in ancient temples along the river, Hinduism having predated the arrival of Buddhism in many places. And not far beneath the surface, animist spirits, inhabiting all living and inanimate forms of nature, remain as very much a part of the culture. Animism, the most elemental source of riverine cosmology, ties together the many forms of modern religious beliefs.

While making its fructifying journey to the South China Sea, the fabled waterway weaves together six nations. Yet the Mekong states do not even agree on a common name for the river. In the stark eastern Tibetan Plateau, the river is known as the Dzachu, "River of Rocks." As it plunges from its headwaters, falling through the uninhabitable gorges of northern Yunnan Province toward China's borders, the river drops 14,760 feet in altitude and is called Lancang Jiang, "Turbulent River." It is known in Laos and Thailand as the "Mother of The Waters" or *Mae Nam Khong*, the contraction of which became the familiar name adopted by European explorers.

In Cambodia, the river feeds into Tonle Sap lake, seasonally increasing the lake's size by 60 percent and forming the largest lake in Southeast Asia, with one of the densest fish populations in the world. It is not surprising that the Cambodian name for the river is Tonle Thom, or the "Great One." In the Mekong Delta, the Vietnamese call their venerated realm of the river Cuu Long, or Nine Dragons—a lucky number and a symbol of power for the former Vietnamese emperors.

The theater of the Vietnam War did not end at some mythical Khmer ruins in Cambodia, as depicted in the movie *Apocalypse Now*. Instead, it spanned another 1,000 miles through Laos and ended at the Chinese border. At the time, the Mekong served as a porous "Berlin Wall" for most of its path upriver to China.

A Trip Down The Mekong

You Like Opium?

Jinghong was the northern-most point on the Mekong traveled by the French on their epic journey over 130 years ago. Based on local advice, the experiences of other overland travelers I had met, and tips along the internet trail, Jinghong seemed to be the best starting point for a casual descent of the river. Off and on for two days, we lurked around the loading docks and the Mei Mei Café, a backpacker hotspot, to try to scare up a boat.

The buffalo burger at the Mei Mei Café aside, the frontier city has taken on a Chinese countenance: a façade of white-tiled concrete buildings glassed in blue, karaoke bars and the ethnic majority Han Chinese outnumbering by a four-to-one ratio the 30,000-strong Dai people, who were pushed into the south of China and northern mountains of Southeast Asia by the Mongol hordes in the 13th century. Filling the streets in uncommon numbers, Dai monks wore saffron, the soothing logo of the Theravada Buddhists of Southeast Asia.

It was easy to pick out the Dai women, adorned in vivid colors with babies slung to their backs. Like the other ethnic minorities, the Dai are not bound by the Chinese one-child policy. They are, however, in theory limited to two children. But as one local woman pointed out, "Farmers need a boy. Boom, boom, boom—until boy."

After a thorough search of the Mei Mei Café and Jinghong in general, we failed to find anyone interested in helping us hire a boat. We did, however, find a rubber dingy below the bridge, and spent a day floating 25 miles to the next village, Galanba. As goalless as vagrant leaves floating down the Mekong; we were beginning to get the feel of the river like a couple of ageing Huck Finns.

Once back in Jinghong, we resorted to our back-up plan: a two-day detour by road crossing the border into Laos. We would put in the river in Xieng

Kok, an opium smuggling village 20 miles south of China. We were on the street at six the next morning, rolling across Jinghong's new bridge with two Chinese drivers in a red taxi.

"Federico Fellini" was the can-do guy riding shotgun, who enjoyed directing things. He bolted from the car at a bus stop to talk to a very naughty-looking young girl. It was not yet 6:30 a.m., and she had trouble written all over her: ample breasts flowing out of a glittering halter top, scarlet lips and dyed blond hair falling along her shoulders, a couple of crude hand tattoos, eyes flashing like beacons. Fellini walked her to the car and tried to slot her in the back seat between Simon and me. Disappointment swept her face as we ungraciously told Fellini to knock it off. She withdrew into the peasant crowd waiting for the bus. Fellini chain-smoked and hacked out the window all the way to the border of Laos.

We passed through several Dai villages, encountering a steady flow of assorted hill tribes on their way to markets and fields, loaded with panniers of vegetables, shoulder poles of firewood, and harrowing blades. Shepherded by a boy and two men in straw hats, a flood of goats and water buffalo filled the road, parting and closing around us like a smelly school of fish.

In the middle of Xishuanbanna Nature Reserve, we stopped in a Dai village walled by spiraling limestone peaks. Fellini got out, pulled off his director's coat, and stopped colorfully dressed hilltribers for our photo-ops. Back at the wheel, Fellini goosed our flashy red taxi around every turn of the tortuous road the rest of the way to the border, while his co-driver enjoyed a drooling sleep. We roared up to the remote border outpost in a cloud of dust.

Third World border crossings are almost always melting pots of diverse cultures, and duty-free zones for smugglers. In the case of southwest China and northern Laos, the crossings are also safe havens for anarchic tribes escaping the Han Chinese yoke. Many tribes in the Golden Triangle border area, mostly in Laos and Burma, continue to cultivate opium. It is processed in local factories owned by drug lords who direct the shipment of raw opium and refined heroin. The forbidding terrain of the region allows the tribes and drug barons to pass as they please through the borders.

In Laos, ethnic groups are neatly classified into three categories based on the relative altitudes of their traditional villages. The largest group, the Lao-lum, comprises 55 percent of the country's five and a half million people. Their dialect is the nation's official language. They inhabit the lowlands along the Mekong and its tributaries. Part of the broad Tai diaspora from southern China, which includes the Thais, settled in Laos toward the end of the first millennium. Not long after, the Lao-lum adopted Theravada Buddhism to go along with their traditional animist beliefs.

The oldest inhabitants of Laos are the Lao Theung tribes—Khama, Htin, Lamet, Loven and more. They are loosely affiliated with the Mon-Khmer groups who mostly live in Burma and Cambodia. Some 9,000 years before the Tai race did, they migrated from southern China, displacing the aboriginal hunter-gatherers who first inhabited Laos. The Lao Theung were, for a time, enslaved and eventually displaced by the Lao-lum. They pushed upward from the plains and lowland rivers to altitudes ranging from 1,000 to 3,000 feet.

Farther up in the mountains of Laos, the Lao Sung people, speaking various dialects of the Tibeto-Burman language group, are relative newcomers from China. They arrived less than two centuries ago, and now dwell in the upper valleys of Laos above 3,000 feet. Like the Lao Theung, the Lao Sung practice animism and favor the healing powers of a shaman—sacrificing a pig or chicken, smearing blood on a sick person, applying dermal treatments, and employing the deterrent magic embodied in amulets and spirit strings worn around the wrist. Fiercely independent, they choose to live in isolation from lowlanders, practicing migratory slash-and-burn agriculture. At the turn of the 19th century, when the British needed more opium to pay for their Chinese tea, the Lao Sung—Hmong, Akha, Mien—with the mountainous, alkaline soil beneath their feet, were willing cultivators and users.

Our bus passed through a caravan of cargo trucks parked near the Laos-China border, their chancy loads wrapped in tarpaulins. The old vehicle lurched and groaned through long tracks of cratered tarmac disappearing into dusty red earth. This wasted road was built by Chinese troops during the Vietnam War. Today, after 30 years of neglect, modern China has plans to rebuild it as an overland link to the markets of Thailand, Malaysia and Singapore.

But for now, the concrete and bricks and glassy tile buildings of China seemed dog-years behind us. Instead we passed through shabby villages of thatched huts with no electricity. The charred hillsides still smoldered, recently slashed-and-burned. Bevies of black pigs shared a play space with pot-bellied three- and-four-year-old kids, their naked bodies tinted in layers of dirt.

Many of the children had blond hair, their noses bubbling with snot and eyes flowing with conjunctivitis—the face of Third World poverty. Dark-skinned women wore checkered head wraps of blue and white, green and red, pink and white, like colorful tatterdemalions. Men, also blackened by the sun, walked the roads in groups of two, some carrying flintlock muskets. They wore olive drab Mao hats and traditional baggy trousers that fell to the shins, with embroidered game pouches strapped across the front, bandoleer-style. Motorized vehicles were outnumbered four-to-one by horses and donkeys, transporting people and products—including opium.

We arrived in a village called Luang Nam Tha just as a bus was leaving for Muang Sing, our destination for the night. The driver happily stopped, for the *kip* equivalent of a couple of bucks, and loaded our bags on top, giving us less than a minute's layover. The bus was mostly filled with women of the Hmong and Mien tribes, who nursed their babies and fidgeted the way white-knuckled flyers do. Their sundry possessions overflowed from the roof and aisles.

Simon, confined as if in a dollhouse, creakily folded his six-foot-two-inch frame into a corner beside two young Japanese women on a field trip to study Laotian culture. I fell into the middle of the bus, my ribcage pressed by the handlebar of a tricycle. Aware of the Lao's predisposition for motion sickness, I kept an eye on the peaked-faced ones sitting within barfing range. Every time I shifted, the tricycle's siren and flashing red light went into action. Barreling down the road trailed by a rooster tail of dusty clouds, the driver doubled as DJ, spinning cassettes of traditional Lao love songs, medleys of stringed instruments accompanied by high-pitched singing.

Once, we stopped to pick up a villager who didn't know which side of the bus to enter. While he circled trying to find the door, the passengers erupted in jeering laughter.

The road twisted indecisively along the upland valley of the Nam Yuan River, a tributary of the Mekong. The mountainous landscape shifted from treeless nubs of freshly toasted hillsides to the luxuriance of primary forest, fleeced in white spring bloom. In a few hours' time, approaching Muang Sing, we drove directly into a fiery sun as it dipped into the crosshairs of the valley's opening.

Centuries of southbound migrations from China have left the Muang Sing area of northwest Laos home to as many as 30 ethnic minority groups, possibly more tribes per square mile than any other place on earth. During the Vietnam War, Muang Sing was by turns occupied by the Pathet Lao—the Vietnamese-supported communist liberation movement in Laos—and the Iron Age hill tribes conducting guerilla warfare operations in the region as surrogates of the CIA.

For a time, the CIA's go-to guy in Laos was a rogue warrior named Anthony Posphepny. Beginning in the early 1960s, Tony Poe, as he was known, conducted his own guerrilla war in the opium-growing Golden Triangle region. He paid cash bounties of a dollar each to tribal operatives, mostly from the Mien tribe, for every pair of ears severed from Pathet Lao fighters. Another tactic was to marinate the severed heads of Pathet Lao soldiers in formaldehyde, then drop them from low-flying planes onto the terrified enemy.

Poe had "gone bamboo," according to fellow paramilitary operatives. He saw it differently, and even defended his collection of ears: "The guy's dead anyway, what's the difference?" He finally ended the bounty system when he encountered a Mien child missing his ears. The kid's dad had cut them off in order to collect on Poe's reward. The American was upset, not because the child was maimed, but because his bounty system had been cheated.

The sobering truth about soldiers like Tony Poe is that they were damn good at fighting and terrorizing whoever was designated the enemy. Such is war. Although Poe pushed his job too far for even military stomachs, the American national purpose was to win; this end justified all means.

Poe was the latter-day inspiration for the Conradian character of Colonel Kurtz, played by Marlon Brando, in *Apocalypse Now*. Although Kurtz got his throat slit at the movie's end, Poe was awarded the CIA Star, the Agency's highest award, by Director William Colby. And this was after a newspaper in 1970 exposed his paramilitary exploits in Laos, and he was banished from the country. Poe retired with his Laotian wife to Udorn Thani, Thailand, before dying, unrepentant, in San Francisco in 2003.

Among Poe's responsibilities in Laos were tapping telephone lines and monitoring road traffic to keep abreast of Chinese and North Vietnamese troop movements, given the threat of China's entry into the larger Indochina war. Muang Sing, just six miles from the border, became one of our paramilitary's prime listening posts.

The American build-up in Laos began after China fell to the communists in 1949, and was redoubled after John Kennedy became President in 1961. The day before taking office, Kennedy was warned of the looming communist menace in Laos by his predecessor, Dwight D. Eisenhower, the lead trumpeter of the "domino theory." Washington saw backwater Laos as a wobbly domino ready to fall and topple the free world with it.

Conflict between the warring princes of Laos had heated up. Sensing the threat of the Red Hordes, the Pentagon dispatched 500 marines with helicopter support to Udon, Thailand, across the Mekong from Vientiane. The Kremlin replied by shipping arms to the Pathet Lao. But the superpowers' open confrontation in Laos soon fizzled. The Geneva Accords of 1962, signed by Kennedy and Krushchev, forbade the presence of American or Vietnamese troops in Laos.

With the ink hardly dry, all parties to the Accords switched to covert operations. With no official government budget to hold back the communist tide in Laos, the CIA and its paramilitary warriors circumvented international law by conspiring in the most lucrative business in the neighborhood—the smuggling of drugs. Nowadays this might seem an obvious option. Conflicts around the globe—in Columbia, Afghanistan, Burma and other countries—are underwritten with drug profits.

The British East India Company showed how profitable it was to create the demand and then cultivate the supply in the 18th and 19th centuries. London fought two wars to preserve their lucrative colonial franchise—the right to foist the "heavenly demon" on the Chinese. After Britain passed the Opium Act in 1878 and withdrew from drug pushing in the East, hill tribes continued to grow small quantities of opium for personal consumption and resale to French colons. Once the French left, the Americans needed local anti-communist warriors. With their planes, arms and access to markets, they turned the rather amateurish cottage industry of family-run farms into an international conglomerate. The region's annual output of opium increased tenfold in just a few years.

Opium became coin of the realm, and during the 1960s and 1970s, one of the epicenters of the opium trade was Muang Sing, where Chinese merchants acted as brokers for the Corsican traffickers. The district still produces several tons of opium a year: some for export but mostly for local consumption by older male addicts, and a bit for recreational use by backpackers wanting to puff some of the "heavenly demon."

Today Muang Sing is a sleepy, backwater village with a main street of stilted homes converted to guesthouses, and a market that bustles for two or three hours each day before dwindling to a few tribal stragglers. As we arrived at dusk, monks in saffron robes and matching ski caps teetered along the road astride bicycles, while kids played badminton beneath the wan glare of a single bulb. The occasional backpacker dawdled by in that tribe's unisex uniform—tie-dyed pantaloons, tattered T-shirt, ears in hoops and bangles, an embroidered, ethnic-style shoulder bag faded by the sun.

In the late light, we found a room on the town's east end, amid the gentle decadence of the Lao Herbal Sauna & Massage, Sing Savanh Nightclub, and Jin's Chinese Restaurant and Disco/Pub. We enjoyed Mekong catfish in the open-air restaurant below the guesthouse. From across the room, in the general vicinity of a slip of girls sitting next to the kitchen, a deep voice rose like the disembodied sound of a ghost, "Where are you from?" One of the young girls—well-formed and handsomely masked in all the red shades of rouge and lipstick—stood proudly as the illusory baritone. As she repeated the question, her Adam's apple rose from her neck like a goiter, "I was asking where are you from?" A Laotian lady-boy in Muang Sing—she could have been a talking poodle and I would not have been more astonished.

Out in the darkened street, the kids were still swatting the shuttlecock and letting go with peals of mockery at the losers. A few market ladies worked the shadows selling hand-woven textiles. In a dimly lit home-style restaurant beneath one of the guesthouses, a few backpackers gathered like tribal women around the village well telling stories of the road. Simon and I skulked in the shadows among the vending ladies, mindful of the traveler's imperative to sample the corn when in Kansas. From out of the dark a voice whispered, "You like opium? I have. You like?"

We were soon back in the room taking our perfumed medicine from the red neck elegance of a Coke-can pipe, inhaling ambrosial vapors tainted by a burnt-cola aftertaste. No cosmic zaps that re-jiggered our lives—just a gush of free-associative babble. I lost my innocence with opium while in the army over three decades ago not so far from Muang Sing. At 18 years old, I had neglected to follow the advice of the wise Chinese opium smokers. They always said it should not be taken by the young but instead savored in old age, a seductive escape from reality. Jean Cocteau, the French surrealist writer and artist, took a similar view:

"Everything one does in life, even love, occurs in an express train racing toward death. To smoke opium is to get out of the train while it is still moving. It is to concern oneself with something other than life or death."

We concerned ourselves with a search for Muang Sing's night life. The only glimmer was Jin's Chinese Restaurant and Disco/Pub, lit up with a single strand of low-wattage fairy lights. Inside, a disco ball sparkled color onto the dance floor as a TV showed syrupy Thai pop videos. A few couples danced with typical Lao reserve, rotating in the circular formation of the traditional *lamvong*, waving their hands in the air but never touching.

After a beer, we walked out into the fresh air, feeling wanton, as in the illusion of revisiting an old haunt. The night sky flashed in pinpricks of silver. More monks padded by in the darkness. A sparrow of a man in bare feet brandished a calumet pipe, inviting us to his hooch to smoke opium. "Not tonight, good buddy. We've seen enough action already. Thanks anyway," I replied airily. He pressed a dollop of opium pasted on a tear of newspaper into my hand. Perhaps transported by Muang Sing's easy-going mood, I stuck the paste in my pocket, handed him some *kip* and in opposite directions, we vanished into the darkness. Lucky I did not accept his invitation to the hooch. I later learned of its dangers.

Our sleep was deep, the "ultimate siesta," matching the countryside's stillness. A chorus of roosters crowed us awake, when, according to Chinese zodiacal folklore, all the demons and ghosts who swirl around the night, depart. Or had the opium kept us sleeping through the pre-dawn cacophony? We tried to catch an early bus to Xieng Kok, the Mekong village where we could hire a boat. But the driver wouldn't leave until the moment the bus was full, a "Laotian moment" that might take hours to arrive.

We killed time strolling around the market populated by tribal women burdened with wooden yokes around their necks, carrying loaded bamboo panniers, bartering, buying and selling. Unharnessed, they gathered at low-set tables where they sat on plastic chairs the size of milking stools. Clouds of smoke hung lazily in the air where stoves heated vessels of hot soup laden with spirals of tripe. The din of diverse tongues wafted through the market like some Eastern Babel.

The women of the Mien tribe stood out in their tightly wrapped black turbans, with red ruffs worn gaily around the neck like cocktail boas out of the Roaring Twenties. The Kaw and Hmong women, when relieved of their yokes, looked like provincial princesses in their beaded headdresses, bedizened with crimson pompoms and half-moon pendants of silver. Strands of silver coins framed their faces, forming necklaces as dense as chain-mail hanging down to the chest. Approaching with smiles of incandescent ivory, their teeth often capped in ornamental gold, Thai lu women peddled handwoven hemp and cotton. Several women of childbearing years walked around bare-chested, their breasts swollen with milk.

I waved some *kip* at a *sawngthaew* driver, and he gathered a couple of fellow drivers and market boys to give his truck a push-start. Soon we were bouncing down the dusty track toward Xieng Kok, tracing the Ma River, another tributary of the Mekong.

The *sawngthaew* was a local taxi, always loading on more people and cargo than letting off. At each village, the stop was easily identified by the barnyard of passengers huddled near the road—screeching chickens, quacking ducks, litters of short-haired, black piglets.

We arrived before noon in Xieng Kok, situated on a rocky knoll above the sandy beaches of the Mekong. Across the dull jade waters were the Shan States of Burma. Xieng Kok is the only legal border crossing between Laos and Burma. An idyllic sprawl of thatched huts and brightly costumed tribal women, the village is a major conduit for Burmese opium and heroin.

By noon, a swarm of river touts emerged from their shaded hideaways. Belying their drowsy demeanor, with staccato swiftness, they offered up an amusing menu of boat options: you want fast-fast boat, slow-fast boat, or slow-slow boat, as they pointed first to a speedboat, then a river ferry and finally a rice barge.

Four speedboats, or *heua wai*, were nosed up on the beach, painted in red and yellow designs along their shallow gunwales. Their tiny propellers were mounted on long engine shafts that stretched 15 feet behind the boat, looking fancifully reptilian. Powered by Toyota four-cylinder engines—souped up with an open-intake carburetor and equal-length headers that meld into a megaphone exhaust—the boat's mosquito-wing prop was torqued by 150 horsepower.

After a long negotiation for one of the Mekong missiles, the captain warmed up the unmuffled car engine in a couple of shore-to-shore bursts, rupturing the stillness with a death roar like a B-52.

A Japanese man, Miyamoto, pitched in with us to share the cost of the boat to Huay Xai. Soon we were being kitted out with orange life jackets and smallish crash helmets. After loading a five-gallon plastic container of gasoline about six inches from my backside, the captain tossed his cigarette into the water and untied the boat. In an act of benign disregard for the region's atmosphere of inertia, we blasted off like a rocket, throwing arcs of silver droplets into the air.

In no time we were shooting through a labyrinth of giant boulders. With every twist of the river apparently imprinted in his head, the captain seemed to see around corners and find the channel, never pausing to study a turn, thinking 20 seconds ahead and veering reflexively at 45 miles per hour.

But it wasn't long before the adrenaline thrill of rocketing down the Mekong took a back seat to the lush scenery and absorbing culture of the river. The sky was a seamless shroud of alabaster—cloudless, lacking depth and texture. The forested hillsides in both Burma and Laos grew thick with jungle-like profusion, steeped in a phosphorous air. Fluted waves of white sand provided the caulking for a gauntlet of basaltic boulders—misshapen monoliths framing the waterway like the tumbled approach of an ancient Inca city.

Our feet and seats were cooled by the pooling residue of the wake. The river smelled of all that had washed into it—an earthy compost of flora and fauna, living and dead—from the yak grazing grounds of the Tibetan Plateau to the tilled vales of Yunnan province.

At distant intervals, riverine villages, or *bans*, were camouflaged as tawny lines of thatch intruding on the verdant forest. Fishing huts, lean-tos of bamboo and thatch, no bigger than a dog's house, appeared on long sweeps of floury beach.

On the port side in Laos, small herds of broad-horned water buffalo rambled down the beach for the cool of an afternoon wallow. Three monks appeared out of nowhere, racing down the beach on bicycles as they gilded the landscape, flowing in sheets of saffron.

On the starboard side in Burma's Shan State, pack horses drank from a glassy pool of jade. After independence from the British in 1948, instability reduced Burma from its position as the world's top exporter of rice to leading in opium instead. Then, as the CIA began using the opium-growing tribes of the region to fight their battles and spy on the Chinese, Burma's annual crop of opium grew from 40 tons a year to 400 tons by 1962, the seminal years of the Vietnam War. Today the output has reached 2,500 tons. Opiate revenues equal the sum from all of Burma's legal exports.

The captain approached a floating petrol-station at Mueng Mueng, killing the roar of the beast by placing his hand over its air intake. Stopped, we slowly unfolded our battered bodies from the snug confines of the boat. The captain motioned us into another boat. Meanwhile, one of the dockhands moved our packs and bungy-corded them in a shallow space on the needle-nosed bow of our fresh Mekong missile.

Mueng Mueng is known as a restaging point on the river, a place to change boats and drivers in some unwritten territorial accord, money and drugs no doubt playing a role.

A few miles south of Mueng Mueng, with the Mekong in a dry season recession, a rice barge was stuck mid-river on a spit of sand. At least 20 boys and men with blackened skin were stripped to their underwear, employing their collective muscle and engineering say-so to rock it loose. Farther downriver, a sleeping fisherman, drifting idly on a raft of lashed bamboo, never flinched when we screamed past and almost swamped him. Only a few minutes had passed when we got our karmic justice—washboarding across the wake of a passing cargo barge, in rapid turns catching air and landing in spine-crushing jolts. The barge was flying the boundary-state flags of China, Laos, Burma, and Thailand, chugging north to the Chinese border.

Soon we approached a turn in the river where the mocha-tinged Mekong bent to the east in a long sweep of fast shallow water. A sprawling, whitewashed building the size of Bangkok's Grand Palace loomed from the prosperous shores of Thailand. To the west was Burma: a narrow tongue of secondary forest jutting meekly from the mouth of the Ruak River as it merged with the Mekong. To the east, hugging the rustic shoreline of Laos, was a shoal of empty rice barges waiting for late spring rains to lift them from the dry-season doldrums. Bobbing there in the middle of the river we found ourselves in the watery bull's eye of the Golden Triangle.

The region was given its name by a senior State Department official in 1971 on the eve of Richard Nixon's visit to China. The term whitewashed China's major role in the cultivation and distribution of opium and heroin, impugning just Thailand, Burma and Laos.

This junction was the site of the Opium War of 1967, a two-day clash that pitted the world's greatest drug kingpins in a three-way battle recounted by such authors as Ed Gargan, in *The River's Tale*. Khun Sa, the self-described "King of the Golden Triangle," led his Mong Tai army in a pack-train of 300 mules loaded with 16 tons of opium to the nearby village of Ban Khwan. Moving up from the south in Thailand were the dusty remnants of Chiang Kai-shek's army, the Kuomintang, or KMT, crumpled 20 years before in China. Now they wanted to reclaim their sovereignty in the Triangle. From the east, General Ouane Rattikone, commander of the Royal Laotian Army from 1965 to 1971, moved his army in. The CIA was friendly with all three parties, and may well have puppeteered their showdown.

Khun Sa's shipment was worth millions of dollars and was destined for delivery at General Ouane's refinery in Huay Xai. But a double-cross unfolded. General Ouane wanted it all and dispatched his air force of T-28s bombers, unleashing 250-pound bombs and CBU's, or cluster bomb units, killing men and mules on all sides. Tony Poe later complained, "For two or three days you couldn't go in there, it smelled so bad from the putrefied dead mules."

With his American planes and ordnance, General Ouane trumped the carbines and machine guns of Khun Sa and the KMT. He shipped the booty to his refinery in Huay Xai, processing the raw opium into his trademarked Double Globe heroin. From there, the heroin was often transshipped by Air America, the CIA-operated airline, to GIs in Vietnam and Thailand and on to the US, with some 750,000 addicts.

Our next stop should have been Huay Xai, but unexpectedly we pulled into a floating petrol station at Xiangchai. The canny captain and complicit friend he brought along from Mueng Mueng motioned us out of the boat. Slow to smell the stench of bait-and-switch, I stayed in the boat taking notes and Simon crossed a couple of other fast boats to get to the dock and smoke a multi-colored Marlboro Light. Soon, a man who spoke decent English arrived and casually informed us a taxi was waiting up the road and would take us on to Huay Xai. This was not our agreement.

In the Lao language, *jai yen* means "cool heart." Lao people, including swindling fast-boat captains, don't scream and shout and show anger. Raising one's voice is just bad form in Laos.

I knew as much. But I detonated with a resounding "Bull! Shit!" They all looked at me as one person—frozen faces in a wax museum—and melted into embarrassed laughter. Simon, jolted out of his stoned reverie by my 400-pound gorilla routine, played the reasonable, even-voiced foil. Miyamoto, favoring Lao-style reserve, was flat freaked out and didn't utter a word.

In moments, after a spew of shouting and a threat to get the police, the grating refrain of "cannot" turned to the more pleasing expression "can do." A new captain jumped into the boat, while the culpable one sheepishly, but with that evasive Lao smile on his face, gathered his belongings. With dampened spirits, I began feeling like a trouncing turd in the Mekong punch bowl.

In less than an hour, staring fixedly ahead, we made our way through several tricky shoals, before pulling up to the busy loading ramp on the east end of Huay Xai. Miyamoto was trying to find a ferry to cross the river to Chiang Khong, Thailand before the immigration office closed. He bade a hasty farewell and disappeared into a rackety snarl of boats and people. It had not been my finest hour: tea and a 20-minute palaver would have sealed the deal; bullying was way out of step.

Once in Huay Xai—home to General Ouane's old heroin refinery—we found a guesthouse near the ferry crossing. Nearby, we settled in at an outdoor restaurant on the river and enjoyed Mekong catfish. Across the water, the lights of Chiang Khong twinkled merrily, advertising Thai prosperity to the dim and sleepy Lao town.

Thais proudly compare themselves to bamboo trees blowing in the wind: bending, leaning, never breaking, surviving. The roots of Thailand's economic success today arguably lie in the 1860s. Bedeviled by Europe's race to colonize Africa and Asia, the King of Siam came to terms with several scowling French man-o-wars anchored near Bangkok. Eventually sacrificing Laos and Cambodia, he saved his nation from the decades of colonization that afflicted the rest of Southeast Asia.

Besides practicing smart diplomacy, the Siamese succeeded by adopting from the West. They borrowed architecture from the colonial French, drove on the left side of the road like the British, sent young royals to Oxford and King Mongkut even offered elephants to Abe Lincoln to help him win the Civil War. Following World War II, after a century of leaning toward Western ways, and centuries more of confrontation with Vietnam, Laos and Cambodia, Thailand naturally aligned with the United States in the Vietnam War and the Indochinese conflict.

At least in economic terms, that alliance paid off. Today, Thailand has more trucks than Texas. McDonalds, KFC and Pizza Hut are as common as pagodas. It would take Vietnam 20 years of growth at eight percent to reach Thailand's current Gross Domestic Product. Sleepy Laos and Cambodia, if not raped of their forests and other valuable resources, might catch up in the next millennium.

Acceding to international pressure and local police action, the Thai hill tribes of the Golden Triangle now cultivate less than one percent of the world opium supply. And once again the Thai army is in a paramilitary alliance with the United States (DEA), this time to combat the Wa militia, the latter-day drug lords of Burma.

The next morning we started off early. In head-snapping acceleration, the prow sliced to the south before cutting to the east. We roared straight into a rising sun, spraying the water in a thousand glints of gold and silver. Long pirogues, choked with rows of people, plied the river in gray silhouettes.

The morning was going by swimmingly until we rounded an elbow of the river cordoned in rocks and were blasted by an unmistakable smell: putrefying flesh. "Water buffalo," I announced knowingly.

Soon I spotted the bloated carcass, salmon pink, 50 yards ahead on the starboard side. Simon chimed in: "If that's a water buffalo, why is it wearing a shirt and trousers?" I did a double-take.

"Whoooa Nellie! We got a dead man floating," I declared, semaphoring to Homphan, our captain, to stop the boat so we could pull the body from the water. He furrowed his brow, flashed that evasive Lao smile, shook his head. He would leave it as food for the fish.

What is the appropriate etiquette when one happens upon a dead man floating in the Golden Triangle? In England it was once a crime to witness a murder or to spot a corpse without making a "hue and cry." I suggested taking a picture. Simon replied with a glare.

Decomposition occurs rapidly in the tropics. The man floating had probably been killed upriver the previous day. Homphan had likely spotted the corpse already while taxiing up and down his route.

So on we went, shorn temporarily of our lively banter, glissading through a peaceful seeming river. Long pools gathered below the limestone rising around us, rock walls stitched in foliage. Then narrow straits interrupted— huddles of large boulders prickled with bamboo poles dragging fish nets. On both sides of the river, palisades of bamboo sheltered a patchwork of vegetable gardens. More bouquets of plumed bamboo arched to the water in graceful lines, while Irish-green banana fronds fell like tresses of untamed hair. A rice barge rolled past, followed by a long passenger boat prowed with the pleasing sight of monks, with a rainbow canopy of parasols shading their shaved heads.

We arrived in Pakbeng, where several fast boats were sandwiched against the floating dock, heaped with crates of eggs, sacks of chili peppers and hefty bundles of sugar cane. But with the many western goodies for sale—Classic Lay's Potato Chips, Kit Kat chocolate, Pringles, Juicy Fruit, Marlboros, and Coca-Cola—it seemed a floating 7-Eleven.

Having been to Pakbeng on several occasions, I knew there would be police lurking around the floating dock—a good spot for all sorts of black market high jinks. The dead man floating seemed like an event they might want to know about, yet each time I caught Homphan's eye, then pointed to the men in uniform standing two feet away, he flashed his no-can-do smile, shaking his head left to right. Making no hue and cry, we kept our sighting to ourselves.

Killing time, we shimmied across a wobbly plank from the dock and climbed like goats up the steep pitched scarp to Pakbeng's high street. The street affords a panorama of the crowded dock, the river and an arc of showy fast boats moored nose-first along the bow-shaped beach, like some Corvette rally in Appalachia. Standing in the same spot on previous trips, I had been approached by young men selling opium, often with police in full view and watching.

The opium peddlers had taken a break and given way to lawless timber merchants, loading fresh-cut colonnades of teak, the dismantled artifacts of an ancient forest cathedral, on a barge destined for Thailand or China. With the wholesale degradation of 80 percent of Southeast Asia's primary forest, such a sight is as ghastly as walking into a Hong Kong apothecary and seeing a jar full of 20 tiger penises—knowing there are less than 5,000 tigers left in the wild.

Soon we were back on the river. Homphan turned his bottle of energizing red syrup, the original Red Bull, bottoms-up for two or three last sips. Several small pirogues weaved in and out of boulders checking nets and removing their spare catches, before untangling the white snarl of filament. Hard to say what might get caught in those big nets.

Downriver from Pakbeng, we could smell traces of smoke. It was the early spring, the end of the swidden season, when the forests are dry and the mountains of Laos are set afire by the hill tribes who practice slash-and-burn agriculture. Swidden farming, the polite term for it, is the oldest method of organic farming. All it takes is a man's ax to fell the trees, a woman's scythe to cut bushes, and a dibble stick to punch seed-holes in the ground. No plowing, irrigation or fertilizer needed.

In Laos, the trees and bushes are cut in January and February. After removing raw materials of value—hardwoods, bamboo, medicinal herbs, bird eggs, fruit, spices and so on—they use dry bamboo for tinder and burn the place to a toast. The charred remains are cleared of stumps and boulders, and left to fertilize the soil with ash, the better to grow dry rice, maize, sundry vegetables, fruits, medicinal plants. Four or five years of farming drains the topsoil of its nutrients, and the swiddeners move on. In 20 years' time, the ground will rejuvenate.

We couldn't see the fires but soon the air whitened in a thin fog. Flakes of ash flew by, engulfing us like a snow flurry. Then it cleared, and we glided past two elephants working in tandem on the south side of the river. At the command of their mahouts, they hurled columns of teak onto a barge. The pachyderms had helped clear the nearby jungle, hauling the wood to the long stretch of sand bar.

Hamphan stopped the boat to take a break on a sand spit, shucked his clothes, shampooed his hair, and submerged in the cool wash of the Mekong. We dawdled on the white shore smoking a spliff, drowsily trying to get our minds around the fate of the dead-man-floating. Who was he, and what had he done to land in the river? Were his executioners anyone we had met that day?

Riding on toward Luang Prabang, we came to the river's picturesque confluence with the Ou, a populous tributary that originates in a mountainous wedge between China and Vietnam. We had reached the pockmarked limestone façade of the Pak Ou Caves.

Beginning in the first millennium, the two main caves—Tham Ting, a vaulted den opening like a gothic mouth to the river and Tham Phum, 100 yards up a winding set of steps, hidden from the river in a shadow of trees—became sites for worship of the animist spirits known locally as *phi*. Martin Stuart-Fox, a leading academic of Lao history and culture, explains the Lao need to propitiate the *phi*:

"In the Lao worldview, opposites interpenetrate: illusion and reality, spirits and human being, jungle and cleared land. For the Lao Lum peasantry, the forest was a fearful place of danger to be avoided. But its demons could be vanquished by those with the requisite merit, and whom divine forces assisted. The supernatural was taken for granted… ghosts and phi were an unquestioned part of everyday life for the Lao."

Around 400 years ago, the cave's *phi* figures were replaced with Hindu statues and wooden images of Buddha. The two caves now house over 4,000 Buddha icons, strewn across the earthen floor like a minefield for the demons, ghosts and praying Buddhists to cross.

Standing on the winding steps in the dank caves, the Buddha images showed a variety of meaningful gestures, or *mudras* as they are called in Sanskrit. But here they were mostly fashioned with arms stretched down at the side and palms faced inward—the "calling for rain" *mudra*, an understandable focus of worship for a people who depend on the Mekong's fecundity.

Legend has it the kings of Lan Xang in the 16th century began paying an annual visit to the tutelary statues in the caves. Royal patronage ended only in 1975, when the Pathet Lao took power. During the three-day Pi Mai festival in April, the Lao lunar new year, pilgrims still travel upriver from the Buddhist holy city and ancient imperial capital of Luang Prabang to worship. As part of that ceremony, they give the dusty statues a ritual wash for the coming year.

Soon we were unloading at the dock and immigration office west of Luang Prabang. After registering with the police, under the duress of monopoly pricing, we hired the only *tuk-tuk* available to shuttle us the three or four miles into Luang Prabang.

We checked into our guesthouse, and then wasted no time in telling the Lao manager and staff about the floating corpse. "Why will no one pull him from the water?" I hued and cried.

After consulting bystanders, the manager said, "Maybe man not so good; he into drugs. Okay leave in the river."

There is logic to this, in the Lao context. In the Golden Triangle, frontier justice and ethics rule; death is no idle prankster. Beyond this, Lao people fear places where demons and ghosts dwell—especially the evil spirits haunting the bloated corpse of an outlaw.

Perhaps the man's violent fate began and ended with opium. We later learned the Thai army had been fighting the Wa militia in the Triangle area in an attempt to stop the flow of narcotics. The Wa—not so long ago a tribe of headhunters and now armed with AK-47s and old American M-16s—are the main producers of opium cultivated in Burma. Ten Wa militiamen had been reported killed in one of many skirmishes over several days while we were there. (A year later, traveling on the same stretch of river with my wife, we came upon another neglected corpse, a man with a gaping hole in his back.)

Simon and I ended our day by trying to bury the dead man's mystery under the shadow of Golden Triangle poppies. We listened to Bob Dylan twanging *Absolutely Sweet Marie*, his gnomic epitaph on karma: "...to live outside the law you must be honest." America and the CIA are finished with their secret war in Laos. Tony Poe is nothing more than a good story. But descendents of their former accomplices still float down the Mekong.

Silky Strides of
Moral Authority

Buddhism reigns supreme in Luang Prabang. Sprucing up the many temples, or *wats*, has been a key ritual here. Almost a millennium ago, when Theravada Buddhism arrived and inlaid the valleys and hilltops with *wats* that sparkle today like gemstones, it was the importance of making merit, or *bun*, to ensure a good rebirth, that inspired Laotians to build and maintain temples. The wholesale employment of artists and craftsmen to build *wats* circulated the wealth in ancient Laos much as the construction of monasteries in medieval Europe generated mass employment there.

Even today, many *wats* remain works-in-progress. You often see craftsmen replacing chinks of the colored glass mosaic, whitewashing the walls, touching up murals or varnishing the intricate carvings. The twinkle of delicate temples lining the streets, the colorful ribbons of saffroned monks padding the early morning pavement for alms, the delicious scent of frangipani trees in fresh bloom, and the sleepy pace of pedestrian life among the French-Lao architecture are subtle and alluring. The town's serenity seduces the soul and opens the heart to compassion and to the local custom of almsgiving.

Luang Prabang is situated on a raised tongue of land that stretches into the muddy confluence of the Khan and Mekong Rivers, a municipal apotheosis suggestive of the Buddhist lotus flower of spiritual purity rising from a mud puddle of ignorance in which it grows. Standing boldly in the heart of the city is Mt. Phousi—a holy promontory that affords a picturesque sweep of the encircling mountains, the emerald river valley and its trove of 30-plus *wats* glancing in the sun. Phousi's summit is crowned with a single golden stupa, shading the modest Wat Chom Si. On the east end of the summit, a corroded Russian anti-aircraft gun installed by the Pathet Lao provides an aesthetic reality check.

Across the road is the Royal Palace. Displayed inside is a copy of the sacred *Pra Bang*, a Golden Buddha, the palladium of Lao Buddhism from whence the city takes its name. The original *Pra Bang*, last seen in the Royal Palace chapel when the Pathet Lao took control of the city in 1975, is rumored to be in a local bank vault. As for the pictures of the last royals adorning the palace walls, the guides become embarrassed when asked about their fate. They don't know the answer and the communist regime won't say.

Every year during celebration of the Laotian New Year, or *Pi Mai*, the cloned *Pra Bang* is paraded through the streets and taken to Wat Mai for cleansing. As the story goes, in the 14th century a Cambodian king, Jayavarman Praamesvara, gifted the sacred image to Fa Ngum—warrior, statesman and religious man—Laos' answer to George Washington. By dint of his military prowess, Fa Ngum merged a handful of tributary states into a feudal union known as Lane Xang, making Buddhism the official religion there for the first time.

When the Pathet Lao took power over the Kingdom six centuries later, Fa Ngum's descendants, King Sisavang Vatthana, Queen Khamponi and Prince Vongsavong, three of the last twigs on the royal family tree, chose not to flee. Instead they hung around, in the Lao spirit of cooperation, to help their beloved and beleaguered country transition from being a Cold War pawn of the West to a dogmatic communist nation state. But the Bolsheviks of Laos feared the Thais would enlist the Lao monarchy to orchestrate a coup. They shipped the royals off to a re-education camp in Sam Neua province in the remote jungles of the north in 1977. They were never to be seen again, *a la* Romanovs.

In 1991, the Party allowed Prince Vongsavong's daughter, Princess Kampha, to return to the family residence, now known as Villa Santi, located on Sisavangvong Street, the main road in Luang Prabang. I have visited the Villa Santi for booze and ballast on several occasions, hoping to meet my first princess. Each time I have asked after her, I am always told she is off to Vientiane or unavailable. She declines all interviews, favoring silence in Luang Prabang to the alienation of exile in France or Thailand.

Luang Prabang plays host to a jangling hive of backpackers, seen marching about in transparent cocoons of decided aloofness; they are the intrepid travelers of the day, descending from all walks of life and a pageant of countries. They roam around Asia in small platoons and solo, clutching dog-eared copies of the Lonely Planet travel bible, all sworn to uphold the Three Commandments of Overland Travel: I shall frequent guidebook-touted cafes and eat banana pancakes; when conscious, I shall obsess about money; and not only shall I stay in glorified barns, I shall show disdain to anyone who doesn't.

When questioned about the risk of traveling in Asian countries after the outbreak of SARS (Severe Acute Respiratory Syndrome), one "Pancaker" told the *Bangkok Post*, "After a nuclear war wipes out humanity, the only creatures that will survive will be cockroaches and backpackers." Their oddly considered apparel and fetish for banana cuisine aside, Pancakers have unwittingly—and at once—carried the olive branch and sown the seeds of Western culture as the doors of postwar Indochina have creaked open; they are the Voice of America and the BBC with legs.

During the Pi Mai celebration in April, four days of revelry that rivals Mardi Gras in pageantry and passion, Pancakers emerge from their cocoons and shake off their rapt expressions. Laotians have traditionally celebrated the holiday with a gentle rite of cleansing, sprinkling water on each other to vanquish the sins of the past year and start afresh in the New Year. In recent times the ritual has become more aggressive, especially among visiting young foreigners. Armed with plastic pastel assault water guns, they maraud through the streets of Luang Prabang in uniformed gangs, attacking Laotian kids, many of whom are equipped with the same playful weaponry.

During the celebration which takes place at the hottest time of the dry season, locals form a gauntlet along the main streets, like a bucket brigade in lieu of fire trucks, and pour cool water down the steamy backs of passersby. Many local revelers carry bags of tapioca starch and toss handfuls on the moistened bodies and faces of pedestrians... better known as being "tapioca-ed." As the festival progresses, across the river from Luang Prabang, beneath the celestial gaze of Wat Long Khun, the empty, incandescent beaches are transformed into a forest of sand stupas, glazed in white tapioca and crowned with stylistic prayer flags.

When I attended the festival, the opening day parade featured Buddhist priests riding on palanquins, seated in golden belvederes and surrounded by a saffron sea of novices and monks. Lao Thueng men and women wore black tunics and trousers, wrapped their heads in crimson bands, and performed a tribal dance to an ominous drumbeat. A rowdy troupe of dancing and drinking Laotian gays and lesbians, their faces painted grotesquely in Kabuki fashion, stirred laughter out of the reserved local spectators. Lao-lum maidens hoisted golden filigreed parasols as they led the way for Miss Laos, who lounged like a royal nymph atop a giant paper-mâché tiger. Standing in a heroic cruciform with a sword in her right hand and walking stick in her left, she portrayed Luang Prabang's patron spirit, the tiger princess, from an ancient Lao legend of love and betrayal predating the arrival of Buddhism.

A few years earlier, in the fall of 1998, I had the good fortune to stumble into another great festival here along Sisavangvong Street, as if I were some touristing Forrest Gump. Boun Ok Pansa celebrates the end of the life-giving rainy season as well as the conclusion of three months of Buddhist Lent, or Buddhist Rains Retreat. The pomp and circumstance of the event—steeped in ancient royal traditions when the king presided over the sangha, the Buddhist brotherhood—was another festive glimpse into the city's golden age.

A parade with floats began on the west end of Luang Prabang and moved east along Sisavangvong Street for about a mile. One after another, jubilant tribesmen and villagers processed by, hoisting paper-dragon-floats—typically 30-feet-long, intricately designed and hued in greens and reds. The dragons symbolize both royal might and the power of the river, which is imagined to be a dragon's vein containing spiritual energy. Fireworks burst all around, their flares puncturing the sky in arcs of red, green and white. A full ivory moon hung with a god-like presence over the golden stupa of Mt. Phousi. The parade inched along for two hours as the revelers melded into one hypnotic heap, driven by a collective gratitude for the river.

After a pass-and-review in front of the high monks at Wat Xeng Thong, the floats were hoisted down stairs that fell to the Mekong. The opposite riverbank glowed with torches and candles. Along with the candle-lit lotus blossoms, the dragon boats were placed in the sacred Mekong as votive offerings, drifting downriver like a flotilla of aquatic fireflies pursuing an armada of fire-breathing reptiles.

Slowly, they faded into the darkness. The fishermen seemed to be working a little overtime, double-dipping perhaps. They silently paddled into the gloom, making sure the votive offerings of local currency, *kip*, made it to the appropriate river spirits.

At our guesthouse, the *Auberge Calao*, next to the great Wat Xeng Thong, Simon and I sat on the verandah overlooking the Mekong, both of us anticipating our first cheeseburger in a week. The absence of constant motion and the stone silence of the waterfront were spooky, as if the town had been abandoned, leaving us behind. Nothing stirred. It was mid-afternoon, when the sun blazes and vapor locks all of Laos into a fetal curl.

On the subject of tropical torpor, Simon imparted to me the story of his maternal grandmother, a daughter of the Raj, who apparently gave Noel Coward his first paid employment. She was a dancer and minor silent movie star back in the early 20th century. As her career faded, Coward's would blossom as a writer of musicals and plays. Among other songs, he went on to compose "Mad Dogs and Englishmen," the inspiration of which was the crown jewel of the British empire, India, where only mad dogs and Brits would dare brave the midday heat.

The burger arrived topped with cold white cheese, not melted, despite the broiling sun. There was no mustard, only mayonnaise and catsup. And forget the dill pickles. But if it was bungled, at least the burger was beef, not water buffalo. Simon declared it "the best burger since Jinghong," forgetting it was his only burger since Jinghong. He drank a few beers, then took to Sisavangvong Street's myriad stalls selling brightly colored textiles woven by ethnic minorities. He purchased a wall hanging embroidered with the primitive image of a stupa, a fitting memento of this spiritual capital.

I meanwhile hired a *sawngthaew* driven by a chubby young man named Phone, who wore flip-flops, a slept-on shirt, and came topped by a haystack of mussed coal-black hair. He had just finished his nap. We set out to the east of Luang Prabang, twining through the weaving village of Ban Phanom. After three or four miles, the road mated with the Khan River, following its course through an immature forest of teak.

Near the village of Ban Naphao, we stopped on a wooded hillock overlooking the river. The French explorer Henri Mahout is buried nearby. Phone locked up his *sawngthaew* and we descended a footpath to the water. Having taken many foreigners to visit Mahout's grave, Phone wanted to know more about him. "Is true he discover Angkor Wat and Luang Prabang?"

"No, no, not at all," I corrected him, taken aback at the suggestion that a European discovered anything so monolithic in Indochina. "He travel only, he no discover."

In April 1858, kissing his faithful wife and family goodbye, financed by the Geographical and Zoological Societies of London, Henri Mahout left England aboard a merchant vessel sailing to Siam (Thailand). He spent the next three years bumbling around Siam, Cambodia and Laos, shooting wild game, collecting animal and plant specimens, penning a copious diary and being feted by the royal courts.

In January 1860, Mahout wandered into the Khmer ruins of Angkor, the prodigious network of tombs, temples, palaces, moats, reservoirs and causeways, much of which languished in a tangle of riotous jungle like some botanical Pompeii. After spending months filling his diary with notes, drawing in pen-and-ink the razor-fine details of Angkor architecture, he departed the fabled temple complex and traipsed around the eastern frontiers of Siam with his butterfly net and insect collection in tow, before finally returning to Bangkok.

From the capital of Siam, he made his way up the Mekong, arriving in Luang Prabang on July 25, 1861. He was the first European to travel there in over 200 years. "The Lake of Geneva does not present scenes more beautiful than many here by the river," Mahout wrote. Within a few days, he was received "with great pomp" by King Chantharat, who squatted on a gilded couch-like throne, shadowed by a brood of prostrating princes.

After two weeks amongst the imperial ambiance of Luang Prabang, Mahout departed on his final expedition, traveling up the Khan River only to die from "jungle fever," malaria. His last diary entry was on October 29th, "Have pity on me, oh my God...!" He died on November 10, 1861.

A posthumous French account of his travels was published in 1868, *Voyage a Siam et dans le Cambodge*. An instant success, the book buzzed France and the rest of the West with intoxicating descriptions of Angkor: "...a rival to that of Solomon, ... it is grander than anything left to us by Greece or Rome." "See Angkor and Die," became a catchphrase in France. But Mahout never claimed to have discovered Angkor, as there are firsthand travel accounts of Angkor going back to the 13th century.

In 1867, the French expedition up the Mekong led by Doudart de Lagree arrived in Luang Prabang. The expedition leaders were greeted by King Chantharat in the same Royal Palace hall which Mahout visited six years earlier. Lagree was under orders from his superior, Admiral de La Grandiere, to give his fellow Frenchman an appropriate burial and monument—the least they could do since the French had admittedly neither supplied "help nor encouragement" to the wandering naturalist.

King Chantharat agreed to provide raw materials for a sandstone monument, while Mr. Delaporte, the artist of the expedition, designed the tomb. After paying their obligatory tributes, leaving Mahout to rest in European fashion, the French expedition moved on up the Mekong, ending their trip in China in 1868.

Mahout's gravesite was left to be rediscovered in 1991 by some anonymous aid workers. His tomb lay strangled in the aggressive clutches of the jungle, much as Angkor was when Mahout found it.

Phone, my driver, had learned his history from guidebook-toting tourists, passing along tidbits of the European paradigm of history. Like many young men in Laos, his only education came from studying Buddhist scripture during his time as a monk.

We walked up the tamped-earth steps to a clearing, surrounded by a handsome stand of blue gum trees. Long-stemmed, orange irises grew like weeds around the white tomb with its black sandstone panel inscribed: *Henri Mahout, 1826-1861.*

Only months before Mahout succumbed to malarial fever he penned his reflections on dying in the tropical jungles of Southeast Asia:

I candidly confess that I have never been more happy than when amidst this grand and beautiful tropical scenery, in the profound solitude of these dense forests, the stillness only broken by the song of birds and the cries of wild animals; and even if destined here to meet my death, I would not change my lot for all the joys and pleasures of the civilized world.

In silence we descended the line of steps back down to the shallow river, its limpid waters dashing off the rocky shoals. Two men in fishing pirogues at the head of the shoals, stripped to their underwear, cast their spacious nets with the graceful tempo of fly fishermen. Black-and-yellow winged butterflies flittered among the stripling willows as the sun fell over the water like a peeled mango, splattering the stream in a savory tinge of gold.

The following morning, an off-key crescendo of cock-a-doodle-doos stole our last snatches of sleep as a rhythmic backbeat of quavering gongs echoed from the nearby temples. I hurried out of bed, dressed in tropical austerity and treaded quietly up to Sisavangvong Street in front of Wat Saen.

The temple grounds were awash in pink and white frangipani blossoms perfuming the fresh morning air. In devout silence, still rubbing the sleep from their eyes, almsgivers trickled onto the streets, placing bamboo mats, dwarf-size stools and vessels of food in a serving line next to the road. A market lady sold me several packets of sticky rice enfolded in banana fronds. Soon a steady stream of monks flowed from the *wats* in sinuous lines of saffron. In shaved-head-sameness, bandoleered in slings with lacquered begging bowls attached, they padded their daily rounds for alms, not in the strident step of military cadence but in silky strides of moral authority.

It didn't take long to drop my packages of sticky rice into the monks' bowls. In doing so I noticed two begging bowls filled with candy bars and packages of potato chips. Seated beneath a fecund mango tree, one family of devotees removed their shoes as a sign of respect, donned white scarves and spooned three-finger dollops of rice into the begging bowls. In turns, each monk removed the lid on his begging bowl, averted his eyes and gave no gesture of thanks to the almsgivers—the monks are doing them a favor by accepting the food.

From an early age, Lao Buddhists are taught that daily almsgiving nurtures generosity in their hearts and accrues piles of merit for them at the karmic bank. In Lao Buddhism, merit and karma feed the cause-and-effect cycle of countless rebirths, *samsara*, a legacy of Hinduism wherein the next life is dependent on the previous ones, guiding adherents to be more conscious about their conduct. Unlike the Biblical afterlife of heaven and hell, reincarnation works like an eternal merry-go-round: a deserving dog can, in a succeeding life, switch position with its own master. At variance with monotheistic religions, which have a creator set apart from or above nature, Buddhism is holistic and eternal, lacking a clear alpha or omega.

Yet *samsara* does have a destination. The "endless cycle" of rebirth can be ended by attaining *nirvana* or enlightenment. *Nirvana* is, however, regarded as a shot-at-the-moon target beyond the ordinary aim of Laotian Buddhists. And it may be this resignation to modest spiritual gains that gives Laotian women solace in accepting the common local belief that only a man can achieve *nirvana*.

Over 60 percent of Laos's five million people are Theravada Buddhists, mainly lowland Lao-lum people. Most young male Buddhists spend up to three months living in a *wat* as monks usually during Buddhist Lent, or *phansaa*, or else before getting married. A few young women similarly become nuns.

At the temple they live as ascetics, eating only food collected by begging. They can own only meager essentials provided by almsgivers: a razor, needle, filter for clearing their drinking water of insects, begging bowl, an umbrella, three robes of saffron for men, or of white for women. The novice monks, or *samaneras*, adhere to 10 vows, covering the usual moral grounds and reinforcing a simple and disciplined lifestyle: no stealing, no killing sentient beings, no sex, no sauce, no lying, no food after noon, no cash, no sleeping on comfortable beds, no song and dance, and no ornamentation.

The day is spent studying the teachings of Sakyamuni, the historical Buddha. The teachings, or *dhamma*, are taken from the Pali Canon, the Bible of Theravada Buddhism, committed to writing about 400 years after Sakyamuni's death in 483 BC. The novices, when not studying or meditating, are occupied with odd jobs, such as keeping the *wats* in fresh paint and lacquer, or practicing their English with visiting tourists.

During the civil war in Laos, the *sangha*, or monastic community, found themselves aligned with the communist vision of a better world—redistribution of wealth and succoring the poor were appealing goals. However, the Pathet Lao betrayed their monastic partners. The *sangha* was replaced by the Lao United Buddhist Association, run by party ideologues who attempted to meld 2,500 years of Buddhist thought and practice with the theoretical doctrines of Marx and Lenin. Almsgiving was banned, monasteries were turned into cooperatives, and monks were required to grow crops and breed livestock, corrupting their time honored vows to abstain from killing and to only live by the merit-making charity of almsgivers. By 1979 their numbers had dwindled to 1,700. After tilting against the windmills of reality for several years, the party lightened up and the ranks of the *sangha* have swollen back toward pre-1975 levels.

I circled back near the Mekong. As far as the eye could see, a wavy line of yellow frocks passed along the receiving line of improvised buffets. In measured silence the boys returned to their respective temples after another successful forage. It felt like the dawn of a world reborn with grace and compassion.

It wasn't long before Simon and I loaded our packs on another fast boat and thundered off in the direction of Vientiane, shimmying and shaking once again through the Mekong's slow minuet.

Pirogues worked the creases among the rock fields, men checking their nets. The fishing was congested and as the day reached mid-morning, many fishermen were already displaying their fresh catch for sale—perch, carp, mud and channel cat—with a set of counterweights stashed nearby.

Along the Mekong, fishing is the most common industry—a family enterprise that provides the Laotian's main source of protein. Piscatorial skills are learned from infancy and practiced daily. Men, women and children ply the waters in dugout canoes setting trotlines, laying cavernous traps of bamboo and rattan, setting bamboo poles along the sand reefs, casting spacious trammel nets from dugouts, and harpooning the bigger fish, or just standing in the shallow margins with a string and hook.

The river's trophy catch is the *pla buek*, or giant Mekong catfish. Growing up to 600 pounds, it is the largest scaleless freshwater fish in the world. The *pla buek* also provides an oil used in the production of cosmetics. A full-sized catfish fetches between one and two thousand dollars. Because of the huge financial incentives, the *pla buek* has been overfished in the Thai and Lao waters of the Mekong, causing a predictable decline in numbers. The dams being built in China pose another human-induced threat to the future of the giant catfish; the *pla buek* can no longer migrate to spawn in their natal headwaters.

Soon the sun turned white hot and the river unfurled like a belt of glistening silver. A clutch of women in palm-leaf hats squatted along a rocky shoreline with broad circular bamboo trays normally used for winnowing rice, but here used to sift for gold. Not only do Lao-lum women pan for small quantities of gold, their culture is matrilineal, giving them final say on money matters. When a couple marries the husband moves into the home of his wife's parents. Eventually they build their own thatched hut nearby and farm the land. This cycle continues until the youngest daughter is married and moves in with her parents. It is her responsibility to live with the parents and take care of them until they die. It is usually the youngest daughter who inherits the home, land and other family assets. "[Lao women] tend to operate within an informal women's solidarity framework, a concept popular in Laos long before it entered any Western feminist's mind," wrote Dervla Murphy in *One Foot in Laos*.

Behind a rampart of 30-foot boulders, a barge was inching upstream, salmon-like. It was too dangerous for us to thread the slim chute at the same time.

We pulled up to a rice barge moored along the shore, and jumped atop its deck, hearing the churning bellow of the advancing boat without seeing it. After half an hour, the screaming, big-bellied, serpentine-green barge finally chugged into view, draped with laundry fluttering in the fluvial breeze. It was now our boat's turn to pass through the rocky gauntlet. Under the gaze of several onlookers across the river, we quickly donned our lifejackets and hit the fast water like rock stars, almost swamping at first in a shower of white water, before emerging drenched.

We stopped at the floating petrol station at Paklay, ostensibly to get fuel and lunch. But it turned out we were also getting another taste of Mekong knavery—our captain began switching our gear to another boat. He had told us back in Luang Prabang that he'd take us all the way to Vientiane. Fortunately I had only paid half the agreed fare. And also fortunately I had mellowed since the incident upriver near Huay Xai, realizing the futility of trying to change something unchangeable. A parley ensued without the aid of a common spoken language, using an exchange of numbers written on a piece of paper, before we agreed to our new captain's terms—a Hobson's choice at best. (As it turned out, his skills as a fast boat captain were the best we had seen.)

We left Paklay in a light rain, while the sky turned smoky and dark. Soon, a golden Buddha carved into the side of a mountain heralded the shores of Thailand. Forming the border of Laos and Thailand for the next 600 miles, the river makes an abrupt turn to the east at this point, bent by earthquakes tens of millions years ago. But for those cataclysmic events, our trip down the Mekong would have taken us almost due south to Bangkok and out into the Gulf of Siam. Such tectonic whims prompted one historian to conclude, "Civilization exists by geologic consent, subject to change without notice."

Near the turn in the river, the city of Chiang Khan, Thailand, came into view on the south shore, dotted with red-roofed temples protected by flying nagas, or dragon-headed serpents. Many of the temples there are fronted with colonnades and fenestrated with painted shutters, an influence of the French. Chiang Khan was historically a local power center, one of the clan-based city-states known as *muang* in ancient times.

Before the French imposed the European custom of rigidly defining colonial borders in Indochina, the more familiar local notion of a loose dominance or *mandala* held sway. *Mandala* is a concept drawn from Indian political philosophy that describes the loose and shifting allegiances of *muangs* with the dominant regional power centers to which they paid tribute in return for military protection. Today, obscured in the shadows of colonial history, *mandalas* are nonexistent other than as lingering spheres of economic influence and exploitation.

A few miles downstream from Chiang Khan, above the rapids at Kaeng Khut Khu, and along a very crowded beach on the Thai shoreline, several trucks were being loaded with freshly harvested teak wood, ferried across the river from Laos. In 1989, all logging was banned in Thailand, making Laos and Cambodia the primary sources of old-growth timber in the region.

Beyond the rapids, the air thickened in a miasma of smoke. Once again, we were careering through a swarm of gently falling ashes before entering a long valley that was wedged beneath a set of lofty ridges. But the valley was on fire. Towering columns of flames climbed the once-forested slopes on both sides, spitting out thunderheads of ebony smoke and darkening the sky. It felt like a boat ride through one of Dante's circles of hell.

But this conflagration was relatively benign. Hill tribes were simply slashing-and-burning the old growth forest, selling off the hardwoods, and they would in due time broadcast the slopes with seeds of rice.

We emerged from the mountains into a sea of open water where the Thon River flows into the Mekong. The banks were low and flat and fell to the horizon in simple and soothing relief. The river was calm, yet lightly ruffled in irregular patches.

In the time it takes to hiccup and say Jiminy Cricket the bruised sky erupted in claps of thunder. Bolts of lightning cracked the horizon and a fierce wind howled, as torrents of rain slashed down and stung our bare skin. The boat shuddered severely, seeming on the verge of break-up. But the captain neither throttled back nor did he blink. We were running wide open through the eye of a Mekong storm. Soon, we swept wide around a bend. The boat dock on the west end of Vientiane came into view. In an instant we were out of the boat, waving the captain goodbye, and scrambling for cover up the muddy embankment.

When the French explorers arrived by boat on the shores of Vientiane, the city's ancient glory had been overtaken by the web of jungle much like Angkor had been. "We hastened to enter the thick forest which hid the ruins of this unfortunate city," wrote a wide-eyed Francis Garnier. "Fire and slavery after victory are, for most of the Asian races, the final outcome of a conquest. In the ruins and the solitude of [Vientiane] we find a striking example of this brutal destruction."

The great temple Pha That Luang, today fashioned in the form of a long-nippled lotus blossom and glistening in a wash of gold leaf, captures the psychic imprint of the Laotian Buddhist spirit—making merit and a good rebirth. This and a few other vestiges of civilization were left partially intact in 1828 when Rama III of Siam ordered Vientiane burned to the ground.

The razing occurred after Vientiane's King Anuvang returned from the Vietnamese court with 1,000 soldiers. It was then that they decided to rebel against the Siamese garrison stationed there as a condition of Vientiane's subservience to the neighboring kingdom. Pumped by the blood of martial success, Raxavong Ngau, the crown prince of Vientiane, upped the stakes by fomenting a popular rebellion against the more formidable Siamese imperial *mandala*. The Siamese army dropped back to marshal their forces, then quickly put the meager Lao army on their heels, defeated them and razed the city. King Anuvong was captured, taken to Bangkok in a cage and perished there.

Killed in battle, the rebellious prince Raxavong was posthumously honored by the Pathet Lao in 1949 when they named their first resistance unit the Raxavong Brigade, as they and the Vietnamese launched guerrilla activities against the French.

Over a century and a half later, the rebellious Simon crashed the Vientiane night scene with a vengeance, like a sailor on an overdue shore leave. After casing most of the joints around the circular fountain near the river, he settled on the Wind West, a new cowboy bar in town. Owned by an enterprising local buckaroo, the bar was festooned in a log cabin motif, complete with swinging saloon doors, wagon wheels, and paintings on the walls of cowboys and Indians doing battle. A Lao band played Pink Floyd tunes to the room full of cowgirl prostitutes and Simon.

Travel writer Paul Theroux visited Vientiane in the early 1970s and later described the city's endemic vices in the *Great Railway Bazaar*: "The brothels are cleaner than the hotels, the marijuana is cheaper than pipe tobacco, and opium is easier to find than a cold glass of beer." After the communist takeover in 1975, the Lao People's Revolutionary Party set out to eliminate social evils—drugs and sex at the top of the list. In the 1980s, after years of obsessive surveillance and dispatching women to Girl Island, a re-education camp, the Party authorities announced that they had eradicated prostitution. No one really believed it with Thailand just across the river: the Land of Smiles and a million prostitutes. In frustration, the Party officials softened their rigid posture by concluding that some women "just like to do it."

The traveler's lodestone in Vientiane is the dusty plaza Nam Phou, where the old waterless fountain and unkempt beer garden run by an affable Croat man once did a booming trade. It has since been transformed into a tasteless, octagonal-shaped park with fresh mowed grass encircled by a modernist strand of wrought iron streetlights. An incongruous socialist edifice, a six-story gray office box built in the early days of Pathet Lao glory, hulks above the low-rise plaza. A bulbous hibiscus tree flowers on the east side of the park. Frangipanis bloom in the shadow of the *Bibliothèque Nationale du Laos*, the colonial library on the south end of the plaza. All is washed in a dusty patina of red laterite, the film through which most of Vientiane can be seen.

I grabbed a table outside of Nam Phou Restaurant and ordered a cheeseburger —pickle-less, but loaded with onions, and slathered in French mustard.

Charlie Parker's "Night In Tunisia" played on the outdoor sound system. As I scanned the square, the eclectic sampling of bars and restaurants constituted a United Nation's quorum—L'Opera Italian Restaurant, Le Provencal, Scandinavian Bakery, Gourmet Mediterranean Deli, and Khob Chadeu—all set amid drooping flags of the communist hammer and sickle.

Over the past year a spate of mysterious bombings had occurred around Vientiane, beginning with a firebomb tossed over the wall at Khob Chadeu one early evening when a friend of mine happened to be having dinner there. He was sitting across the courtyard from where the firebomb exploded. He assumed a cooker had exploded. A few people were injured. The restaurant was back in business the next day.

Since then explosions have also occurred on the Friendship Bridge to Thailand, killing several people, and in front of the Vietnamese embassy on one of Vientiane's main roads, which caused only minor injuries. The Orwellian local papers have been silent on the bombings, sticking to Big Brother's poppycock about Party successes. At the same time, the cadre does not want to scare off tourists, which is probably what the attacks were meant to accomplish—sabotaging the stability of the government. On the street and in the international media, the finger of blame seems to point to Vang Pao, the former CIA proxy known as the "King of the Hmongs," living in well-financed exile in southern California with at least two of his six wives and his 26 children.

Simon and a new English acquaintance, Toothless Dave, were sidled up at the Khob Chadeu bar. Toothless Dave, wrinkled and wasted beyond his early-40 years, maintained that he had been living in Vientiane for the past year with his Thai bride, working as a motorcycle mechanic. Judging from his demeanor and several inconsistencies in his story, I would guess his rap sheet would stretch from Vientiane to Venus.

As I straddled a stool at the bar, the two of them were lamenting the death of the Queen Mum while downing beers costing just a dollar for six. Sloshed and sappy, with no details of her death, at 101 years old, they were both ruling out a suicide and seemed loath to accept their own suggestion of a royal-repeat of death-by-car-wreck. Simon wondered if Elton John might rewrite "A Yellow Brick Road" and sing it at the Queen Mum's funeral.

An attractive Irish woman of 30-something, Maeve, joined them at the bar. The three of them toasted the Queen Mum as the best of the royal lot. But soon Maeve was overwhelmed by Catholic guilt—admitting to a high level of anxiety about what her mum back in Dublin would think of her getting drunk on Easter Sunday. Visibly stressed, Maeve left after two beers and didn't return. (No regrets, I presume, about the swell company she was keeping at the bar.)

Simon and Toothless Dave picked up some ganja from a *tuk-tuk* driver and started touring Dave's haunts. They began at a Vietnamese gin-bar, where Simon endeared himself to the female owner and bar staff by singing a couple of tuneless and toneless strains of a Hanoi ballad. They eventually landed in Toothless Dave's favorite cathouse... dancing with the cats and drinking with the local police and government officials.

Shore leave in Vientiane was almost too much inspiration for the visionary artist from London. Meantime I, sober and bloated, walked down along the esplanade embowered in mature acacia and jacaranda trees. The river makes a sharp turn to the south, in a pell-mell confluence of East and West, the gilded resplendence of the Buddhist temples and the colonial-era Presidential Palace share front row river space with Pizza Xia, Mixay Massage, Nazim Indian Restaurant, and thatched huts advertising Pepsi and Tiger Beer.

Across the river lies the northeastern Thai region known as Isaan. At the turn of the twentieth century, with the anti-colonialist blessing of Siamese officials, over 20,000 nationalist-minded Vietnamese found sanctuary in Isaan. In the late 1920s, as the ferment of anti-French sentiment stirred, a Vietnamese man in his late 30s posing as a Catholic priest and using the alias of Father Chin arrived in Isaan.

Father Chin soon began organizing and networking the Vietnamese patriots in the communities of Udon Thani and Nakhon Phanom. He cross-pollinated them with the ideologies of nationalism and Marxist-Leninist social revolution. The firebrand priest, a linguist of note, formed the Indochinese Communist Party in October 1930. The Central Committee of the new communist party issued a foreboding statement:

"Although Vietnam, Cambodia, and Laos are three separate countries, in reality they are from only one region. In an economic sense they are tightly linked together, while politically they have all been ruled and oppressed by the French imperialists. If the workers and all the laboring masses in the three countries want to overthrow the imperialist, the monarchs, and landlords to restore their independence and liberate themselves, they cannot struggle separately. So the Communist Party, the vanguard of the working class and the leader of all the masses in waging the revolution, must also not just separately represent Vietnam, Cambodia, or Laos. If the enemy of the revolution is composed of a united force, then the Communist Party must also concentrate the force of the workers in all Indochina."

Father Chin would later become known as Ho Chi Minh, "the hidden figure in the carpet," whose revolutionary thread would ultimately wrap around the world.

Amid the steady background din of *tuk-tuks* winding their gears, I made my way to the quiet of a thatched hut perched above the Mekong. The water level was low, exposing all the dry season sandbars, spits, reefs and islands—postcards from my past.

Over three decades ago, my final days in the U.S. army were spent in Isaan at a listening post occupied by the Army Security Agency—radio reconnaissance minions of those whiz kids running the secret war. The outpost Ramasun Station was aptly named for the local "thunder god," the same one Simon and I had encountered in the storm upriver. In the Army post, we worked and dwelled in the shadow of possibly the world's largest radio receiver dish. Shaped like half an eggshell, but the size of a football field, the dish plucked fresh waves of North Vietnamese war talk from the sky. It looked like a flying saucer casting its beam to some empyrean receptor.

I landed in Isaan because my superb typing skills had won me a promotion from general clerk to the finance corps, a group of mostly college graduates. With my police record duly waived and expunged, the army even gave me a top security clearance, and a 45-caliber side-arm to go with my M-16. I was charged with paying paramilitary operatives, cryptograph operators, and other less notables in the region. We were at the edge of the war, attempting to plug the holes of insurgency started in the time of Father Chin.

When I was not sitting in a vault or iron cage camouflaged by cash, a handful of fellow REMFS (Rear Echelon Motherfuckers) and I hung out on the Mekong, catching a sampan at Nong Khai, near the present-day Friendship Bridge, to a random postcard island in the middle of the river. Only an occasional shrub or willow sprouted on those islands, leaving us scant shade to while away a day at the beach smoking "Laotian tops," harvested by monks under the holy *Wesak* moon, or so the seductive sales pitch went. When we tired of drinking hot wine, we would run hot beer sorties to the eastern shores of Vientiane—an illegal destination for GIs at the time, unless one was "sheep dipped," a term used for soldiers-turned-spooks. Sometimes after a beer run we'd take a splash in the margins of the big muddy Mekong with one of the Isaan girls, all the time watching and listening to the steady migration of metallic birds crossing overhead—C-130s, Uh-1s, AC-47s, F-4s, T-28s, Ch-3s, H-34s, AC-119s, 0-1s, C-123s, F-105s, A-1s, U-17s. We, out-of-uniform voyeurs of the secret war, had a front row seat at the Pentagon's Parade Day—set on some provincial Potomac. Only a few miles away, and divided by a river, life was quite different.

The fighters and bombers were dropping their payloads over the Plain of Jars, the Ho Chi Minh Trail, and sundry targets in North Vietnam, all widely known by the press and public at the time. Working beneath the radar of common wisdom, the transports, helicopters, spotters and vintage bombers, piloted by a bunch of CIA cowboys and air force mavericks known as Ravens, were all destined for Long Tieng, "Spook Heaven," the CIA base northeast of Vientiane. Some flights hauled refugees or the wounded or dropped rice supplies on war-torn Hmong villages. Until discovered by the press in 1970, Long Tieng was the second largest city in Laos and arguably the most secret spot on earth.

The real folly of those languid and transforming days on the Mekong, for us little guys looking up, was "truth is the first casualty of war," which called to task many of the iconic influences in my life. All versified with God and Country, inflicting mass carnage was known as pacification; the military invasion and occupation of another country was called liberation;

and search-and-destroy really meant destroy-and-search. This reverse speak, coupled with the deceptions of the secret war, were tell-tale signs of a wider condition where one only listened to those who were in agreement, reinforcing ideologies and presenting a situation ripe for miscalculation. During the Johnson and Nixon years, almost all those who disagreed with the President on the prosecution of the war were not invited back to discuss the topic, or else they were simply fired.

One man who certainly did disagree was Daniel Ellsberg, the defense strategy analyst who made history by leaking the Pentagon Papers. In November of 1968, long before Ellsberg went public with his views, Henry Kissinger acknowledged Ellsberg's expertise saying, "I have learned more from Dan Ellsberg than from any other person in Vietnam."

Despite this, Kissinger failed to heed Ellsberg's advice. For the next three years, as Kissinger and Nixon secretly bombed the bejesus out of Indochina, they started to resemble caricatures in a *Saturday Night Live* sketch rather than level-headed public servants. This was revealed by Nixon's White House tapes:

President: How many did we kill in Laos?

Kissinger: … In the Laotian thing, we killed about ten, fifteen [thousand]….

President: See, the attack in the North [Vietnam] that we have in mind…power plants, whatever's left—POL [petroleum], the docks… And, I still think we ought to take the dikes out now. Will that drown people?

Kissinger: About two hundred thousand people.

President: No, no, no…I'd rather use the nuclear bomb. Have you got that, Henry?

Kissinger: That, I think, would just be too much.

President: The nuclear bomb, does that bother you?… I just want you to think big, Henry, for Christsakes.

They did think big: talking about casualty numbers as dispassionately as a stockbroker recounting last year's trades. Even with Kissinger's mild objection, they were capable of much grander deeds: in one period of a year and a half, they authorized 75 times the explosive equivalent dropped on Nagasaki to be rained over Indochina. We were then, and even more so today, in the age of mega-death, when victims' voices are silenced in abstract tabulations known as "body counts." As genocidaire Joseph Stalin once quipped, "A single death is a tragedy, a million deaths is a statistic."

Guernica without a Picasso

imon and I rented a jeep and driver and traveled north from the Mekong to the Plain of Jars, then beyond to the old Pathet Lao headquarters in a complex of caves in Sam Neua province. Beyond the mysterious appeal of the prehistoric structures of the Plain of Jars, my military past left me feeling a sense of responsibility to visit and comprehend the defenseless places that had been targets of our severe aerial bombardment. Mostly, I am the converse of the guilt-ridden civilian described by 18th century English writer Samuel Johnson: "Every man thinks meanly of himself for not having been a soldier." Although I feel fortunate that as a soldier I never danced with the wartime ghosts who shadow Tuck Freeman, I am haunted by my youthful apathy. Mine was the course of least resistance while others more committed gave their hearts and souls, if not their lives… peaceniks, privates, pilots and peasants alike.

Joining us for the ride were a couple of American wannabe Pancakers, Cynthia and Lilly, who were exactly my children's ages, 25 and 27. They had stumbled on to us on a Sunday afternoon, shortly after their arrival in Vientiane, while they were looking for an ATM machine. They had no money, and the banks were closed. They soon found Vientiane had no ATM. Cynthia, a recent anthropology graduate from the University of California and Lilly, a textile importer living in San Francisco, struck me as worthy traveling companions, so we offered them a ride. We would work out their money problem later. I sat up front with the driver, while Simon dazzled them with expatriate tales of *Indochine*.

Within three hours of traveling up Highway 13, the jagged karst pedestals of Vang Vieng loomed into view, shadowing a bend in the west bank of the Nam Song River, a tributary of the Mekong. A few years ago, Vang Vieng began devolving from a scenic Iron Age hill tribe enclave to its present circus atmosphere, the hottest new G-spot for imported culture. As our jeep reached the carnival-like midway, Cynthia and Lilly seemed to tingle with excitement. They had heard yarns from seasoned Pancakers of Vang Vieng's hedonistic glory. Neon signs shouted at us: Real Bangkok Pancakes, Best Pizza, Banana Pancakes, Hand Woven Trousers (Pantaloons), Kayaks, Pancake Breakfast, Inner Tubes, Laundry Service, Bike Rental and the ubiquitous Israeli Salad Served Here. In a single bound, we had leapt from the Iron Age into Disney World.

Among the gathering of young nations, an army of Israelis filled the streets uniformed in Pancaker regalia. Israelis have become a common sight in Southeast Asia in recent years, particularly in Laos and Thailand. Menus appear in Hebrew in certain establishments in Chiang Mai, in Bangkok's Khao San Road and now Vang Vieng. Many Israelis take off six months or a year after their mandatory army service, typically beginning an ascetic *Wanderjahr*-to-the-East in Bangkok. Because they are Israeli, they skip Muslim Malaysia and Indonesia. Their collective migrations are as predictable as the annual monsoons.

Strains of "Santana" drifted through the neon arcade. The façade of restaurants and bars swelled with Pancakers sitting cross-legged on raised bamboo and mattressed platforms. They circled around low-set tables, Laotian style, eating Israeli salads and pizza and watching foreign videos. Barefooted practitioners of inner-tubing, a recently introduced American fraternity sport, walked the streets with the self-satisfied bearing of swamis.

Abandoning a hopeless search for a bank or moneychanger, we went to the river and watched the inner-tubers arrive at the take out point. For the Hmong and other hill tribes, this scene—a vulcanized school of half-naked foreigners flopping around like half-baked fish, stoned to the gills on grass and opium and using the sacred and succoring waters for nothing more than gratuitous merriment—must have been like watching Reality TV.

After a few beers and provisioning, with daylight waning, we returned to the highway, pushing north to Kasi. Cynthia and Lilly were tempted to abandon us old farts and join the jamboree, but decided instead to hang on for the free ride. They promised themselves a full week in Vang Vieng after circling back from Luang Prabang in a few days.

After dark we arrived in Kasi, a wide spot in the road with a newly-built guest house across the highway from the Nam Lik River. Kasi, were it any more laid back than it already is, might fall off the planet. It was the antithesis of bustling Vang Vieng. After we ate Laotian truck-stop food next to the road house, Cindy and Lilly disappeared to their room. Simon and I carried on until a herd of cows ambled up to our miniature plastic blue table, sniffing around our Beer-lao and leftover food, as if they were sacred Hindu bovines enjoying command of the place. Laotian cows aren't the kind of cultural companions to pique Simon's attention though. We called it an early night.

At dawn's break the Nam Lik River revealed itself in full, snaking through rice paddies in an emerald mist. Whatever its beauty, this locale has yet to see the end of the secret war. Government soldier camps of stilted huts mingled with hill tribe villages. In 1998 anti-government Hmong guerrillas, alleged followers of the exiled General Vang Po, attacked vehicles on Highway 13 in an attempt to disrupt tourism. The road was believed to be safe from such attacks until recently.

Only two months after my visit with Simon, some 20 Hmong rebels greeted a bus near Vang Vieng with a spray of automatic weapons fire, killing seven locals and three foreigners. The government claimed robbery was the motive, but at least one Western diplomat pointed out that the attackers went into the bus to kill people who were wounded. Two similar incidents involving Hmong rebels occurred along the same stretch of Highway 13 a few months later when my wife and I were visiting for the Pi Mai New Year celebration, killing seven government soldiers in one ambush and 12 students in another. Countless similar incidents are all rooted in the secret war.

Yet it is difficult to pin down the truth about all this, thanks both to the Lao government's silence and the hyperbole put out by Hmong-dominated exile groups in the U.S. It is clear, however, that Hmongs in Laos and Thailand—who admit a connection with the insurgency—often receive support from relatives in the States. And if Vang Po's claims of supporting a Lao insurgency are true, then one might infer that the United States is guilty of sheltering terrorists.

We dropped Cynthia and Lilly off at a hilltop village, Phou Khoun, at the junction of Highways 13 and 7. They waited at a roadside teashop where a bus to Luang Prabang would shortly arrive. I loaned them $40 and gave them my children's addresses in the States to mail the money. I enjoy being around my children's friends and people their age, so would miss their company. They waved with grateful smiles as we pulled away. Simon was ever his sentimental self, "Well they hit the jackpot big time: a free ride in a comfortable jeep, loads of inside travel shit and cash for the road to boot."

Fortunately the guidebooks give short shrift to Highway 7 and beyond to Sam Neua: "Not a lot to write home about." I interpret this as a euphemism for a jamboree-free zone.

As we descended from the lofty crossroads, a sheet of morning clouds wrapped the darkened glens. The jagged peak of Pha Thao sliced open the cottony duvet of sky, letting cerulean blue pour through. Banks of Mexican sunflowers brightened the shadowed road with tall stalks forming a canopy of yellow that shifted in gentle waves, nudged by the morning breeze. Bamboo disks of red chili peppers dried on thatched gray rooftops. Armed with crude scythes, Hmong women in tartan green-and-blue headscarves emerged from forests beyond the flowery banks with panniers of fresh cut wood. A woman with matted hair falling down her back like the bushy tail of a raccoon walked the middle of the road, shoulder-poling vessels of water.

We stopped on the edge of a small village, near a rice hut the size of a dog-house, placed just beyond the village in case of a mass fire. A young man in shin-length black trousers stood atop a primitive ladder standing straight up from the ground, appearing to defy gravity as he leaned and poured baskets of golden rice into a perfect wind. On closer inspection the ladder turned out to be anchored in shallow holes in the ground. He was "fanning" the grain, letting the dust-like chaff blow away with the breeze. A young girl wrapped like a woman in purdah to keep out the airborne chaff scurried around below on a pad of bamboo, whisking the winnowed rice into a pile.

The tarmac road traversed and tracked the Nam Jut River in a rolling matrix of ridges and ravines. The pragmatic ingenuity of the people of the Nam Jut and other rivers here evoked constant wonder. At one rocky shoal, they had built a partial dam and placed long, crudely built bamboo boxes as catchment devices across the river, open at the upstream end. At the downstream end of each box, a metal pole protruded, crowned with a fat metal disc attached with wires and splayed into a confusing web, like a backlash of filament. Each wire led to a thatched hut nearby, providing electricity to light perhaps a single bulb. This was Lao hydroelectricity on a micro scale.

After stopping at a bombed-out Buddhist temple atop a knoll forested in bamboo, we reached the village of Ban Souy. Our driver Sommay, who resembled a Laotian version of the Pillsbury doughboy, brought us to a stop in front of his friend's stilted house. His friend raised turkeys. His five or six year-old son poured loose seed for the turkeys into a small feed trough fashioned out of a cluster bomb casing. Before we got out of the truck, Sommay leaned over and whispered conspiratorially, "Don't tell anyone you are American."

Craters as large as baseball diamonds dotted the village of Ban Souy. Sommay's friend soon appeared bleary-eyed from the back of the house and greeted us in a *wai*, with clasped hands and slight bow. They talked, while Simon and I strolled around the village.

Amid a flourish of poinsettia, the man's stilted house was propped up on 500-pound bomb casings, their noses pointing upward, their fins planted into the ground as cornerstones. Many of the nearby houses were constructed with the same scraps of war—pigsties and yards fenced in a palisade of cluster bomb casings. School girls and boys streamed by in white shirts and blouses, stopping out of curiosity to watch us and see what we were photographing. The bombing had stopped 15 years before they were born, but the bombs remain. Chances are frightfully high that at least one of these kids would be blown to bits by a leftover American bomb.

Sommay was trying to buy a "little bird" from his friend—marinated swallows, a local delicacy. After coming up empty, he drove us on toward Phonsavanh, departure point for the Plain of Jars. Not far out of Ban Souy, we turned off the tarmac and passed a fenced area where Lao de-mining personnel were scanning the moonscape with mop-handle-size detectors, wearing coveralls with flak jackets and blast-proof helmets. They were from UXO Lao, an international NGO (nongovernmental organization), charged with removing unexploded ordnance.

Twisting up a dusty road, we stopped briefly at Tam Pha, a Buddhist shrine, before hiking to a former Pathet Lao hospital cave. Thousands upon thousands of spent penicillin and morphine ampoules littered the earthen floor, testament to the human carnage once visited upon the area.

It wasn't long before we reached Phonsavanh, a market town that serves as the new capital of Xieng Khouang province. The old provincial capital, Xieng Khouang town, no longer exists. During the secret war it was bombed to dust.

We arrived in time for a late lunch at the Sangah Restaurant, located on the main drag, a de facto museum of war scrap. As recently as 1998, according to Sommay, the drive from Vientiane to Phonsavanh took up to 12 days. It was quicker to get there by bullock cart or walking. We had made it in less than 20 hours: driving time, a night's sleep and other stops included.

Gerry Duckitt, a Canadian doing rural development work around Phonsavanh, sat at an outside table writing a letter the old-fashioned way. We asked him to join us inside the restaurant, out of the crosshairs of the sun and swirling dust. With his sun-bleached hair, year-round tan, boyish good looks, dusty flip-flops, faded jeans and T-shirt, he looked more like a surfer than an NGO worker.

Speaking fluent Lao, Thai, and bits of local tribal languages, Gerry had for the previous four years chosen to live in a small village about 10 miles away rather than "downtown" Phonsavanh. His work focuses on sustainable management of soil, water and forests. But dearer to his heart is his own project to revive the ancient art of making paper umbrellas, known locally as *khan nyu*. The handmade umbrellas were traditionally crafted by monks and novices living in pagodas, using spokes and struts carved from two different types of specially selected bamboo. The parasol paper is made from the bark of the indigenous mulberry tree, painted with decorative designs done in organic pigments.

Umbrellas were traditionally used more for protection from the sun than for staying dry, but their production declined after many local pagodas were bombed to smithereens during the secret war and the monastic order dismantled by the communist government. Later they disappeared entirely beneath a flood of cheap Chinese imports. Gerry's umbrella project will actually support his conservation work because villagers making the crafts will earn extra money, reducing their need to practice unsustainable farming or fell hardwood trees.

Gerry could not stop talking, spitting out local lore with staccato swiftness. After a plate of *laap*, a spicy salad of minced chicken, Gerry took us to a friend's house where he had stashed several bundles of umbrellas. They cost just a few dollars a piece, but there was no telling how many hours of work each one took. We bought a few as souvenirs and wished him luck before driving on to the principle site of the Plain of Jars.

It wasn't until after leaving the army that I first saw old pictures of the Plain of Jars. Those strange photos piqued my interest in the ancient history of the place. The images showed fields that were not yet pocked with bomb craters, just grassy sweeps of undulating plains, with their enigmatic adornments. Cradled in the bosom of low slung mountains, the plain looked like a dining table set with stone urns. Some observers have compared it to a giant's tea set.

The Plain of Jars is the only flat ground in northern Laos. From 1960 to 1973, during the dry season—November to May—the Pathet Lao and North Vietnamese armies would clash with the American-supported royalists and Vang Pao's tribal soldiers, until one wrested control and the other retreated. It wasn't until 1964, however, that the sky erupted, when American planes first let true terror rain. By 1969 the air over the fabled prairie was blackened in a torrent of falling bombs, code-named by military masterminds as Operation Rain Dance. To add to the cascading apocalypse, planes returning to Thailand from bombing missions in North Vietnam would often jettison their excess ordnance over the archaeological site. More often than not, the Pathet Lao or North Vietnamese were not the victims. They had fled to the hills and forests. It was innocent villagers who suffered.

In October 1969, Pop Buell, a secret war legend and aid worker whose job description was not so different from what Gerry Duckitt's is today, wrote to his children back in Indiana:

"The unblevable [sic] has been done, we do have all the Plain D Jarres [sic] area. I flew all over the Plains yesterday. There is nothing left in the whole area, blown up or burnt. Nothing left but shell holes. Maybe can make fish ponds out of them."

Simon and I ambled up to the reception pavilion at Thong Hai Hin—Site 1 on the Plain of Jars. We were greeted by a beaming barricade of cluster-bomb casings, and were *wai'd* by a sleepy cluster of Laotians. To the north, beyond a scattering of stone jars, was an air base with several planes moored along the runway. No planes came or went. We wandered cattle-like up a nearby grassy hillock where some of the biggest jars were located. Though I had only seen photos before, the jars and sweeping plains seemed uncannily familiar, like the face of a celebrity finally seen in person.

A few of the sandstone megaliths rose to a height of eight feet, weighing up to seven tons. Others were laid open like cracked eggs, while many were filled with stagnant rainwater, glazed in a coat of algae, like abandoned cisterns. We saw only one stone lid, and it was lying on the ground, the size and weight of a village millstone. Long gone are the contents of the jars: bronze bracelets, earrings of stone and glass, cowrie shells, glass and carnelian beads, hand axes, and human bones. One quickly senses that the jars are funerary urns, collectively forming an ancient cemetery.

Steeped in mystique as the megaliths on Easter Island, the locals believe the jars were put there to make and store rice wine, in celebration of a great military victory by a Chinese chieftain over a local despot. Thanks to wars, Laos's self-imposed isolation and an apparent lack of local interest, the first and only serious archaeological survey of the mysterious jars was completed in the 1930s, by the Colani sisters, Madeleine and Eleonore. These French women mapped the location of each jar, and catalogued the remaining funerary offerings in situ. They concluded the jars were ancient burial urns dating back 2,000 years ago, a finding corroborated today by modern techniques. Miraculously, according to the Colani sisters' survey, few of the jars were destroyed during the American bombings.

The majority of the 300-plus jars at Thong Hai Hin are scattered in no discernible pattern in a shallow downhill slope. A whispering wind lifted the tall grass and coiled through the puzzling maze of death urns. Simon, donning his beret, photographed the jars up close and examined them with the skillful eye of a potter, mystified by their purpose and where they might have been cast. Nearby a karst pillar stood like an islet in a sea of grassy plains, penetrated by a deep grotto—a womb in Buddhist cosmogony. The cave opening was chiseled in a perfect half-moon expression, a gnarly smile into which the villagers fled to escape bombardment. On either side of the mouth of the cave were two deep craters, like giant dimples whiskered in stubby, yellow wildflowers.

Leaving the deserted ruins, we backtracked to the main dirt road and drove south another 10 miles. Along the way were a couple of small lakes, possibly bomb craters upgraded to become a source of food. The lakes were rimmed by thatched hunting blinds—constructed like miniature lean-tos and fronted by a cleared swatch of barren earth. Flying swallows, known locally as *nok ann*, alighted on the earthen squares for a dust bath, and were quickly snared in a net. Sommay, our Laotian doughboy, called the swallows "little bird." He was bent on buying some, searching in every village we passed. Once caught and killed, the swallows, or *nok ann*, are de-feathered, gutted, marinated, fried and, if desired, stuffed with salt as a preservative. So embalmed, they keep for up to 10 days—long enough for Sommay to share some with his wife back in Vientiane.

Soon, we halted next to a patch of forest, the entry point to Hai Hin Laat Khai, or Site 3. Clanking cowbells rang through the flaxen valley, while we danced for footing across narrow and soggy paddy bunds. As we approached several haystacks of harvested rice a distant murmur of voices grew to a cackling crescendo. Women—cloaked in clouds of chaff—shared the ancient task of threshing cut rice.

On a flattened eminence leading up to a rocky ridgeline, a grove of trees sprouted above the surrounding paddies. Scattered beneath them, like the disorderly remains of some rowdy tea party, were over 100 of the sacred jars. Spilling beyond was a breathtaking view of the plains, a broad expanse of unmottled gold. We crawled in and out of the jars hide-and-seek style, like elves frolicking amid the giant's tea service.

We returned to Phonsavanh after dark and tried to find a decent guesthouse. No neon signs here. Instead the guesthouses posted their names on top of cleverly stacked bomb casings, hugging the road like mailboxes. The local architectural motif blended buildings with their natural surroundings— scraps of war. At most places we stopped, the reception area doubled as a souvenir shop... selling spent mortar shells, grenades, landmines, rockets, projectiles, howitzers, bomb casings of all sizes and the favorite and most plentiful item in stock, bomblets the size of tennis balls, called *bombies* by the Laotians. *Bombies* were everywhere, as plentiful as seashells at the beach and sold the same way conch shells are in Florida.

Fredric Branfman, an aid worker in Laos in the late 1960s, who helped expose the saturation bombing, wrote at the time of the devastation,

Never this century has there been so much bombing for so long in such secrecy by such a great power against so weak a people. Nine years of bombing, two million tons of bombs, whole rural societies wiped off the map, hundreds of thousands of peasants treated like herds of animals in a Clockwork Orange fantasy of an aerial African hunting safari.

According to UXO Lao, between 1964 and 1973 over 500,000 bombing missions occurred in Laos, dropping some 2.3 million tons of ordnance. About a third of those bombs were dropped in or around the Plain of Jars. The rest showered the Ho Chi Minh Trail in eastern and southern Laos. Of the 2.3 million tons dropped, up to 40 percent of the munitions were anti-personnel cluster bombs, each filled with up to 670 *bombies*. The "dud rate" of bombs, mortars, and rockets is routinely projected to be about 10 percent, but the empirical evidence at ground zero in Laos falls closer to 30 percent.

Landmines are designed to maim, *bombies* are meant to maim and kill. *Bombies* are armed with a variety of triggering devices—timing, impact, static electricity and rotation, to name a few. With their attractive yellow markings and ball-in-hand fit, children love to pick up *bombies*, toss them from hand to hand, spin them around. In one playful moment, they are blown to bits. In Laos there have been more than 11,000 "reported accidents" caused by unexploded ordnance since 1975, an average of more than one a day for 27 years.

Laos's devastation has been variously described as the raping of a virgin, or an apocalypse in a vacuum. Another suggestion might be a Guernica without a Picasso, after the Spanish artist's memorial to history's first aerial destruction of a defenseless city, the 1937 bombing of the Basque enclave of Guernica. Even Vietnam has its iconic images to remind us—a naked little girl running down a road with her skin melting from napalm burns. The secret war would produce no such artifacts; photographers weren't allowed in.

Simon and I walked to the Maly Hotel for dinner, almost stumbling over a canoe-sized napalm cylinder on the way. Inside we grabbed a table next to four Dutch women. They had flown in for an overnight on one of the ageing Russian planes used by Lao Air. The room was dimly lit, rustic with wooden floors, and decorated in the local form of folk art. Each table was set with a *bombi* "candleholder" in the center. Rockets adorned the walls as fin-tailed flower pots. Standing next to us at the spot where one might place a luxuriant fan palm was instead a captured M-60 machine gun on its tripod. On a pedestal in the center of the room, was a hand-held rocket launcher pointed skyward.

Since their guide didn't speak Dutch, the four women held forth about the decor in English: "Those Americans bombed here more than anywhere."

I chose not to fuel their disgust by correcting their rankings, but I am fairly certain the Plain of Jars came in third as the most American-bombed place in the Indochina region. (South Vietnam and the Ho Chi Minh Trail in Laos would come in first and second.) In any case, I was as moved by what I saw that day and wondered to myself what the pilots might think if they could visit here and see the mess they had left. Did their military duties absolve them from moral responsibilities?

Simon made a strategic decision to lay low in Phonsavanh, in order to recharge his batteries for the bright lights of Sam Neua the next night. By dawn we were sitting street-side, the air crisp and foggy, waiting on fried eggs and what was described on the menu as "American fried rice." In light of local history, Simon mused aloud on what might be contained in a dish by that name.

Emerging sleepy-eyed from the blanket of fog, a Chinese man with a chiseled face and Mao hat pushed his dumpling cart past us, clouds of charcoal smoke rising out of his steam pots. Lao boys on bicycles equipped with TV-size tin boxes welded to the pillion seat squeezed their air horns and sold hot baguettes, a pleasant legacy of the French era. Hmong women in laceless tennis shoes shouldered baskets bristling with produce to the market around the corner. Six monks clasped their begging bowls and halted next door, where a woman draped in a white scarf ladled spoons of sticky rice. After each scoop she wai'd with fingertips held at the highest apex of respect.

A slice of magenta cut through the fog as we rolled out of town traveling in an easterly direction on Highway 6. We zig-zagged up through the jungled mountains, the mist gradually thickening. The mountains were immense, swallowing us like a jungle enveloping the flight of a few bees. Every bend in the road seemed to open new glimpses of an imaginary land. Mexican sunflowers stippled the steep embankments and grew riotously in the valleys like canary-tinged clover. Gin-clear rivulets spilled from the forest into bamboo aqueducts that stretched above the road.

Lao-Sung villagers appeared randomly out of the mists. Wearing a Mao cap and black trousers, a bird hunter, armed with a primitive crossbow, stared cat-eyed into the gossamer forest, searching for his quarry. Barefooted, half-naked kids playfully shepherded goats, sat astride loaded pack horses, pushed miniature wooden carts full of wood and of bagged rice. Cheerful knots of women wrapped in tartan scarves with tumplines strapped across their foreheads dutifully carried more than their own body weight in chopped wood.

High mountain villages of stilted homes were festooned in sprawling poinsettias and studded with leafless trees, masts for drying sheaves of golden corn. Traffic was so light that packs of dogs lay sleeping in the road. We stopped in a weaving village where women circled us like a shoal of pilot fish. Dressed in colorful sarongs, they followed us from one household loom to the next; they were more interested to inspect us, the long-nose aliens, than to sell us cloth.

We looped wide around a blind turn in the road and found something to spoil our fantasy of a hobbit's shire: a row of cluster bombs stacked like cord wood against a shallow embankment. Nearby a legless man dragged his nubs on the shorn grass next to the highway; we would see many more like him. On the six-hour drive to Sam Neua, UXO Lao trucks were more plentiful than the scant traffic of cars and buses. In northern Laos, the grim relics of war are found in every remote jungle nook and mountain cranny.

Sommay came to a stop near the market that skirted the Nam Sam River. We had arrived in Sam Neua, a sleepy town tucked into a narrow valley surrounded by rolling ridgelines. After a look at the hill tribe market— featuring barbecue bats among other tasty repasts—we drowsily strayed down an alleyway of shops and homes before ducking into the most obscure flyblown restaurant. There were four other customers: three heavy-set American men with close-cropped hair and one well-fed American woman. We had stumbled upon an MIA (missing in action) search team from the Joint Task Force-Full Accounting.

"Captain Porkchop," the man in charge of the group, and Simon and I had a couple of mutual American acquaintances formerly of Hanoi, both of whom had been killed in a recent helicopter crash while on an MIA search mission.

According to current statistics published by the Joint Task Force-Full Accounting, there are still 1,872 American MIAs in Indochina, 375 of whom went missing in Laos. America's diplomatic favors to Laos and Vietnam are preconditioned on their active assistance in finding these MIAs, a much-resented policy in both Asian countries. The resentment runs deeper at the realization that tens of millions of dollars are spent every year on this quest rather than, say, efforts to remove the American bombs that continue to kill people here.

I asked Captain Porkchop if they had found any remains. "Yes, sir, we have identified the wing markings of a C-119 Flying Boxcar piloted by quite a character, Captain James McGovern, better known as 'Earthquake Magoon,'" nicknamed after the burly Lil' Abner comic strip character.

As a young fighter pilot with General Claire Chennault's Flying Tigers during World War II, Earthquake Magoon was credited with shooting down four Zeros and seven "probables." After the big war he became an anti-communist soldier of fortune. In his leather pilot's helmet, goggles pulled up on his forehead, sporting a long, bushy goatee, he looked more like a Hell's Angel biker than one of Chennault's finest. In the late 1940s, he flew supply runs for the Civil Air Transport, operated by the CIA as a paramilitary arm of Chiang Kai-shek's nationalist army, the KMT. Once while flying over an advancing Red Army, Earthquake sent communist troops scattering for cover by tossing empty beer bottles at them; the whistling noise resembled the sound of falling bombs.

The stories abound. On one supply run both engines failed, but he refused to parachute due to his weight—260-pounds. So he crash-landed the C-47 in a dry riverbed—not far from a Red patrol. He was immediately captured, but hardly contrite. According to Christopher Robbin's book *Air America*, Magoon's "delicate" feet bothered him as he was marched off to a mountain jail, so he sat down and massaged them, while his captors prodded him to move. "I'd rather be shot than walk any farther on these feet of mine," he insisted. The soldiers seized a horse from a nearby village, and permitted Earthquake to ride while they walked.

Once incarcerated, Earthquake would bellow maddeningly between meals for more food, leaving the prison guards so frazzled they gave him some of their own to shut him up. Saving up his daily ration of rice whiskey for one big birthday bash, he celebrated by busting out of his tiny cell. In the chest-pounding fashion of a charging gorilla, he destroyed the prison furniture as well. He was promptly locked back up.

As he approached six months in captivity, he taunted his PLA captors for calling themselves liberators. "Prove it by turning me loose." After escorting Earthquake to the border, giving him the local equivalent of five dollars, they happily released the recalcitrant man. A few days later in Hong Kong, when Earthquake arrived at his favorite bar, Gingles, the legendary *bon vivant* placed his order: "Set them up, I've got half a year's thirst."

On May 6, 1954, the morning of his 45th mission over the besieged French battleground of Dien Bien Phu—bordering Laos in the northwest of Vietnam—Earthquake and his wingman Steve Kusak talked about going on leave in Saigon the following week. They would hang out at the fashionable Majestic Hotel bar and at the *Croix de Sud*, known as the "Crock of Suds." With American co-pilot Wallace Buford, their C-119 "Flying Boxcar" lifted off from an air base in Haiphong, carrying several tons of ammunition and an artillery piece. For most of the day at Dien Bien Phu, the French had successfully suppressed the flak emplacements of the Viet Minh, communist troops of Ho Chi Minh. But once in the danger zone, Steve Kusak heard Earthquake's voice over the radio, "I've got a direct hit." Earthquake feathered the engines, as oil squirted onto the window of co-pilot Wallace Buford.

About the time Earthquake stabilized the Flying Boxcar, the plane took another hit in the right tail boom. From a short distance away, his friend Steve Kusak radioed and asked Earthquake if he was going to make it, while at the same time calling for a helicopter rescue. The swashbuckling veteran pilot replied, "Piece of cake," as he was known to say in the face of danger. The hulking plane rapidly lost altitude over the northern hinterlands of Laos. Earthquake declined to parachute, as the ground rushed upward, and the plane's shadow grew longer. In fearless tones, apparently addressing his younger co-pilot, Earthquake bade an aviator's farewell, "Looks like this is it, son." The Flying Boxcar's wing dug into a hillside, sending the plane into a cartwheel before exploding. The next day, May 7, 1954, Dien Bien Phu fell to the Vietnamese communists, ending the French colonial period and beginning the era of the Vietnam War.

Over 48 years later, people were still talking about Earthquake Magoon. Captain Porkchop invited Simon and me to join them for drinks and dinner later in the evening after our trip to the Pathet Lao caves. Although Simon was reluctant, I agreed to look them up.

The caves are near the village of Vieng Xai about 20 miles south of Sam Neua, nestled in the shadow of a beautiful rampart of karst formations. The upper reaches of the karst form a shaved, bone-colored face of pitted limestone, splotched in vegetative tufts and crested in a tumble of boulders.

Once part of a single mountain plateau, now decayed by time, the porous remnants are honeycombed with 102 caves, some of which served as the headquarters for the Pathet Lao during the secret war.

We were greeted by silence at the permit station as we stared upon the paternal mugs of Ho Chi Minh and Kaysone Phomvihane, a guerilla fighter for over 30 years and the father of communist Laos. In time, a young man stirred from a nap, scrawled some entries in a ledger, and handed us a permit to see the caves, which had been off-limits until well into the 1990s.

The myriad bomb craters at the mouth of each of the caves have been cleared of unexploded ordnance, and in some cases filled with dirt and blanketed in gardens of flowers and towering trees. Khamtay Siphandone, the current president of Laos, occupied the cave complex that now bears his name—Tham Thaan Khamtay. As we wandered through the musty catacomb, it branched off into bedrooms, meeting rooms, primitive ground toilets, a drive-in garage—many with concrete floors. A bomb shelter room had hermetically sealed metal doors similar to those found in a submarine. While the bombs were falling outside, which was often, the command center troglodytes would gather around a pumping device with Iron Age mechanicals and hand-crank outside air into the tomb-like room.

Making our way through limestone corridors to the back of the karst mountain, we found ourselves in a puddle-filled, vaulted room that was used as a barracks by lower ranking Pathet Lao soldiers. Next to the earthen barracks was a cavernous room, breached at both ends with broad thresholds of light. Silhouetted in the entrance opposite where we stood was a proscenium stage, hooded in teak latticework. Below the stage an orchestra pit had been dug from the cave floor. In the rustic theater setting, famous "anti-imperialist," Laotian folk singers and entertainers—such as Phu Vong and Phou Vieng, both of whom are still living—would perform revolutionary songs in front of hundreds of troops temporarily shielded from the war.

The morale-boosting performances in the rustic theater were the Pathet Lao equivalent of Bob Hope's traveling Christmas show, which I witnessed in Thailand on Christmas Eve of 1969. That evening, one of the featured entertainers was Neil Armstrong; with his unassailable credentials, he gave a rousing speech full of can-do exhortations. Across the Mekong in Laos, your average peasant wouldn't have known about Armstrong's walk on the moon five months before. When a lunar eclipse occurs here, rural Laotians are known to shout and shoot at the moon, scaring away the "cosmic frog" that is trying to gulp it down.

Simon and I indulged in an antiphonal pantomine of Woodstock's Country Joe McDonald on the Pathet Lao stage, "Give me an f... What are we fighting for..." Then we sauntered out into an Elysian Field of all manner of butterflies, poinsettias, buttercups and a purplish ground cover shadowed by the white blossoms of frangipanis and yellow acacia trees. Across the valley of mystical karst pedestals, splattered cream-white in their melting decay, Sommay drove us to Tham Thaan Souphanouvong cave where the "Red Prince" had been holed up during the secret war.

Souphanouvong was born to a concubine mother and a father of royal blood. A dashing figure with a penciled moustache, upon earning his engineering degree in France he returned to Laos during World War II to a terminally depressed job market. Like a host of French-educated elites in Indochina, he had developed an anti-colonial bent and soon found himself in Hanoi in the company of a sympathetic Ho Chi Minh. He married a Vietnamese woman, also avidly anti-colonialist, and joined the Indochina Communist Party, which by 1951 devolved locally into the Lao People's Party, or the Pathet Lao.

The Red Prince and his older half-brother, Prince Souvanna Phouma, prime minister of the Royal Laotian Government, represented their parties in more than one coalition government, all of which ended in chaos and calumny. From 1962 until near the end of the royalist-controlled government, they were at war in every sense of the word. On April 3, 1974 with the war drawing to a close, the Red Prince returned to Vientiane for the first time in 10 years, amid an outpouring of support the likes of which had never been seen there. During that day of glory he promised in a grandiloquent speech that the victorious Pathet Lao would support an "independent, democratic and prosperous Laos ...under the august auspices of His Majesty the King, Sisavang Vatthana."

Ho Chi Minh and the Pathet Lao used the Red Prince as a front man because his royal status boosted their credibility in the diplomatic arena. Although the Red Prince became titular president upon Laos's liberation and held that position until 1986, he was seventh or eighth in the party pecking order. As for his promise to His Majesty King Sisavang, the Pathet Lao has been fighting shadows since the war's end. They eventually starved and denied medical treatment to King Sisavang along with other royals after holding them at a jungle gulag near the Red Prince's cave headquarters. The communist government has never said where or whether they were buried, only that they died of natural causes.

We walked in the shade beneath a bower of pomelo trees; their fat, ripened fruit hung by tenuous stems and fell to the walkway here and there with surprising thumps. The garden-like path led to the Prince's Lao-French house, which was built after the bombing stopped. Our guide Phaeng kept referring to "before" and "after" the bombing period—1964 to 1973— in mantra-like repetition. It reminded me how Westerners mark history from the time of Christ. A garden nook featured a stone stupa built as a shrine to the Red Prince's son—also a Pathet Lao guerrilla fighter—inscribed with his name Alijathame, 7-10-39 to 12-23-67. I recalled that a Hanoi friend had attended university with him in Moscow in the early 1960s.

The Red Prince's cave headquarters was equipped with rooms for his son, daughter, doctor, an armory, meeting rooms, and a bomb-proof chamber plumbed with one of those Iron Age air pumps. A rustic kitchen consisted of a few stacked rocks, with natural notches in the limestone for chairs, and a fire ring. It looked out over a garden and beyond to more craters.

A short distance from the Red Prince's headquarters was the wartime home of Kaysone Phomvihane, the founding father of the Lao communist revolution. Born to a Lao mother and a Vietnamese father, Kaysone was educated in Hanoi and, like his mentor Ho Chi Minh, became an accomplished linguist. He enlisted in the resistance movement in the mid-1940s and fought for Ho Chi Minh and the Viet Minh against the French. Once the French left, he fought in Laos, leading the North Vietnamese and Pathet Lao against the Americans and royalists. Upon "liberation" in 1975, he became Laos's Prime Minister, a post he held until his death in 1992.

Under Kaysone's leadership Marxism-Leninism took the same pattern seen in other agrarian cultures—Vietnam, China, North Korea, Cuba and more: a strong military exacting obedience; the abolition of non-residential private property and concurrent "nationalization of all human and material resources;" the elimination of basic freedoms including free speech and an independent media; totalitarian rule by a single, all-powerful party, often headed by a cultish figure.

Kaysone never had the flair or international name recognition of other third world communist icons—Fidel Castro, Che Guevara, or Ho Chi Minh. In death, however, his myth and cult of worship is burgeoning. With the help of the minds responsible for the Ho Chi Minh Museum in Hanoi, Kaysone has been honored with a shrine palace on the outskirts of Vientiane. It falls short, however, of the Lao-Buddhist architectural style intended, instead resembling a Mississippi riverboat casino and brothel.

As for Kaysone's cave lair, befitting his role as Chairman of the Central Committee of the Politburo, it is more grandiose than the other caves. A great room mushrooms out of a long corridor where the Committee used to meet, each seat clearly marked, with the head of the table reserved for Kaysone. An arc of light pours through a natural opening, grated with reinforced steel bars like a prison. Gas lamps placed around the room were used when bombs had knocked out the power generators running electric bulbs.

Kaysone's private study was furnished with a desk, dusty tea set, and several books. In the chapel-like atmosphere of an anchorite, positioned centrally on the desk as a religious treatise might be, was a well-thumbed anthology of Ho Chi Minh's political writings, *Tuyen Tap*. To the left of the mentor's collective works, was a book of V. Lenin's in French, *L'Alliance de la Classe Ouvriere et de la Paysannerie* (The Class Alliance of Workers and Peasants). Above and behind the pulpit-like desk, a white bust of Lenin was placed next to a picture of a bewhiskered Che Guevara in his signature, stylishly tilted beret. The place was aloft in history, yet in our three or four hours there, we saw no other visitor. As for the local hill tribes, who comprise the majority living in the rural province, their seasons come and go, none of which have these people deemed in need of renaming as Lenin, Ho Chi Minh, Che or Kaysone.

We got back to Sam Neua as the sun was setting across the paddy-filled valley. We found a room in a row of A-frame huts perched along a hillside across from a rustic air strip. There were no planes on the short tarmac, only the helicopter being used by the MIA team. As the somnolent village settled into darkness, the only glimmer was the fairy lights across the street lighting up a shabby hut named the Airport Restaurant. Sommay sauntered over and sat beside me on the porch steps. Wearing an animated smile, he leaned over and asked in a half-whisper, "You want girl, ten dollars?" He pointed to a young lovely who had just finished bathing, walking into the sunset with her wet hair shimmering and wrapped in a sarong.

"Too damn expensive, Sommay, but let's get dinner with the Americans. Simon will wait here. Artists and the armed forces don't mix."

I went to check on Captain Porkchop and his team, but found them missing in action. We circled the sleepy town a couple of times, left a message with their Laotian army translator, before returning to our hillside digs. We found Simon immersed in the dubious pleasures of chewing shoe leather—a water buffalo steak—while chatting it up with a Laotian beekeeper who was there to buy bees and honey at the nearby Vietnamese border.

As we followed the twinkling lights while carefully descending the steep gradient to the road, Simon stepped in a fresh pile of cow manure. Two friendly dogs took up his scent and followed us into the Airport Restaurant, which boasted a Karaoke bar. It wasn't long before we had become the two most popular guys in Sam Neua, particularly so with the short-tailed dogs who stretched at our feet. The beekeeper showed up and bought us shots of rice whiskey, his face beet red from a day of drinking, radiating heat from its sheer redness.

The pleasantly plump proprietoress took a shine to Simon, scowling at anyone on the dance floor who threatened her territory. When not spinning traditional Laotian songs, the local maestro played Credence Clearwater Revival's hit of the late 1960s, "Have You Ever Seen the Rain?" Simon turned Pied Piper and coaxed the crowd out of their usual staid tribal minuet—no touching, all in a circle, arms outstretched like tentacles—into a hilarious, out-of-beat, bump-and-grind-pantomine of John Travolta and disco dancing. Even the drowsy curs perked up and took notice of the melee.

Simon had stolen their hearts and minds.

Captain Porkchop never showed up that night. Over a year later, I spoke to the public affairs officer at Joint Task Force-Full Accounting, and learnt that the remains found at the crash site of Earthquake Magoon's Flying Boxcar had been repatriated. As for identity of the bones, the forensic tests were inconclusive. After half a century, there were still no remains to put under Magoon's epitaph.

Gauguin on the Mekong

Having satisfied our curiosity about the horrors visited upon the inhabitants of the Plain of Jars and beyond, our Mekong journey carried on from Vientiane. After reading the *Vientiane Times*, a state owned newspaper, and having breakfast at the Scandinavian Bakery, I went to collect Simon following a night of white mischief. We got into Sommay's jeep and I threw him the newspaper with the headlines, "Crackdown: Night Clubs and Brothels Closed in Vientiane." As we bounced down the red earth road, Vientiane receding in the rear view, Simon gave me the garbled version of dancing with the cats in the government cathouse.

We picked up the tarmac and drove east out of Vientiane on Highway 13. Built in the 1930s by the French, the road tracks the meander of the Mekong from a discreet distance, converging with it at the larger villages, and stretches all the way to Saigon (Ho Chi Minh City). Near Pak Kading, as the Mekong begins to turn south toward the panhandle of Laos, we crossed a bridge built by the Soviets over the pristine Kading River. The bridge was constructed in the early 1980s when the Soviets were playing sugar daddy to the newborn communist regime. At the confluence of the two rivers the Kading River broadens into a sea of jade before melting into the silt-laden Mekong.

The Kading originates in the Annamite Mountains bordering Vietnam, a wilderness home to such rare animals as Asiatic black bears, langurs, gibbons and elephants. To the east of Pak Kading, running alongside and often braiding the Mekong catchment area all the way to the delta of Vietnam, is the jungly track once known as the Ho Chi Minh Trail.

During the Vietnam War, there were 12,000 miles of trail having five main tracks, 29 major branches, and myriad cutoffs, all of it pulsing with caravans of martial materiel. The trail spread from Laos and Cambodia into the border frontiers of South Vietnam like seismic fissures in a perpetual state of aftershock. Today, the trail is essentially extinct, although still alive with unexploded ordnance. In many places it has been overgrown by the primeval forest from which it was carved.

Several miles south of Pak Kading, we cut through the Hmong village of Ban Tong Na Me. Stilted homes of thatch and wattle gave way to fallow wet rice fields. An air of poverty hung over the place. Before being resettled at Ban Tong Na Me in 1996, the entire village had spent 21 years as refugees. Sommay was sympathetic to their plight and explained how they have not adapted to living in the lowlands. Instead they have attempted to drift back into the mountain fastnesses where they once lived. Regarding the uplands as their exclusive domain, they had recently slashed-and-burned several acres of government tea plantations to plant their own crops. According to a Hmong proverb, "Fish swim in the water; birds fly in the air; the Hmong live in the mountains."

For centuries, the Iron Age Hmong have distinguished themselves in China and Southeast Asia by maintaining their ethnic identification without the cultural glue of a written language; it is instead their deeply embedded animist world-view that makes assimilation into other cultures extremely problematic. Anne Fadiman, author of *The Spirit Catches You and You Fall Down*, describes Hmong traits: they do not like to take orders; do not like to lose; would rather flee, fight or die than surrender; are not intimidated by being outnumbered; are rarely persuaded of the superiority of customs of other cultures, even those more powerful than their own. And they are capable of getting very angry.

The Hmongs, as historic enemies of the Vietnamese, were recruited by the CIA as anti-communist soldiers. Known in the quirky military parlance as "irregulars," they became the main force fighting the communists in Laos. But after the war, the United States denied them any compensation or veterans' benefits despite their role as surrogates for U.S. GIs in fighting communists for as long as 15 years. In fact, the communist takeover forced more than 120,000 Hmong to flee Laos. They had been sucked into the secret war, spin-cycled through its havoc, and then centrifuged across the Mekong to the Ban Vinai refugee camp, among others, in Thailand.

A refugee has three options, none easy for the Hmongs: integrate into the first country of refuge (which Thailand refused to allow); eventually repatriate when the situation stabilizes (which it did not within a reasonable time); or convince a third country to open its doors. Ideally, the Hmong should have returned to Laos, but in 1975 the Pathet Lao announced a policy of genocide against them.

The fleeing families were forced to live in the cramped, deracinating confines of the Thai refugee camps for several years before they could find a sponsoring country. Finally, honoring old CIA promises, the United States opened its doors to the homeless Hmong veterans and their families. Many, as it happened, were processed into the United States at Fort Chaffee, Arkansas, and later settled in nearby Fort Smith, my hometown.

By choice, the Hmong living in the village of Ban Tong Na Me never made the leap from the Stone Age to the Space Age. The remote upland valleys, with pristine rivers bountiful with fish, and spirit-inhabited forests where they hunt, forage and gather herbs, are the settings for their world view.

Before long we passed the turnoff for Highway 8, which leads through Kaew Neua Pass into the north of Vietnam, a distance of about 60 miles. We stopped for lunch in Thakek, a river town where the population is mostly Vietnamese. The Mekong around Thakek has always been an unspoken buffer zone—for centuries a watery Great Wall separating the *mandalas* of Thailand and Vietnam. In the first half of the 20th century, many Vietnamese emigrated to Laos as colonial administrators, doing the bidding of the French over the less industrious locals. Those Vietnamese stayed and then more arrived *en masse* after the French left the north of Vietnam in 1954.

We found a Vietnamese *pho* shop along the forlorn promenade on the river, next to the colonial square, with its shabby stucco buildings in blue and buff-yellow. The French buildings wore a mangy face of chipped paint and crooked shutters. Thakek was a ghost town where all clocks had stopped. The loudest noise was the buzz of flies. I walked down the waterfront and found a couple of monks sitting on the floodwall. A leper cowered under a tree, fitfully scratching his sloughing skin and avoiding the sun.

In a typical pairing of Thai and Laotian cities along the Mekong, across the lazy slick of muddy water was the ancient *muang* of Nakhon Phanom, smiling back with glints of urban fluorescence at its country cousins. Many anti-colonial

Vietnamese settled in Nakhon Phanom in the early 20th century to escape the yoke of the French. The most famous of those settlers, whose house and garden now stand as a tourist attraction, was Father Chin, Ho Chi Minh.

During my REMF days as a finance clerk, I used to pay an army detachment at Nakhon Phanom, or NKP as we called it. The detachment was part of a special operations group attached to a gaggle of Air Commandos flying the panhandle of Laos and the Plain of Jars. NKP was blessed with having one of the largest statues of Buddha in all of Thailand for protection. It was the perfect location for a special operations unit also because of its proximity to the Ho Chi Minh Trail.

Beginning in 1959, and lasting for the next 16 years, over a million North Vietnamese went south on the Trail, toting countless tons of supplies and weaponry. By the mid-1960s, activity on the trail was like "the Long Island Expressway during rush hour," in the words of one Special Forces commando.

The Pentagon and Secretary of Defense Robert McNamara, were bedeviled by how to stem the flow. Old fashioned bombing as a means of interdiction had failed. The US techies had already unleashed the latest products from Dow Chemical: silver iodide to make rain, Calgon to make mud, and Agent Orange to defoliate the forest. Then operation "Igloo White" was hatched. The busiest sections of the trail were "wired" like a pinball machine with tens of thousands of seismic and acoustic sensors. When the system detected movement, it beamed coordinates to drones circling above. Back at command center in NKP, circuit boards flashed with lights to indicate bombing targets. It was the control panel for the biggest blitzkrieg in history. By 1970, our best fighter planes were flying almost 10,000 sorties a month over the trail and our B-52s were averaging 900 missions a month. Lower Laos and the Ho Chi Minh Trail became to many American military leaders what Moby Dick was to Captain Ahab—the object of a self-defeating obsession.

In the first century A.D., the Roman historian Tacitus wrote, "They made a wasteland and called it peace." Two millennia later we dubbed it "peace with honor."

Near the crossroads town of Xeno, at Highway 13's intersection with Vietnam's Highway 9, we turned west on a tributary road leading to the Mekong. By mid-afternoon we arrived in Savannakhet, a larger, dustier version of Thakek.

I had been to Savannakhet once, crossing from the Thai sister city of Mukdahan by ferry. On that trip a dry-season island emerged in the middle of the Mekong, blocking the ferry's passage. The boat was stacked with tins of Thai coffee, plastic containers of detergent, tires, canned goods and piles of packaged incense. It was crowded with day shoppers from both countries, who cross the river border freely without passports.

I stayed on that trip at a courtyard-style guesthouse frequented by international aid and development staff and owned by the Donald Trump of lower Laos— a man nicknamed Souvanna. There were more SUVs parked around the courtyard than I had seen in all of Vientiane. When I checked in, Souvanna's daughter Tina invited me to go swimming across the street in a large pool, perhaps the only one in the panhandle of Laos. Unlike the surrounding streets of tamped earth, the road in front of the motel was paved in concrete.

Souvanna was pudgy for a Laotian, and dark-skinned. As the local big wheel, he seemed to benefit from crony capitalism in the mode of Russia, via good connections in Vientiane. He owned, among other assets, "the" concrete and dredging company P.P.S. Sand & Rock, three cash-ginning ferries, including the one on which I had arrived, a travel agency, a 10,000 square foot palace in Vientiane, a Mercedes, and Lexus. He was President of the Chamber of Commerce and Vice President of the Savannakhet Red Cross. Eyes shining like a boy showing off his Christmas gifts, he conveyed all this within 10 minutes of meeting me, offering his business cards and various snapshots as proof.

I didn't get to meet Souvanna's wife. She had left for Bangkok to do some shopping. I spent my time drinking beer and talking to Tina. She took her anglicized name when she attended the International School in Vientiane. After leaving that pricey institution (with tuition of $12,000 a year), she moved to the States to live with an aunt and attend high school in Baltimore. While in the States she tooled around in a $25,000 Toyota Camry. After graduating high school, she went to live with a sister in Fayetteville, North Carolina.

Tina's sister was married to an enlisted man with the 82nd Airborne based there. Tina had not yet told Dad, but she, too, was in love with one of those rangers. The American called once a week and they exchanged daily emails. She showed me a picture of him in his Persian Gulf uniform. "On soldier's pay he can't afford a ticket to Savannakhet from North Carolina," she moaned. And no Laotian father would ever consider buying his daughter a ticket to the States to see a boyfriend.

Tina had been to Paris, and then Fort Bragg. She was smitten with America. "There is no way I will date or marry a Lao man." But as long as she lives in Savannakhet, she has to keep both feet in Lao tradition. She stays in at night unless chaperoned. Otherwise she would be looked down upon as having low morals, or worse still, as a prostitute. Her real dream is to marry her "ranger dude" and move him to Savannakhet to be a part of the family business.

As darkness fell, Souvanna burst into the office and opened the vault. He and Tina counted out what must have been a trillion *kip*, the equivalent of about a thousand dollars. It was payday for P.P.S. Sand & Rock. Seventy or eighty funky-smelling laborers fell in line, and Tina counted out a week's pay, about $15 a piece. They were all tongues a-wagging, thirsty for a night of rice whiskey, or *lao-lao*.

While Tina paid the crew, Souvanna showed me snaps of himself with the former American ambassador. His favorite, however, was an eight-by-ten glossy with the American MIA team who stay at his motel when in Laos searching for remains. He handled all their field logistics, another tidy profit center, compliments of Uncle Sam.

After drinking the first half of a case of beer and seeing Souvanna's MIA-team pictures, I mentioned having been stationed in Isaan while in the army. He stood up in surprise and shook my hand as if I were some long-lost relative. He considered us members of the same club; which club, I was unsure. His sudden warmth pointed at some collaboration with the Americans during the war, although he wouldn't say so. But he had not left the country after the war. And now he was a tycoon.

An educated Lao friend later told me that a figure like Souvanna was probably "owned by the Politburo," a group of nine who control all policy in Laos. "They send their kids to the U.S. to be educated," my friend warned. "Be careful what you say if you ever see him again." Even without the warning, I was as skeptical as I was intrigued by Souvanna.

We decided not to stay at his courtyard motel on this trip, although I was curious about how Tina and the "ranger dude" were doing after the passage of a year. Instead, we settled on a newly-built guesthouse a few blocks away from the river with air conditioning and a private shower.

Extending from the modern, box-like customs building, the river promenade was a cluster of plastic tarps slung over Lilliputian red and blue stools, where Laotian women served skewers of barbeque chicken and fresh fish. A block away, at the end of the town square, was a colonial church used by Vietnamese Catholics. The usual complement of dilapidated French buildings peeling from humidity flanked the square. Dotting the surrounding area were Chinese and Buddhist Temples, home to a kraal of half-painted, concrete *stupas* housing the ashes of deceased votaries. An inordinate number of dogs roamed the old part of Savannakhet, baring teeth at *farangs*. One Pancaker, with head wrapped in a red do-rag, his purse strapped across his chest, sat at the end of the colonial plaza beneath a shade tree, surrounded by kids as he sketched Savannakhet's faded elegance.

Late afternoon I found Simon at a riverfront bar with a couple of Pancaker women. As travelers do, we exchanged stories of our journeys. Reflexively they asked how much we had paid for rooms in places like Muang Sing. We had paid five dollars. They stayed on one dollar, but had to take cold showers from a bucket and walk a gauntlet of goblins in the middle of the night to use a squat toilet.

They told of fellow Pancakers who had been invited to a hooch in Muang Sing to smoke opium. By the time the calumet-pipe got cooking, the police showed up and threatened to arrest them unless they paid hundreds of dollars on the spot. Our angels had served us well.

The Pancakers ordered Lao vegetarian dishes for dinner, while Simon and I requested hamburgers. We had to settle for water buffalo steak. They were appalled, tossing light jibes across the table. Buzzed on the booze and full of mischief, Simon morphed into a Walter Mitty persona… "How about a Banana Pancake tour boat down the Mekong? Paint it yellow, shaped like a banana. Banana-scented, cold bucket showers, and a crew in yellow pantaloons. Banana pancakes served round the clock…"

After Simon's shtick, our neighbors put their hound-dog faces back on. They had waited since early afternoon for their run-down guesthouse around the corner to turn on the water. It was ten o'clock and they hadn't bathed in a few days. I had offered the shower in my room, but they were too proud— Pancaker pride. Simon and I disappeared into the sleepy silent streets.

Next morning, Simon recounted his descent into Savannakhet nightlife. He had followed an echo of music to an obscure alleyway at the back of the hotel. There a guitar and organ duo played Laotian ballads—sappy love songs—that blended into one another with no apparent beginning or end. The only foreigner present, Simon settled into a table by the stage. From that vantage point, he watched in amazement as a dance pageant unfolded.

Women of all ages and shapes swayed gracefully, at intervals lining up back to back, and twisting their elegant hands like enchantresses. In a seamless segue they glided around in a circle while the men slowly formed an inner ring, hands on hips, mirroring the women's pace. Elegant, gentle, bizarre, the dance was the *sala vhan lamvhong*, a kind of mating dance peculiar to Savannakhet. The décor was 1960s neon, but the dance seemed to recall tribal ritual. Female companionship soon was offered, and the visionary artist found himself performing his own version of the dance.

We left early the next morning for Pakse, 150 miles to the south and the last town of any size before Cambodia. Colonial Highway 13 to Pakse was recently asphalted by a consortium of countries—Thailand, China and Japan—each taking an equal share in the construction. The highway bisects several tributaries of the Mekong—the Bang Nuan, Bang Hiang, and Don Rivers—all flowing out of the Annamite Mountains that border Vietnam. Except for one leftover iron bridge built by the French, the spans were made of concrete, by the ubiquitous Soviet and Australian bridge builders.

The market city of Pakse was built by the French at the turn of the last century as the southern-most of their administrative centers in Laos. They opted for Pakse instead of Champasak, the capital of the ancient kingdom of southern Laos, to avoid interference from the royals.

The Boun Oum Palace, as wide as it is tall, is a white monstrosity that dominates Pakse's truncated skyline. The last Prince of Champasak, Boun Oum, was the third of Laos' warring princes, and a devout anti-communist. He once commanded a revolutionary army based in the panhandle of Laos. In the early 60s, the CIA used him as a front for an airline, Boun Oum Airways, equipped with a couple of American planes and piloted by Asians.

Prince Boun Oum began constructing the palace in 1968 as a 1,000-room repository for his collection of fine art, including treasures he pilfered from the nearby pre-Angkor Wat Phu. Although his indulgent lifestyle of gambling and debauchery bloated him to the size of a Sumo wrestler, the roly poly Prince of Champasak was reputed to have indulged himself with over 20 wives. As the Pathet Lao neared victory, he fled Laos in 1974 for France, and never returned, dying in Paris in 1980.

Boun Oum Palace is now a Thai-owned hotel—whitewashed, rimmed in balustrades and wide verandahs—the Lego fantasy of a *nouveau riche* oilman from Dallas. In over three decades of traveling in Southeast Asia, I have never seen any building so out of place.

Road 13 in front of the palace was abuzz with *tuk-tuks*, *sawngthaews*, motorcycles with sidecars, *saam-laaws* (three wheeled bicycles), and motorcyles with women riding pillion, side-saddled under colorful parasols. There were many vintage American cars left by the CIA in the 1950s and

1960s, now serving as taxis. It was a scene from the streets of Havana.

Pakse is an ethnic crossroads, with the Bolaven Plateau and its ethnic minorities situated to the east, the Thai border a few miles west and the Khmer frontier not far to the south. Vietnamese comprise 40 percent of the local population, and there is the usual concentration of Chinese merchants. Throughout the town, a continuous flow of saffron-robed monks poured forth from the two-dozen temples there, while rifle-toting militia in camouflage uniforms patrolled the streets.

We tooled out of the hurly-burly of the streets to the surreal opulence of our hotel palace. A forest must have been sacrificed to build it—we found ourselves entombed in walls, floors and doors of musty teak. I decided to be Prince-for-a-Day, and took the royal suite on top with the whole floor to myself, for a pittance.

From my chambers, a spacious view of the Mekong unfolded—a shimmering band of bluish-green shaping the southern shores of Pakse. The muddy brown waters of the Don River snaked around from the north and west, encasing the city on a palm-shrouded tongue of land. Only a handful of French-era church steeples and one modern commercial building pierced the umbrella of palm trees.

Around dusk, I wandered down to the commoner's floor to Simon's room and tapped on his door. A Teutonic blond opened it, standing *au naturel* but for a towel teetering on the pointy ends of her tanned breasts. She was fine as frog's hair. I took a deep breath and turned away: "I'm sorry, sorry, sorry! Do—do you know Simon?"

She adjusted the unruly towel. "No, and who are you?" I strained to keep eye contact, explaining who I was and apologizing again for knocking at the wrong room. She was unfazed. "I just came from Don Khon Island. It was sooo hot. Now I get a bottle of red wine and celebrate my 40th birthday in the air conditioning," ending with a giggle and a smile.

A long silence; it was my move.

"Phil, I've been looking...," Simon approached from behind and stopped mid-sentence as he clapped eyes on my nude Hildegarde.

"Oh, Simon, do you know... I didn't get your name," I said, still trying to steady my breath. With my marital vows intact, I hurried after Simon down to the verandah next to a garden of follies. The grounds in the back of the palace, nestled above the Don River, feature a Buddhist shrine flanked by a concrete menagerie of zebra, giraffe, kangaroo, elephant, lion, deer and cranes.

Over drinks and a few laughs about my encounter, we ordered burgers. The kitchen made its half-baked attempt: a baguette with ground beef, Thousand Island dressing and cucumbers.

The next morning Simon claimed his room had been visited by a poltergeist. Perhaps just bats and bad dreams. But I thought of the barrier of just six inches separating him from Hildegarde. My royal suite night was remarkable only for a gaggle of geckos hanging on the walls, shrieking with the lungs of raptors.

We drove south along the Mekong to the ancient imperial *muang* of Champasak. Going back to the early years of the first millennium in lower Laos, population centers such as Champasak coalesced wherever people were drawn together by ample local resources—food, water, tin, copper, iron, and salt. But these centers were unstable. Their chieftains augmented their authority by adopting Hindu deities from the Indian traders and holy men wandering the region. Lao historian Martin Stuart-Fox wrote:

"Indianization occurred... as a slow and complex [process] which owed more to the needs of the local elites than to any [missionary] impetus on the part of the Indian informers. Worship of the great Hindu god Siva reinforced the belief that kings were imbued with divine powers, and thus carried with it a powerful notion of [legitimacy]."

The sacred temple of Champasak, Wat Phu, was the center of a cult that worshiped the Hindu god Siva. Siva was formerly represented there by a phallic megalith, or *lingam*, where sacrificial rites were held. Khmer kings worshiped and sent priests to serve at Wat Phu during the ninth to thirteenth centuries. As in the case of Angkor, which began as a complex of temples dedicated to Hindu gods, in time the priests of Wat Phu overlaid Buddhist iconography and ritual in a seamless mix of the two Indian-born religions—a foreshadowing of Theravada Buddhism found throughout Southeast Asia today.

The white-sand beach at Ban Muang—the ferry crossing to Champasak—was teeming with food and drink vendors operating from a cluster of thatched huts. A picturesque row of pirogues were nosed up on the white sand. We drove warily onto the jerry-rigged ferry. The crudely built decking, with several gaping holes, was laid atop two deep-hulled metal pontoons, formerly U.S. Army patrol boats.

Three *sawngthaews*, overflowing with people and possessions, finessed their way onto the vessel. Market ladies sold skewers of sun-dried fish, golden balls of bitter apricot, gelatinous rice wrapped in banana fronds, and icy coconut juice mixed with sugar and rice. Kids in the water hung on to the anchor rope for a tow, shrieking with laughter. When the ferry approached the middle of the river, they let go and swam back to shore.

We passed through Champasak before skirting a muddy lake, shrunken almost to sludge by the dry-season heat. Except for a few kids astride the backs of water buffalo, the broiled landscape was empty of people. At the end of the lake was a run-down French-style villa, a residence once built for kings to occupy during the annual festival at Wat Phu. Rising above the villa in a haze of smoke was Linga Parvata, the pyramidal mountain thought to resemble a phallus by the Hindus who built Wat Phu.

A tumbled promenade, surrounded at its base by dried-up lotus ponds, led up the mountain through a long archway of blooming frangipani. Before antiquities thieves arrived, it had been bracketed with lions' heads and nagas. A couple of snotty nosed temple urchins in tattered clothing, with incandescent smiles as captivating as those of my own children, joined us. They guided us through two decrepit pavilions amid a sandstone forest of carved *lingams*, lintels, statues and bas-reliefs showing Siva, Parvati, Ganesh and Nandi, a who's who puzzle of Hindu Gods.

Walking up the narrow stairs to Wat Phu, the soothing shade of the frangipanis drew my thoughts to the ancient Khmers who must have enjoyed the same picturesque vista of the Mekong valley below. On top of the mountain, shrouded in a sprawl of ancient trees, a statue of Buddha wrapped in golden yellow stood next to the half-crumbled Siva sanctuary, which once housed the sacred *lingam* of the Hindu worshipers. Although many carved dancing apsaras (heavenly nymphs) and other Hindu images remained in the sanctuary, a statue of Buddha now presides in the inner sanctum, where the *lingam* once stood.

I followed the temple urchins beyond the sanctuary, past a blackened boulder incised with a crude relief of the Hindu triumvirate—Siva, Vishnu, and Brahma. A short walk from there, up a small outcropping, was a sheer wall indented with a shallow grotto from which a plastic pipe released trickles of fresh spring water. In ancient times, the purifying water was funneled there from the cave to wash the *lingam*. In the heat of the day, the cool water was rejuvenating. Locals say it is charged with sacred molecules of good luck. Along the same rock ledge, about 50 yards away, a giant footprint of Buddha was etched into the mountain. As an offering, I placed a nosegay of frangipani mixed with the orange blooms of a nearby acacia, given to me by the urchins.

When the French explorers arrived at Champasak in the 1860s, Mr. Delaporte, the expedition artist, wrote in a state of nostalgic passion:

"Indeed, what vanished beauty... after having wetted my lips with this fresh, limpid water, I lay down in the shadow of the rock, my head resting on an old, admirably worn-down stone which was lying in front of the cave. Looking around me, at the ruins which surrounded me, my spirit was transported to the days when we were visiting Angkor the Great..."

Now seated on the rock ledge described by Delaporte were a couple of German travelers. They had been battered for 12 hours on a provincial bus traveling to Champasak. Grousing at what they saw, they said they had expected the grandeur of Angkor.

Travel is an attitude, which often imitates the disciplines of a method actor: purge all preconceptions and replenish with fresh impressions. Although

Wat Phu is a flyspeck next to "Angkor the Great," the French explorer seemed to bask in its romance. In today's shrunken world—where so many destinations are fair game for tourists swarming from pink tour buses—there is great solace in the solitude of such places as Wat Phu.

To the east of the old temple, beyond the monk's residence, is the crocodile rock, believed to have been the site of human sacrifices conducted by the ancients during the annual Wat Phu festival. We and the urchins sat nearby in the shaded daydream of an old banyan. Its low-hanging branches framed a view of the Mekong valley's timeless patchwork of field and forest.

Farther south on Colonial Highway 13, approaching the border of Cambodia, we left the tarmac for a pot-holed track that led to the riverside village of Ban Nakasang. Taking a shaky pirogue ride in shallow waters, we threaded our way through a flooded forest of willows where clusters of submerged water buffalo peeked out from the branches. We entered a narrow strait with stilted bungalows on either side. To the west and ahead was the French-built railroad trestle. And a few miles beyond the antiquated bridge, the mountains of Cambodia were amassed into a hazy sky.

We were in Si Phan Don, or Four Thousand Islands, a 30-mile section of the Mekong littered with inhabited islands. Here the river widens to almost nine miles, before narrowing at the Khone Falls, the doorstop to commercial boat traffic and river trade with China.

Louis Carne, a member of Doudart de Lagree's 1866-67 expedition, wrote in his book *Travels on the Mekong*, "These cataracts offer an insurmountable obstacle to steam navigation... steamers can never plough the Mekong, as they do the Amazon or Mississippi; and Saigon can never be united to the western provinces of China by this immense river-way." Van Wuysthoff had reached the same conclusion over 200 years before on his exploration of the river, but the French were not convinced. They persisted like salmon migrating upriver to spawn, attempting to hurdle the falls and scatter the milt and eggs of *mission civilsatrice* all the way to China.

By 1920 docking facilities were built on the south end of Don Khon island, complete with steam cranes and Vietnamese coolies. From the loading dock, a narrow gauge railroad track was laid, linking the islands of Don Khon and Don Det. When a boat arrived from downriver, the cargo was painstakingly offloaded on the south side of the falls. From there the freight was transshipped by miniature locomotive to another docking station on Don Det, where a fresh steam barge awaited.

When the Japanese occupied the region in 1940, the French abandoned the railroad. It had proved less than efficient. Even with the train, it took 37 days to ship cargo from Saigon to Luang Prabang by boat, longer than it took to travel by sea from Saigon to Marseille.

We debarked from the pirogue at the village of Ban Khon Tai and walked a shaded path of coconut palms to the old French hospital, now converted to a guesthouse of four rooms. Stilted huts along the path were strung below with fishnets, untangled and drying like gossamer curtains for the women and children sprawled in tropical torpor beneath the buildings on crude wooden divans or in hammocks. Sprinkled amid the hammocks and beds were bevies of pigs, chickens, fish traps and barrel-sized clay vats filled with water, in the Khmer style. A man on a bicycle selling hammocks pointed to his product, smiled broadly, and pedaled off. In the shadow of parasols, several women strolled by in brightly hued sarongs. They welcomed us with dulcet chirps of *sabai dii, sabai dii*. We felt as if we had been greeted by a covey of tropical birds.

A riotous garden of red and white bougainvillea fronted the hospital-turned-guesthouse, where we met Yoi, the manager and part-owner. The spacious rooms were carpeted in bamboo mats and strung in a cat's cradle of mosquito nets. French doors and shuttered windows opened to a fluvial breeze, brief respite from the blazing sun. The walls were adorned with prints of Tahitian scenes by Gauguin.

After dusting off in the ward-size room, we walked in the direction of the bridge, coming upon a sullen group of 50 or more men constructing a coffin and drinking beer on the water's edge beneath a cluster of coconut palms. The last conductor of the French train—the Casey Jones of the Mekong—had died the day before, at the age of 90 or more.

Until the coffin was finished, his body would lay exposed in his home across the footpath, protected from evil spirits by his vigilant family. There would be a wake of several days, with food, drink, card playing, and offerings of flowers to festoon his coffin, before they would take him in a cortege led by monks to a nearby temple where he would be cremated.

In some overgrowth near a rice field was the rusted-out carcass of the miniature French locomotive, once operated by the deceased man. Further up the path was the temple of Wat Khon Tai, set in a clearing of palm trees on the site of an ancient Khmer temple. Crowding the fenced grounds of the traditional Lao temple, a fanciful forest of gaily colored *stupas*, scored in arabesque designs, housed the ashes of generations of local families. The deceased conductor's ashes would be placed here.

We doubled back, following the rail-bed across the old bridge and met a mad Welshman carrying a couple of fiberglass spinning rods. When I asked about the fishing, he wasn't clear about what kind of fish he hoped to catch, but he held up a cup of worms with a stoned grin: "They love these things." On down the footpath, several demi-locals, Pancakers-Plus, were stashed in the porch shade of small bungalows that faced the river, idling away the afternoon heat in hammocks, enmeshed in clouds of ganja. We settled into a thatched restaurant hovering over the water and enjoyed a plate of *laap*, spicy minced chicken salad, and a couple of beers before going to the falls.

By mid-afternoon, with the mercury still spiked, we were sweating like a couple of sundrenched cheeseballs. Two boatmen picked us up in a long pirogue, steering us back through the flat swirls of flooded willows. The half-submerged water buffaloes there reminded me of hippos I'd seen in the pools of East Africa. Weaving through islets and boulders, the light jade waters gave way to a sheet of silvery ripples, where solitary gulls and herons perched on rocks and the rumble of the Khon Phapheng Falls droned nearby.

Pirogues of fishermen plied the shoals above the rapids, working perilously close to the rocky bilge—the point-of-no-return. On the east side of the falls, plumes of white fell into a turbo of surging foam, before settling in a swollen channel of fast moving sage-green water. On the west side, the falls threw up columns of spume like geysers jetting skyward.

The captain maneuvered onto the east bank of the river. Following a well-trodden path, we circled downstream below the falls. Fishermen had fixed a scaffolding of bamboo ladders, extending from a shale ledge to a three-story sandstone monolith, high above a frothy pool of distilled turbulence. From the ladders, maneuvering downward like salamanders on the slick surface, they slung their spacious nets over the crest of falling water—the most precarious effort to trap fish I had ever witnessed.

After coming upon a hollowed-out cirque of flat rocks, fed by a secondary fall of water, we stripped and slid down into the natural whirlpool, our searing flesh practically sizzling as we entered the coolness. Several locals modestly took baths in a terrace of pools leading up to the rocky embankment, surmounted by a line of trees. Other visitors stayed dry on the high ground, picnicking on bamboo mats in the shade, sipping the juice from fresh-fallen coconuts.

Once cooled down, we trudged back to the boat, and powered upriver against a subtle but strong current. We were escorted by iridescent kingfishers that wheeled and skimmed the water in short bursts of flight before alighting on rocks in mid-stream, a cautious distance ahead of us. Fish darted among rocks in the limpid waters below. We turned in and out of a labyrinth of islets, happening upon small groups of women bathers and shrieking kids jumping in and out of the water. In less than an hour, we were back into the main channel, shallow but sea-like in its breadth.

With near perfect timing, the sun dropped across the water to present the vast skyborne shape of some mythical bird—spread-eagled with copper wings of flattened clouds, its head a fire-breathing orb. It stalked us with its radiant stare. In the dancing waterscape, two silhouetted fishermen stood waist deep beside their pirogues, casting their nets. As we stared back into the face of the fiery bird, the fishermen appeared to be lassoing pools of gold with strands of shiny silk.

In this reposeful scene, we drifted onto the sandy banks of Ban Nakasang village, pushing up alongside a row of retiring fisher folk who had slivered their pirogues onto the beach for the night. Saronged women gathered the fish and nets, while kids swam among the lapping waves. Lao tunes wafted from the jam box of a nearby *sawngthaew*. Many of the fishermen gathered along the sandy banks with us drinking *Beerlao* and *lao-lao*.

Once covered in darkness, we pushed off from the beach to return to Don Khon. The whiskey-happy captain and his equally sloshed first mate, with the aid of a dimly-lit torch, guided us through the flooded forest.

Back at Don Khon, we joined Yoi by the water's edge and ordered fresh catfish cooked in a coconut sauce, presented atop a bed of rice—all fresh staples of the self-sufficient islanders. The meal would take a while to prepare. As we waited, the beacon light hanging over the water was clouded in a steady swarm of insects. It was the beginning of an aquatic food chain: the fecund water churned with silver flashes of fish surfacing to feed on the light-crazed insects, the bigger fish eating the smaller ones, the frogs leaping down the banks for their share.

Through the evening, the conversation with Yoi drifted over several subjects. Of Lao-lum lineage, Yoi's family fled the country in 1975 to a refugee camp near Ubon, Thailand, as did 90 percent of the nation's educated people at the time. Before fleeing across the Mekong, Yoi's family lived on rations for several months as the war drew to a close. "It was very difficult. No opportunity for my family," he lowered his voice while shaking his head. After a year in the refugee camp, they were re-settled in Australia, where he lived for 20 years.

During Yoi's time in exile, Laos was cut off from the rest of the world, and known as the "Albania of Asia." In part Laos's isolation was self-imposed. But Thailand and other anticommunist U.S. allies embargoed the little country. During the 1980s, 95 percent of Laos's trade with Thailand and other countries disappeared. A few supplies trickled in from Vietnam, but that country was working through its own difficult period of economic isolation. Both Vietnam and Laos were struggling to recover from the tatters of war and from dependence on the Soviet Union.

In due course, a sea change in economic policy occurred, coinciding with the breakup of the Soviet Union and Vietnam's *doi moi* policy of economic liberalization. The doors of Laos were swept open in 1991. At the same time as in Vietnam, a capitalist lifeline was tossed into Laos' economic backwaters to rescue Karl Marx from drowning. Yoi returned to the Panhandle a couple of years after this ideological back flip. He had not seen his homeland since fleeing as a young adolescent.

I asked him why he would sacrifice Australia's modern comforts, and the presence there of much of his family, in order to return to Laos.

"It's peaceful here, there is opportunity. Besides there is no stress. I will live longer," he replied in a soft, philosophical tone. "We smile when we are happy, we smile when we are sad. But most important, Laos is my home."

But what about freedom of speech?

He laughed at my question: "We have *Playboy*, we can talk, we just can't spread influence."

Yoi kept raising the subject of U.S. President Bill Clinton's errant member, baffled by all the hoopla over Monica Lewinsky. From Yoi's point of view, such mischief should be considered a duty of office. And Clinton's mere wanderings could hardly compare to the epic appetites of Champasak's last prince.

As the night wore on, we heard what sounded more and more like an uprising, coming from across the channel where the Pancakers were staying. Yoi noted they had been loud the night before, partying on booze, grass, and ecstasy and methamphetamine brought in from the Golden Triangle. Prostitutes will be next, wait and see," he predicted.

Yoi obtains sexual relief every two weeks when he goes to Pakse, where he visits the brothels and bar girls. There are no women for him here on the island, unless he should marry one. This is in keeping with the Asian principle of "loving the one you marry, not marrying the one you love."

Our meal had still not arrived after an hour and a half, but Simon and I were enjoying the conversation and didn't mind. Yoi felt a need to explain the delay, pointing to the ongoing convulsion of fish beneath the dangling bulb, "Lao people don't need jobs: say something wrong and they quit. They have all the fish and rice they can eat. In Thailand they have 70 million people and Vietnam 80 million. They have to compete for food and jobs. Lao people's needs are few, maybe some new clothes and someday a bicycle or motorcycle. That's all." He paused and framed his thoughts, "For example, I sit here and wait on food. And wait. And then I get up and go cook myself. I go around the problem, not confront it."

Finally arriving at the glacial pace contentment affords, food was served. Yoi left to cook his own meal. While hastily swallowing my sweetened catfish, I was reminded of Yoi's words and the French saying about Indochina, "The Vietnamese plant rice, the Khmer stand there and watch, and the Laotians listen to it grow."

Morning broke in a medley of creature sounds... frogs, cicadas, geckos. Birds were cooing and warbling from the palms and bougainvillea, roosters crowing everywhere. We set out for the beach on the west end of Don Khon where we hired a dugout to take us downriver to see some remarkable creatures.

The Irrawaddy dolphin, or *Orcaella brevirostris*, adapts to both salt-and-fresh water. For thousands of years, they have inhabited the warm coastal and fresh waters of south Asia and Australia. Their inland migrations have led them up several rivers—the Mekong, Burma's Irrawaddy, the Mahakham in Indonesia and the Padma in Bangladesh. Rarely are they observed at sea, and when sighted they are often confused with porpoises and dugongs.

Under unstressed circumstances, the average family size is six, but can be as large as 15. The dolphins can live to be 30-years old, growing up to nine feet in length and weighing as much as 300 pounds. The river people from Laos through Vietnam feel a mystical connection to the dolphins. They are considered sacred protectors—reincarnated humans, maidens turned mermaids, who pull fishermen from the jaws of crocodiles or save people from drowning.

Now the dolphins themselves need protection from the humans. The dolphins get caught in the fishermen's nets and cannot surface to breathe. In a major dolphin habitat in Cambodia, near Sambor Falls, locals have used dynamite to harvest fish, but this kills dolphins.

The deluge of dam-building on the Mekong and its tributaries also bodes ill for them. The dolphins follow seasonal migrations of quarry fish when the river is flooding, then seek deep-pool sanctuaries during the dry period.

There are few such pools in the Mekong, and there will be fewer still as the dams go up and reduce the river's eco-diversity.

Through the 1960s there were countless dolphins in the Mekong. Then, in a matter of a few years, the Khmer Rouge slaughtered thousands of them to quash local superstition and to obtain dolphin oil for greasing their weapons and boat motors. Vietnamese soldiers occupying the country in the 1980s used them for target practice with their automatic weapons. Now there is a fragile genetic pool of fewer than 100 animals, blowholing for life.

As with many endangered species, when the numbers become critical, people get interested. After all, extinction is a modern idea. Fish Conservation Zones are being established in deep-pool habitats to curb net fishing. Eco-tourism is beginning to boost both conservation awareness and the funding needed to implement sustainable, community-based resource management programs. A conservation group working in Phnom Penh reports that eco-tourism has encouraged fishing communities to successfully stabilize the dolphin population near Sambor Falls.

Because the Irrawaddy dolphins are considered sacred, fishermen do release them when they catch them in their nets. River people have never hunted them for food. In one village fishermen even claim that dolphins help drive fish into their nets. There are tales of locals holding cremation rites for dolphins they find dead.

As we scrunched into the shallow and cramped dugout we must have looked like a thousand pounds of sausage being squeezed into a hundred-pound crate. Water flowed over the gunwales when we hit the first set of rapids. At the foot of the rapids, a heron stood on a prominent rock, letting us pass closely as if it were a gatekeeper punching our ticket. Along one stretch, the channel was rocky and lined with cypress-like trees. Kingfishers wheeled in iridescent flashes from tree to tree, while crows fished the rocky shoals. Soon, the fast water gathered into an open expanse. A couple of fishermen cast their nets in the distance. We idled to the middle of the Mekong, cut the motor and drifted in silence.

Answering our need for instant gratification, within 10 minutes two dolphins sounded a loud blow and slapped the water 50 yards away.

Their tapered, dark gray bodies blended with the water. Their lumbering pace resembled fresh-cut logs floating downstream, but their dorsal fins gave them away. Our pleasure was unbridled as we harpooned them with pointed cameras. And almost as quickly as they surfaced, time for 20 or 30 unmemorable clicks, they disappeared. Another pod of three soon appeared and sounded—rolling, then diving in arcs, giving us a flash of their white undersides. Over the span of an hour, we watched eight individual dolphins broadcast their whereabouts with tailfin slaps to the water. Even though the dolphins are known for their friendliness, we were not able to observe them from any closer than 50 yards away.

We motored back upriver to Somphamit Falls, passing by elaborate fish traps of bamboo built into the frothy crevices like sluice gates, with a flock of crows standing on the framework.

Back on land, we treaded over a sandy knoll to a leafy umbrella of spiraling kapok trees. In the shadow of the gnarly, prehistoric columns, webs of cascading water fell from a series of five or six discrete cataracts, their beauty sublime.

Nearby we joined a French couple beneath a roof of thatch for a coconut shell of fresh juice. Soon a stream of Thai tourists poured in from the larger island of Don Khong, day-tripping to see the dolphins and waterfalls. Simon and I breathed sighs of relief at having seen the animals under pristine conditions, when we, as eco-tourists, were fewer than the remaining dolphins.

Coming into Khmer Country

Early the next morning, we paid some fishermen to bicycle our bags to the west side of Don Khon. From there, it was only a short pirogue ride to the Lao village of Voen Kham, where the customs office was located.

There we would be entering Cambodia across a border that was closed to foreigners for most of the 30 years the Khmer Rouge controlled the area. In 1998, on April 15th, the Khmer Rouge leader Pol Pot died. By early 1999, most of his withered band of followers had put down their weapons and accepted the amnesty they were offered by the Cambodian government. Today it is relatively safe to travel anywhere in Cambodia, although there are plenty of armed robberies thanks to the many weapons still around. As for crossing the Lao-Cambodian border, it is done every day with the help of bribes, but it is still unclear whether it is a legal border crossing for foreigners.

So we paid our bribes in Voen Kham—a reasonable sum of $5—and soon were crossing the river in another boat to Cambodia. We made a deal with a Cambodian fast boat captain to ferry us to Stung Treng, a major outpost 30 miles south on the Mekong.

The national flag, emblazoned with an image of Angkor Wat, fluttered atop the customs house on the Cambodian side. Inside, a picture of King Sihanouk, a figure now back in favor, was framed above the customs official's desk. Across the room was a small armory of grenade launchers and Kalashnikovs at rest in a metal gun rack, gun barrels pointing up the loins of a blonde *Playboy* foldout pasted on the wall above. The armaments seemed to warn against bargaining too hard on the bribe.

Henri Mahout wrote about custom officials in Cambodia in the 1860s: "... they are licensed beggars. A little salt-fish, a little arrack, a little betel, if you please—such are the petitions; and the more you give, the less strict will the search be."

After affecting a grave face, the official behind the desk demanded, "Excuse, twenty dollars for one." Round numbers and a couple of words were the extent of his English, and my Khmer was zilch. I pulled out a sawbuck. His swarthy, handsome face spread into a toothy grin—the smile of a guy who owns the cookie jar—as laughter settled upon us. He repeated, "twenty dollars for one." Seeing the futility of resistance, Simon and I laughed as we each handed over the crisp and familiar face of Andrew Jackson. We had already paid for our visas before beginning the trip, but it would take this impromptu processing fee of $20 to get them stamped for entry. The men never so much as glanced at our bags.

Our fast boat had arrived by the time we came out, and two armed and uniformed soldiers jumped in the front, catching a ride to Stung Treng on our nickel. Who were we to argue? Welcome to Cambodia!

The prow sliced southward. Mountains stood port and starboard, and as our journey wound on, slowly receded to flat low banks. In 1866, Francis Garnier called Stung Treng the "commercial intermediary" between southern Laos and Phnom Penh: "The village itself of Stung-treng still probably has about eight hundred inhabitants, all Laotians." Khmer Rouge militia hid out in the jungle here during most of the time they ruled the area. Stung Treng was a safe haven for the guerillas, thanks to its remoteness and proximity to the mountain fastnesses of the hill tribe region of Ratanakiri.

We were greeted on Stung Treng's banks by a wolf pack of young hustlers. Their guile was not hard to detect, virtually leaping out at us. They offered a commission-based menu of products and services: hotels, boats, cars, women, dope, buses, food, booze and guides to the mountains of Ratanakiri. Their most valuable commodity, however, was spoken English. They flashed a cell phone. I suspect that for the right price they could have dispatched the mayor to lead a parade for us.

In the business of predation they enjoyed a monopoly, and we were certain prey. We decided against spending the night in Stung Treng unless necessary. But the river was low, and a king's ransom would be needed to hire a fast boat to Kratie. Luckily it was still before noon, early enough to travel to Kratie by car and arrive before nightfall. It was just 120 miles south along the river, on Colonial Highway 13.

Our young fixers made a couple of calls while coaxing us to have a seat at a hot and dusty streetside cafe for food and drink. Before long, a 1970s model Toyota arrived—three-toned corrosion, no shocks, a full set of bald tires, and an engine that coughed more than purred. The driver, old and weary looking, was a perfect match for this hapless heap of metal. But it was as good a day as any for misadventure. With daylight wasting we paid half the agreed-upon price and chugged southward in the rattletrap, molting loose parts along the way.

My map showed the thick red lines indicating a primary road. Nevertheless we had not steeled ourselves for the battle we soon were facing: well-evolved potholes now used as pig-wallows and rickety, metal bridges with big sections of planks missing. "On the road," as it were, we spent more time in the sandy margins avoiding slabs of broken tarmac than on tarmac itself. In short, the road was an obstacle to be avoided rather than driven on. It was easy to understand the warnings we had received regarding road bandits: with all the detours and impediments requiring a stop, they could have developed a thriving trade in waylaying travelers.

But the route did unveil Cambodian village life. In the first hour of driving, we saw three cars, a few stilted huts and a herd of bullock carts. The poverty was disarming, with a severity we had not seen in Laos. In the tidy enclaves of stilted huts and gardens, men seemed to come and go in aimless excursions—tea, a cigarette, a brief word—as if on holiday or taking a break from a relay of naps. They were often shirtless, wrapped in sarongs, and wearing the *krama* (the red-checkered Khmer scarf) as a headband. When carrying heavy loads, the women wrap the checkered *krama* around their head and use it as a platform—an influence from India, like the use of spoons instead of chopsticks and the wearing of sarongs rather than loose pants.

All of the villagers were dark-skinned, and would automatically be looked down upon as peasants by the lighter-skinned denizens of the cities. It was not uncommon to see women with massive goiters swelling from their necks, a consequence of a lack of iodine in the diet. Malnourishment appeared widespread, seen in the excessive number of kids with ginger hair and pot-bellies. Plenty of food is available, I was told, but the children don't get the right balance. Most of the kids' eyes were runny with conjunctivitis, by the age of three or four they had acquired the rheumy eyes of old people.

None of the remote hamlets we passed through had electricity. The thatched-roof homes were perched on stilts, with walls of bamboo matting and an open byre below for the pigs, similar to houses we had seen all the way from China. Beneath each home was a large clay vat of drinking water sharing space with an idle bullock cart. The margins between huts were slotted with fecund trees of banana, mango and coconut. However remote the hamlet, there was always at least one home of someone active in politics, with an archway festooned as a kind of permanent campaign sign for the favored party—Sam Rainsy Party, Cambodian People's Party (CPP), the National United Front for an Independent, Neutral, Peaceful and Cooperative Cambodia (FUNCINPEC) and the Buddhist Liberal Democratic Party (BLDP).

Cambodia is a destitute country, but its people are proud of the patronage benefits—money for campaign signs and votes—offered by their nascent if shaky democracy. It may be politics shaped by venality, but Cambodians clearly value their right to speak out against the government, a freedom not known in Laos and Vietnam.

Cambodia's current era of multi-party politics essentially began with the Vietnamese invasion on Christmas Day, 1978. Vietnam's combat-experienced army overran Phnom Penh, putting an end to Pol Pot's four-year reign. The Vietnamese, with an occupation force of 200,000 troops, remained in Cambodia for the next 10 years, reconstituting a nation gutted at every level. In some ways, it was just an example of a strong country exploiting a weaker neighbor for its resources: food and timber to name a couple. Even so, the occupation force was an economic drain on Vietnam.

Under international pressure, mostly from the United States, the Vietnamese pulled out of Cambodia in 1989. Within a year the country again found itself immersed in a bloody civil war with the Khmer Rouge. After a few thousand more Cambodians were killed and 150,000 refugees fled to the Thai border, the international community stepped in under the auspices of the United Nations Transitional Authority in Cambodia (UNTAC), and ran the country.

The UNTAC supervised elections held in 1993 ended in a dead heat. Prince Norodom Ranariddh, leader of FUNCINPEC and son of King Sihanouk, was named as the first prime minister. He failed to win the two-thirds majority needed to govern alone and a second prime minister was named—Hun Sen—anointed by the Vietnamese, a former member of the Khmer Rouge, and head of the communist CPP.

Hun Sen's control of the military doomed the uneasy coalition. By 1997, a coup in July forced Prince Ranariddh to flee the country. Hun Sen and his CPP party won the 1998 election, but again lacked the necessary majority. The two adversaries switched places to form a new unholy alliance—Hun Sen is now first prime minister, and Prince Ranariddh is second.

Our rusted-out heap broke down in a FUNCINPEC village. An assembly of locals convened to jawbone the problem until a shade-tree mechanic arrived. For the next hour we watched him crawl around the hood of the car, testing the plugs, the battery, the fuses, the ignition. Valves, springs, rings and screws were scattered beneath the hood and dashboard. He pulled out the backseat, disassembled the console panel in front and rewired some wiring. Soon the poor beast was coughing with life. We pulled out of the village sincerely concerned for the car's well-being.

Less than half an hour down the road a front tire blew. Our scruffy driver flashed an embarrassed smile, hurried out of the car, rolled up his sleeves and traded the spent tire for a fresh bald one in a matter of minutes. It was our last spare, in a place where flats could not be fixed.

Our driver tried to help by making up for lost time. Crossing a bridge, we nearly smashed into a bullock cart and herd of water buffalo. Before long, the road mated with the Mekong once again and we arrived in the village of Samdan. The traffic circle in the middle of the town featured a pirouetting silver dolphin raised on a blue pedestal, herald of the nearby Sambor rapids, the Mekong's largest dolphin habitat.

We reached Kratie in an hour, and settled in a river-front restaurant watching a CNN replay of the Queen Mum's funeral. Later as I wearily drew shut my door before collapsing into bed, I overheard the night attendant asking Simon if he would like a massage girl. Simon sniffed the unalluring scent of desperation, however, and declined.

Kratie had not impressed the French explorers in their gunboats. They sneered at its subsistence lifestyle, "Nothing provides a sadder idea of the carelessness and indolence of the Cambodians, than the sight of these small squares of rice, lost amidst the fertile land left fallow." To this day it is a fairly idle place, but not without the charm of decaying colonial villas and buff-yellow administrative buildings left by the French.

We stayed across the road from the Kratie port, where the fast boats depart each morning for Kampong Cham and Phnom Penh. Beginning at daybreak, the loudspeakers along the waterfront screeched with shouting voices that read public service announcements and socialist news of the day; then followed the haunting strains of a Khmer opera singer.

By the time we made our way down to the fast boat, striped red and blue, the seats inside the metal capsule were taken. People were massed on top of the roof—soldiers in floppy hats, monks, armed policemen, *krama*-shrouded men and women. Market ladies worked the crowd selling dried fish, eggs, chicken and sticky rice in banana fronds. We joined the roof-riders on the rounded top.

The overloaded boat listed under the shifting weight of the many people on its roof. The captain blasted ahead, however, without adjusting for the imbalance. The cabin below had a couple of exit doors in the front, but none in back: no chance of escape should the boat capsize, as Khmer boats at sea often do. According to a French wire service, international maritime authorities have assessed Cambodia's global shipping record and concluded the nation should stay on dry ground. Following its rapid growth as an international shipping registry, Cambodia has incurred "an appalling rate" of sunken ships. So there on the express boat, I calculated I was better situated on the roof, from which I could leap if the captain was determined to uphold his nation's record.

Ferries brimming with cars and people crisscrossed the broad river. The occasional pagoda loomed into view, fronted by two pillars, roofed in red and laced in a golden twist of flying *nagas*. Within a couple of hours, we stopped beneath a modern bridge built by the Japanese at the old French trading post of Kompong Cham.

Our craft gave up a few passengers, and took on many more before roaring away with a starboard tilt. We glided by floating fish farms surrounded by palisades of bamboo. A long sandy beach was littered in fresh cut teak, strewn about like tinker toys.

After Thailand banned logging within its borders in 1989, the price of teak spiraled from $1,900 a metric ton to $10,000. Conveniently for global timber barons, 70 percent of Cambodia's hardwood forests remained intact as of the early 1980s. Western Cambodia then saw a boom in illegal logging. The devastation was so rapid and intense that UNTAC banned the export of Khmer logs.

But in 1995 the Cambodian government secretly awarded 32 concessions covering a third of the nation's land area. The logging was not selective and gradual. Global Witness, an environmental group monitoring logging in Cambodia, estimates that in the past 20 years, the forest cover there has been reduced by 70 percent.

The result has been a deluge of floods in the last 10 years. Healthy forests in the Mekong basin absorb the excessive rains of the monsoon season, then slowly release them during the dry season. But deforestation forces brute gravity to take over the ecosystem: the unanchored soil gives way and the rivers rise.

Prime Minister Hun Sen, under persistent pressure from the international donors on which his government depends for most of its funds, suspended logging indefinitely in January 2002. In May that year he declared no more permits would be issued for the transport of logs. Yet illegal logging continues, in line with the excessive bribes demanded by government officials.

Opposition leader Sam Rainsy blames it on Hun Sen's CPP. "They resort to corruption to survive. It's a warlord system with senior army officers and civilian officials exercising power in the different military regions and provinces of Cambodia." Hun Sen gives the warlords control of valuable resources in return for their political support. "The result is institutionalized corruption and lawlessness," Rainsy concludes.

We reached Phnom Penh around mid-afternoon, veering right as we passed the Naga, a riverboat casino. We turned up the Tonle Sap River, passing by the Royal Palace on the capital's flag-shrouded esplanade. A hot white sun shimmered off the ceramic-tiled roofs in painful radiance. The low-slung waterfront is like a movie façade of glinting temples, palaces, ministry buildings, shops, hotels and restaurants, all washed in faded French elegance, splashed with the saffron of Buddhist robes.

As we climbed the embankment, we were met by a hard-bitten lot of guys in baseball caps and floppy hats offering us a variety of conveyance—Honda motos, *tuk-tuks*, taxis, *cyclos*, *remorques* (a trailer pulled by a motorcycle), buses, boats and bicycles. Edging our way past a couple of legless war victims with their beggar's hats extended, we emerged on Sisowath Quay, the riverfront road.

Their Foreign Correspondents' Club is housed in a French-era building, the open-air bar and restaurant overlooking the confluence of the Tonle Sap and Mekong rivers. The opposite side of the club affords a view of the terra-cotta *nagas* that crown the National Museum. Fans hum from the club's musty ceiling, geckos spackle the dull yellow walls and cats skulk the floor beneath. Furnished with a clubby scatter of low-set tables, padded armchairs and reading lamps with dusty shades, the nostalgic atmosphere leaves one expecting the arrival of a band of *colons* sporting tropical whites and pith helmets.

As I cleaned up the remains of an exquisite cheeseburger of New Zealand beef, dripping in fried onions and French's mustard, a balding man with a small ponytail sat at the bar stool next to me. His deep tan gave away his tropical residency. Taking a *café latte*, he introduced himself as Bud Gibbons, a friend of a friend of mine in Hanoi.

Bud came to Vietnam the first time around as a soldier in the U.S. army. He was stationed near Ben Tre in the Mekong delta during the famous Tet Offensive of 1968. After returning to the States, he married, started a family and a landscaping business. By 1982 his life was reeling out of control from alcohol abuse. Divorced and having lost his business, he gave up the sauce. Once his youngest daughter graduated from secondary school in 1993, he decided to begin a new life in Vietnam, a place his thoughts had never left.

Around the same time, he met Bobby Muller, a former marine who was paralyzed during the war. Bobby had established a non-profit organization called the Vietnam Veteran's of America Foundation (VVAF) and encouraged Bud to go to work at their clinic in Phnom Penh where they provide prosthetic limbs and physical therapy to war victims.

After opening a sister clinic in remote Preah Vihear province, where almost 40 percent of the villages are seeded with landmines and cluster bombs, Bud realized the amputees needed not only prosthetics, but also a way to earn a living. Cambodian amputees are usually reduced to begging or total dependence on their families. Maimed women have no hope of ever marrying and leading a traditional life. Even today, as many as 20 people a week are either killed or maimed by landmines and unexploded ordnance in Cambodia.

Bud converted some of that gloom to hope by starting a silk weaving factory in Preah Vihear, reviving a craft that had disappeared under the tyranny of Pol Pot. Bud's vision took the name of *Joom Noon*, meaning "gift" in Khmer. *Joom Noon* now employs 85 people, all but 15 of whom are disabled. Counting their family members, it thus supports an extended family of over 500 people. At *Joom Noon* they weave expensive scarves and sarongs, exporting them to First World markets. Many employees now have their own homes in an expanding compound of 30 huts, with sanitary boreholes, electricity and a pre-school. At least two of the disabled employees have married and become parents.

As Bud told us his story, several fortyish Westerners with four newborn babies settled into a pair of tables at the other end of the club. Although they had the look of Americans, pear-shaped and in baseball hats and Nikes, they were Australians. The U.S. had banned child adoptions in Cambodia, which costs up to $12,500—not an excessive price in the region. But in a country with a per capita income of $300 and rife corruption, such big sums encourage mothers to deliberately bear children for sale. Middlemen sell the babies on to adoption agencies.

Soon, Simon and I left Bud to visit Café Freedom, a place to catch the sunset over Boeng Kak, the oxbow lake located in the middle of Phnom Penh. Riding along the quay, we noticed police filling a bus with hookers whose nonchalance suggested they might be hitching a ride to a friendly destination. Nearby a chained monkey stood on top of a beat-up taxi, wearing a hat and entertaining a crowd of locals with a magic routine. His handler gave onlookers the chance to purchase medicinal herbs, in a Khmer rendition of an old-time American snake-oil promotion.

We reached Café Freedom riding in *cyclos*, or bicycle chariots. Brian, the Scots proprietor, and a wee bit out of kilter, greeted us bare-chested, his eyes like pencil-drawn slits. "Let me get you a beer! Sit down, let's talk." Simon had visited before, but this time found he was in for a shock. He glanced around and proclaimed his haunt had been "spiritually castrated" since last time. A Zen garden had been replaced with a spartan slab of concrete shaded by a bland pavilion. Brian clued into Simon's astonishment, and waved his beer in the air, crowing, "I met my September 11th on October 10th when the guesthouse burned!" A fire had snuffed out 20 homes thereabouts.

A nearby table of rough-and-tumble Western men vegetated with their shirts off, exposing badly drawn tattoos. Ned, a long, skinny guy who resembled a praying mantis, joined us at our table with Brian. They had been hanging out since noon—drinking beer, smoking pot, fishing in the lake. Brian has been hooking the same fish there for years. He considers them his own pet fish—he feeds them bread and scraps from a nearby pier every day. A year earlier Brian had planned to move to East Timor and open a "girly bar." He is a junkie for hot spots, the world's shifting lawless reaches. His Thai wife, however, saw some Dili riot footage on CNN, and put the kibosh on his startup dreams. Brian takes a certain professional pride in being a renegade, bragging about the hard time he did in an English prison for armed robbery as well as an incarceration in Japan.

Ned, in contrast, was a bit of a "techie." He had set up planetary headquarters in Phnom Penh for the secret advancement of what he called the "hologram," a three-dimensional imagery that, according to Ned, will "replace the digital age." Ned flailed his bony arms in a reptilian manner, speaking ominously of "them" and things "up there," which considering Ned's presentation, I initially took for references to extraterrestrials and outer space. But it eventually became clear that by "up there" he meant Laos, and "they" were the CIA. The Agency desperately wanted his research, it seemed, because it was needed to reinforce America's military and economic dominance of the world.

Brian had heard Ned's spiel many times, and sought to cut it short with an illustration. The Scotsman pulled out a Visa card—hard to imagine where that came from—and pointed to the iridescent square illustration of an eagle in the middle, "There, that's a goddamn hologram!"

Ned had once had a bright future—the son of two doctors, a doctoral candidate at the University of Texas, a mathematical genius. But he took a detour a few degrees south of reality in the early 1970s, washing ashore in Phnom Penh in 1993 amid Brian and other expatriate flotsam. That was the year of the UNTAC elections when billions of dollars from worldwide aid and relief organizations were flooding into Cambodia. Eventually the swell of money and expats receded, leaving behind a few success stories like Bud, along with Café Freedom's many bottom feeders, successfully angling for pet fish.

As the rogues' gallery grew, we departed Café Freedom for the "Heart of Darkness" bar, a name-brand venue where sightseeing dabblers can take a walk on the wild side. It was empty, but for a side room of local gays shooting pool and camping it up with the cue sticks. After 11 p.m. the nightly rave would start taking wing. We smoked a spliff at the bar, which quickly put Simon back into shore-leave mode. I left him to his work, "an artist living the artist's life." Returning to his hotel alone much later that night, he would admit the next morning that it seemed unsuitable to take one's pleasures in a city that had felt so much pain.

Pol Pot and his madness defy explanation. He died without volunteering any regrets. There was no Nuremberg-style trial to force him to confront the truth of his crimes against humanity. His life remains shrouded in secrets and mystery. In contrast, a vast library has been written about Adolf Hitler. But after myriad attempts to identify a single personality flaw or childhood trauma to explain Hitler's tyranny, one writer concluded, "There is no real mystery: he was no more than the sum of his atrocious actions. He was what he said and did what he thought." Pol Pot's life, too, should be seen for what it is.

Pol Pot was named Saloth Sar when he was born in 1928 in the village of Prek Sbauv near the provincial capital of Kompong Thom. Although his father and mother were farmers, they had connections to the royal palace in Phnom Penh. In 1935, Saloth Sar and his older brother Chhay were sent to the live in the capital where he began his education as a novice at Wat Botum Vaddei, a Buddhist monastery favored by royals. From there he went to Ecole Miche, a Catholic primary school attended by the children of French bureaucrats and Vietnamese Catholics.

By 1942 he was selected to attend the College Norodom Sihanouk in Kompong Thom. While pursuing his French-sponsored education, he took up the violin, played soccer and basketball. Saloth Sar's classmates knew him as a quiet, mediocre student. His best friend at school was Lon Non, brother of Lon Nol who in 1970 would become Cambodia's president, ousting King Sihanouk in an American-orchestrated coup.

Saloth Sar left for France in 1949, where his academic pursuits gave way to political interests. He never took an examination and eventually lost his scholarship at the City University of Paris. He did, however, absorb the literature of Marx's *Das Kapital*, Lenin's *On Imperialism*, and Stalin's *The National Question*.

World War II had laid bare the Achilles heel of France and other colonial masters, lending strength to the independence and nationalist movements in Asia and Africa.

Before returning to Cambodia in December of 1952, Saloth Sar joined the French Communist Party (FCP), just as Ho Chi Minh had done 31 years before when living in Paris.

In 1954, the Vietnamese defeated the French at Dien Bien Phu. The ensuing Geneva Accords partitioned Vietnam at the 17th parallel and ended French control of Indochina.

The Geneva agreements called for Cambodia to elect a National Assembly in 1955. Back in Cambodia, Saloth Sar's job was to prepare for the election by recruiting candidates and pushing a communist agenda. The Geneva agreements mandated Vietnamese elections in 1956, and pre-election polls made clear Ho Chi Minh was the overwhelming favorite. Buoyed by Ho Chi Minh's popularity, Saloth Sar and the Cambodian communists hoped to gain control of the National Assembly.

In a shocking turn of events, however, King Sihanouk abdicated the throne, crowned his father as the new Cambodian king, and entered the election himself as "citizen Sihanouk." Using all the heavy-handed tactics at his disposal, Sihanouk's party won every seat in the Assembly. As Cambodia's prime minister for the next 15 years, Sihanouk ruled the country like a personal fiefdom, while dabbling as a movie producer, director and leading actor. The 1956 elections in Vietnam never took place, under pressure from the U.S., which feared a Ho Chi Minh victory.

Saloth Sar continued his underground work and married Khieu Ponnary, a frumpish school teacher at the Lycee Sisowath, older than him but like-minded in politics. At the same time Saloth Sar began teaching French, civics, history and geography at a newly established private school. In Cambodia, teaching was a respected profession in the ancient tradition of the Hindu Brahmans and later Buddhist monks. Students remember Saloth Sar as engaging and passionate, softly eloquent, reciting French classics by heart.

Having risen to be secretary of the central committee of the Communist Party of Kampuchea, his double life ended in 1963 when he gave up teaching and became a full time *maquis*, a guerilla fighter, in the remote jungles of Ratanakiri province. Similar to the guerilla experiences of Ho Chi Minh and Mao Zedong, he lived among the hill tribes. Applying his Marxian theory of social development, Saloth Sar viewed the Brao and Jarai people with whom he lived as "noble savages," unsullied by money or social class and operating within a primitive framework of subsistence solidarity, aboriginal communists.

In 1966, Saloth Sar traveled to China to witness the beginnings of China's Cultural Revolution. Engineered by an aging Mao Zedong, this authoritarian dissembling was designed to attain "continuous revolution, class warfare, and the empowerment of the poor." Saloth Sar befriended China's head of secret police, K'ang Sheng, "Mao's pistol," who used the interrogation techniques he learned in the Soviet Union during Stalin's purges. He then unleashed the same horrific genocidal methods in China.

Saloth Sar and the Khmer Rouge, with abiding respect for their Chinese ideological mentors, would later adopt Mao's penchant for purging "class enemies." Saloth Sar labeled the Khmer Rouge's plan for an agrarian, barter economy the "Great Leap Forward," in spite of the fact Mao's same misguided economic initiative in the late 1950s caused as many as 20 million Chinese to starve to death.

By 1970, General Lon Nol managed to topple the government of Prime Minister Sihanouk, thanks mostly to assistance from the U.S. Lon Nol then declared Cambodia the Khmer Republic, ending almost 2,000 years of various forms of imperial rule. But however feudalistic Sihanouk's government, the vast majority of Cambodians supported him. This U.S.-backed coup would destabilize Cambodia for the next 30-plus years.

Concurrently the Vietnam War against communism in Vietnam was shifting more and more into Cambodia. For many years Sihanouk had allowed the North Vietnamese to use Cambodia as an extension of the Ho Chi Minh Trail (known in Cambodia as the Sihanouk Trail) and as a jungle redoubt for staging their raids into South Vietnam. When Sihanouk fell, the Khmer Rouge engaged Lon Nol's army throughout Cambodia, and also were enlisted by the North Vietnamese against the South.

As the Khmer Rouge tightened the noose on Phnom Penh in March 1973, the U.S. ratcheted up the B-52 bombings. America had no combat troops in Cambodia, never declared war there, but nevertheless dropped a quarter of a million tons of bombs in the countryside over a five-month period. The casualty estimates of Cambodians killed, mostly civilians, range from 30,000 to 250,000. By spring of 1973 most American troops had been withdrawn from Vietnam, Thailand and the secret war in Laos. As far as Americans were concerned, Cambodia was left as "the only war in town," in the words of one U.S. official.

America's indiscriminate bombardment of the countryside produced a flood of peasant refugees in Phnom Penh. By the time Khmer Rouge troops arrived on April 17th of 1975, the city had mushroomed to two million people, mostly refugees. Shadowed by an eerie sense of uncertainty, they welcomed the heavily armed, young soldiers. By all accounts the troops resembled Boy Scouts carrying their RPGs (rocket propelled grenades). They paraded through the streets as menacing victors.

In a new twist to the Marxist-Leninist notion of class struggle, these peasant refugees were tarred with the same broad brush as city dwellers, and were regarded by Saloth Sar and the Khmer leadership as "enemies" of the revolution. Even though the fleeing peasants had not actively participated in the armed struggle, they became known as "April 17th people," a new class of undesirables. Women, children, the elderly and all others were ordered to evacuate Phnom Penh and Battambang within 24 hours—coaxed to hasten their pace with warnings like "Quick, Quick the Americans will drop bombs." They marched for weeks to rural collectives without adequate food and water during one of the hottest months of the year. Over the weeks that followed, tens of thousands died, families were separated—in some cases forever. The genocidal terror of the Khmer Revolution's "Year Zero" had begun.

After almost 12 years of anonymity as a guerrilla, Saloth Sar emerged as the architect of the revolution under the *nom de guerre* of Pol Pot. He became prime minister of Cambodia, renamed Democratic Kampuchea. Managing and growing a self-sustaining economy would prove a tougher challenge, however, than leading a bunch of privileged, French-educated ideologues to foment a revolution underwritten by rich patrons, such as China.

Pol Pot's four-year plan of economic and social reform envisioned rice as the wellspring from which all else would flow. In a ruthless attempt to destroy all cultural identity, the Khmer Rouge forced everyone to wear black pajamas like the Chinese instead of the sarongs traditionally worn by both men and women. Buddhism was suppressed along with folk culture, private property gave way to collectives. Pol Pot initiated these reforms and went on to abolish money on the premise that private markets and industrial development was of no concern.

The Khmer Rouge targeted families as a capitalist conspiracy, one which prevented communist revolutions in both China and North Korea from gaining full flower. Thus, family members were not allowed to eat together in collective dining halls. Health care was assigned to traditional healers and 15 year-olds. Youths were put in charge of the collectives, where tens of thousands of the "April 17th people" met their deaths by malnutrition, disease, or execution Khmer-style, a club to the head. Before this genocide was ended by the invasion of the Vietnamese army in late 1978 and the Khmer Rouge's flight from Phnom Penh, at least 1.7 million souls had perished—one of every four people in Cambodia. An ancient, dignified Buddhist kingdom had been transformed into a charnel house overnight.

On my first trip to Cambodia in 1997, when Pol Pot was still alive and the Khmer Rouge still controlled pockets of the countryside, I went to Choeung Ek, a Chinese cemetery and the site of mass graves where bodies were dumped after being bludgeoned to death. I was greeted at the entrance by an army of legless men, all extending their beggar hats. Better known as one of the "killing fields," a 50-foot-high glass memorial tower (stupa) holds shelf upon shelf of the victims' skulls. Bones remain strewn about in open graves, never to be identified.

While walking around the tower, I looked closely at many of the skulls. Only a few lacked the cracks and indentations indicating massive blows to the head. Executions were usually carried out at night, with the prisoners blindfolded and made to squat beside an open trench. Saving ammunition, their heads were smashed with ox-cart axles. Below the memorial tower were piles of the victims' blood-stained clothes. It does not take long, as you look upon the mass of darkened clothes and then the mass of skulls, for the sense of horror, for the sense of the enormity of man's capacity for evil, to seep in.

To one side of the skull tower, was an 80-foot row boat used today by local villagers in the annual holiday races on the Mekong and Tonle Sap rivers. After a guide explained its purpose to two chirruping matrons from London, they replied, "In England we have the same competition between Oxford and Cambridge."

Upon returning to Phnom Penh, I found myself walking numbly around the Holocaust Museum at Tuol Sleng, a secondary school that was converted in 1975 to a prison and interrogation center, code named S-21. When the prison was first discovered by the invading Vietnamese army, it was the stench of putrefying flesh that drew them there. The only identifying sign at the former school was a red placard over the gate, "Fortify the spirit of the revolution! Be on your guard against the strategy and tactics of the enemy so as to defend the country, the people and the Party."

The victims came from a variety of socioeconomic backgrounds: professionals, intellectuals, *petit bourgeois*, soldiers, factory workers and any citizen who wore prescription glasses—a sign of education or elitism. In a strange contrast to the Nazi genocide of the Jews, most of the 14,000 victims at S-21 were loyal Khmer party members who were fingered in some paranoid ritual to cleanse the "microbes" infecting the army, the collectives, the ministries, and the revolution in general.

My guide at the museum lost his father, two brothers, and a sister. When the Vietnamese arrived at S-21, only decomposing bodies were left—there were no prisoners to set free. Otherwise, the Vietnamese left the torture rooms as they found them. They took photographs and later had artists paint pictures of the ghastly site.

Van Nath, a painter and one of only seven who survived torture at S-21 and still escaped death, provided many stark images, two of which hung in an interrogation room: vultures eating the viscera of torture victims chained to beds and scorpions crawling about the gaping wounds of chained women whose breasts had been partially removed. Some say the paintings are an exaggeration, but when I recently met Van Nath, he said that they are what he and fellow inmates witnessed.

The floors are still stained with blood. Neighbors say they heard howls of death echoing from S-21's torture chambers almost every night. These are the stains that shape the psyche and culture of contemporary Cambodia.

Like most soldiers and functionaries, the henchmen, often boys wearing Mao hats, were obedient to their superiors; imbued with the sense of impunity and detachment of those who blindly obey orders. Systematically, they took the victims' pictures, then tortured them into a signed confession of disloyalty, and finally executed them with all paperwork in order. I sat in the chair where the photo IDs had been taken. Hundreds of the victims' pictures blanket the walls. It put faces on the skulls I had seen earlier. S-21 was but an urban microcosm of the paranoid, genocidal tyranny that swept the entire country during what is now called "The Pol Pot Time."

Welcoming the Khmer Rouge in Phnom Penh in April 1975 was Saloth Sar's best friend from College Sihanouk, Lon Non, who offered his help to the new regime. Within days Pol Pot had him executed.

Saloth Sar's older brother Chhay, who had arrived in Phnom Penh 40 years before with his younger sibling, was one of the tens of thousands of April 17th people who perished on the road to the rural cooperatives in 1975. Chhay would not have known Pol Pot though. He last saw his brother Saloth Sar sometime in the early 1960s.

As for America's political intruders in Cambodia, Richard Nixon is dead, having never apologized for the Kent State killings, much less acknowledging the faceless thousands of innocent Cambodians who died as a result of American bombings. Henry Kissinger won the Nobel Peace prize in 1973, receiving the award at about the same time Cambodian refugees were fleeing the countryside being devastated by B-52s sent as a result of his policies. Today the former secretary of state is usually treated as an eminence, enjoying a lucrative practice as advisor to governments and leaders around the world, including the U.S. president. He recently published a book, *Ending the Vietnam War*, in which he defends the Nixon Administration's policies in Indochina. Like Augusto Pinochet, Kissinger has had to limit his overseas travel for fear of being arrested for international war crimes by some local judge bent on sending a message to despots.

Prince, King, ex-King, Prime Minister, ex-Prime Minister, citizen Sihanouk, spent three years under house arrest in the royal palace during the Khmer Rouge reign. Only because the Chinese intervened was he not executed. He continued to make movies and was crowned King Sihanouk once again in 1993. Like the ancient Khmer kings, he took the title "varman," meaning protector, much to the objection of the many Cambodians who have suffered because of his whimsical political exploits.

Ieng Sary, Saloth Sar's old friend from student days in Phnom Penh and Paris, defected from the ranks of the Khmer Rouge in 1996 and was given a royal pardon. Like many of the Khmer Rouge leaders who have struck it rich in gems and timber, Ieng Sary now lives prosperously in Pailin, a Khmer town near the Thai border.

Even after the damning movie, *The Killing Fields*, was released in 1985, the United States, Thailand and China were only mildly embarrassed by their ongoing support of Pol Pot and the Khmer Rouge. In each case, national foreign policy favored tactics over principles, following the pattern of the-enemy-of-my-enemy-is-my-friend.

A Dutch non-governmental organization estimated that over one-third of Cambodia's populace—approximately four million people— is suffering from post-traumatic stress disorder. The sickness that took over a country left its survivors with another sickness, one which pervades and has changed the culture. The gentle-cultured people, the gestalt of an earlier time, have been replaced by a culture characterized by emotional volatility. Violence erupts daily in families, disputes are settled with hand grenades, and vigilante street gangs take the law into their own hands.

On January 29, 2003, a Thai actress was "rumored" to have said that Angkor Wat belonged to Thailand. Once word hit the streets, raging vigilantes in Phnom Penh marched on the Thai embassy, looting it and burning it to the ground. They danced on portraits of the King of Thailand, an offense the Thai neighbors cannot forgive. The prestigious Royal Phnom Hotel and many other Thai-owned businesses were torched, as Thai merchants fled the country under threat of violence and death.

This rage now lies beneath Cambodia's surface of Buddhist calm and humanity. As a war-torn, impoverished country, Cambodia was deprived of any cathartic process to mourn its holocaust. There were no "truth commissions" like in South Africa, or "criminal tribunals" such as those in Rwanda. In place of the healing that might have come from a process of grieving, truth finding and justice, Cambodia is plagued by thinly suppressed blind rage.

Van Nath, the artist and survivor of S-21, was given his life by the prison guards because he could paint, mostly portraits of Pol Pot. He told me at his open air studio above a tea shop on a quiet street in Phnom Penh, that he could not allow his thoughts to be consumed by the talk of a tribunal unless and until it happened. In addition to his prison torture, Van Nath and his wife, Kith Eng, lost two boys in the collectives during the Pol Pot Time. His sorrow forced him to quit painting for over a decade, and he now prefers doing therapeutic landscapes.

In 1988, Pol Pot married a second wife and had a baby daughter, his first child. He was once sighted holding his daughter, a loving father. In 1997, suspecting treason by Sun Sen, a long time friend and comrade, Pol Pot ordered his assassination and the murder of his children and grandchildren. Only then did several outraged Khmer Rouge members put Pol Pot through a public tribunal, sentencing him to life in prison solely for the murder of Sun Sen. Armed guards escorted Pol Pot away from the jungle courtroom to his two-bedroom house, where he died of a reported heart attack in bed 10 months later. He was wrapped in a tarp and cremated over a fire made of scraps of furniture and old car tires.

He never issued a *mea culpa*, except to express regret about his abolition of money, calling it "a drastic measure." Even though Pol Pot had attempted to abolish Buddhism in Cambodia, friends and comrades have built a *stupa* in his honor, housing his ashes in the foothills of the Cardamon Mountains on the border of Thailand. Former Khmer Rouge officials are now building a casino and "five-star hotel" nearby, hoping to cash in on the macabre celebrity of Pol Pot.

As for isolating the trait that might have predisposed the likes of Adolph Hitler and Pol Pot to be able to lead their nations to practice genocide, what mostly comes to mind is blind ideology, and the ability to inflict a nation with its inherent sickness and proclivity for true evil. The "banality" of evil is illustrated throughout Indochina. It was not just certain evil people that devastated a land and people—it was a confluence of factors, not the least was foreign aggression.

Himalayan Fantasies

O n two previous journeys to Cambodia, I visited the ancient ruins of Angkor near the provincial capital of Siem Reap by crossing Tonle Sap lake. Producing over 100,000 tons of fish a year, the lake is a honey hole that made a great civilization like Angkor possible. It is the fourth largest captive fishery in the world, providing Cambodia's 11 million people with up to 70 percent of their annual protein intake and irrigating vast acreage of rice paddy.

What makes the lake so fertile is its link to the Mekong. Each year in June at the beginning of the annual monsoons the rising waters of the Mekong force the Tonle Sap river to reverse direction and flow into Tonle Sap lake. At the height of the rains in September the lake swells to a depth of 30 feet and covers up to 10,000 square miles, an increase of 60 percent in size.

In November as the monsoons end and the lake begins to recede, the Tonle Sap river flows once again southward into the Mekong. That is when Cambodia holds its biggest annual festival—the Bom Om Tuk, or Festival of the Reversing Water—to mark the end of the floods, to ensure a bountiful rice and fish harvest, and to honor the Mekong. And so it was in ancient times, as told in a 13th century account by Chinese envoy Zhou Daguan:

"In front of the royal palace, a great platform is built, capable of holding a thousand people, and decorated with lanterns and flowers... The rockets are released and the firecrackers lighted... the festival goes on like this for fifteen days."

Today as well, under the spell of a full moon, Angkor Wat hosts great firework shows, monks row golden-prowed ceremonial pirogues around the moat, and in Phnom Penh, boats race up the Tonle Sap river. The royal family attends in both places.

By February, fishermen are gathered at the mouth of the lake with nets and bamboo traps plucking fish from the water as brown bears would at an Alaskan salmon run. Henri Mahout was amazed: "...they [fish] are actually crushed under the boats, and the play of the oars is frequently impeded by them."

In April and May, the lake has been drained so low it becomes like a giant holding tank for fish. Elephant fish flop across the mud flats looking for deeper pools, able to leave water for several hours at a time. But that makes them easy prey, and they're considered a delicacy, selling for up to $60 each.

The hydrological wonder starts anew in June with the seasonal symbiosis of monsoons, rivers and lake engineering a refuge of Mekong biodiversity. Kings and ideologies will come and go, but arable land and fish-filled waters will always be the basis of local beliefs here, just as pre-biblical Mesopotamia was founded on water cults.

Simon and I boarded the commercial fast boat to cross Tonle Sap lake. The smell of marijuana wafted through the hold from the half-closed cockpit. Working the crowd of staid tourists and a few Pancakers, a cabin boy passed out glossy flyers for Siem Reap's Sok San Club: "Private Karaoke Lounges. And Full of Lovely Girls. Massage and Pay as You Go Dance Partners." Not that many of the brochures fell on the floor.

We throttled to the northwest up the Tonle Sap river's narrow straits before it slowly widened into an oceanic sweep, the Great Lake. The boat was listing uncomfortably, to the point where I was trying to counter the tilt by leaning the other way. The captain, possibly stoned, sent the cabin boy to balance the oblivious sprawl of people on top. He had to shuffle and reshuffle every half hour or so.

After about two hours, a chain of low-slung mountains appeared to the west, fronted by a floating fishing village where television antennas crested each roof, whether thatched or tin. Across the otherwise redundant waters, a fishing scowl acting as a tug boat towed a family and its floating farm: a tin roofed house with kids playing and dad soaping down on the front porch, trailed by a vegetable garden and banana trees, piles of chopped wood and fish traps. A dog sniffed around the garden in this moveable estate; it could have doubled as a movie set.

On the opposite side, the shoreline was a muddy swamp of flooded thickets that receded seamlessly into a forest. Those wetlands are home to a variety of aquatic plants and provide breeding grounds for fish and migratory birds. In the last several years, the lacustrine forests have been trimmed in half, leaving parts of the waterway clogged in silt.

In the relatively shallow waters, a wind threw up whitecaps. The stippled grayish expanse was garnished in drifting clumps of water hyacinth, aquatic plants that spread like duckweed on a warm summer pond. In many parts of the world, the purple-flowered plant is considered a pest. But around Tonle Sap, in addition to being used for pig fodder, the water-resistant fiber makes it useful for baskets and other woven products.

This is not always the case, however, in the peasant fishing villages of Cambodia. Along a major tributary of the Tonle Sap we attempted passage that felt as if we were driving through a Kansas cornfield: for ten miles the vegetative flourish slowed boat traffic to a standstill, as it completely engulfed the river and its floating villages. A Cambodian friend described the mounting ecological dilemma these peasant fishermen are faced with, "They live from hand to mouth; they don't have time to clean it up. Only 60 percent of the country is literate, so these people don't understand the long-term dangers of water hyacinth."

After six hours in the roaring bowels of the capsule, we entered calm water and idled slowly through a floating Vietnamese fishing village. In 1177, armies of the ancient Chams of coastal Vietnam followed the Siem Reap river another 10 miles to the fabled city of Angkor, before pillaging it and putting the Khmer king to death. The next year the Khmers led by Jayavarman VII defeated the Chams in a naval battle, and memorialized the event in detail on the bas-reliefs in the temple-city of Angkor Thom. The Vietnamese now living in the fishing village are descended from people who arrived in the 19th century, then fled back to Vietnam during the Pol Pot Time, and after that returned.

Fishing skiffs with small thatched compartments for cooking and shelter plied the waters around us. The occupants wore the cone-shaped peasant hats peculiar to Vietnam. We wove through a corridor of tattered, thatched-roof houseboats. Heaping pyres of branch wood pruned from the lake's canopy of trees provided charcoal for cooking. The more prosperous floating homes were mounted on pontoons, with mesh fish tanks below their docks. Storks, ibises and pelicans perched and plodded on the docks as tourist photo ops. Scattered in the floating mishmash was a primitive hospital, post office, petrol stations and a police headquarters.

Several barges of oceangoing size were being loaded near a spit of land occupied by Khmers in their traditional red and white scarves. We debarked along a skinny canal that smelled of the dried fish spread in silvery sheets along a dike, where we were met by a group of local touts and drivers attempting to monopolize the transportation options on to Siem Reap. As we rode west along the dike in a taxi, straight ahead was Phnom Krom, crowning a hillock like a medieval salient. It is an 11th-century temple dedicated to the Hindu gods Vishnu, Siva, and Brahma. It seems to guard the approach to Angkor and bestow bountiful harvests upon the Great Lake.

The point of departure for touring Angkor's ruins is the city of Siem Reap, which Cambodians proudly point out means "Siam (Thailand) Defeated," an allusion to a 16th century battle when the Khmers routed the Thais and retook Angkor. The city is built along the banks of the southward-flowing Siem Reap river, which during the dry season comes to a muddy standstill, mirroring the somnolent pace of the locals.

Like some Klondike town, the crazy waterway is cluttered with the Old Market, temples, many new hotels, fewer old ones, Sihanouk's residence, colonial French villas, franchise restaurants, branches of Phnom Penh bars, a host of legless beggars, prostitutes, pimps, and motorcycle taxis. The palatial grounds of the Grand Hotel d'Angkor, with rooms at $300 a night—about the average annual income of most Cambodians—offer a profound contrast to the fetid squatter huts that line the trash-choked river.

Most visitors overlook the many faces of poverty around Siem Reap, unless the tour bus makes an unscheduled stop. On one occasion, while catching a ride in front of my hotel on the back of a motorcycle to the Old Market, a ring of pubescent girls played in a circle on the earthen ground a block from the Grand Hotel d' Angkor. When the driver slowed, the children looked up, leapt to their feet and shrieked, "Hey mister, hey mister, come for me." I waved them off.

Surprised by my lack of interest in the young girls, the middle-aged, scruffy driver assumed I had other desires, "You want boom boom young boy, $10. You boom boom my young friend, $8. Boom boom me, $7."

As the motorcycle driver took several wrong turns—hard to do in little Siem Reap—he persisted with his sales pitch. "I don't want to boom boom anyone," I barked, and got off short of my destination. He was sunken at the loss of business, only trying to stay afloat in a soulless sea after a long storm. Pederasty is not new to Siem Reap, as recounted by the 13th century Chinese emissary, Zhou Daguan:

"In the market place groups of ten or more catamites are to be seen every day, making efforts to catch the attention of the Chinese in the hope of rich presents."

Today's givers of rich presents are mostly Western sex tourists. At the end of the day, it is the pimps, prostitutes, pushers and politicians who take home the big bucks in Cambodia, while school teachers are paid $60 a month and policemen take home $15 plus all they can steal. Minesweepers risk their lives every day for a monthly salary of $150. For most well-heeled tourists, all the poverty and decadence around Siem Reap becomes a colorful backdrop for the ancient monuments. "Great Angkor" was built by half-a-million Khmer slaves, after all, and Siem Reap is home to their descendants.

My first impression of Angkor was formed by a Life magazine photo spread showing Jackie Kennedy at the ruins with Prime Minister Sihanouk. It seemed fascinating, equal to any of antiquity's Seven Man Made Wonders. Since Jackie's visit, years of war, particularly during the Khmer Rouge period, have taken their toll on the complex. So have antiquities thieves. Even so, its 100 temples spread over 80 square miles remain one of the summits of human culture, still alive with architectural magic.

Officially the Angkor period begins in 802 A.D. with Jayavarman II, referred to in inscriptions as devaraja, or god king. Undoubtedly those Sanskrit writings are an allusion to the king's association with a popular Siva, a belief that survived in Cambodia into the 1960s. The period of Angkor's greatness would close when Siam sacked it in 1431 A.D., and many Khmers were enslaved or scattered. Although much of the Angkor complex was abandoned after the Siamese invasion, the royal city of Angkor was restored in the 1570s. At the temple of Angkor Wat, an architectural acclamation to the Hindu gods and the largest religious building in the world, Buddhist statuary has been placed there every century since it was built; its last inscription was carved in 1747.

Although most of the ancient monuments had been consumed by the jungle when Henri Mahout arrived in the middle of the 19th century, the temple of Angkor Wat was still cared for by more than 1,000 hereditary slaves. Even today, most of the monuments are only slightly spruced up—the encroaching forest, with its vegetative rage, lends extra charm.

The recent influx of tourists often leaves the causeway leading to the ethereal towers of Angkor Wat resembling the Champs Elysees on a busy day. Yet strolling the celestial corridor across the temple's spacious moat, it is hard not to be mesmerized watching the young Buddhist monks in saffron blazing against the gray backdrop of Hindu sanctums. Angkor Wat is a working temple, where on the first and 15th days of the lunar month worshippers come to pray and burn incense before a dwindling galaxy of *naga*-headed Buddhas. Cambodian men smile impishly just inside the portico, fondling *apsaras'* breasts rubbed slick from years of veneration.

It takes more than a moat to keep Himalayan fantasy apart from the tropical jungles of Cambodia. Built by Suryvarman II in the first half of the 12th century, the temple and tomb known as Angkor Wat were dedicated to Vishnu, the preserver. Spiraling from the center of the temple complex is a stepped pyramid symbolizing Mt. Meru, the center of the universe in Hindu cosmology. Surrounding the holy mountain are four lesser peaks of pointed cupolas marking the corners of the universe. They overlook courtyards that represent continents and a rectangular moat that symbolizes the ocean.

Atop Mt. Meru stands an astronomical observatory. From this mystical aerie was the site of the cremation ceremony of Suryvarman, whose ashes would ascend to heaven. There he would be met by flying *apsaras*, heavenly nymphs dedicated to eternal lovemaking. Today the summit features Buddhist statuary encircled in the reverent smoke of incense.

On Mt. Meru's aerial sanctuary, once reserved for high priests and the royal caste, Simon and I took a spliff break, enjoying the sepia-stained views, flecked in saffron and spilling out like a cosmic potion. Wobbly, we descended a steep fall of narrow stairs into the spiritual realm of the commoners—the cloistered gallery of bas-reliefs. The carved images stretch continuously for over half a mile, flowing counter-clockwise through an open hall of ornate sandstone. Afternoon light streamed through the galleries and porticos, illuminating stone carvings that depict Heaven and Hell, scenes of Khmers battling Chams in Vietnam, the Hindu epic *Ramayana* and the famous *Churning of the Ocean of Milk*, a Hindu allegory of good and evil conspiring with Vishnu to extract a bottle of the elixir of immortality from a swirling sea.

Heaven and Hell are depicted in the southern gallery, orchestrated by the Hindu deity *Yama* sitting atop a water buffalo and dispatching a column of people either to a reposeful heaven, or to one of 32 infernal chambers, each designed with a macabre torture to fit the transgressors' crimes. *Yama*, with his inventive tortures, has often been likened to Pol Pot.

In the late afternoon, hotter than Hindu hell, we found a breezy, shaded space along the eastern gallery's great bas-relief, the *Churning of the Ocean of Milk*. Our guide Rith Roeurm told us the story of the antigod Rahu, who succeeded in obtaining a sip of the elixir of immortality. Alerted to Rahu's devilry, Vishnu the protector, the referee of good and evil, had Rahu's body severed from the chest down to prevent him from having complete impregnability. To this day Cambodians attribute eclipses to Rahu trying to swallow the sun or moon. Darkness comes as the celestial body passes through his truncated body, before emerging in full luminescence. Similarly Laotians blame eclipses on the appetite of a cosmic frog noshing on the sun or the moon. Laotians shoot guns and make whatever noise they can to scare the demon away. Cambodians, on the other hand, beat drums and gongs out of happiness at Rahu's folly.

Leaving the terrestrial confines of Angkor Wat via *tuk-tuk*, Simon and I arrived at the Victory Gate of Angkor Thom. The gate is approached by 54 heads of antigods known as *asuras* on the right and an equal number of benevolent gods known as *devas* on the left. Many heads have been pilfered and several originals have been replaced with copies to prevent further theft. Staring down from the imperious gate is Avalokiteshvara, a *bodhisattva* or patron Buddhist saint of the temple-city, his smiling gaze like an enigmatic death mask.

Hinduism has remained in India, whereas Buddhism traveled on. Jayavarman VII, the founder of Angkor Thom, learned the mystical teachings of Mahayana Buddhism, and introduced this new religion to the Khmer empire in the 12th century. Yet he kept many Hindu practices in place. The ancient Khmer kings enjoyed the powerful status of demigods. Sihanouk squandered the remaining influences of this tradition, though, to some extent, this holy status still attaches to the Thai monarchy. The king is both the *sangha-raj*, or leader of the Buddhist community, and considered an incarnation of Rama, thus the reigning king's title, Rama IX.

The center of Angkor Thom is the temple-mountain known as the Bayon, framed in sago palms and kapok trees. Elephants and their mahouts take tourists on short excursions around the ruins. Dominated by the imposing faces of the patron *bodhisattva*, the pyramid temple looks like a grouping of forest sprites petrified in place. Of all the carvings in Angkor, it is the most mystical. At one time it boasted 54 gothic towers adorned with over 200 larger-than-life faces of the smiling *bodhisattva*, with "the eyes of a pineapple."

Elderly monks gain merit in their golden years as caretakers of Bayon's remaining Buddhist shrines. They pass out joss sticks, take donations, and take the typical diet of older Khmers—watermelon and dried fish. The French explorer Francis Garnier wrote that Cambodians of the day had an apt nickname for Bayon. Suggesting its many hidden chambers, its narrow corridors of ornate bas-reliefs, and the encroaching forest, they called it, *preasar ling poun*, "the pagoda in which one plays hide and seek."

A short distance east of the Bayon is Ta Phrom temple, where we were greeted by several enterprising policemen selling their badges for $5 a piece. Beneath a shade tree a band of landmine victims played traditional

Cambodian instruments for tips from tourists. Westerners know Ta Phrom as the set for several sequences of the movie *Tomb Raider*. Ancient kapok trees rise as leafy towers with serpentine carpals and metacarpals for roots, strangling and dislodging the temple remnants, leaving a tumbled wake of fractured *apsaras* and fallen lintels. Local guides don't see this as yet another case of tropical eagerness, but instead as an example of nature being more patient than man.

For a donation of $10 to the park police, Simon and I and a few others enjoyed a private sunset on the second tier of Pre Rup temple. Enjoying a view of the towers of Angkor Wat, we drank Tattinger champagne, munched on European comestibles and communed by candlelight with the vestigial Hindu-Khmer spirits. Good ambiance has never fetched a high enough price.

Once back in Phnom Penh, Simon and I spent our last evening at the Foreign Correspondents Club engaged by Dihrya, a Javanese dancer who had spent the last several years teaching Indonesian folk culture and traditional dance at the University of California in Los Angeles. She laughed as she told us about rushing into the FCC to get off the street, "The police are outside picking up prostitutes. I was afraid they might confuse me for one!"

One of Dihrya's good friends, now living in the States, is a Cambodian woman who survived the collectives of the Pol Pot Time. Her friend was left with many psychological scars, and fingers permanently disfigured from carrying heavy loads of water, her punishment as a child slave in the Khmer work camps. Inspired by her friend's story, Dihrya had recently been awarded a Ford Foundation grant to write a book on the survivors of the Pol Pot Time. She would be staying in Phnom Penh for a year, documenting as many stories as possible throughout the country and keeping alive the memory of the Cambodian Holocaust.

The next morning we left for Chau Doc, a border town in Vietnam. Riding in a Pancaker shuttle, we were slowed behind a funeral cortege—an open-air hearse with a stylized casket showered in flowers and leaves and encircled by praying monks. Behind the decorative hearse were family and friends dressed in the traditional garments of grief: the women covered their faces in gauzy white veils and wore muslin robes cinctured at the waist with banana-plant-fiber belts; the men wrapped their heads in white bands of cloth. A wake of leaves and flowers preceded us like potpourris of spring and fall.

Following the Mekong by road for an hour to Neak Luong, a ferry-crossing town heavily populated by Vietnamese, we caught a fiberglass boat the size of a hot tub, with a 40 horsepower motor. A family of six Vietnamese with as many boxes joined us.

The river was fast, ever widening, and banked with shallow walls of red earth. For an hour and a half, we passed through the Khmer Plains of fallow cornfields while the young captain, at full throttle, slammed the square bow into wake and wave in tortuous repetition. Using my arms as shock absorbers, I winced from back pain, while holding on for dear life. The Vietnamese family took naps, laughed in conversation, and generally enjoyed the ride as if we were on a cruise ship. Simon shared my misery.

We docked next to a couple of armored naval boats. An arched blue sign with white lettering read, "Kaamsamnar Kohrokar International Border"— from the land of Sihanouk to Ho Chi Minh's Vietnam.

After a bribe-free pass through Cambodian customs, on the Vietnamese side of the border all the customs policemen were lying shirtless in their hammocks for a noonday nap. Hardly vigilant, they would periodically thrash about and spout an order, then go back to sleep. After a short wait, one of the protectors of the border spun out of his mesh cocoon and stamped our passports. His body was covered in crimson circular welts like natural polka dots. It's common practice in Asian traditional medicine to apply heated cups to the body to draw blood and disease to the skin's surface, leaving such temporary marks.

The ferry on to Chau Doc had engine problems and would take a while to fix. We passed the time in a flyblown food joint overlooking the river, competing for space with a clutch of scrawny dogs sniffing the dirt floors for scraps. Time passed drowsily. Once on the spacious ferry, we were joined by two other foreigners, an American law professor living in Saigon and a 50-something German man, self-proclaimed sex tourist and almost certainly a pedophile. He bore a strong resemblance to Anthony Hopkins' character Hannibal Lecter.

Hannibal had overstayed his 30-day visa and was on his way to Chau Doc to get a new stamp. It didn't take long to figure out that he was an authority on the regional flesh trade, as he spouted expertise on cohabitation laws in Vietnam, and the crackdown on discos and prostitutes in Phnom Penh. When I mentioned I had been to Svay Pak, a boomtown of distressingly young Vietnamese prostitutes seven miles north of Phnom Penh, he lit up: "I go there many times, very nice girls."

A year before, I had visited Svay Pak with my wife Joellen, who works in the reproductive health field, and to some extent with HIV-AIDS education. Svay Pak is a brothel village with only a couple of streets which are lined with hotels displaying doll-faced girls as merchandise for sale. Our passing car provoked a flowering of smiles and ogles. Joellen said some of the girls were 13 or younger.

Chaos and extreme poverty have fueled prostitution in Cambodia and Vietnam's Mekong Delta. According to Asia correspondent Mark McDonald, Hannibal's "very nice girls" are well protected by their owners, who have procured them for a few hundred dollars in the impoverished paddies of Vietnam's Mekong Delta or villages in lower Cambodia. The young girls are brought to Svay Pak by middle-aged women procurers who promise them a housekeeping job or a position as a waitress. Once there, they are indentured as prostitutes and not allowed to leave until their owner has recouped his cost several times over.

It is estimated that 64 percent of these prostitutes working in Cambodia are HIV-positive, twice the rate in Thailand and Burma. Many customers will pay extra to have sex without a condom. If the girls refuse, they are beaten by their pimps or owners. Sex tourists, if not mostly locals, are willing to pay hundreds of dollars for a virgin, an experience the men believe imbues them with virility. Some also believe intercourse with a virgin cures HIV-AIDS, a bit of folklore that generates significant market demand for these sad victims.

The status of women is paradoxical in Asia; they have been elected as heads of many Asian states and "dragon ladies" abound, wielding power in business and government beyond the traditional role of controlling the purse strings at home. Yet beneath the skin of poverty, lawlessness and moral drift in Cambodia and the larger Indochina today, the chauvinist practice of polygamy is still deeply ingrained. Polygamy relegates women to a low rung on the food chain; Confucius summed up the underlying attitude 2,500 years ago: "a woman without talents is virtuous."

Perhaps as an outgrowth of these ancient belief systems, a permissive culture survives that quietly but often openly accepts the adulterous cavorting of older men with much younger women—prostitutes, mistresses or wives. Even today in Southeast Asia, where there are laws against polygamy, it is still common for men to have second wives, reflecting the substantially Chinese character of local culture.

In almost seven years of living in the region, I have met but a few local men who don't routinely visit brothels—it's a rite of passage. Simon had recently spent a weekend visiting ancestral grave sites with a prominent Hanoi artist, the artist's father and three male relatives in their 50s. On the first day of the traditional family weekend in the ancestral village, they drank jugs of rice whiskey diluted with pureed goat gonads, while also eating slivers of tiger bones provided by the commune chief. The morning after, washing the goat gonad taste from their parched mouths with warm tripe soup, they began swilling more of the teste punch—a libido tonic. Once they had caught their stride of the night before, they set out for a nearby brothel village. Drunk on nature's Viagra, the family of Vietnamese men raged in the crowded van like a flock of crowing roosters. Simon is no shrinking violet, but the whole ritual became simply more fun than he was ready to cope with. He caught a quick bus back to Hanoi.

In his novel *The Quiet American*, Graham Greene helped mythologize Vietnamese women as "twittering doves on a pillow." The objectification of these women was relatively civilized then, seemingly part of the natural order compared to the treatment they would receive in the 1960s and 1970s on behalf of testosterone-sated American GIs. The doves were scooped off their pillows and put into neon birdcages. Witness the sex carnival that continues to this day on Patpong Road in Bangkok where hundreds of young girls pole-dance nightly, or demonstrate how their vaginas can manipulate balloons, cigarettes and goldfish.

Once the war ended and the R&R scene was over, Bangkok was a natural host for "sex tourism" to spontaneously generate, fertilized with local baht, German marks, U.S. dollars and Japanese yen, where anything goes for a price, and everything did: boys became girls, girls became boys, men went after girls, boys took men, men chased men, women enjoyed girls, and virgins male and female were much in demand. It's not that Bangkok invented any of this sexuality, it's that rarely if ever before had sex been placed so massively in the service of commerce.

Fortunately Thailand has cracked down on underage prostitution and targeted foreign pedophiles over the past 10 years. Regrettably, poverty-stricken Cambodia then became a choice destination for traveling predators of children.

Hannibal had visited Cambodia seven times in the past two years, staying for over a month at a time, all for pleasure. He was hoping to find a girl in Chau Doc who he had met the year before in Phnom Penh. If he could not find her, Hannibal would return upriver the next day for two more weeks of preying on the young residents of Phnom Penh's brothels. Thanks to decades of war, economic embargoes and little effort at remediation, the child prostitute's poverty is Hannibal's honey pot.

We followed the main channel of the Mekong which parallels the Bassac, a branch of similar size that flows to the east and southeast. Both branches fissure in Vietnam after crossing the border from Cambodia and flow into the delta in nine fingers, giving rise to the area's traditional Vietnamese name of Cuu Long or Nine Dragons. Transecting the mythical tributaries was an elaborate system of canals, designed by Thoai Ngoc Hau and commissioned by Gia Long, the emperor who unified Vietnam at the turn of the 19th century.

Hau is revered by the Vietnamese as a visionary who saw public works projects like canal building as the force that would drive settlement of the Mekong Delta. He also oversaw the building of the Vinh Te Canal that stretches for more than 50 miles from the Gulf of Siam to Chau Duc. Because building the canal took 55,000 laborers, mostly Khmers, Cambodian accounts describe the project as yet another example of Vietnamese cruelty.

Today, the narrow Tan Chau Canal connects the main trunks of the Bassac and the Mekong. As we entered the Bassac, the Vietnamese quickly lived up to their reputation as worker bees—riverine life buzzed and teemed like nowhere we had seen since joining the Mekong in China. Granary warehouses lined the shores and big-bellied rice barges with eyes painted on the prows loaded, unloaded and cut deep wakes through the water. Three boys in a trio of pirogues tethered end-to-end latched on to one of the barges for a joy ride.

Well-built wooden homes and tin huts floated on the water, dragging submerged wire cages bubbling with catfish. Accompanying each fish farm was a cooking vat shaped like a gigantic teapot, and exhaling pillars of smoke. These vats are used for making cakes of gruel mixed with fish offal. We later stopped at one of the farms. When the owner opened the cellar-like tin doors to reveal a churning mass of boiling catfish, Simon described it precisely, "It looks like some place 007 might retrieve Pussy Galore."

There are over 500 species of fish in the Mekong floodplain, from which an estimated half million tons are harvested each year, or five times the take from Tonle Sap. Once the Vietnamese sniff out a niche in agriculture or aquaculture, as in the case of catfish, their enthusiasm to produce becomes uncontainable.

As happened in the coffee trade that is now depressed worldwide because of the sudden glut created by Vietnamese farmers, American catfish growers saw their prices plummet and market share fall as "*basa*" and "*tra*," two species of freshwater catfish farmed in the Mekong Delta, appeared in grocery stores in the States at half the price of domestic catfish. A brouhaha erupted as Southern catfish growers appealed to Washington for relief, couching their got-whupped-dilemma in a labeling argument that contended "*basa* and *tra*" should not be called catfish so as not to be confused with homegrown U.S. catfish. Of course, when battered, golden fried and placed on a buffet line beneath a heat lamp, which is the way most catfish in the U.S. is served, it's impossible to tell them apart.

We passed a long stretch of catfish farms, then at least a half-mile row of sawmills with columns of new teak from Cambodia piled along the banks. To the south and east the venerated Nui Sam, or Sam Mountain, the highest eminence in the Mekong Delta, looked over Chau Doc and the Khmer frontier, peeking through the hazy afternoon sky.

At the foot of the sacred mountain stands a temple dedicated to Lady Chua Xu, a Pygmalion local saint who came to life from a stone statue that once crowned the top of Sam Mountain. From this mystical pilgrimage site, which I have visited on two occasions, the glassy mosaic of flooded paddy and canals stretches forever: mirrors signaling the fecund face of the Mekong Delta. That view exemplifies why the Vietnamese word for rice, *com*, is the same as their word for food.

At a bustling bend in the river at Chau Doc, once again the shore was lined with floating fish farms, and an armada of houseboats draped in laundry, their braziers spewing smoke. The boats flew Vietnamese flags, yellow star centered in red background.

To the west, retreating up a long sloping hillside, a higgledy-piggledy crush of shanties stood candled in a riot of antennas. A French, neo-colonial hotel stood smack in the vortex of this riverine swarm.

In neo-colonial decadence, I enjoyed a cheeseburger poolside on the verandah of the French hotel. With a half pound of Australian beef covered in tangy French mustard, it was a repast to relish, despite the lack of pickles. I listened to the cicada cries of boats chugging by, watching darkness scatter across the sky.

As with many frontier Mekong towns, Chau Doc is a tropical melting pot of cultures—Chinese, Cham, Khmer, and Vietnamese. The river entrepot is home to several domed mosques built by the ancient Cham who live along the water in stilted houses. The Cham are no longer coastal traders, pirates of the sea or conquering warriors; instead they are fishermen and weavers, with names like Salama, Muhammed, Ali, Fatimah and Maridam. Religion has been a revolving door for the Cham—animism for openers followed by Hinduism in the first millennium, Buddhism in the ninth century, and today in Chau Doc, Islam. Other than the mosques and the occasional Muslim greeting, *salam aleykum*, they keep their religion low key: no veils, prayer caps, or robed clothing.

More apparent are the Cambodians, who still refer to the larger delta region as "lower Cambodia," or Kampuchea Krom. At least one million ethnic Khmers still live in Vietnam's Mekong Delta. The border clashes during the Pol Pot Time were the brutal culmination of Cambodian resentment over Vietnam's annexation of large tracts of the Mekong Delta at the turn of the 19th century. The entire delta spreads over about 10 million acres, or some 15,000 square miles, about twice the size of the state of New Jersey. Vietnam now controls almost 70 percent of the Mekong Delta, leaving Cambodia with about a third of this fertile area.

I hired a left-behind American army jeep and went to the nearby Khmer village of Thot Lot, a dusty hamlet of a few thousand almost black-skinned inhabitants, set beneath a forest of coconut palms, with an air of delta laziness. Porches were filled with hammocks and not stools, the women wore *sampots*, or traditional Cambodian skirts and not trousers. Many wore the red-checkered scarves, or *kramas*. They all wore the face of economic despair.

Surrounded by palms and several flaming hibiscus trees, a 400-year-old pagoda, Chua Van Rau, was being refurbished by a huddle of resident monks with their saffron robes wrapped around their heads. I knew they were Khmer by the bright color of their habits. The Vietnamese monks, or bonzes, wear gray and brown habits with stocking caps. The Khmers of Thot Lot have held on to their heritage in the face of abject poverty, the result of being marginalized by the governing Viets.

From Thot Lot I traveled to the village of Ba Chuc, famous for its "Skull Pagoda." A stone's throw from the Cambodian border, Ba Chuc is an idyllic delta village built into the side of Elephant Mountain, with a thriving central market and a couple of fanciful Vietnamese pagodas.

In April 1978, the Khmer Rouge massacred 3,157 Vietnamese, Khmers and

Chinese in the village, often employing torture as they slaughtered. There were only two reported survivors, one of whom now sells soft drinks to the few tourists who drop in. Ha Thi Nga, 64, was shot in the neck and clubbed over the head, then left for dead alongside her six children, husband, parents, and siblings; a total of 37 of her family members were killed that day. Nga fainted and awoke to the grisly aftermath. She was not rescued for another 12 days.

Nga arrived from her next door neighbor's shanty to greet me wearing a bronze-colored tunic and trousers, mirroring the sundrenched shade of her skin. Her hair was pulled back in a tight pony tail, taut like her face, which only yielded a twitch for a smile. As we idled through a couple of hot Pepsis, I brought up the prospect of war tribunals in Phnom Penh.

"I am scared. I do not want to go there. It will bring back memories," she said.

Similar to the Killing Fields memorial near Phnom Penh, the ossuary across the dusty road from where we were talking commemorates the massacre at Ba Chuc. Here the skulls are arranged by age—babies, pre-adolescents and so on. Higher up on the glass pagoda are stacks of bones, many of which were Nga's relatives, piled like kindling.

A wagon train of ox carts formed a *kraal* 50 feet away around a mountain of freshly harvested and bagged rice. Local men, women and children loaded the bags onto their carts with hardly a glance at the pagoda. Vietnamese tourists from Can Tho, the next province to the east, burned incense and prayed in ritual obeisance to the shrine.

Before leaving, I asked Nga if she wanted her family's executioners brought to justice.

After a deep sigh, she said, "All I want is to forget everything and live in peace."

Waking from a night's slumber in my Chau Doc hotel room, I watched a golden sun rise across the river above the Mubarak Mosque and the stilted homes of the Chams.

Simon had spent the preceding evening at the Café Koala, owned by an Australian who had landed in Chau Doc a couple of years before. An elegantly dressed, flirtatious tour guide tried to tempt Simon to invest in a local culinary wingding of fried porcupine, roasted dog and dried squid, followed by dessert at a Karaoke bar. He settled instead on quaffing *bia tuoi* (draft beer) while soaking up morsels of the Aussie's world view.

We rented a sleek-as-*basa*-catfish fiberglass boat—the Mekong equivalent of the Pope Mobile—to take us to Can Tho, 70 miles down the Bassac, or Hau Giang, as it is known in Vietnam. Traffic on the river was considerable. The shoreline was a corridor of provincial industrialization blended into a hedgerow of sugar palms. Cranes crisscrossed the river dredging the channel of silt, to keep it clear for transport and irrigation. A fuel dump with a short six-pack of giant tanks gleaming in the sun verged the water next to a couple of grain silos, the skyscrapers of the delta.

The smell of burnt sweetness poured from smokestacks atop sugarcane and sugar palm refineries. Ocher, conical-shaped brick kilns fueled by mounds of paddy husk competed with rustic sawmills for status as the most prevalent industry. Newly built, fresh painted barges rested on sawhorses at a boat factory snuggled up to a cemetery of rotting gray cadavers of sampans.

Ocean-going freighters, car ferries, fishing gondolas, skiffs, barges, sampans, and pirogues all play leading roles in the Delta's water ballet. Mekong artistry in motion is a sampan piloted by a peasant woman in a conical palm-leaf hat, standing astern manipulating a set of double oars in a dance-step cadence through crowded waters.

About halfway to Can Tho, we took a short excursion to the Bang Lang Stork Garden in Thot Not district. Flanked by spiraling palms, several branching trees were billowed in smoke as farmers stirred bees out of their hives to harvest honey. Many palms had pink pouches of snail eggs clinging like barnacles to their lower trunks, out of range of the jaws of fish. Once hatched, the snails fall into the water. As we rounded the bend of a side-canal, four boys stood in the water. They held up a headless dog they were skinning. Eating canine meat brings good fortune. Further on, piles of jute were spread along the canal banks, stripped and hung to dry in sheets like blond curtains; they would later be woven into mats or twine.

Cuongs, or waterside altars, stood on pedestals sprinkled with offerings of lotus blossoms and incense for the river gods. They lined the fronts of the canal homes like mailboxes. In the delta, the annual floods generally bring great benefits to farmers by dumping tons of nutrient-rich silt over their fields, yielding bumper crops and record fish harvests. But for more than a decade now, the floods have exceeded normal levels, partly due to deforestation upriver. The floods have caused massive damage to homes and crops, seen the outbreak of waterborne diseases such as cholera and chronic diarrhea, resulting in great loss of life. Although the technological key to flood control is upgrading the floodgate systems—the dikes and canals— farmers along the Mekong see their fate as rooted in daily communion with the river gods.

Approaching the stork refuge, we edged through rampart-like walls of bamboo filled with the birds' screeching cries and the stench of ammonia. A gnarly cluster of trees was painted white with bird droppings. Many trees had slumped over and died. The branches were weighed down with a few thousand nesting storks and several hundred cormorants. As the male storks came and went, searching out food for the nesting females, the forest roost echoed with discordant cries and the flapping of wings, sounds evoking some primordial world.

Traveling on, we viewed the river's fecundity in fields of beans twisting on bamboo arches, low-slung orchards of *longan,* a grape-like fruit with a hard skin, tracts of bitter melon nestled on the ground in neat rows, and boundless paddies of emerald rice—the heart and soul of the delta.

Through the 1970s and into the 1980s Vietnam was an importer of rice. Due to increased irrigation in the delta, higher yield seed varieties, privatization of land and markets, Vietnam now enjoys food security, ranking second in the world to Thailand as an exporter of rice. The delta yields two to three crops a year in most places, with some areas reporting up to seven in a two-year period. It is a year-round anthill of food production.

Shortly after noon, with the smell of saltwater in the air, we arrived at Can Tho which is only 50 miles from the South China Sea. During the dry season and periods when water flows decline due partly to excess irrigation, the sea tides push up through the maze of canals and waterways, affecting almost half the Mekong Delta. Known as "shaking hands with the flood," many communities on the delta's edge have diversified their agricultural options by irrigating fields with the brackish water to earn additional income from shrimp farming.

Once the tide had risen sufficiently, we took a pirogue up Cai Son Canal, worming our way through a tranquilizing trellis of bamboo. The canal banks were a fertile shrine adorned with linear patches of yellow marigolds and fruit orchards of mangos and *rambutan*, a prickly red ball with a sweet, juicy core. Other plants and produce grown were areca nut for the betel chew favored by older women, custard apples, water palms, and swatches of morning glory brocading the water's edge, anchored by stakes of bamboo.

The fragrant smell of incense filled the air, as we stopped next to a flower-strewn altar, or *coung*, at a farmer's home. The family elder, in his 60s, was a runt of a man, his belt circling his waist twice and pants hanging like a potato sack before piling atop his plastic sandals. Blessed with a gentle face, he served us green tea next to a riotous bougainvillea where grazing bumblebees the size of hummingbirds flitted from bloom to bloom. Once the farmer had figured out I was American, former Private Do Van Be showed me his certificate of completion for a "Refrigerator Maintenance Course" held at Fort Bellevoir, Virginia. The certificate issued by the U.S. Army was signed by Colonel Sidney Killibrew, August 16, 1968. Through translation, he kept assuring me of his affection for America and Americans. After discovering that he had spent a year in one of the brutal re-education camps after the war ended in 1975, I was touched by his pluck and his candid remarks in a place where too much sincerity can mean trouble.

He gave us a tour of his small, canopied farm, which utilizes a method known by agricultural advisors as the "garden system." Stands of sugarcane, plots of vegetables, fruit trees of all varieties—spotted with pouches of pink snail eggs—crowded his three ponds stocked with catfish, fed by the droppings of his chickens and ducks. His well-fattened pigs, the pride of every Vietnamese farmer, fed off the rice husk from the paddy nearby, which was fertilized by human fecal matter. Planted among the dripping, hothouse verdure were the bones of his ancestors. Someday Do Van Be's bones will join those of his forebears, and nourish his descendants.

The late astronomer and prolific writer Carl Sagan, was fond of saying that human beings are made of "star stuff." But farmers like Do Van Be might better be described as a bit of "Mekong stuff."

After saying goodbye, we moled back through the tunnel-like canal, approaching the lean arches of a monkey bridge. Through a feathery frame of water palms, I spied the profile of a peasant girl in mauve blouse, black trousers and conical hat crossing the bridge to a nearby seed paddy. She stooped and began transplanting the germinated shoots. Nearby on the narrow paddy bund, a boy astride a dawdling water buffalo played the clear tones of a bamboo flute, a scene straight from a Chinese scroll painting.

Can Tho is the commercial heartbeat of the Mekong Delta, home to a slew of rice-husking mills, and the former site of a large U.S. Air Force base during the Vietnam War. I spent my evening there cocooned in a French hotel, having drinks on teak verandahs, enjoying the quavering tones of the Vietnamese sitar, or *dan bao*, and the intoxicating scents of jasmine and frangipani.

Simon disappeared early in the evening and scoured Can Tho in search of a decent guesthouse. He settled on an "International Hotel" in the center of Can Tho where an old chamber maid awaited him on the fifth floor in the doorway of her linen cupboard. She looked like she had not left the floor of that building in 20 years, as she ushered him into a decrepit and musty room, which reminded him of one of the psychiatric units he had worked in. The Hitchcockian atmosphere unnerved him, but he had already turned over his passport and paid his $10. He was trapped. Having just visited my garden paradise, he felt a bit like Adam banished from Eden.

So out he went wandering the streets, seeking Can Tho's feral nightlife. Failing to sniff out an expatriate scene, he bounced aimlessly from one outdoor restaurant to another, with a few stray hookers picking up his scent along the way. He settled on oblivion in the bottom of a glass, then returned to his dreary confines for the night through the vacated streets of Can Tho. Back in his isolation unit he found the ageing chamber maid suddenly more attractive; together they finished our pad of opium and passed out in rapturous embrace.

Next day, at Can Tho's Cai Rang floating market, the empty streets and sidewalks sprang alive with the same hocus pocus a magician uses to pull a rabbit from a hat: Women in conical hats carrying shoulder poles suddenly morphed into *pho* (soup) stands, tea shops, fruit, fish and vegetable markets; an old man arrived on bicycle with a box and within minutes a mirror hung on a tree and a chair unfolded into a barbershop. The key makers, the tire fixers, the lottery stands, the mobile hardware stores selling nails, brushes, dusters, screw drivers all unfold in the same unmarked spots everyday, then fold up again at night and flow back into the recesses of Can Tho, or any city in Vietnam.

The floating market was a logjam of wooden skiffs, buyers and sellers. The rustic live-a-boards—they are the wholesalers—were more firmly anchored than the smaller craft. When the boats had to make way, mooring ropes would loosen, the extended props would lift from the water and a skinny wedge would open for pirogue-bound buyers to edge through. It was like swimming through a parting school of fish.

Many vendors advertised a fruit salad of products—dragonfruit, pineapple, lichee, jackfruit, durian (the Limberger cheese of fruit), mangosteen, coconut, star apple, rambutan, plum, mango, grapefruit, and oranges— hung on a decorative string from a makeshift mast. The market ladies' mastery of product presentation borders on Madison Avenue brilliance, always stacking items—tomatoes or whatever—in neat rows, shapely humps or picture-perfect pyramids, splashing them with droplets of water like sparkling rubies, and slicing open the ideal specimen to display a fresh, juicy core. Bunches of grapes hung from leafy vines as if you were plucking them straight from the orchard. Sticky rice, fish and pork were packaged in banana fronds and tied in a bow with a string of bamboo.

Barking dogs jinked about the boat decks as several fishwives hoisted stringers of *basa* and *tra* catfish onto portable scales, suffusing the whole market with their odor. A grocery boat beeped its horn nonstop, weaving in and out of the squeezed armada, selling *ruou thuoc* (rice whiskey), *nuoc mam* (fish sauce used in almost every dish in Vietnam), sugar, chili sauce, noodles, quail eggs, and 100-year-old eggs, a delicacy in which the egg is steeped in ammonia until it turns black like gummy charcoal.

Before mid-morning, the floating market began to scatter like an ice floe breaking up in all directions. I boarded the Pope Mobile II for a final sprint to Saigon. Tuan, the boat captain, was an affable 30-year old who has a sister living in the States. Tuan's father had worked for the Americans during the war.

His father burned incriminating documents when the communist victors reached his doorsteps, avoiding the re-education camps. Tuan wanted to buy more Pope Mobiles to make a regular run to Phnom Penh and Siem Reap, and "maybe in a couple of years have a few in Laos." He envisioned a Pope Mobile empire.

We sliced through a couple of long arroyos linked to the other main branch of the Mekong, better known as the Tien Giang in Vietnam. The banks were lined with the usual fecund sweep of fruit orchards fronted by water hyacinth, its shadows haunted by fish. Drift nets flanked the canal's main channel staked on long bamboo poles rising like goal posts from the shallow water.

Along the populated banks, tatty delta homes—thatched, whitewashed, or painted in tropical peach, buff yellow and sky blue—backed up to the water, often with a street bounding their fronts. Beneath one of the many hogback bridges, a reptilian-eyed barge was stuck in the channel with a full belly of rice, waiting for a higher tide.

At a ferry crossing, a wave of schoolgirls on bicycles wore flowing white *ao dais*—the traditional form-fitting long dress and matching trousers.

On Thoi Son island, a favorite stopover between Saigon and Can Tho, pet gibbons shrieked in the trees above the drooping branches of dragon fruit. Cobras and eels were displayed in side-by-side cages as top delicacies.

From a distance we spotted the gilded arches of one of the Delta's many Cao Dai cathedrals. Founded in 1926 in the delta, the eclectic religion once commanded a formidable anti-communist army in the south. Their numbers have diminished as a result of the intolerance of the communist regime, but there are still a few hundred thousand devotees, mostly assembled near the Cao Dai headquarters in Tay Ninh province. There, I once watched a noon prayer service conducted by female cardinals and a look-a-like pope, who often invoked the names of Cao Dai saints: Dr. Sun Yat Sen, Trang Trinh, a Vietnamese poet, Victor Hugo, Joan of Arc, Winston Churchill, Buddha, Confucius and Christ.

We arrived in My Tho around noon to refuel and for Tuan and his sidekick to have lunch at the appropriate time, a ritual normally followed by the Vietnamese siesta. Cutting the nap short in businesslike haste, we were back on the water within an hour, passing vast forests of coconut palms, and encountering barges brimming over with the fibrous husks, used for making ropes and mats. Nearby, a factory broadcasted the invisible but noxious stink of the fish sauce.

Before long, we saw the first of the colorful shrimp boats—red, blue, and green—chugging in from the sea. The grayish-brown water of the Mekong melded into jade, then a sea of aquamarine, an estuary, the mother of watery hourglasses: filling the shores of Vietnam with sandy silt from the top of the world in Tibet.

Two ebony-tinged fishermen kept the sun off their heads with black headbands. They were checking their nets and collecting black fishing markers, adorning their fishing scow with them like prayer flags.

The Ty To mountains hulked above the coastal city of Vung Tau through a liquid haze of heat. Surf-tipped waves creased the sea, traversed by the silhouettes of fishing scows trailed by clouds of gulls. We had first joined the Mekong almost 1,500 miles before in a Dai village in China. Now we were at the Dai Gate—a coincidence of unrelated names—which led into the South China Sea, one of the nine mythological estuaries of the Mekong. With the Pope Mobile bobbing as trivially as flotsam lost to the sea, Simon and I waxed lyrical about our journey for a few minutes: from hill tribes and pack horses to trawlers and gulls. After popping a couple of imagined champagne corks, we proceeded dutifully on to Saigon for some unfinished culinary business.

Skirting the white sand beaches of Vung Tau we headed inland, networking through a couple of tributaries—the Long Tau and Thieng Lieng—before joining the Saigon River. Soon, the glassy new high rises of Saigon loomed into focus. The river filled with freighters hoisting registry flags from Shanghai, Singapore and Panama. A forest of gantry cranes crisscrossed the water like daddy-long-legs loading and unloading containers. Opposite downtown Saigon, a neon wall curtained the water's edge advertising foreign products—Mercedes-Benz, Hitachi, Suzuki, and Siemens.

We unloaded on the pier next to an imperious statue of Tran Hung Dao. The 13th century Vietnamese commander and mythologized kicker of Chinese ass stood in the center of a busy Me Linh Square beneath the shadow of the towering new Renaissance Hotel. Dressed in warrior garb, he pointed a threatening finger downward. Saying goodbye to Tuan, and also to Simon briefly, I took a *cyclo,* or bicycle taxi, along the waterfront, passing the colonial Majestic Hotel before cycling ahead to the former colonial customs building. In 1866, the French expedition up the Mekong had taken two years on their epic journey to reach China. In less than a month, we had just finished our own jaunt.

After dropping my bags off at a nearby guesthouse, I took a *cyclo* through the back streets of Saigon's District 1 before turning in front of the Continental Hotel, site of many scenes in Graham Greene's *The Quiet American.* Circling behind the municipal theater, a petite but sublimely sculpted Saigon hooker on a street corner motioned for me to join her in the Club 97 karaoke bar. Her footwear was a telltale reminder of our return to modern civilization: she wore heels she could not walk in. Touching as her invitation was, I kept on riding to Mogambos, a restaurant and guesthouse where Simon was staying. After greeting the proprietor, a Vietnamese woman named Hoa, I asked her to call Gary Dale Cearly, a girthsome friend from Arkansas who is a regular there. Hoa quickly obliged. She has time on her hands, spending most of her days flopped on a long banquette couch like a banked fish, thrashing to life at intervals to feed and to school with customers.

Five well-bellied Caucasians sat speechless at the bar across from Hoa, taking up eight seats in an all-day beer-drinking seance. I call such adherents Buddha Bellies. Two acquaintances slipped away from the holy alliance, and walked over to say hello, but they didn't seem to notice our Cambodian tans, much less the mystical layers of spiritual and social silt that we secretly believed must have shrouded us like monks' cowls. When we told them we had just arrived from China via the Mekong, in a ho-hum gesture Frank-from-London didn't find the idea of the journey interesting enough to ask a question, going on to tell us about a new product line of sports memorabilia he was marketing. Johnny-from-Australia was even less interested. "Hmm, oh really. Well, good to see you mates," he managed to say, and walked out.

The Buddha Bellies are a familiar order in Hanoi and Saigon. Drinking is an indoor event, so their color is always pasty. Seasoned Buddha Bellies sport noses laced with fiery spiderwebs. Mostly talkers, not listeners, their origins are usually steeped in myth and mystery. They are no Asian Argonauts; they are far from home but don't really like traveling. They have journeyed to Vietnam for the affordable, carefree lifestyle and female adulation. Their mission is best expressed by a manifesto I saw scrawled in the john of their Hanoi sanctuary, The Spotted Cow, "If you have tried everything in life and failed, try Hanoi."

We weren't at Mogambos pining for a parade, only a good hamburger and some barroom banter. While I looked over the menu, pleased to see there were no banana pancakes, Hoa, having emerged from her vinyl reef, handed me a cell phone, whispering that Gary Dale was on the other end. "Hey Gary Dale, Phil Karber here. Simon and I traveled from China down the Mekong and just arrived in Saigon. We were wondering what to order here at Mogambos. Any suggestions?"

Like a seasoned doctor, Gary prescribed the right medicine: "Phil, get the bacon cheeseburger with chili-cheese fries on the side." We talked a few minutes, but he asked nothing about our epic journey. The burger, however, answered my query faultlessly: pure U.S. Angus beef, marbled ground chuck with a meat-to-fat ratio of 3:1, piled with a half rasher of fresh cooked bacon, sliced tomato, rings of white onion, well-melted cheddar cheese; and served on lightly toasted white bread buns, slathered in American mustard and most critically, garnished with at least four round slices of dill pickle. At the end of our 1,500 miles it was manna from the Mekong gods.

I went to bed fat and happy as any Buddha Belly. Simon of London enjoyed a sublime shore leave, prowling Saigon's dark corners for the next three nights.

Saigon to Hanoi

Your Power Has Collapsed

Saigon's morning rush hour of motorcycles leapt *en masse* from alternating intersections like the staggered start of a Grand Prix event. The onslaught of exhaust merged into a single soaring scream, then dissolved in a shimmer of heat. After living almost five years in Hanoi's din, I was numb to traffic noise, padding along in a vacuum of silence. Walking past Pasteur Street—one of only two streets that still had foreign names—I crossed Khoi Nghia Street and moseyed up to the gilt-iron gate of the former Republic of Vietnam's "White House," its Presidential Palace, now called the Reunification Palace.

A stooped crone chewing betel nut greeted me with a black-stained smile. Hawkers descended upon me selling postcards, Chinese fans, fresh coconut juice, and local currency for dollars. Two *cyclo* drivers, as implacable as Moroccan rug merchants, jived and bantered until I fled behind the spiked fence surrounding the palace, to the quiet of its lawns.

The 65,000 square foot palace, a modernist structure curtained in a glass-and-masonry screen, was the brainchild of the American-supported President Diem. Construction of the palatial monument began in 1962, after two rogue South Vietnamese army pilots bombed the 1868 colonial Norodom Palace, home of the French Indochine Governor General. The modernist palace, Diem's two million dollar folly, was dedicated by Vice President Nguyen Cao Ky on Halloween day, 1966, which happened to be my 15th birthday.

Two freshly painted Soviet T-54 tanks are displayed near the entrance beneath a manicured forest. These are claimed to be the very two tanks that crashed the gates of the Presidential Palace on the morning of April 30, 1975, symbolizing the final conquest of the South.

What's paramount in Vietnam's war museums is the message, not the exhibits' authenticity—the tanks may not have been the ones that crashed the gates. That message usually boils down to "reunification, revolution and victory." The palace probably would have been reduced to shards of rubble in keeping with the traditions of Vietnamese conquest, except that it had such utility as propaganda. It stands today as an alien icon of everything American, of the "imperialist enemy" and its decadence.

I made my way to the rooftop, passing through hallways and spacious meeting rooms appointed with 1960s-period chrome-and-vinyl furniture, waxed floors covered in rangy silk and wool rugs scored in local designs. There are a menagerie of tiger skins, a stuffed cougar, elephant tusks, and the ubiquitous mug of Ho Chi Minh. On the rear section of the rooftop is a heliport where an American UH-1 helicopter remains moored. To the front is a pole flying the victors' flag, a bright yellow star in a field of blood red. From the roof I surveyed Ho Chi Minh City's panorama. Dwarfing all else on the skyline were the Manulife and Prudential office buildings, built by those who lost the Vietnam War but won the Cold War.

The communists were vindictive conquerors. When the "liberation forces" crashed through the palace gates, a humbled Big Minh, president of the South, was there to meet them. The highest-ranking communist soldier present happened to be journalist Colonel Bui Tin, there to cover the war's end, so he handled the surrender. Big Minh greeted Bui Tin decorously by explaining his final duty as commander-in-chief of a defeated army, "I have been waiting since early in the morning to transfer power to you." Bui Tin replied coldly, "You have no power left to transfer. Your power has collapsed. You cannot transfer what you do not possess." It wasn't long before Big Minh defected to the United States. Bui Tin continued to serve in the Communist Party until 1990, when after 44 years of faithful membership, he defected to Paris, vehemently calling for political reforms and an end to corruption. By speaking out against the communist regime, his power, too, collapsed.

On that April day, as a victory celebration engulfed the Presidential Palace and streets of Saigon, the first wave of approximately 130,000 refugees fled for their lives. In "Operation New Arrivals," over a third of those refugees landed laden with taels of gold at Fort Chaffee, Arkansas, where I used to scrub pots and pans. Some 3,000 of those refugees settled in my nearby hometown of Fort Smith. There, Vietnamese soon became the second language, Buddhist temples sprang up among enclaves of Southern Baptists, Tet celebrations greeted each lunar New Year, and Saigon restaurants flourished. The refugees were natural-born entrepreneurs, and after a few years were neighbors in my middle class environs—extended families, ancestral altars, chickens and all. Their children were my kids' schoolmates. They soon became the town's valedictorians and scholarship students, thanks to their Confucian heritage emphasizing family and education.

Many South Vietnamese left behind were less fortunate. Countless thousands who supported the Americans were forced into Stalinist re-education camps, some for up to 15 years, and others were never heard of again. Many were evacuated from the cities into the Mekong Delta countryside, or the Central Highlands, forced to live in "new economic zones." To the victors went the spoils —carpetbaggers besieged the south of Vietnam, taking over the homes, businesses and farms of the defeated enemy.

From 1978 through the mid-1980s, up to a million people left Vietnam in one long tidal wave. It was a brain drain: a case of reverse evolution, where the needy and dependent survived and the finest and fittest departed. Many desperate refugees took to the sea, becoming known as the "boat people." Many drowned, or were murdered by pirates. The lucky ones washed ashore to wallow in refugee camps in Southeast Asia or Hong Kong before going on to host countries.

Mobilizing hatred was nothing new in communist revolutions. Soviet and East German advisors arrived *en masse*, full of doctrinaire paternalism, and filled the vacuum of foreign influence created by the exit of the French and Americans. The Marxist seeds of dialectical materialism would be broadcast in every classroom, commune and coffee shop from the Mekong Delta to the Ben Hai River, the former DMZ. For the next decade and beyond, in the streets and the paddy fields alike, it was feudalism revisited, this time with a Stalinist stamp on it. Yet in many ways it was but a short leap from the authoritarian Confucianism of the past to the new dictatorial communism.

For America, the war had never been about the Indochinese people. Our mission was Cold War geopolitics, not battling for moral high ground or humanitarian ideals. Terrorising Indochina through 10 dark years of war, we then did little to clean up the mess we left behind. For two decades the war-torn region would struggle to produce enough food. Hospitals, schools and other basic services would be woefully inadequate. Despite this postwar devastation, America's bitterness over the outcome of the war congealed into economic sanctions that further impoverished communist Indochina. Incrementally the Cold War was being won, but at the expense of Third World peasants, who didn't know *sic 'em from come here* about communism and geo-strategy.

Later that morning, I met up with a remarkable pair of sisters, Tao Thieu Thi and Tan Thieu Thi, who were bound together like Siamese twins by shared battles as well as sibling blood. A journalist friend had given me their telephone number, telling me I would find their story interesting. Tao urged me to call them by the French names they were given as schoolgirls—Mado and Dany.

Mado arrived to meet me driving her own car, an uncommon luxury in Vietnam. Dany was only a few minutes behind her, climbing from the backseat of a taxi. As she crossed the hotel lobby she favored her right leg, wincing with each step. After the introductions, Mado told me that all I had heard about them was true—their legendary exploits as former child soldiers for the Vietnamese communists. "There is nothing fictional about us, we are real," she said matter-of-factly, and in perfect English.

As a young soldier imbued with a shadowy and two-dimensional image of the Vietcong—the American slang term for the communists—I used to have nightmares about girls like Mado and Dany. GI folklore conjured up bizarre tales of fanatic women with razor blades up their vaginas or wearing explosives strapped to their waists. They were alien enemies, like crazed Indians attacking in cowboy movies. They didn't value life as we did. Worse still, girls like Mado and Dany were intoxicated by the sinister drug of communism. And like most of my comrades, I believed all this.

Remembering my youthful folly, I glowed at the chance to meet two individuals like Mado and Dany—age-mates of mine, and dyed-in-the-wool revolutionaries. I especially welcomed the opportunity to get to know them as people, not as examples of the propagandistic lies pumped into me when I was young and gullible.

In their youth, both girls were scholarship students at a French school in Saigon, Lycee Marie Curie, where they learned to speak French and English fluently. Dany is the younger, born in 1953. As she approaches 50 years of age, her face has taken on a ceramic quality: glazed, rounded cheeks, a youthful beauty cracked with age but far from broken, and liquid brown eyes fired with purpose. Her older sister, Mado, born in 1950, is a classic Vietnamese beauty, with hair swept back in a ponytail, and placid eyes that twinkle and dance when she talks. Her effervescent personality infects you with laughter but equally mesmerizes you when she pontificates on poverty, political repression and social injustices, as she often does.

Mado and Dany both agreed they got their dogged determination and sharp sense of right and wrong from their mother, Nguyen Thi Binh. She was a single parent of five children, a hard-working market lady who sold textiles. Throughout the second Indochina War, her anti-colonialist bent turned to anti-Americanism. Along with their mother, Mado and Dany attended anti-Diem demonstrations in the summer of 1963 when Buddhist monks first immolated themselves to protest the oppressive regime of that leader, who was Catholic.

Dany had no leaning toward communism, or even understanding of it, but she grew angrier and angrier as the Vietnam War imposed its foreign fury. "All I wanted to do was kill the Americans that were bombing my country. Why did they have the right to kill my people with bombs? So, I joined the Vietcong when I was 13."

When the Vietcong recruiter asked Dany what she wanted to do for their cause, she laughed and assumed a rifle-firing pose, saying she would "do anything" to help.

"I was a good shot with an AK-47 but I needed someone to help me hold it. I wanted a weapon to blow up the planes."

Mado joined at the same time. She was 15. It was 1966.

After being spotted at several anti-war demonstrations in Saigon, two years later, in 1968, the two sisters were approached by Huynh Van Dai, another Vietcong recruiter, to lead a commando unit to blow up the Saigon Central Police Station. The CIA kept an office at the station, where Vietcong suspects were tortured. Many disappeared. The Vietcong delivered 30 pounds of C-4 explosive stolen from an American base to the girls' home. With a gas expansion rate of 26,000 feet per second, 30 pounds of C-4 would be enough to vaporize the entire police station.

Meantime, a woman by the name of Ton Kim, who worked in the police headquarters, had moved into Mado and Dany's house. Her home had been demolished by a U.S. Army tank in the street fighting in Saigon that took place during the Tet Offensive of 1968. Mado and Dany knew a kindred spirit when they saw one, so they recruited her to plant the C-4 in the police station, to be detonated with a mercury-drip fuse.

Each day over a period of weeks, Mado and Dany filled a milk carton with the explosive and covered it in rice. Disguising it as a lunch pail, Ton Kim each day smuggled a portion of the 30 pounds of C-4 into the police station.

It was the first week of May of 1968, and the Vietcong had staged a second wave of Tet Offensive. Saigon was a principal target, and there was fighting in the streets. Sections of the Chinese district of Cholon were occupied. The outskirts of Saigon were ravaged, bombed out by the Vietcong. It was the deadliest week of the entire war for the American side.

Ton Kim, in the end, did not deliver all the C-4 explosive. Instead she betrayed the rebellious young sisters, enticed by the reward of being given Mado and Dany's house in return for exposing them. When the police raided their home on May 11, 1968, they found the remaining cache of C-4 explosive, along with Vietcong leaflets and flags.

The whole family was arrested. Even their five-year old brother, Hieu, went to jail for 10 days, where he begged the guards to give him leg irons like his big sisters. Their mother Binh and siblings were released, but Mado and Dany spent the next six years in seven different prisons. For most of that time they served hard time in the barbarous "Tiger Cages" on Con Son Island, a prison built by the French for the worst of anti-colonialist criminals, and then taken over by the Americans. Dany was only 15, the youngest person ever sent to the Devil's Island-style prison.

Released in 1974, they both lived in Vietcong camps until "liberation," when they were finally hospitalized with debilitating injuries from years of starvation, wearing leg irons, and other forms of torture. Not surprisingly, by that time they had both been swayed by Marxism and Leninism.

Soon after her release Dany married a fellow ex-prisoner, Nguyen Van Ut, a poor farmer from the Mekong Delta, who she had met on Con Son Island. Ut has since risen to a prominent position in the Saigon Communist Party, rewarded by a system that has put many uneducated "war heroes" into Vietnam's corridors of power.

Naturally Mado and Dany, too, were rewarded by the new regime, given plum jobs in Saigon handling the spoils of war, supervising the takeover of abandoned and expropriated real estate. Each vacant home was inventoried. The valuables were placed in cabinets and taped shut until the assets were reclaimed by the rightful owners or formally ceded to the State. Mado and Dany often found the cabinets opened and plundered, a disturbing manifestation of the corruption already embedded in the new communist government.

After a variety of jobs, Mado attended Vietnam National University in Saigon where she studied marine biology, falling just short of attaining her doctorate. She felt by studying marine biology she could contribute to feeding the young nation, which she has since done by operating a shrimp co-operative in a flooded mangrove forest in the Mekong Delta. The farm helps 12 families in their struggle against poverty. A few years ago, Mado told an American documentary filmmaker that she feels a need to remain politically active in ways like organizing the shrimp co-op, "In the war time, solidarity is easy, maybe because during the war, the people were needed for the resistance. Now no one needs the poor people. So the revolution is not over..."

In 1988, Mado married Huynh Van Dai, the Vietcong recruiter who had spotted her 20 years before in the crowd of demonstrators and asked her to bomb the police station. When they were married, Mado asked Dai, "When did you fall in love with me?"

"Since the beginning, since our first meeting."

"Why, if you loved me, didn't you prevent me from taking those risks and placing the explosives at the police headquarters?"

"Because it was your duty. Only when we have freedom, we can have love. If our people, our country, is dominated, we can't have happiness."

Love was less happy for Dany. She and Ut had a son, but eventually divorced—the result of cultural differences between an educated, outspoken urbanite and a Party apparatchik from the countryside. "No common style of life," Dany shrugs.

Twelve years ago she married a Frenchman, Marcel, older than herself, an idealist and diehard apologist for the Vietnamese brand of communism. Marcel designed and built them a bucolic, traditional house—a love nest of sorts—set among palm trees on the outskirts of Saigon.

As a solid and respected member of the elite Vietnamese Communist Party (VCP), which counts only three percent of the population as members, Dany was taking a risk by marrying a foreigner. For years after "liberation," the government did not allow ordinary citizens to speak to foreigners on the streets or in cafes. Even today, there are laws that prevent Vietnamese married to foreigners from working for the government, the predominant employer in Vietnam.

It wasn't long before Party members began to target Dany for derision. Last year, Marcel got fed up with the harassment heaped on his wife and moved to Sihanoukville in Cambodia, where he opened a restaurant. Describing Marcel as "a very good man," Dany remains as loyal to him as she does to her sense of justice. Anger sizzles beneath her warmhearted demeanor.

These tales and more had all started to unfold during that first breakfast meeting I had with the women. When we finished with the guesthouse buffet, Mado suggested Dany should meet Simon and me in a few days in the coastal city of Vung Tau. From there we would take a helicopter to Con Son, the notorious prison island where the South shipped captured Viet Cong.

Nursing our cups of green tea, Mado showed me old news photos of anti-war protestors all over the world waving placards that read, "Free Tao [Mado] and Tan [Dany]." Then she handed me a tattered copy of *Life*, with a glossy cover photo of a bejeweled Rose Kennedy striding into a gala celebrating her 80th birthday, followed by Ted and Ethel Kennedy. The date on the magazine was July 17, 1970. Inside was a black-and-white photo expose, by a little known congressional aide named Tom Harkin. The appalling subject was the conditions of the Tiger Cages on Con Son Island. Mado and Dany became international *causes celebres* when the magazine hit the streets.

After I thumbed through the magazine, Mado threw a picture in front of me of a fortyish-looking, Western woman. "Do you remember Norman Morrison?" she asked. I did, but I had no idea what he had to do with the woman in the picture.

On November 2, 1965, two years to the day after President Diem was assassinated, a Quaker protesting the war in Vietnam by the name of Norman Morrison walked onto the steps of the Pentagon, just 40 feet from Secretary McNamara's office, and lit a match to his gasoline-soaked body. At the last moment, at the urging of a bystander, Mr. Morrison handed his 18-month-old girl to another onlooker. Secretary McNamara stood in his window and watched the grim aftermath.

The woman in Mado's picture was Emily Morrison, the baby girl on the steps of the Pentagon. She had recently visited Vietnam, and met Mado and Dany. Today, in the United States, even in peacenik circles, they mostly don't remember Norman Morrison, or if they do, they think of him as a crazy man.

In Vietnam Norman Morrison is a hero. Poems have been written about him, a postage stamp has been dedicated to his memory, and every kindergarten kid in the country learns a nursery rhyme about his "anti-war heroism."

I said goodbye to Mado and Dany in the lobby of the hotel, while also taking a phone call at the front desk to argue with a man about a train ticket he was supposed to have purchased for Simon and me. Dany came to my rescue: "I have a very good friend who can help you. We can go there now." We were about to leave when the ticket middleman called the front desk and said he had managed to score: "Only 50,000 dong ($3.50) for the policeman."

Dany and Mado rolled their eyes in mild disgust, then we all laughed together.

"That's Vietnam," Dany sighed.

"I'll see you in Vung Tau in a few days."

Ascending the Lam Vien Plateau, we passed through rubber plantations partly shrouded in morning mist as peasants in plaited palm-leaf hats tapped the scored trunks, collecting the milky latex out of cups affixed to the trees. We were traveling north in the direction of the French hilltop resort of Dalat.

We stopped for a late lunch at a wild game restaurant in the mountain village of Bao Lac, nestled in a sea of rolling green hills braided in coffee plants. As we exited the car, a legless man dragged himself toward us, using wooden blocks as handholds to elevate his nubs and posterior, where he wore a leather pad. He muttered the noise of an explosion, throwing his hands up and outward, to indicate he was a landmine victim. He then stuck his hand out for money. He fought on the losing side during the war, otherwise he might have had prosthetic legs, or at a minimum a wheelchair. There is no Veterans Administration for those who fought for the South. Probably lacking pension and disability pay, his safety net is to pick himself up every morning and catch the noon tourist crowd on their way to Dalat, as he found us. A white placard with red lettering hung around his neck:

CONGRATULATIONS TO LADIES AND GENTLEMEN BEST WISHES ON YOUR TRIP BY SENTIMENT PLEASE HELP ME SOME MONEY FOR MY

LIFE WE HOPE THE LORD WILL BLESS DOWN ON YOU THANK YOU
VERY MUCH INDEED.

I had seen him in front of the same restaurant six years ago. As before, I
decorated his open hand with a couple of small bills, then retreated inside
to feast on wild boar, deer and porcupine.

It was mid-afternoon before we passed through the last of the tea
plantations, filled with pickers clipping the neat rows of tea like barbers
working an assembly line. Masked and shaded in parasol hats, the pickers,
mostly women, gathered around a field boss who weighed the brimming
baskets and paid them piecemeal for their labor. The comfortable sight of
tea plantations gave way to the pleasing smell and shade of pine forests that
wicketed the mountainous road, like an arbor leading to the inner-sanctum
of an enchanted garden.

Occupying the natural hillside amphitheater encircling picturesque Xuan
Huong Lake, the French villas of Dalat were once residence to Saigon's
colonial elite. Now they are weekend cottages for the communist *crème de
la crème* of Ho Chi Minh City. Bao Dai, Vietnam's last emperor, had three
villas in Dalat. His old golf course has been upgraded into a respectable
scheme of baize swatches that crowd the lake. In times of plenty, Dalat was
where Bao Dai and his wealthy fellow sportsmen set out on tiger and rhino
hunts. Now the pursuit of big game is the secret sport of poachers in the
area. Their quarry is nearly extinct.

Hill tribes, known by the French as *montagnards*, have inhabited the
upland region of Dalat for centuries. Waterfalls abound in the area; exotic
flower gardens scent the air; candied strawberries are a favorite repast;
and artichoke tea and mulberry wine are beverages of choice. Over the last
decade this has attracted artists, writers, and Vietnamese flower children
who now call Dalat home.

Simon and I decided to stay in a villa on the outskirts, country-quiet on a
spit of Khasia pines and Chinese firs. The place was thick with cultivated
orchids, their shapes and colors so extraordinary that they appeared
artificial. I stayed in the modestly priced pink suite, former bedroom of
Madame Nhu, known to the international press corps in the early 1960s

as the "Dragon Lady of South Vietnam."

Madame Nhu was the wife of President Diem's brother Nhu. In the late 1950s and early 1960s, her fiery rhetoric and mindless meddling fueled local and American outrage against her and her brother-in-law's regime. Her well-publicized woes with Vietnamese culture may have begun with language: she spoke French and English fluently but could barely read or write Vietnamese. As a Roman Catholic convert, her lack of sympathy with the Buddhist majority was legend. She taunted radical monks by saying they had accomplished nothing politically, describing their ultimate sacrifice—immolation—as "not even of self-sufficient means since they had to import the gasoline."

She also organized the Women's Solidarity Movement, and had laws enacted banning polygamy, concubinage, abortion, prostitution, contraceptives and adultery. According to the new Family Laws, a conviction on the charge of adultery merited a jail sentence. The self-anointed arbiter of Vietnamese morals, completely out of step with her own country and the larger world, even took on Saigon's taxi dancers: the bar girls selling sex. She went on to teaberry shuffle all over Western social dancing, and even had square dancing banned at the American Embassy.

President Diem would not muzzle her, whatever her extremism. She was his brother's wife. Family harmony persisted until the end. Madame Nhu has lived on the French Riviera since the coup. She charges for interviews, and is still bitter at Vietnam, President Kennedy and the United States.

As a mantle of darkness crept across the sky, Simon and I gave up the pinkness of Madame Nhu's pad, and had Tuan drop us at an outdoor bar below the old cinema building, the centerpiece of the colonial town square, which once enjoyed a sweeping view of the lake. After a few drinks and stiff-arming a steady barrage of beggars and boys selling shoe shines and postcards, we crossed the busy street to the Golf 3 Hotel, the high-rise culprit that stole the town's once-pristine views, and the alleged hotbed of gays and lesbians.

The cavernous disco was packed with a shimmering scatter of metallic chairs amid a fog of white air and colors flashing across the dance floor. The place was half-full, with a college-age crowd, all same-sex couples. No one asked Simon or me to cut the vitreous rug. Perhaps they were shy, but in any case, this is the only time in five years either one of us had been to a disco in Vietnam and not been approached with the sale of sex of some variety.

After going to the market to pick up a bottle of mulberry wine, we retreated to Madame Nhu's cozy pink shelter. We sat outside, where the air was crisp, bats jinking in and out of the natural light. We smoked ready rolls picked up from a Saigon *cyclo* driver, and choked down the wine, which tasted like a musty bottle of cough syrup. All was nicely quiet, until Simon heard cooing in the garden—seemingly the voice of a woman in rapture. Then came a crescendo of groans followed by a woman's death cry loud enough to fill the entire resort valley. A few more blood-curdling screams roused the dogs in the neighborhood before we went downstairs to check on the aggrieved parties.

The night watchman sat on a couch watching television, indifferent to the commotion. He apologized for the disturbance, and pointed to the gate near the road, signaling that the couple in the garden had left, "Everything is okay," he said. Although he was shy about giving details, we gleaned from his scrappy English that after what sounded like a dalliance under the moon, the woman was accused by her lover of infidelity. And to emphasize his point, the man clobbered her. The guard, however, hardly thought to console her, much less call the police. We went on to bed, haunted a bit by the ghost of Confucianism lurking there at Madame Nhu's villa.

We had breakfast the next morning on Xuan Huong Lake, a local lover's paradise where Donald Duck paddleboats churn the sparkling blue waters. Simon and I took a stroll through the flower and fruit market, then made our way to the epicenter of Dalat's avant-garde movement, "The Crazy House."

This Disney-like creation is a collection of fantasy bungalows clustered in a bamboo garden, each shaped from concrete in the form of a giant tree trunk. The Crazy House is the brainchild of Hang Viet Nga, a Russian-trained architect, sometime artist, and active environmentalist, who also happens to be the 63-year-old daughter of the late Truong Chinh, the former Party General Secretary and President of Vietnam.

The Crazy House is significant both for its wacky charm and for the fact that Nga's father led the brutal land reform movement in the 1950s, when thousands of innocents were executed by landless peasants. Late in life, in an hour of redemption, Troung Chinh would introduce *doi moi* to Vietnam, the nation's opening to market economics.

Then, the socialist pipedream of a world without private property smouldered toward a natural death. Truong Chinh died in 1988 without seeing the spring flowering of *doi moi*.

Nga greeted us, her hair in long cascade of curls falling from beneath her blue beret. Wearing a full-length skirt, only her face and hands revealed her pale, almost transparent skin, with the delicacy of classic Chinese beauty. She spoke English in short, breathy exhalations, embellishing her already pixilated persona.

She first came to Dalat in 1983 and fell in love with "the mountain coolness and the nice, kind hill tribe people." With two grown children and one failed marriage behind her, she made the break from Hanoi in 1990 and moved to Dalat to try out her own rendition of dad's *doi moi*, creative architecture and hotel landlordism.

Nga, whose name means Russia in Vietnamese, spent 14 years in Moscow getting her doctorate in architecture before going to work in Hanoi with the Ministry of Construction in the late 1960s. In a departure from the Soviet utilitarian creations of her past, she has built 10 rooms of a whimsical hotel, has one more underway and will finish a restaurant, bar and dance hall within three years. She is also working on a magic mountain and simulated sea. "I would like the people of the world to be near to nature, through architecture," she told me.

We admired an aviary of Japanese doves. Hanging on the outside of the cages were some paintings by Nga and other local artists. Simon and I burrowed through several of the hotels' theme rooms—tiger for the

Vietnamese, giraffe for the Africans, bear for the Russians, eagle for the Americans, pheasant for the Brits. I was never clear which nationality of customers might get the equally enchanting rooms designated "termite" and "ant." The rooms were decorated like a love hotel, but a love hotel built in a giant tree house. Each was appointed with honeymoon beds reflected by spacious ceiling mirrors, oversized bathtubs that curled to the contour of the concrete trees, barren portholes for window-peeping Japanese doves, colorful bedspreads woven by local ethnic minorities, and gooey, heavily lacquered walls and built-in furniture.

On parting, I asked Nga what her father would have thought of her Disneyland in Dalat. "If alive now he would like because there is a new sentiment in the world, which is globalization. Crazy House is for all the people of the world."

Dalat is a resort town with a perpetual holiday atmosphere. It is a place to stroll around and enjoy the faded elegance of the colonial past, including the three villas of Bao Dai, the last emperor of the Nguyen dynasty.

Born as Prince Nguyen Vinh Thuy, Bao Dai was the only non-Buddhist emperor of the 150-year lineage of Nguyen rulers. Like President Diem, he was a Catholic and out of touch with grassroots Vietnam. His true loyalty was to a lifestyle befitting his Francophile tastes and aristocratic status: French women, good wine, tennis, casinos and in the main, life in Paris. He lived a long life, dying in 1997 at the age of 84, and was buried in the Passy Cemetery in Paris.

Bao Dai's summer villa was built in the early 1930s on a forested hilltop, trees thinned to give a panoramic view and to make room for a maze of terraced paths and gardens. Vietnamese tourists took to the art deco furniture, perching on couches, chairs, beds and thrones for imperial snapshots. Simon and I took turns sprawling in the emperor's office, pretending to make calls on vintage metal telephones beneath a library of French books and plaster busts of the Nguyen emperors.

The second floor of the two-story villa was ablaze in sunny yellow, the royal colors. At the top of the teak stairs, spanning out from a throne-like couch used for parental consultations, were separate suites for Bao Dai, Empress

Nam Phoung and their five children.

When Truong Chinh brought Nga and the rest of his family to Dalat for three weeks in 1983, they had stayed in Bao Dai's sumptuous summer villa. Bui Tin, the "Conquering Colonel" who was also Truong Chinh's biographer, accompanied the Truong family on that holiday, described in his book *Following Ho Chi Minh*:

One day, Truong Chinh asked me to come to his bedroom. There he pointed out the bed with sheets of gold brocade embroidered with dragons and phoenix. The pillows were the same. Speaking softly as if he wanted to awe and impress me, Truong Chinh invited me to take a close look and asked whether I was aware that the bed and bedclothes had belonged to Bao Dai and Empress Nam Phuong. I looked and also saw Truong Chinh's wife sitting there as if she were on the throne.

I was half amused and half surprised to the point of amazement. I had discovered a diehard communist leader who had been determined to get rid of the royal family. Yet here he was now being so proud and emotional about sleeping in a room where he could use sheets and pillows embroidered with the symbols of royalty!

Our final stop was the Palace Hotel, the grandest of all Dalat colonial estates. It was here that Vo Nguyen Giap—who is credited with defeating the French at Dien Bien Phu and the Americans two decades later—met French negotiators to determine the colonial fate of Vietnam after World War II. Following the rehearsal meetings at the Palace Hotel, the French broke off negotiations with Ho Chi Minh in Fountainebleau; 30 years of war thus ensued.

Located on a hillock across the road from the striking Dalat Cathedral and enjoying a bird's eye view of Lake Xuan Huong, the colonial hotel was restored to its former glory by an American tycoon named Larry Hillblom, who is the "H" in DHL, the international air courier. On Hillblom's first visit to Dalat in 1990 the hotel was in shambles, but that didn't keep him from falling in love with the area and dreaming up his own vision of Xanadu.

Loaded, and willing to pay dearly for his own bit of neo-colonialist glory, Hillblom was *doi moi*'s wildest dream come true. Forty million dollars later, the Palace Hotel opened its 43 rooms at a cost of almost one million dollars a room. At the time of the grand opening, there were 18 expatriate staff and 170 Vietnamese.

Hillblom never enjoyed his Xanadu, though. He died in a mysterious plane crash off the island of Saipan a week after the hotel opened. Most of his estate—estimated at $600 million—was to have gone to a charitable trust for the benefit of the University of California, and to the University of California San Francisco Hospital, where he had been treated for injuries from another plane crash.

Although Hillblom was a lawyer by training, his will, for some reason failed to include the standard clause disinheriting illegitimate heirs. For years, he had been using intermediaries throughout the Asia-Pacific region to indulge his fetish for 14-year-old girls. Fearing disease, he preferred virgins.

Four of Hillblom's former girls who had had children by him banded together and filed a class-action lawsuit against his estate. After a lot of dissembling by Hillblom's family, business associates and prospective beneficiaries over the search for DNA samples, it was determined that the four children indeed had the same father, who was no doubt Larry Hillblom. The estate reached a settlement, paying the youngsters a shared $90 million.

We left Dalat corkscrewing down the mountain in heavy morning fog and rain. Blue broke through the clouds only when we reached the arid coastal plains of Phan Rang. Rising from the plains like a ruddy mirage were three medieval towers on a cacti-splattered knoll—the Po Klong Garai, the Cham monument of Phan Rang. Built over 700 years ago by the ancient race, the tiered, rounded towers symbolize holy Mt. Meru, as do the Khmer temples of Angkor. It is the Cham warriors of this region—Phan Rang and Nha Trang—who are featured in many of the bas-reliefs at Angkor.

Simon and I tiptoed through an army of four-inch scorpions that scouted the parched earth pathway up to the towers. Atop the terraced promontory where the towers stand—built brick-on-brick without any mortar—the wide-angle view to the north reveals the Quonset hangars of a former American airbase, and to the south, French pillbox bunkers that once guarded the railway going to Dalat. The mostly monochrome landscape is dashed with emerald green paddies stretching along a seasonal river basin.

A statue of Nandin, the divine bull, faces toward the sunrise, guarding the main sanctuary entrance. The brick and sandstone outer walls are etched with a cosmic band of *apsaras* and dancing elephants. A Pancaker family, a pantalooned couple and their child, the first Pancaker tyke we had seen on our journey, took charcoal rubbings from the Sanskrit relief fronting the temple. Inside the tower, the cool, incense-sated sanctum sanctorum houses the *lingam* of Siva, the presiding deity of the Kingdom of Champa. During the annual Kate festival in October it is customary for Chams to drink the holy water that has washed the Siva's phallus, while remembering their ancestors and celebrating ancient Cham heroes.

The Viking-like Chams originated somewhere in the region of present-day Malaysia and Indonesia. The first signs of Cham settlement in Vietnam are around the port city of Danang in the second century A.D. From there, they migrated south and for a thousand years, the Chams ruled from Quang Binh province in north-central Vietnam to the Mekong Delta. Before converting to Islam centuries ago, the Chams were Hindus as a legacy of trade with ancient India. Sanskrit, their sacred language, is often found on stelae alongside the Cham language.

Boasting a population of 2.5 million at their cultural pinnacle a thousand years ago, their demise came at the hands of the southward-advancing Vietnamese in 1471 A.D., with 60,000 soldiers killed and 30,000 taken prisoner near the present-day city of Quinhon. By the 19th century the Cham aristocracy had disintegrated, and they no longer dominated the coastal waters. They gave up piracy and their military centuries ago, and are now an ethnic minority group of just 100,000 people in Vietnam. Like in Chau Duc, they are known for their weaving and crockery, as well as farming and fishing.

Passing more Cham ruins along the highway, we soon arrived in Nha Trang, a resort city defined by a four-mile stretch of Vietnam's most scenic beach. We stopped by the Cyclo Café, part-owned by an American veteran and Hanoi friend of ours, Chuck Searcy.

By day Chuck manages a landmine awareness and removal program in Quang Tri province, where some of the heaviest fighting occurred during the war. Having served a year's tour in the army in Saigon, he came back eight years ago to live and work in Hanoi. His attachment to Vietnam is deep. He will eventually retire there. The Cyclo Café is intended to spin off a morsel or two of his retirement fare. Since foreigners are required to have a local partner to own a business in Vietnam, Chuck has teamed up with an enterprising local man, Bui Viet Khuong. They celebrated the grand opening of the Cyclo Café the day before we arrived, and to our disappointment, Chuck returned to Hanoi shortly thereafter.

After ordering a couple of plates of fresh calamari, we noticed an advert on the wall for Mama Hanh's day trips to the nearby islands. I asked Chuck's partner, Khuong, about the storied tour operator. The mention of Mama Hanh on this trip always produced the same response, giggles and laughter. Like everyone else would, indeed Khuong giggled, then froze his expression in a vague smile, "I am very sorry to tell you that she go to jail for one year."

"No way, man. What for?"

"She make up funny song about Ho Chi Minh and sing for tourist. I think policeman come in regular clothes and watch her give marijuana cigarettes to tourists and then they all sing song."

"So did she go to jail for marijuana, or for singing a song about Uncle Ho?"

"They say marijuana but I think it because she sing funny song about Ho Chi Minh."

Even in the South where people tend to be more open and Western, Mama Hanh pushed the envelope too far. Free speech is not an option. Neither are satirical ditties about the most revered man in Vietnam's pantheon of gods and heroes.

Short, dusky and busty, wearing a green wide-brimmed hat, Mama Hanh had been running boat tours to the islands off the coast of Nha Trang for 15 years. Charging just a few dollars for a ride on one of her red-and-blue junks, Mama Hanh mostly had Pancakers as customers. She had started her entrepreneurial career over 30 years ago as a young waif selling crabs and clams to American soldiers and other English-speaking beach visitors. For a decade after the war, she had to cater to locals and Soviets. Then *doi moi* made the beaches of Nha Trang a prime destination for Western tourists.

When Simon joined her island tour eight years ago, she led her flock of passengers in a ritual of mulberry wine shots, then flashed her aging breasts. As the tour party puppeteer, she would order the singles to sit on top and the couples below: "Don't be lazy, don't be lazy," she would tease. After depositing her customers in the azure waters for snorkeling, she would float by on her plastic raft pouring shots of mulberry wine and retrieving ready-rolled joints from her signature green hat, firing them up and circling the crowd.

Disappointed at Mama Hanh's fate, Simon decided to take a room around the corner from the Cyclo Café, and get a quick start soaking up Nha Trang's beach amenities.

Tuan drove me along the beach to the south end of Nha Trang to yet another of Bao Dai's palaces, where I would sleep with the royal ghosts for the next couple of nights. Second only to the pleasure of being rich is the pleasure of pretending to be rich when traveling. I took the emperor's suite at a kingly 40 bucks a night. The rooms may have been bigger than the entire house I lived in as a child in Arkansas. It was a little musty, but had a fine view.

Situated on a high point at the end of a jut of land, the palace grounds host a nursery of exotic plants and palms. My palace suite overlooked a scimitar-shaped beach of white sand, studded with shrimp boats washed in loud hues of red and blue. In a distance, islets of bearded karst rose out of the aquamarine sea, mantled in a runaway fluff of cloud.

Daily flights from Saigon now arrive via a flight path that skirts ever so closely the palace's rocky promontory, before landing in the downtown airport. The aiport is the former home of the U.S. Army's 5th Special Forces, the unit my brother Stan served in for almost two years. We used to talk a couple of times a week on the secured army telephone system, and met several times in Bangkok on R&Rs (Rest and Relaxation breaks). As a supply clerk with the Green Berets, he used to start his days in Nha Trang by getting a friend and driving a jeep up to a cliff above Bao Dai's palace. It was a tranquil escape from the deadweight of servicing a war, with views of navy ships slicing the placid seas below, and planes and helicopters lifting from their nightly roost.

After a light night at the Nha Trang Sailing Club—the local G-spot for nocturnal action—I roused Simon and we went to find a good friend of mine, Bobby Chinn, at the Yasaka Nha Trang Hotel, a Japanese-owned glassy skyscraper located on the beach.

Bobby lives in Hanoi, and owns the most chi-chi restaurant and bar there. He is the Rick of Rick's Café in Hanoi. His father is Chinese-American; his mother Egyptian. Approaching 40, his brash personality complements his boyish good looks—half pharaoh, half Oriental potentate. He was raised in British boarding schools, was a trader on Wall Street, a stand-up comic in California, and through the test of time, has remained a Mick Jagger wannabe on stage and off, a five-star chef, a practicing Muslim and a Yankee-doodle-dandy to the bone.

Bobby was in Nha Trang to play a speaking part—enough to get his union card—in an upcoming American movie *Beautiful Country*, starring Nick Nolte, Tim Roth, and an upstart named Damien Nguyen playing the lead. After the remake of the *Quiet American*, *Beautiful Country* is only the second American feature movie ever filmed in Vietnam. The movie is about a refugee on a boat coming to America to start a better life and search for his estranged father, played by Nick Nolte. The crew had been filming for weeks in Hanoi, where Simon had been hired to play an aristocrat at a dinner party, a non-speaking role. Only a few days before, the cast and crew had arrived in Nha Trang.

We met Bobby in the lobby along with Damien, the Vietnamese-American protagonist in the film, and an American girl named Sue, a beguiling Pancaker-turned-groupie. After introductions and a few minutes of catching up with Bobby, they sat in silence and then bolted for the elevator. It was unclear to me whether Simon had farted, or if the couple were just horny and not willing to waste time being polite about it.

Their departure was timely, though. Bobby, Simon and I were on a mission to find Mama Hanh and to learn more about local business intrigue known as the Nha Trang "Banana Split Wars." We walked down the palm-lined beach, where condoms were scattered like seashells. It had been a *doi moi* night for Nha Trang's working girls. The sky shortly burst open in an early monsoon frog choker. We were without rain gear but too far from the hotel to turn back. We slogged through the hammering rain and flooded streets like big, dumb kids at play.

Arriving at Quang Trung street, several young women waved menus at us. "Come here, we better, here, please, please!" they shouted above the din of the squall. We had reached the banana split battle zone. It was just as Simon had described. Two ice cream joints—"The First Original 60 Banana Split" and "58 Banana Split"—competed side by side, separated by just six inches of shared wall, in a contest for customers that looked like a college football cheerleading face-off.

With our skin pickled from the downpour, we peeled off our shirts and socks, wringing pools on top of pools of water on the restaurant's floor. "The First Original 60 Banana Split" restaurant was the older of the two, and it made our decision much easier that the "58 Banana Split" joint was full of meditative Pancakers nipping away at stacks of banana pancakes like mice attacking cheese. Deferring to tradition, we ordered a late breakfast of banana splits—scoops of lime, strawberry and coconut ice cream dripping in a chocolate sauce and topped with pistachio nuts, with two fresh banana halves buried in Neopolitan Nirvana. All that fruit would be good for us.

Both places advertised Mama Hanh's tours, pulling out photo albums with glossy snapshots of the loose-lipped owner and her boats. But they giggled when we mentioned her name. An older man arrived pedaling a *cyclo*, sat at the next table with his ears pricked, and joined in after recognizing our accents as American.

In almost perfect English, he introduced himself by saying that during the war he worked with Americans, "Me no communist," he asserted.

"Do you know Mama Hanh?" I asked.

As did the ice cream girls, he clasped his wrists like handcuffs to pantomime her arrest. "She go to jail for one year," he said glumly.

Bobby focused on the *cyclo* driver's English. In the movie *Beautiful Country*, Bobby plays a Vietnamese refugee who speaks a few words of street English in a camp card game. Native Vietnamese speakers using English as a second language have difficulty with consonants. More often than not they clip their consonants a bit, or dispense with them entirely. The Vietnamese language features soft endings not hard—because becomes "becau" and a word like lose gets pronounced as "wose." Waiting to be called to the movie set at any moment, Bobby enlisted the *cyclo* driver to help authenticate his accent. An audience gathered as they rehearsed:

Bobby: "Three tens I win again."

Cyclo driver: "Why I alway wose, fuk Ameica!"

Bobby: "You don't fuck America, America fucks you."

Cyclo driver: "Why you win so muc?"

Bobby: "I learn to play on boat, on boat you live or die."

Repeating the punchy script several times, the grizzled old *cyclo* driver had trouble staying in character—laughing and embarrassed at once, not completely understanding the context. The ice cream girls, for their part, got up a chorus of "fuk Ameica."

Parodying accents is fun but it cuts both ways. In 1627, a French Jesuit, Alexander de Rhodes, arrived in Vietnam. Upon hearing the rapid, high tones of the Vietnamese in conversation, he referred to them as "twittering birds." Seeking to spread the word of the Bible to a wider audience, he developed the Romanized script known as *quoc ngu*, replacing a bastardized version of Chinese ideographs called *nom*. Although widely used for three centuries, *quoc ngu* was not formally adopted as the written language of Vietnam until after World War II.

Vietnamese borrowed its tones from the Tai Language family, of which modern Thai and Laotian are part, but is a member of the Mon-Khmer family, like Cambodian. With a range of six tones available for every word in Vietnamese, one minor slip of the tongue and the dinner plate can change features. For instance, the word *ran* with one diacritical mark means snake, which some Vietnamese consider a delicacy, while the same word with another phonetic tick denotes cockroach.

The language reflects the culture. In the main, the Vietnamese language is less direct than English and more accommodating to poetry and romance than to *doi moi* introductions such as memory chips and stock markets. An American friend and colleague, who speaks fluent Vietnamese and manages an office of 20 English-speaking Vietnamese professionals, explained the complexities of communication in the office environment.

The Western paradigm of management identifies job functions with a simple organic chart. But the Vietnamese are by dint of their culture forced to sift through a maze of added organizational filters, often defined by age. The company driver might be an older male, given the respect of a grandfather, *noi*; the secretary might also be older and addressed with the esteem accorded an aging aunt, *ba*; while the male boss may be a fresh university graduate called younger brother, *em*.

Beyond the age hierarchy and the complex matrix of language, social hierarchy, and political nepotism, conveying Western ideas is truly complicated. Company tasks tend to be constructed in the Vietnamese way, indirect and circular like the path of Buddhism, instead of following a linear progression—from point A to point B.

After Bobby's comical rehearsal, we grabbed three *cyclos* and set out for the north end of Nha Trang to the Po Nagar Cham Towers. En route, I had to endure my driver's pitifully narrated saga of his parents having been killed during the war. He told his tale like Khmer Rouge survivors do, marking time before and after 1975. His acting job, however, was only slightly more convincing than Bobby's was. Unfortunately this is a well-known con game used by the *cyclo* drivers of Nha Trang to garner extra tips, hogging the sympathy that real victims do indeed deserve.

We rolled up April 2nd Street, which commemorates the day in 1975 the communist army "liberated" Nha Trang, to the estuary of the Cai River. Serenaded by the exotic twang of loudspeakers blasting out plaintive love songs, knots of fishwives crowded the road, squatting around bamboo baskets and selling a variety of fresh clams and mussels. Past Xom Bong Bridge, up a tree-lined hillside, were the ocher-hued Cham Towers.

According to archaeologists, the site was first used for Hindu worship in the second century. The baked-brick towers were built between the eighth and 13th centuries to serve as the Holy See of the Champa Kingdom of Panduranga. In the 16th century, Nha Trang was the last Cham bastion of power to fall under the inexorable southward push of the Vietnamese.

The meditation hall, or *mandapa*, is an open space of octagonal, stand-alone columns. In ancient times, a pass through this ethereal space of brick columns was a spiritual warm-up before the main event of prayer in the Cham Towers. We ascended the steps up Cu Lao hill into the Hindu kingdom of heaven, which was crowned in statuesque palms, a sprawling banyan tree, feathery casuarinas and flowering acacia trees. The North Tower, the biggest of the remaining four towers, houses the shrine of Siva's divine mate, Uma.

Cham creation myth has Uma emerging Noah-like out of a Great Flood, recreating the world and teaching her unskilled flock how to fish and farm. Once finished with that task, she morphed into a piece of sandalwood and drifted into the Eastern Sea before returning to heaven.

Facing eastward in sandstone relief above the doorway, Siva and Nandin hailed us. We made our way upstream against the current of a prayerful group of locals—travelers, fishermen and masses making offerings and praying for good fortune and safe passage on land and sea. Entering the main chamber, a smoky pyramidal vault festooned with ceremonial parasols, we burned incense on the altar, bowing three times to the bare-chested, ten-armed ebony statue of Uma.

The author (left), on his first travel adventure, enjoys a Corona with Arkansas friends in a Tijuana bar, August 1968.

Carl Bates at Fort Bliss, Texas, January 1968.

Jackie Gilker at Camp Pendleton, California, December 1968.

Simon Redington (left) and the author relaxing on a Mekong fast boat.

Mien hill tribe women in the market at Muang Sing, an opium village in northern Laos.

A local beauty lounges on a paper-mâché tiger at the Pi Mai celebration in Luang Prabang, Laos.

Monks collect alms from merit-gaining devotees in Luang Prabang, Laos.

A portrait of the peripatetic Ho Chi Minh, delivering a speech to the French Communist Party on Christmas, 1920.

A guesthouse near the Plain of Jars advertises using salvaged metal signs fashioned out of unexploded ordnance.

James McGovern, aka Earthquake Magoon, who was shot down at Dien Bien Phu, Vietnam on May 2, 1954.

The author, on the leeward side of the war, in Isaan, Thailand, 1969-1971.

The mysterious stone vessels found on the Plain of Jars.

Adorning the cave headquarters of the Pathet Lao are books by Ho Chi Minh, a bust of Lenin and a picture of Che Guevara.

166

The "killing fields" pagoda, where victims' clothes and skulls remind us of the Pol Pot Time.

A portrait of Pol Pot.

Van Nath, an artist, survived the S-21 torture center in Phnom Penh by painting portraits of Pol Pot.

Ha Thi Nga (right), a Vietnamese survivor of a Khmer Rouge massacre in the Mekong Delta.

Monks on causeway to Angkor Wat, the largest temple in the world.

Tan Thieu Thi, aka Dany, standing on the catwalk above the Tiger Cages where she was imprisoned in May of 1968.

Dany and Mado (center), at home in Saigon supervising impoverished kids in martial arts, math and reading.

Second lieutenant John Lancaster (left) outside of Hue during Tet Offensive, 1968.

John Lancaster returns to the battle site where he was critically wounded on May 5, 1968.

De-miners removing unexploded ordnance near Dong Ha, Vietnam, 2005.

Truong Son Cemetery near Dong Ha, the largest of Vietnam's martyr cemeteries.

Vietnamese boys dawdle beneath a flame tree on Hoan Kiem Lake, Hanoi. (photo by Billy Tudhope)

Do Van Du, former child warrior and double amputee, in a Hanoi hospital checking on hydrocephalic children.

Flower Hmong in the north of Vietnam near the Chinese border

Suel Jones, a marine veteran, wounded near Dong Ha in May 1968, together with disabled kids at the Friendship Village near Hanoi.

General Giap and Ho Chi Minh in the early days of Vietnam's independence struggle.

The Wild Bunch next to Lenin Stream, below Pac Bo, Ho Chi Minh's cave redoubt during World War II.

Leaning against a bas-relief of Makara the sea-monster, Uma is crowned with an indescribably complicated headdress, and seated cross-legged on a lotus pedestal atop a three-foot high Yoni-base, a vaginal symbol honoring the essence of womanhood.

Emerging from the serenity of Uma's crypt, we heard Bobby's voice resounding from a nearby tumble of boulders. Bobby stood alone on the stage-like pinnacle of the tallest boulder as if in a Shakespearian soliloquy. He was dressed like a Latino drug lord in a black, silk do-rag, matching dark glasses and his signature black t-shirt. He screamed into his cell phone, "Why I alway wose, fuk Ameica."

Tini Tran, a Vietnamese-American and the Associated Press correspondent in Hanoi, was on the other end taking the place of the *cyclo* driver to coach him with his accent.

When he spotted us, he broke out of character momentarily, "Hey you guys. Where you been? I've been looking all over for you."

"Wait, wait, Tini. One more time, I found them. Why I alway wose, fuk Ameica. Okay, okay, goodbye."

Together we climbed up on the boulders, looking over the Cai River, its rain-stirred waters parted by the fecund beauty of Coconut Island. Out of the urban sprawl of the ancient city rose a giant white Buddha, its head piercing the clouds, hidden and revealed at once.

Bobby, however, had the attention span of an outhouse fly when it came to monuments and history. It was the end of Ramadan, the Muslim fasting period, and Bobby was ready to party. He had devoutly endured the sacrificial lunar month without a drink. "Builds discipline," he said.

All roads led us back to the Nha Trang Sailing Club, one of the better open-air beach bars in Vietnam. It was rama-dama-rama-time: after a long month of abstinence, Bobby began chugging beers at a furious pace, while I ate and Simon worked his way through several gins.

The monsoons arrived with a fury—the drubbing din on the thatched roof drowned out a Shirley Bassey album and sent the beachside Pancakers diving for shelter. "A port in a storm night," quipped Simon.

Before I returned to my palace, Bobby resumed practicing his lines with the English-speaking Vietnamese bartenders and waitresses while juggling a conversation with a young, beautiful French Canadian model. With shooting shot by the monsoon, the cast and crew poured in, drenched but dry-mouthed. Damien's starstruck friend Sue, her feminine wiles at play, arrived on the arm of Tim Roth, the ship captain in the movie, who did a superb job of acting out his amorous intentions. They sidled up next to Bobby and Simon, and began a long night of dancing and drinking. It was Nha Trang at its best: exotic, erotic and for many, narcotic.

Tiger Cages of Con Son Island

The next morning at Cyclo Café, I was introduced to an elderly man in his early 70s sitting at the next table, Mai Phouc Linh. Having learned English on language tapes provided by the U.S. Army, he spoke in a clear Texas accent, compliments of the tapes' narrator. During the war he worked as a translator for the U.S. Army, and taught English to the South Vietnamese Army. He spent almost a year in re-education camps for his association with the Americans and their "puppet army." In spite of his excellent English and experience as a translator, he is not allowed to work for the communist government.

In a wearied voice, Linh delivered his summation, "I don't like politics. I don't believe anything they say, Americans or communists. I just teach English to private students and don't worry anymore."

Simon arrived and we set out traveling south on the coastal highway to Vung Tau to meet Dany. Beyond the turnoff to Phan Rang, along an arid landscape of prickly-pear cactus, we passed the sleepy, postcard-perfect fishing village of Ca Na, with its giant boulders, turquoise waters and shimmering white sand. Soon orchards of green dragon fruit crowded both sides of the road.

Brought to Vietnam from South America by French missionaries, the epiphytic dragonfruit grows on thick, climbing vines of cacti. The burry oblongs of green fruit turn magenta when ripe. Its black-seeded white flesh is a Vietnamese favorite and an export in high demand. Wrapped around a tree or trellis, the dangling tails of the plant resemble spiny serpents, or dragons I suppose.

We motored along the coastal plains, golden sheets of corn, dun-colored swatches of rice and paddy straw, and fluffy piles of cotton resembling white duvets lay drying on the tarmac. The gray harvested fields and sandy terrain stood in relief to emerald paddies, speckled with the white of egrets flocking.

Bullock carts competed in the traffic against waves of schoolgirls wearing flowing white *ao dais*. Peasant women walked the roadsides with baskets balanced on their heads, a practice of the Indianized Cham. The unsteady approach of the antiquated French Renault buses, listing as if they had loaded chickens on one side and concrete on the other, afforded many sign-of-the-cross opportunities. Splashed in Day-Glo red and yellow, the buses sported oversized tires, like toys on steroids.

Looking for a beachside hotel or restaurant for lunch, we left the main highway at the city of Phan Thiet. A Cham enclave, Phan Thiet is also the hallowed ground where for seven months Ho Chi Minh was an instructor at Duc Thanh secondary school, teaching Chinese, *quoc ngu*, and martial arts.

Red and blue fishing skiffs packed the Phan Thiet River like sardines. The satellite villages were scored by paddy-like grids of fish farms producing *nuoc mam*, the fermented fish sauce eaten with every meal. Fumes of fish ferment sate the air in a year-round pall. A couple of miles before the sublimely sculpted sand dunes of Mui Ne Beach, stood a Cham tower hovering over the road like a decrepit sentinel house.

Gazing out over the bold blue sea, we ate a lazy lunch of fresh white fish, before motoring on to Vung Tau, a beach resort and port occupied in the past by the militaries of the French, then Americans and later Russians. With the Bach Ho oilfields located nearby in the South China Sea, and the terminus of the recently completed Nam Con Son Gas Pipeline, today Vung Tau is the main distribution center for Vietnam's growing petroleum business. Percolating into this industrial mix is the free flow of Saigon's sewage and trash, including the dregs of the sex tourist scene, polluting the once pristine waters and littering the alabaster beaches. On the beach promenade we were chased by hawkers on motorcycles, who passed out leaflets for massages, whiskey, dog races, dancing girls, pizza and fine dining.

Dany was waiting at the top of the circular drive near a nondescript high-rise beach hotel, owned by the National Oil Service Company of Vietnam. She greeted us by the car in the European way, cheek kissing, before pointing to a neon sign next to the entrance and praising her choice of accommodations, "See the hotel even has a massage parlor for you men."

Dany led us to the front desk where we turned over our passports to be registered at the police station, before she herded us to the elevator and on up to a room. I slowly began to suspect that Dany planned on staying in our room. She had rented a two-bedroom suite, and ordered up extra linen so she could sleep on the couch. I argued with her about the arrangement, contending she should have a bed and her own bedroom, but Dany had made up her mind, and that was that.

Assuming the role of tour guide, Dany brought us to a nice beachfront restaurant a couple of miles from the hotel. Flagging off a phalanx of motorcycle hawkers circling us as we drove down the strand, we were soon honking for the guard in front of Ba Ninh, a walled bungalow complex with a fashionable restaurant catering to both locals and foreigners.

Years of leg irons having left her with a pronounced limp, Dany held on to me like a crutch to get down the steps into the split-level bar and restaurant. A large table of Vietnamese sat on one end, but we were led across the room and seated in a foreigner's nook next to two bloated Russian men in their late 50s or early 60s, oilfield workers of some ilk. Woefully shy of Baryshnikov's looks, they were well into their vodka cups, enjoying the company of two of the most tawdry-dressed hookers I had ever seen. The men bellowed like beasts, and their consorts twittered like birds—this was one kind of cross-cultural gathering introduced by *doi moi*. We ate our seafood, and soaked up more of Dany's saga.

After the war, Dany spent time in the hospital, and made a partial recovery. Once she was ready to restart her life, she took on a succession of jobs and learning experiences, all meant to help her achieve her dream of building a socialist utopia. After supervising the transfer of expropriated real estate in Saigon, she committed herself for the first time to study communist doctrine, which she did for five years while also helping to organize youth groups. After she completed her political education, she joined the Ho Chi Minh Medical College where she taught pharmacology students the fine points of Marxist-Leninist doctrine.

With tongue-in-cheek, I asked Dany how she presented Marx and Lenin to the young doctors.

"I told them we don't need it," she said. She then began exorcising some deep-seated anger, crinkling her face and spraying her words, "We need another revolution. It was wrong from the beginning. The government has nothing to lose and all to gain. I have suffered more since prison than while there."

The suffering she referred to began in South Vietnamese prisons, shortly after the Paris Peace Accords were signed in February of 1973. Dany along with Mado and a small group of like-minded women inmates on Con Son Island protested the dire prison conditions, steadfastly refusing to perform hard labor after the Accords were signed. Most female inmates, seeing light at the end of the tunnel, were not willing to stand up to the guards, who were South Vietnamese and supervised by American advisors. Threatened with more torture, the inmate leaders called an end to the acts of civil disobedience that had become a part of their daily life.

"They just wanted to go along with prison conditions as they were," said Dany. They chose to work in the quarries, live in squalor, be fed and go free in a couple of years when inevitably the war would end. Dany, Mado and the other protestors were bitter and hardened to prison life, and willing to die fighting for their dignity and principles.

Over an eight-day period, three of the protestors were beaten by the inmate leaders and their followers, deprived of food and medicine before they died. Many of those inmate leaders who turned on or failed to support their protesting comrades in prison are now Party notables in Hanoi—Vice President Truoug My Hoa and Vo Thi Thang, Chief of Vietnam Tourism. They reaped the rewards of being political prisoners, a cachet that continues to pay huge dividends in Vietnam. "The VCP is proud about the history of Con Son Island," Dany stated assuringly.

Although she had some minor confrontations with the Party over the ensuing two to three decades, it was not until Dany married Marcel, the

Frenchman, 10 years ago that she was forced to revisit these old hatreds. "They cannot interfere in my private life," Dany fumed, "'Why you marry foreigner?' they ask me." Once Marcel moved to Cambodia, Dany's anger crescendoed, often putting her in hostile confrontation with the VCP. More dangerously, she began to speak publicly against the Party's suppression of others' views.

Back at our beachside aerie, Dany put on her black pajamas and curled up on the couch, while Simon and I locked ourselves into our master suites for the evening. By midnight, I was blowing it out both ends. It felt like germ warfare: a stray microbe taking anti-colonial revenge perhaps. Through the night I wore a path to the toilet, passing Dany at least 10 times while she slept on the couch. She never woke.

As the false light of dawn beckoned, she was up and rapping on my door. Once informed of my condition, she got out her black bag of Asian remedies, a sideline she picked up while teaching Marx and Lenin at the pharmacy school. She soon reappeared at my bedside with a razor and a sticky patch of traditional medicine to sooth my stomach, "Oh, I think you too hairy, I shave."

"This ain't no VC camp, Dany. I have some anti-nausea medicine right here I am going to take before we go to the heliport."

"What is it. Tell me, I know about drugs."

"It's Phenergan, and it works. I've used it before."

"Yes, I know but Phenergan will make you sleepy."

"But I won't be puking on everyone in the helicopter."

She acquiesced, and put her razor and remedies away.

Once at the heliport, the nausea contained for the moment, I stretched across a row of chairs to watch an oilfield-produced safety video on riding in Russian helicopters. Ready to travel, we strapped on life jackets and sound-muffling headsets, and were the last passengers to board the 24-seat whirly-bird.

Joining us on the flight were two septuagenarians in white shirts and slacks, one slightly built, wearing a fedora, and the other thickset, trimmed out with a baseball hat. Both men left the prison almost 40-years ago, and were on a pilgrimage that included family members. They were political prisoners during the brutal years of President Diem in the early 1960s. Dany whispered that the man in the fedora had lost a brother on Con Son Island, tortured to death.

My nausea came and went, buffeted by the shuddering roar of the rotor blades. As we skirted the coast and headed south, Dany recounted the first time she had ever flown. In 1968, a short time after being arrested, she and as many as 200 other women prisoners—*toc dai*, or "long haired" soldiers— were loaded in the back of an American C-130 cargo plane and flown to Con Son Island, where she and her sister would eventually be put in the Tiger Cages.

An hour after lift-off, we were skimming the island's foliaged cliffsides. As we descended to the remote heliport, the surrounding turquoise waters gave way to white sheets of surf and empty, clean-swept beaches. It was a stunningly beautiful island, but it didn't seem like Vietnam. I would soon discover that not only are the footprints of history found in curious places, but Con Son Island bears the heart and soul of Vietnam.

As we boarded a small bus Dany dumped a chalky packet of re-hydration powder into my water bottle. Tracing the furrowed base of a jungled ridge, we chugged up a twisting track of sublime scenery, the Yellow Brick Road of a Fantasy Island. But each of the road's eight miles was built with the blood and sweat of French *corvee* and prisoner labor, and later improved by RMK-BRJ, an American joint venture that included Halliburton subsidiary Brown and Root, with mega-contracts in Vietnam during the war.

After unloading our bags in the Saigon Tourist guesthouse near the jetty, we walked up to the former prison director's villa, a French colon's dream house in the tropics, with a roofed porch looking out onto manicured gardens and beyond to the sea. Now the Revolutionary Museum, the house was built in 1862 at the same time the prison was opened. Con Son Island was then known by its European designation, *Iles Poulo Condore*, one of 15 in the Con Dao Archipelago.

Dany is a celebrity around Con Son Island. She worked there as the director in 1988 when the museum opened, catering to former prisoners returning to make their peace. Today Simon and I were the only non-Vietnamese on the island.

After a stir of excitement from Dany's arrival, she introduced us to the museum staff and the current director Linh, also a former prisoner. Linh invited us for a drink in his tent sprawled to one side of the museum entrance. But saving this refreshment for later, we spent over an hour reading the inscriptions and perusing the faces in the black-and-white photographs lining the musty walls of the museum. Most of the pictures were from the colonial era—a roll call of nationalists and future communist leaders, virtually an index to street names throughout Vietnam.

One of the first nationalists to be imprisoned on the island, Phan Chu Trinh took his *pho bang*—doctorate degree—after passing the imperial exams in Hue in the same class as Nyugen Sinh Sac, Ho Chi Minh's father. At the turn of the century, as the French were attacking the time-honored institutions of Confucianism in Vietnam, imposing harsh taxes on salt, opium and alcohol, and exacting laborers to work long hours for low wages under squalid conditions, Trinh spoke out against these inequalities. Acknowledging all the positive aspects of French rule, he also called for educational and legal reforms, as well as the overhaul of the political system, the creation of democracy perhaps.

In 1907, a demonstration in Hue turned nasty when the French opened fire on the protestors. They arrested everyone directly involved, even those they merely suspected to be sympathizers. Trinh was apprehended in Hanoi, and transferred to Hue for trial where the prosecutor pushed for the death sentence. Following an appeal to the French resident superior, he was given life in prison on Con Son Island. After three years in Phu Hai Prison his sentence was commuted and he was exiled to France.

While living in Paris he often shared his nationalist ideas with other dissidents, including Ho Chi Minh, with whom he worked as a photo retoucher. Working within the French system, eschewing organizational politics, he returned to Vietnam after a long absence and spent his final years promoting nationalism through non-violent reform. He died of cancer in 1926 at the age of 53. "His funeral became the occasion of a mass national outpouring of grief; thousands lined the streets to watch his bier as it was carried from Saigon to a grave site near Tan Son Nhut Airport...," wrote Vietnam scholar William Duiker.

Le Duan, a founding member of the Indochina Communist Party in 1930, was imprisoned on Con Son Island twice: once from 1931-1936 and again for four years during World War II. Converting hard time to political currency, Phu Hai Prison was his springboard to the top. He became Party Secretary and the most powerful man in Vietnam from 1960 until he died in 1986.

After it became evident that there would be no democratic elections in Diem's Republic of Vietnam, Le Duan started the communist underground network in South Vietnam that led to the founding of the National Liberation Front, the VC as they became known to Americans. He pushed guerrilla warfare and the invasion of the South as the inevitable solution to reunification.

Phan Van Dong, prime minister of North Vietnam beginning in 1955, had also been imprisoned on Con Son Island from 1930 to 1936. In his youth, Dong joined Ho Chi Minh's Association of Revolutionary Youth, the forerunner to the Indochinese Communist Party.

Dong served as prime minister until 1986, and although he was guilty by association with Le Duan's heavy-handed policies, today, more often than not, Dong is compared by historians to Ho Chi Minh—a nationalist first and a communist by default. Some would argue that with independence as their goal, in the face of Western reluctance to prize the French from Indochina after World War II, they had no one but the Soviet Union and China to turn to for military support and financial aid.

Speaking out against corruption and bad governance until the end, Dong died at the age of 94 in 2000, a life that spanned the breadth of the 20th century he helped to shape. I was living in Hanoi at the time of his state funeral.

The roll call of Phu Hai Prison, often called the Revolutionary University, goes on: Le Duc Tho, best known internationally for putting the britches on Secretary of State Henry Kissinger at the Paris Peace Talks; Ton Duc Thang, who became President when Ho Chi Minh died; Pham Hung, who became Prime Minister; and a host of noted scholars.

The imprisoned dissidents were as irrepressible as quicksilver. The French applied the heavy thumb of punishment and torture, but once it was raised, the prisoners coalesced again, stronger and more united. In attacking the nationalist movement which ultimately became the communist revolution, the diehard colonialist French faced an impossible dilemma: political dissidents became more empowered or worse yet, martyred, pushing the independence movement forward geometrically. Phu Hai Prison—whose remote location implied its brutality—provided Exhibit A in the court of Vietnamese public opinion.

We walked to the front grounds of the museum where a couple of miniature rusted tram cars rested on a narrow-gauge track, similar to the one we encountered on Don Khon Island in the middle of the Mekong. Completed in 1873, they say at the cost of almost 1,000 lives, the track was used by prisoners to bring rocks from the mountain quarry miles away to the nearby jetty.

Leaving the museum grounds, we crossed the road to the jetty, where Dany had arrived by boat in 1973. At the end of her tether with the hostility of her fellow inmates, she was returning from four months of psychological evaluation at a Ben Hoa hospital on the outskirts of Saigon. Resting on the seawall, Dany pointed out where the prisoner boat had been moored at the end of the jetty, and where fishing skiffs now bobbed in the idyllic waters.

Back in 1973, a double row of guards greeted the boatload of women prisoners as they debarked down a wooden plank. To soften the fresh arrivals up, each of the guards beat the women with a cudgel as they passed. Not new to the prison scene, the *toc dai*, or "long haired" soldiers, charged the guards, and briefly overcame them, only to be punished for their rebelliousness later.

Shaded in spiraling broadleafs and a line of palms, the frontage road and seawall were lifeless. Far away, pearl divers fished the sparkling waters along a sandy cove. Nothing stirred on the jetty, as if the evacuation of prisoners in 1975 had just occurred, leaving the island tranquil.

We ambled around behind the guesthouse and joined the two other former prisoners and their families for a tour of Building No. 3. The cellblock was encased in a jaundiced rampart of concrete wall, fronted with a circular guard tower. Dany led us over to Cell No. 1 where Nguyen Van Ut, her then future husband, was held in isolation. On the same side of the prison yard but at the opposite end of the building was Cell No. 7 where Dany and Mado were kept in isolation from the hostile inmates—those accused of killing their friends—until the time of their release.

Spartan, oven-like and infested with mosquitoes, each cell was the same, with a horizontal slab of concrete extending from the walls to make one continuous bed. In the same French style as at Hoa La Prison in Hanoi, at the foot of the concrete slabs were built-in leg irons, spaced for narrow body widths. Dany and Mado were permanently disabled from wearing them every night.

Saving the Tiger Cages and cemetery for the next day, we returned to the guesthouse, where I immediately went to bed. Just after dusk Dany came to my room with a bowl of *pho ga*, the Vietnamese version of chicken noodle soup. Nurse-like, she filled my water bottle again with more of the re-hydration powder. She then flopped on the other twin bed while I sat up and spooned the soup down tentatively.

Gushing with pride, she told me about her children—65 homeless, impoverished or otherwise disadvantaged kids to whom she opens her house every day for martial arts training, Chinese unicorn dancing, and math and reading lessons. With her husband gone, the children are her life.

Dany is a black belt in *Vovinam*, a form of martial arts that originated in Vietnam and now practiced worldwide. She told me the story of first being introduced to the sport—a way of life—about the time she joined the Viet Cong. Mado's high school sweetheart and first love was their instructor, a black belt in Vovinam named Le Cong Danh. They practiced in a training house near An Dong market, where the walls were papered in slogans teaching the way to live, "Vietnamese should learn paternal Kung Fu," admonished one poster.

It was a star-crossed romance from the beginning. Danh's family was devoutly anti-communist. Torn between the timeless charms of Aphrodite and a son's devotion to the bone-deep Confucian principles of family harmony, Danh painfully refused Mado's wishes for him to join the VC. Signaling the knell of their youthful romance, a week before being arrested, Mado broke it off with him.

It wasn't that easy, though. Danh had been observed coming and going at Mado's house in the weeks leading up to her arrest. After being detained under intense interrogation, Mado took full responsibility and Danh was released.

Still under Mado's spell, he waited on her for five years until after the Paris Peace Talks. Once the talks concluded, with no word from Mado, he married another French-educated Saigon woman. In 1975, after the war was declared over, and hearing of Mado's release, Danh hastened to her house for a brief reunion. He brought his little girl, and after a long silence, he said, "It's amazing how my daughter looks like you." That was their last tryst. Prison and the politics of war had forever changed the tack of Mado's life. She was left with no return passage to the romance of youth.

Danh and his family joined the "boat people" and fled Vietnam, eventually emigrating to Australia. Last year, Dany's son Nhut competed in the Vovinam World Cup in Paris, and Mado's first love was one of the judges.

After forcing a pink pill and then a white one into my hand, both herbal concentrates of some manner, Dany left to phone her son and see how her adopted kids had done that day.

The next morning, feeling like a svelte Rip Van Winkle, a few pounds lighter and refreshed by 12 hours of sleep, I joined our group for more *pho ga* before getting on the bus for the Hang Duong Cemetery. We stopped in the market and bought bouquets of marigolds and white sunflowers, three heads of dragonfruit and two packets of incense, as offerings for Dany's fallen friends.

Despite the cemetery's starkness, Dany seemed to see the past there coming back to life, tears filling her eyes. She sobbed, wailed and sobbed again. "Why them? Why them?" she screamed, recalling friends who had been tortured to death. I draped my arms around her shoulders, despite feeling poorly equipped to play the role of comforting soul.

We drifted dumbstruck through a sea of triangular stone markers, each cartouched with a Red Star, the sovereign's touch. They say over 20,000 souls are buried in the cemetery, but beneath just 2,000 headstones. Of these, only 600 are engraved with names.

The other former prisoner in the fedora and his family scattered to find the grave of his brother, whom he had last seen alive over 40 years ago when they arrived at the prison together. Soon they found his granite marker near a line of willow trees. A contagion of cries circled the family like a burning ring of fire. He was killed decades ago, yet his death seemed as painful to them as if it had happened last week.

Traipsing through high grass around a lotus pond, Dany knew where she was going. When she worked at the museum, she came to the cemetery every night with offerings. Once in front of the gravestones, where her three friends lay together in a row, Dany collapsed on her knees and wept child-like in a paroxysm of grief. After a time she gathered herself, still sobbing, and began lighting incense.

With intermittent lapses, she told us of Nguyen Thi Houng, her closest friend of the three, "She was very pretty, and she loved to sing and dance. She would dance for us at night and sing us her favorite songs. She had no husband but had a son in one of the VC camps. When she was dying she gave me a VC contact to find her son. I have looked for 30 years! I don't know what happened to him."

Her voice grew louder, echoing with anger, "There were 400 of us. We could have saved them."

There was not a dry eye among us. My senses were numb, as I fumbled with matches to help Dany light more incense, and burn paper money and clothes to comfort her friends in the afterlife. The wind sloughed through the trees like a paean. The sky broke into an ambivalent blue infinity, then darkened into night. Emotion weighted the air like heavy mist. It refused to be shaken off.

Dany had unwittingly insinuated us into her private but intense reality. We became her witnesses as she exorcised the ghosts of her past, in a place and moment where suffering souls come together with the better angels of the departed. Perhaps out of this sepulchral force field, she found a confluence of heaven and earth.

Gathering our belongings and tattered souls, we left the gravesites of Huong and the other two friends, Thanh and Cuc, weaving through several mass graves represented by larger, blank stones. We stopped to pay homage at the grandiose headstone of Vo Thi Sau, the 17-year-old martyr who tossed a bomb into a patrol of French *gendarmes* near a market in Baria-Vung Tau, killing four of them. She was executed in 1952—in the heat of the French war, when Emperor Bao Dai was gallivanting from palace to palace—the only girl ever shot to death on the island. Her defiant spirit seems to have been reincarnated in later revolutionary girls like Dany. In Dany's case especially, this notion seems plausible. She was born a year after Vo Thi Sau's death, enough of a gap in time to accord with the Buddhist belief that there is an interregnum, a benign purgatory, before rebirth.

Vo Thi Sau's gravesite altar was lined with combs and mirrors, a sign of her youth and reputed to be her last possessions. Honoring her like an adolescent Joan of Arc, today there are shrines, temples, schools and streets throughout Vietnam named Vo Thi Sau. In her memory, Dany bowed, burned incense, arranged flowers and cried out for lost youth.

We met the other visitors back at the bus and drove the short distance to Camp Four, surrounded by thick walls of stone. The prison barracks bookended a tree-shaded courtyard, formerly a place of public beatings and the hard labor of breaking rocks. The museum has installed mannequins with emaciated bodies in the prison chambers, vaulted rooms that could be a jailhouse anywhere—shackles, concrete and iron bars.

Dany led us to cell No. 15, where her friends were killed. As she recounted the grim details to us, a man named Quy, a Russian-trained MIG pilot, war hero and recent government retiree in Hanoi, overheard. He stepped over to express his sympathies to Dany.

Quy had apparently tweaked the whiskers of the tigress the day before, because Dany leapt into a tirade about the Hanoi women who had not shown solidarity three decades before. The biting tones of her anger were familiar, and judging from Quy's chastened recoil, her words were sharpened with the claws of truth. All was starkly silent when Dany finished, her eyes turned to puddles, her oval face veined in tears, pooling on her cheeks before she washed them away with her shirt sleeve. A few bystanders stepped up and expressed their regrets. Others wandered away staring at the dusty ground. Her prison ranking seemed undisputed.

Once she had pulled herself together again, I asked her if Quy could make trouble for her by reporting that she had criticized government officials in the presence of foreigners. She didn't think so, "Privately is okay to speak out but not publicly."

We walked to the perimeter wall near the entrance and turned left at the site of a former vegetable garden, the same pathless route Senator Tom Harkin, then a congressional aide, had ventured in 1970 when looking for the Tiger Cages. Harkin was with two congressmen, William Anderson of Tennessee and Augustus Hawkins of California, on what might have been just another of the many congressional junkets that rarely merit more than small headlines in local papers. Except on this occasion, Harkin had a chance meeting with Don Luce, a social worker and the executive secretary of the World Council of Churches. At the time, the Tiger Cages were only a rumor outside of the need-to-know prison circles. Luce had recently met a former inmate of the Tiger Cages, and had asked him to draw a map pinpointing the location.

The Con Son Island prison was already part of the delegation's scheduled tour, which Luce would join. They would be informed on conditions there by an American, Frank "Red" Walton, a former Los Angeles policeman. He had been in charge of the Watts District—the scene of out-of-control race riots in 1965—and parlayed his police work into a new career as chief advisor to the Vietnamese on law enforcement and prison practices. According to the *Life* expose, Red called the island, "a correctional institution worthy of higher ratings than some prisons in the United States… This place is more like a Boy Scout recreational camp."

Harkin suspected otherwise. Straying from the staged tour, he snooped around. "I was in a vegetable garden when I saw a wall, and a door that didn't seem to go anywhere, and I was sure that was it," he wrote in the 1970 *Life* expose. Luring the Con Son Commandant Colonel Nguyen Van Ve into the garden and making small talk about vegetables, an unsuspecting guard heard the colonel's voice and opened the door. By Harkin's account, "He looked mortified. But before the colonel could say anything, Congressman Hawkins and I barged through the door, and inside, there were the tiger cages."

With the exceptions of Dany and Mado, almost all the prisoners were from peasant backgrounds and spoke only Vietnamese. Seeing Harkin, Dany and Mado tried to get his attention by speaking French. When he didn't respond, they spoke to him in English. Harkin replied, "Is there anything I can do for you?"

Dany and Mado answered in a voice, "A drink of water would be nice." After a guard retrieved some water and they slaked their thirst, Mado made another request, "Please contact our mother in Saigon and tell her we are alive." Harkin wrote down the Saigon address of their mother.

We retraced their steps, breeching the once-secret gate, and followed Dany up a steep set of stairs. From a small platform at the top, a tumbled catwalk stretched the length of the building, overlooking the remains of 30 grated cells, or Tiger Cages. Buckets of "quicklime" still lined the catwalk. The guards used to perch on the catwalk and disgorge the caustic white powder on the prisoners as torture, burning their skin until they bled and causing severe breathing problems.

We tightroped down the crumbling catwalk, Dany holding onto my backside, until we reached a point overlooking cell numbers nine and 11, where she and Mado were confined for over a year. The wind slammed a cell door shut, metal clanging on metal, jangling our nerves. The cages—or concrete boxes—were blackened from years of mildew, and stained with circles of green fungi growing out of the quicklime-encrusted floors.

Each cell measured just three feet by six feet, and was packed with five women, most shackled in irons. Sleep was furtive, thanks to bedbugs, mosquitoes and malarial fevers. A typical day began at five in the morning, with, if one was well behaved, a dollop of jelly and salt. Dany calls it "Continental style."

Each cell contained a small bucket for use as a communal toilet. There was a *Guigoz* milk carton, which on good days was half-filled with water. There was no paper for cleaning, no pads for menses. "It was terrible, Phil. You would not believe," Dany groaned.

Minutes after Harkin arrived came Henry Luce who spoke Vietnamese. He described the scene in detail:

"All the prisoners were sick: with TB, open sores, eye diseases and malnutrition. The sickest lay on the floor while others fanned them with bits of cloth. Few could stand—the result, they claimed of being constantly shackled. One prisoner said they stole handfuls of grass to eat on the way back from beatings, and snared lizards, beetles and other insects and ate them alive, biting off and sharing pieces."

When not being punished, the prisoners were given sparse portions of rice and dried fish for lunch or dinner, to be eaten by bare hand. More often than not, though, the inmates were protesting. They refused to work and screamed in synchrony with all the strength they could muster. They were usually repaid with a bucket full of quicklime. Dany and Mado both told me in separate conversations that after being tortured they were afraid to pass out, not knowing whether they were falling asleep or dying.

Colonel Ve understood the likely political consequences of Harkin's discovery. He became defensive, claiming the prisoners deserved harsh treatment. "Very bad people. They will not salute the flag. They will not even salute the American flag," he said. When the American advisor Red Walton got wind of Harkin's surprise intrusion, he fumed, "You have no right to interfere in Vietnamese affairs. You aren't supposed to go poking your nose into doors that aren't your business."

During the two hours the delegation was at the Tiger Cages and on Con Son Island, Harkin took pictures. Upon returning to Saigon, he fulfilled Dany and Mado's request to contact their mother, Nguyen Thi Binh. On the trip back to the United States, an unnamed member of the congressional delegation asked for Harkin's film. "I have a higher obligation," Harkin told the official, "to those 500 human beings who are jammed in those cages." Three months later the Tiger Cages were partly dismantled and closed for good.

In 1995, on the 25th anniversary of the delegation's trip, Dany and Mado were honored to escort Senator Tom Harkin back to the place where they first met, that infamous dungeon.

Dany arranged for us to borrow a motorcycle from Linh, the museum director, who greeted us in front of his tent at three in the afternoon, red-faced and wearing only his pajama shorts. His folding camp table brimmed with crushed Heineken cans and the bony remains of an afternoon feast of dog. The unpleasant smell of purple, fermented shrimp paste—*mam tom*, a dip for the meat—lingered in the air. American soldiers used to call it VC tear gas.

He handed me the key and pointed to the automatic starter. Simon jumped on back, and we followed Dany and Vang, the assistant museum director who is a young Loretta Lynn look-a-like. Everything on Con Son is of an island scale and the roads all interconnect, so we opted for the scenic route, following the seaside before turning inland to Con Son village. We made a quick pass by the new Vo Thi Sau secondary school and headed out a couple of miles to a farm owned by Ms. Dong, a friend of Dany's from the late 1980s when they worked together at the Revolutionary Museum.

Recently remarried, Dong and her new husband had in the last year bought the two-acre farm for $1,300. They had built a one-room house with a trellis of hanging squash for a porch, where we all gathered. There was a fishpond out back, next to a large vegetable garden, and at least an acre of mature sugarcane. Dong went out in the field and cut some sugar cane for us to chew on, while her teenage daughter Xuan made us green tea. Six years before, unsettled by her parents' divorce, Xuan moved to Saigon and lived with Dany for a couple of years. The mentoring worked: Xuan finishes high school this spring in the village at Vo Thi Sau, and aspires to go on to university in Saigon.

After getting caught up, Dong cut us more long stalks of sugarcane, before we took off for a hilltop pagoda next to a dilapidated French salt mine near the waterfront. Dany used a stalk of the sugarcane as a walking stick to climb the 172 steps to the top, dominated by a statue of the Buddhist Goddess of Mercy (*Quan Am*), shrouded in a flowing white cape and trimmed in gold.

The view was timeless, an ecological *tabula rasa* of bluish shades. Clouds laid gingerly across the island peaks, a tissue-like relief to the infinite blue sky. Fish hawks caught thermals against the rugged mountainous backdrop, rising and falling through the fluffs of white. Colorful fishing scows cut the turquoise waters, tinged beneath with darkened lines of coral and perhaps the unseen dugongs, or sea cows, that inhabit the marine park.

We finished the afternoon sitting outside at Vo Thi Sau's shrine along the seafront. Locals came and went, praying for better health and making offerings—often a comb and mirror—to a golden bust of the teenage martyr. Above the altar emblazoned in red was a tribute from Ho Chi Minh, heralding Vo Thi Sau as a Vietnamese hero and encouraging all women to follow in her footsteps. As we sipped soft drinks and green tea, Dany and Vang sang a ballad about her—praising the island's mountains and streams and urging all to visit Vu Thi Sau's tomb when the red flowers of spring come into bloom.

That night the museum staff and other locals held a dinner to honor Simon and me, but in fact it was Dany's night. She was seated at the head of the table, shining like a Nguyen princess before her court, clearly much adored by the women there. While the men drank beer and local rice whiskey, *ruou thuoc*, the women decked the long, linen-covered table with an orgy of food—hot pots of noodles, vegetables, blood organs, duck, beef, shrimp salad and French fries.

The director of culture on the island, Mr. Thieu, a modest gentleman of moderate habits, sat next to me and with limited English skills, patiently answered my questions about tourism.

"All we need is reliable air service, maybe two years, then it will happen."

Dany weighed in from across the table, "The ex-prisoners do not want it—pizza cafes and backpackers everywhere. I think we cannot stop it, though."

In the middle of dinner, Mr. Le Xuan Ai, Director of the Con Dao National Park, also known as Mr. Lovely, arrived wearing a fresh glow of whiskey. Mr. Lovely talked like a big shot, telling us of his trips to Thailand, the Philippines, and Malaysia. Kitted out like a Japanese tourist in a floppy safari hat and matching multi-pocketed khaki jacket, he soon turned the dinner into a drinking competition, *tram phan tram*, a favorite local sport. Once Mr. Lovely realized I was a diver, he wanted to take me the next morning to see the dugongs. One woman tried to dash my hopes, however: "I've lived here for 22 years and never seen one." After a toast given by Dany and myself, the young women joined in the drinking, taunting Simon and Mr. Lovely to duel on with the shot glasses.

Simon took on all comers, leaning over to me at one point, "Why hit the wall at 50 when you could be going 80?" I agreed but still felt too tender for dueling drinks, something Mr. Lovely and the other men refused to accept.

Feeling guilty about being a stick-in-the-mud at the generous reception, I ran to my room and snatched up my stash of Cuban cigars. Once back at the boisterous banquet I ceremoniously circled the table and gave each of the four Vietnamese men a #4 Monte Cristo, $7 a piece in Hanoi. As each of them inspected the fine stogies with obvious puzzlement, I should have recognized my misjudgment. They had never seen a cigar before, and worse, they were drunk.

They lit up the wrong end and neglected to slice the tip of these very fine specimens of tobacco—it was painful to watch. I stepped in with some guidance, and luckily had my knife. Cigars lit, they each exhaled four or five thick clouds of smoke, caricaturing 10-year olds taking their first crude puffs. This failed to impress the women, who fell over like dominoes in fits of laughter. The men soon thought better of their cigar schtick and smashed the stogies out, leaving them in unsalvageable condition. They lit up their usual 555 cigarettes. They would not remember any of this treat the next day, despite the $28 I had spent in an effort to share goodwill.

Yet the bonhomie continued, as Simon passed around a photo in uniform of his significant other in Hanoi, Pham Kim Quy, a stage and television actress and officer in the army for 24 years. Many of the women recognized her, prompting one of them to sing a popular folk song about Hanoi lovers, and dedicate it to Simon. The celebration died a natural death. Mr. Lovely had already staggered off, liquefying into the pitch, which left the last Vietnamese competitor in a drool. Amid gales of laughter, he admitted he had finally hit the wall. His concession speech was slurred but to the point, "I'll be dead before Simon quits!"

The next morning broke splendidly. With Dany and Vang, we had a breakfast of croissant and cheese on an ocean-view verandah, listening to a French Jazz singer. Simon arrived late, sheepish but proud of his victory the night before.

After lazing around the breakfast table an extra hour due to a delay in our flight, we boarded the bus with the same group that had arrived with us, following the beachfront back to the heliport. At low tide, the sea exposed a rocky shoreline and a long sweep of mollusk-rich mudflats. The Russian chopper was waiting on the tarmac, but there were no pilots in sight. Everyone waited patiently, Simon and I reading, Dany talking to her fellow ex-prisoners.

After an hour, the two pilots, in uniform—gilded epaulets, billed hats and golden wings on white shirts—emerged from a white shack next door, walking in gallant strides across the tarmac. They had been busy the past two hours, judging from the two hookers accompanying them.

The chopper was overloaded, with two guys sharing a jump seat and loose bags piled against the bulkhead. Simon had the hookers and pilots line up with Dany for a group photo. The hookers boarded last, squeezing into the pilot's cabin, while everyone shrugged off the delay with laughter. It wasn't long before we were tracking the colorful coastline of the Mekong Delta, the river's muddy tentacles laden with silt, spilling out miles into the vast blue sea like a fantastic inkblot. Dany's head fell against my shoulder. She was fast asleep, exhausted from the events of the last few days.

Her psychological resilience, her will to live courageously despite anguish and trauma, left me feeling grateful never to have suffered so much myself, and also regretting missed opportunities. Perhaps I too could have played some role in opposing crimes against humanity. She has rebounded better than many survivors of torture do. Jean Amery, who survived Auschwitz, wrote about an unshakeable despair:

"Anyone who has been tortured remains tortured... anyone who has suffered torture will never again be at ease in the world; the abomination of the annihilation is never extinguished. Faith in humanity, already cracked by the first slap in the face, then demolished by torture, is never acquired again."

In 1978, 33 years after being liberated from Auschwitz, he committed suicide. Dany, however, has managed to live by championing the indomitable human spirit. At the low point of her wretched existence in prison, as Harkin left the island and returned to his secure and sensible world, Dany told me her thoughts at the time, "Harkin opened our hearts. When people understand each other, there is no war."

General William Westmoreland, commander of American troops in Vietnam until after Tet Offensive of 1968, was interviewed for the Academy Award-winning documentary *Hearts and Minds*, about the Vietnam War. Relaxed in his civvies, waxing philosophical, the retired general proffered his assessment of the Vietnamese mindset, "The Oriental doesn't put the same high price on life as does the Westerner, life is plentiful, life is cheap in the Orient. The philosophy of the Orient expresses it, life is not important." Indeed, dehumanizing the enemy makes it easier to justify and prosecute a war.

As the chopper touched down, Dany woke up excited about getting back to Saigon and seeing all her kids. Tuan was waiting for us outside the terminal, and within a couple of hours we were back in the crush of Saigon traffic. Before dropping Dany off, I asked Tuan to circle the former Saigon Central

Police Station, the building Dany and Mado attempted to blow up, which now houses the offices for immigration and customs. Dany has been there many times to help her husband Marcel obtain his residence visa. On one occasion when a clerk at the immigration office attempted to charge her double the price for a visa renewal, she reminded him, "Just where you are sitting, I once planned to detonate a bomb." He understood what she was talking about, and gave her the visa at the official rate.

We passed slowly down Nguyen Trai Street in front of the building, now obscured behind high walls and towering trees and guarded by a flank of gun-toting soldiers. As I raised my camera, Dany panicked, "Stop, stop! Be careful—you will get in trouble for taking picture."

"Calm down Dany, I am only taking a picture. Unlike you I have no intention of blowing this place up."

"That was a long time ago," she laughed.

The next afternoon, before catching the night train, Simon and I went to Dany's house in District 13 on the southern outskirts of Saigon. Down a quiet side street in a rural setting tucked into the urban sprawl, we entered through an arching gate, following a gravelly path festooned in potted plants, palm trees, decorative cart wheels and a fully outfitted antique bullock cart. Impaled by a coconut palm, her thatched-roofed home seemed to invite people in like a treehouse to inspect its curious nooks.

VTV (Vietnam Television) had just arrived to film her kids unicorn dancing, an ancient Chinese performing art rarely seen in Vietnam anymore. Two dancing boys formed the body of the unicorn—one peered through the open mouth of a mask and the other was joined by a cloth body and plays the tail. Children wearing blue Vovinam habits—Kung Fu clothes—filled the yard, some taking reading lessons from the martial arts instructors. They sat in a makeshift library where nine, thick Vietnamese volumes of Lenin and Marx were prominently displayed among many shelves of children's books. Simon searched the library for his illustrated book of Oscar Wilde's *Selfish Giant*, translated into Vietnamese only recently, but it was not to be found. In another corner of the red-tiled verandah a group of kids worked on math problems.

Outside and above the doorway—hung like a family coat of arms—was a historical portrait of a young Ho Chi Minh, wearing a double-breasted, blue blazer and a red tie, as he stood at a table delivering a speech among a crowd of mustachioed Frenchmen. It was the inaugural event of the French Communist Party held on Christmas day in 1920 in Tours, France. He ended his oration with a plea for independence, "In the name of all humanity, in the name of all socialists of the right and the left, we appeal to you, comrades, save us!"

Mado arrived and we gathered around a low set table for green tea. Dany introduced her son Nhut, also a martial arts instructor. A portrait of Dany's husband Marcel, handsome at sixtyish and wearing a bushy pioneer's beard, hung on the wall. A shuttered window opened to the back, framing the vegetative flourish of bamboo and corn crowding the house, nipping at our necks as we sat on the couch.

Joining us briefly, Dany complained about the police demanding a bribe in lieu of a permit for her ad hoc school. As she walked off, I commented on the Ho Chi Minh portrait, and Mado grew wistful, "We were so lucky to have Ho Chi Minh, he was pure."

I gulped at the suggestion of HCM as the plaster saint, then told her the documented story of Uncle Ho in his waning years when he asked a Chinese Party leader visiting Hanoi to bring him a young woman from the Chinese province of Guangdong. Confused, the diplomat agreed but wondered aloud why the local women weren't acceptable. "They all call me Uncle Ho," was his terse explanation.

Mado laughed, and said, "Not so pure like that."

While we talked, Dany darted about with puppyish energy, minding the children's activities with the collective forbearance of mother, mentor and martial arts aficionado, the way of the ancient masters, taking charge of all aspects of her students' lives. Out of Dany's earshot, Mado talked in a stream-of-consciousness manner, "Dany loves her kids. She lost her childhood and this is the way she gets it back. When we were in prison, if we thought about living when being tortured, the protest was over. We didn't care if we died. That was our survival."

She told us about high-level Party members who were trying to take over her shrimp farm, "As naïve communist revolutionaries, we trusted that whatever we do for the good of the people will be protected by the communist party in power. But now, corrupted officials become decision makers, so everything is decided by money."

Dany passed by, freshly outfitted in blue Vovinam garb, and took her place at the front of the formation of kids. She wore a knee brace on the bad leg, and began kicking and stabbing the air, issuing staccato commands to the students. With the lights washing over her, the television cameras rolling, cymbals clashed and drums beat. Dany then switched gears and began directing the two young boys emboweled in the long, writhing unicorn costume. They danced up against a swarm of big-eyed kids, swirling the unicorn's fuzzy and colorful head in dizzying circles. Against this *mise en scène* of dance, music and a commune of children, we said our goodbyes, looking back at a merry vision of a socialist utopia, heralded by these angels of revolution.

Only a few months later, I received an e-mail from Mado telling me that on April 18, 2003, Dany had been expelled from the Vietnamese Communist Party. A similar Party resolution was passed against Mado, but the ruling committee overruled it for the time being. Their crime was to believe in and wholeheartedly embrace the social equalities promulgated by the Party, leading them to speak publicly against the endemic corruption within the government—the "Saigon Mafia" and their old enemies from Con Son Island.

The voice in Mado's correspondence was as ever direct and unwavering, "The fact is that the communist doctrine is fair, but the people in power, who proclaim to be Party members, just implement the doctrine for their own profits... We are now out of a clique that is playing a confidence trick on the people and exploiting and stealing their labor."

On April 30, National Liberation Day, less than two weeks after the resolution of expulsion, Dany and Mado were featured on the covers of two popular Saigon magazines—*Ho Chi Minh Women* and *Family Knowledge*. They are heroes because they refuse to be like all the rest.

The Ghosts of
Old Friends

Built by the colonial French, the *Transindochinois* is a 1,000-mile railway connecting Hanoi and Saigon. Its route links Vietnam's two rice bowls, the Red River Basin and the Mekong Delta. After 33 years of construction, the final stake was hammered in 1936 at Thuy Hoa, in an inauguration attended by Bao Dai and French officials. "By law, every bolt and rail came from France; by custom, every drop of sweat from Vietnam," wrote David Lamb in *Vietnam Now*.

In 1942, only six years after its completion, and while Vietnam was occupied by the Japanese during World War II, the railway was blown up in many places by an unlikely tandem of Ho Chi Minh's Vietminh soldiers and American bombers. The destruction was renewed during the American war. After liberation it was rebuilt and re-inaugurated on December 31, 1976 as the Reunification Express. On a map the ribbon of rail looks like a carpenter's string, nudging the rocky jags and sandy indentations of Vietnam's coastline, ready to snap this geography into alignment.

For buffs of train travel, the railway provides the southern link to an international rail system spanning over 10,000 miles, crossing China, Mongolia, Russia and branching out all over Europe. Piecing together three train journeys, I have traveled from Saigon to the Hook-of-Holland, ferried across the English Channel, and lurched on into London's Victoria Station.

On my first journey aboard the Reunification Express I shared a six-bed cabin with a family of eight Vietnamese *nha que*, better known as country folk in my southern vernacular. Together, we spent 33 intimate hours in a Romanian-built sleeping car riding the clanking cast-iron spans from Saigon to Hanoi. Mindful of my creaky back, I reserved the bottom bunk. The cabin had three bunks on either side of a spacious window protected from rock throwers by a wire screen. When not sleeping, my cabin mates would descend to floor level and crowd onto my bunk and the one opposite, where a mother roosted with her two-year-old baby boy, the focus of everyone's affections.

With only basic pleasantries in my Vietnamese repertoire, I smiled and laughed a lot, like some autistic interloper, making funny faces and hand gestures to show I was tuned in at some level. We shared bags of pumpkin seeds, peanut brittle and a thermos of hot water for green tea. Rather than go to the metallic hole-in-the-floor toilet a few doors down, the young mama allowed the baby to pee on the cabin floor, which she cleaned up sooner or later. I stepped barefooted into a puddle about 10 hours into the trip, sometime in the early morning around Quinhon. When I looked around in disgust, mama smiled and pointed to the cute little boy, shorthand for "It's only baby piss."

Grandma slept in the bunk above me, traditional in black trousers, a matching velvet jacket, a rolled disk of black cloth flanging her bundled hair, and a crimson-stained crease for a mouth. Her teeth were mere nubs turned black from a life of betel-nut chewing. During the day, when not standing in the aisle watching the scenery scroll by, she sat at the end of my bed chewing, from time to time depositing her spittle on the floor.

Just after our stop in Danang, a cabin girl with a rolling cart served lunch, a tin tray of bony chicken parts, rice and fried morning glory. Trying to corral her cute little critter, mama spilled her tray all over my bare feet. With her bare hands, she quickly cleaned the greens from between my toes. After reconstituting the TV tray, she passed it to one of the family members for lunch.

As the Reunification Express was arriving in Hanoi, the public address system played what was supposed to be a bilingual farewell message. Instead we got a garbled departure salutation: "Welcome aboard. We are now leaving Hanoi… Reunification is groovy… American B-52s tried to stop us… and the glorious Revolution triumphed in the end." Leaving the cabin hopelessly littered like the aftermath of a picnic in a public toilet, I gave the little boy his first bag of peanut M&Ms and said a warm adieu to all. They waited in the cabin for relatives to arrive and help them unload.

My trip with Simon would not be so packed with cultural excitement. We were able to get a cabin in one of the new air-conditioned cars, equipped with four beds instead of six, a fresh clean, white duvet for each, and Western flush toilets two doors down. As the Reunification Express ground northward out of Saigon, Simon and I settled into our bottom bunks, at the same time introducing ourselves to Nicholas, a gregarious French lawyer and Diep, a mechanical engineer living in Saigon and eager-beaver when it came to practicing his English. The cabin attendant came by punching tickets, noticed Simon and Nicholas were smoking, and exiled them to the accordion interstices between cars. We chatted and read until midnight, then shut out the lights and locked the vault-like door.

With the colonial spans clanking out a backbeat, night was a rolling ballet. We rocked from side-to-side on uneven parallel rails or caught a level stretch to glissade at seemingly high speeds. The periodic pauses were preceded by raucous crescendoes of screeching wheels. At some point it all became monotonous, inducing sleep.

We were near Quinhon by the time dawn broke, revealing for most of the way into Danang a ticker tape of recurring scenery—coffee-brown rivers, flooded fields of emerald green, periodic glimpses of the South China Sea, and the coastal conurbation of villages succeeding villages, until settlements reached critical mass in cities such as Quang Ngai, Chu Lai and Tam Ky. After steaming past the shallow lagoons of Sa Huynh, a crystalline grid of desiccated salt pools, one of the main sources of salt in Vietnam, we crossed the Tra Khuc River on the northern verges of Quang Ngai, near the turnoff for the once sleepy and unknown village of My Lai.

On March 16, 1968—that memorable year—a rogue platoon leader, Lieutenant William Calley, and his men stormed the village of My Lai, massacring 504 innocent women, children and old men. Evoking the worst face of war, My Lai is now a well-tended memorial site.

In 1998, I attended the premiere in Hanoi of a documentary film, *The Sound of the Violin in My Lai*. The award-winning Vietnamese film was funded by the Madison Quakers—an American church NGO doing humanitarian work in Vietnam during and since the war—and inspired by a veteran friend named Mike Boehm, who returned to Vietnam in 1992 and played

Taps on his violin at My Lai as an offering to the spirits of the dead. I watched the film with an audience mostly of Vietnamese, peppered with a few Americans. After it was shown, there were many emotion-packed speeches delivered by Vietnamese veterans condemning the United States. At times the speeches turned to rants, giving a hostile edge to the otherwise conciliatory packed room.

Into this line of rapid fire, the American Ambassador, Pete Peterson, a former pilot and POW for six years, took the podium. He visibly transformed from a diplomat apologizing for the slaughter of innocents at My Lai, to a defensive colonel explaining the realities of combat and shifting the odium of war to all parties who participate. He explained: "At My Lai and many other places, a handful of soldiers crossed that fine, often blurry, line that separates the heroics of disciplined combatants from the descent-into-madness barbarism of a hair-triggered few." War is a place where "paranoia and schizophrenia are valid versions of reality."

Another four hours beyond the My Lai turnoff, the train stopped in Danang with a screech and hiss, just around noon. Clearing the station in moments, we shared a taxi with Nicholas, the French lawyer, for the hour's drive to Hoi An. We agreed to skip Marble Mountain, a former VC redoubt that bedeviled the U.S. Marines stationed nearby, and a cave network honeycombed with ancient Hindu and Buddhist worship sites. Marble is quarried there now, and cast and carved into a range of miniature-to-colossal figurines, fountains and other follies. It's a magnet for shopping tourists.

Simon directed the cabby to a favorite guesthouse, built pagoda-style with an upward-turning roof like the fore and aft of a Chinese scow. My room suggested the interior of a lacquer box: the walls, wardrobes and beds all made of glazed wood and inlaid in mother-of-pearl with images of peacocks on tree limbs, cranes in the rushes, swans mating, and maidens idling in a bamboo forest. Turned inside out, the room might stand as an artistic mirror of the prim and well-painted medieval city of Hoi An.

At the mouth of the Thu Bon River, Hoi An was, for many centuries, a busy entrepot for European and Asian traders. It became a major hub after the Vietnamese ousted the Chams there in the 15th century, and welcomed merchants from Japan, China, Portugal, Holland and France. The foreigners set up their own neighborhood "colonies," trading in silk, porcelain, lacquer, ivory, and herbal medicines. The Thu Bon River silted up in the latter part of the 18th century, damning Hoi An's commerce. Today it is a Mecca of 18th-century temples, assembly houses and homes, with a population including some 15,000 ethnic Chinese.

The laid-back ambiance of Hoi An begs visitors to slacken their pace and savor every detail. Simon and I walked down Loi Street, with its silk shops, art galleries, and streetside cafes. Dovish hawkers trilled hellos as we passed. Aging European tourists donned peasant hats, mingling with a jamboree of Pancakers in the shops and restaurants. The Pancakers here inevitably swap their frayed pantaloons for newly tailored Capri pants. For custom-made clothes, Hoi An is a poor man's Hong Kong.

Many of the restaurants specialized in Hoi An's signature dish—*cao lau*—a bowl of doughy noodles topped with shreds of pork, leafy greens and fried croutons. A rainbow of Chinese lanterns hung on clothes trees adorning the shop fronts, looking like outsized Christmas ornaments. The air was perfumed with sandalwood. Turning along the river in the trembling shadows of kerosene lamps, we joined Nicholas on the waterfront at the Café des Amis.

Mr. Kim, the proprietor, pretended to recognize us and showed us to a table on the upstairs balcony. As was my custom at Café des Amis, I asked Mr. Kim to play one of his scratchy old Edith Piaf LPs on his equally antiquated phonograph. For me, the *chanteuse* is a sometime taste, but for Kim she is a passion. Following a painful screech of static, we soon basked in the sounds of old *Indochine,* the diminutive French Resistance singer belting out her operatic strains. Not knowing French, Simon and I imagined her ballads must be a bit like those by Bob Dylan.

Waxing nostalgic with Nicholas about the common thread of Vietnam that links France and America forever in an unlikely cultural tripartite, we dined on Mr. Kim's Franco-Vietnamese cuisine of crabs, whitefish, and shrimp, washed down with a bottle of cheap French wine. Joining us, six fat geckos fanned out from the overhead light like spokes on a wagon wheel, feasting on the bugs drawn there.

In a scene recalling a sepia-colored *daguerreotype*, Piaf's voice flowed out into night, our thoughts trailing along. We watched sampans loading bicycles and commuters headed for villages across the river. Materializing from the river's darkness, an old woman paddled a skinny pirogue, cutting the surface with the grace and glide of a rowing team. Two scruffy curs fornicated in the light dancing from a lantern at a table of foreigners dining *al fresco*.

As the French songs trembled down the street, a bit of agony finally broke through Nicholas's usual reserve: "Why do you like her? The music is really terrible. It's simple French. I love you, I love you—that's all she sings. It's nauseating."

"You don't know what you are missing," Simon told the Frenchman, clinging to his own romantic notions of the songs.

We walked back to the guesthouse through the hooker-free streets of the historical district where Simon admired a painting he would later purchase—his first ever. The next morning, I traced the footsteps of a former trip to Hoi An, entranced once again by the lyrical architectural language of Hoi An.

Much of Hoi An's history and special culture can be found along the medieval Tran Phu Street with its many Chinese assembly halls and temples. Their stylized yin and yang tile roofs represent a universe in balance with swirling dragons, symbols of the king, facing the "pearl of prosperity," the iconic fulcrum of life. Many of the courtyards were badged with the sacred frangipani tree, frosted in a nosegay of fresh white blooms. Traditional gardens featured gnarly mountainscapes of rocks bulging from pools of golden carp. Fat columns hewn of ironwood and jackfruit lined the temples coated in a fresh lacquer of sticky, candy-apple red. Joss sticks spiralled ribbons of smoke from the altars as devotees genuflected to a rainbow of demigods and gods. The peal of bells and the quavering of gongs punctuated the stillness. It was the first day of the lunar month, an auspicious day to visit temples.

On the western end of Tran Phu Street was the covered Japanese bridge, known as Chua Cau by the locals. Originally built in 1593 to connect the Chinese and Japanese colonies living in Hoi An, it has been destroyed by floods and fire and rebuilt many times. Constructed of heavy timbers, the covered bridge was washed in a dull pink like the spans over a moat in a fairy tale. Guarded by a couple of carved monkeys on one end, and a duo of dogs on the other, the animals are believed to represent the birth year of the rulers in Japan when the bridge was started and finished. Adjoining the bridge on one side was a Chinese temple, which housed the image of a Tao god to placate the monsters of natural disaster that have haunted the bridge.

The central market, located quayside near the Café des Amis, was shaded in a tattered patchwork of plastic, breached by angles of glistening light. Crinkle-faced market ladies perched on tables. With their scales to one side, they intoned the mantras of the market. Like wizened goddesses, they held court in a garden of plenty.

Nearby fishing smacks unloaded their daily catch. Faceless fishwives in a jabbering sprawl of palm-leaf hats sorted and haggled and weighed and sliced. They winnowed basket upon basket of cockle-sized snails to be sold later on the street cooked in red chilies and onions. They came and went in their smacks, coracles and pirogues.

I took a scenic bike ride out to Cua Dai beach, three or four miles to the east of the old town. If you survived the gauntlet of terrorists who rent beach chairs and sell food, the beach was beautiful, and there were many solitary spots. A few distant islands rose from the turquoise seas and fishing boats trolled the waters.

Where all the Europeans were sun-bathing, six bonzes sat in a neat row—in an attitude of "see no evil, hear no evil, speak no evil." The bonzes were heavily clothed in gray habits and brown robes, their heads covered in knitted brown stocking hats. Three of them wore shades. In their direct line of sight, by no coincidence, lay several skimpily clad European women in thong bikinis, baring in turn their pasty breasts and cheeky derrieres. Normally this would be a juxtaposition to cry cultural insensitivity about. I am not sure who got taken advantage of, though. The young bonzes had much to meditate upon.

In the late afternoon, I hired a boat to take me to the estuary of the Thu

Bon River—it's a two-to-three-hour journey. Five trawlers in various stages of completion sat in a boat yard along the way. Farther along, the shores were dotted with fishing villages and wrapped in loamy fields of golden corn. Stands of areca nut trees segued into balmy lines of lilting casuarinas and feathery marshes of palm. The channel was stabbed with bamboo poles hoisting nylon fish traps the size of trapeze nets. Once the current subsided, the traps would be lowered. As far as the eye could see, the nets were suspended above the glassy water like diaphanous clouds of saffron and red. The hasty tropical sun turned golden, a signal for work to begin. A flurry of fishing boats sliced the water. Their bows were glazed with black-and-white eyes. Silhouettes of women and children lined the shore, waving goodbye for the night.

One of my first memories was of the day in April 1955 when my family arrived in Fort Smith, Arkansas. The day was memorable because Jackie Gilker and his brother were in our garage climbing the rafters before we had time to unload the car. They lived three doors down. Jackie always played hard. Even when we were adolescents, his cheeks were always crimson, as if smeared with rouge. His energy and zest for life seemed to exceed all others.

The mountainous area around Danang has historically registered some of the highest temperatures in Vietnam. In June 1969, there were three days straight when the mercury blasted over 120 degrees. Phillip Caputo, in his eloquent memoir on Vietnam, wrote of that heat, "Numbers can no more express the intensity of that heat than the reading on a barometer can express the destructive power of a typhoon. The only valid measurement was what the heat could do to a man, what it could do to him was simple enough: it could kill him, bake his brains, or wring the sweat out of him until he dropped from exhaustion."

And that is exactly what it did to my childhood friend and drinking buddy, Jackie Gilker, who had also been my wife's high school sweetheart. After those three days of heat wave in June 1969, Jackie fell over dead of heat exhaustion, less than two weeks after coming to Vietnam. He had been in the marines a mere six months—the same time I had been in the army. The disbelief among friends and family was such that his father hired a lawyer and team of investigators to look into what appeared to be dubious circumstances surrounding his death. They came to Danang looking for foul play, and left convinced that the only culprit was the foul heat of the place.

Since moving to Vietnam, I have been to Danang many times, and each visit I am nagged by a sense of the absurdity of Jackie's fate. It seemed so preventable. On the other hand, they weren't doctors; they were young foot soldiers doing what they were told. Fiery red cheeks, is my memory of my friend Jackie.

On a trip in 1998, I took Highway 14 out of Danang and headed southwest to Kham Duc. From there I struck south to the Central Highland cities of Kontom and Pleiku. Travel in the area was forbidden until about 10 years ago, and was restricted again after 2001 because of anti-government riots in the highlands.

I hired a crafty and highly intelligent guide in Danang named Mau, who seemed to know a lot about tribal people. For five days, he told me many tales. The thorns and petals of his life story formed a dubious bouquet, however. His education was French. As a first lieutenant in the ARVN (Army of the Republic of Vietnam), he became a war hero. His dad and brother were VC around Danang, and he sold dope to the American marines to supplement his paltry soldier's pay. (It was a trade he still plied, judging from his attempt to sell some to me.)

After deserting first, then surrendering at Danang on April 29, 1975, he was sent to a re-education camp near Kham Duc. His story was familiar from similar accounts I had heard from at least one other former lieutenant imprisoned there. For the first several days he was denied food and told to pray to his higher being for it. He closed his eyes and prayed, but still there was no food. After several days of that exercise, he was told to try praying to Ho Chi Minh. Which he did, and it worked. He got a few cups of rice a day, and rodents and snake for protein. Then after two years of back-breaking labor, his mind was finally deemed right.

Once released, he worked as a woodcutter and a *cyclo* driver. When tourism took off in the late 1980s, he found a job using his language skills. He now dresses Western—hiking boots and a khaki vest—and has a wife, two children plus a girlfriend in every village. He showed me pictures of his 22 year-old son in the uniform of the Vietnamese army. On at least three occasions he asked if I were military or CIA. Not that it matters to me, but my guess is during the war he wore black pajamas at night, and that today he reports to the internal security department of the Ministry of Interior in Danang.

About 20 miles out of Danang the road turned to dirt, giving a dusty patina to the broadleaf tobacco fields and palisades of drying leaves. The tobacco fields soon gave way to hillsides of pineapple and hollows of peanut patches. Reappearing like an old friend was a single lane of macadam, the raised bedrock used by the French, as we traced the murky meander of the Nuoc My River.

We passed through several villages of Cotu, an ethnic minority group of almost 40,000 people who inhabit the area all the way to the Lao frontier. Other than their darker skin, and the occasional woman wrapped in a traditional dress encrusted with years of soil, only a few tribal traditions distinguish the Cotu from the Kinh (ethnic Vietnamese) settlers. Several older women we passed chomped on cigar-sized cheroots or puffed on pipes. Hewing to their patrilineal culture, the wealthier among the relatively impoverished Cotu men become polygamists. They also follow the practice of wife inheritance, or levirate—when the husband dies, the widow marries one of his brothers—also a practice among some biblical people.

One 30-mile stretch took us four hours, mostly passing through primary forest dappled in flowering shades of yellow, white and orange. At times the road plunged under waterfalls, providing a natural car wash. Straight-as-a-string columns of teak rose up the opposing embankment between glistening fan palms and tightly-webbed foliage. The occasional canoe crossed the river below. Guinea fowl took the point in skittering advances.

Wearied young men, woodcutters, collapsed to rest beneath heaps of rattan in mobile camps on the roadside. With a couple of tents, a plastic tarp, and a fire ring for cooking, they had spent weeks in the forest with their scythe-like blades cutting and stripping the climbing palms. Trucks came by every few days to haul the rattan to one of the factory villages to be woven into baskets or furniture.

The valley widened, and the forest thinned. We turned off the tarmac up a dirt road into an Ede village, a collection of huts that looked more like chicken houses. People here were poorer than the dirt that clung to their skin. The kids were bloated with malnourished bellies, their arms hanging like fragile toothpicks. The women wore vacant stares and picked lice from their matted hair. As did the kids, they took fright at me—the furry bogeyman—and hurried into their earthen-floor hovels beyond my gaze. The men could not be seen, but I heard their drunken roars coming from a cluster of huts. Other than their language and poverty, their culture seemed to have nothing left—no stilted, boat-shaped homes, no traditional dress. The climax of modern civilization in this village was a decrepit Russian motorcycle.

Numbering about 200,000, the Ede are generally found farther to the south in Dac Lac province. Like many of the ethnic minorities in the central highlands, the Ede have been moved into settlements near the main roads, similar to Indian reservations in America. The government wants the minorities out of the frontier areas where the police and military don't have as much control. Much of the arable frontier land has been given to the Kinh, or Vietnamese. It's not a new policy, though. Every regime, North and South—colonial, catholic, or communist—has treated tribal lands as unclaimed territory.

Within moments of arriving in Kham Duc, I met a German doctor who had arrived the same day to do medical exams and pass out medication in several minority villages. She was happy to see me, the only other expatriate in the village. I immediately inquired about the hopeless condition of the *Ede* village I had visited a few hours before. She said that over 40 percent of the ethnic minorities in the area were technically malnourished, surviving on 2,000 calories or less a day. "They have the food. They just don't know the right combinations to eat each day," she said. I had been told the same thing in rural Cambodia, not so far from Kham Duc. Local aid workers had to take the tribal women to the markets and point out the ingredients for a proper diet. "Only about one percent are acutely malnourished," she added.

While we visited for a half hour, the policeman who owned the guesthouse moved six Vietnamese out of a mosquito-infested room and gave it to me. A trail of chirping followed them as they disappeared. A low-slung fog rolled into the town, and the German woman left to have dinner with local health officials. As darkness set in, the streets echoed with faceless voices and the grinding din of invisible vehicles.

Mau had been drinking with the district policeman and guesthouse proprietor since our arrival. With the usual persistence of drinking Vietnamese men, they persuaded me to join them for some local rice whiskey, a potent brown-to-black concoction full of floating detritus—something to rub on a horse. It had a fiery kick, getting no smoother on the second, third and fourth drinks. With more remedies in their libations than a room full of Chinese teamakers, they assured me that the unidentified particles were healing herbs and libido stimulants—that even though the drink left me cross-eyed, I would now be well fortified to have five rounds of sex. Returning to my room, it took me five minutes and a flashlight to get my key in the lock. I fell onto my bed without negotiating the mosquito net into position. The bugs could have a drink, too.

Before 1963, Kham Duc was a market town for *montagnards*. Because of the village's proximity to the Laotian and Cambodian frontier—Indian country as Americans called the area—the 5th Special Forces opened a camp there in September 1963. Kham Duc was used as a launching point for mobile strike forces and observation teams that secretly operated in the panhandle of Laos—the Ho Chi Minh Trail was their target. The camp was overrun in May of 1968 in the second wave of the Tet Offensive. It proved to be one of the most costly battles of the Vietnam War.

A Vietnamese-American friend of mine in Hanoi, Do Van Du, worked with the 5th Special Forces and *montagnards* in the area south of Kham Duc during the second wave of Tet. The 5th Special forces became famous from Barry Sadler's song *Ballad of the Green Beret*, the number one hit in the United States in 1966, as "fighting soldiers from the sky."

The Special Forces recruited Du as a combat interpreter when he was 13-years-old. He was one of the CIDGs—Civilian Irregular Defense Group—a fighting force consisting mostly of *montagnards*. When I asked him how he learned to speak English, he said it was simple: "In the seventh grade I learned by listening to the Beatles and Herman's Hermits over and over, and then talking to the Green Berets."

As a child warrior he worked alongside 12-year old *montagnards* who carried heavy M-1 rifles. "We were used by the Green Berets as bait to make contact with the VC along the Ho Chi Minh Trail," he said in a thoughtful, soft voice, "Then they would call in the artillery, air support and infantry, and the Green Berets would disappear to make new contacts. You know, Phil, you remember Barry Sadler's song, '100 men will die today but only two were the Green Beret.'"

In August 1968, Du was leading an American lieutenant on an observation mission when they were hit by RPG fire, vaporizing the Green Beret and leaving Du with a mangled arm and leg. After Du was airlifted to the 93rd Evacuation Hospital at Long Binh, his left arm and right leg were amputated. He was 15, a combat veteran of two years, and a few months older than Dany when she was thrown into the Tiger Cages.

Blessed with a resourceful mind, Du made his way to the States in 1971, sponsored by a host family in Seattle. He even joined other American Vietnam vets in the anti-war protests of the early 1970s, going to churches and pleading with them to quit supporting the war.

Unfortunately he couldn't join where it counts—neither Du nor any other Indochinese who fought for the Americans receives any veteran benefits. He did, however, eventually earn a college degree and became a part of the information technology boom of the 1980s and 1990s.

Returning to Vietnam for the first time in 1988, he helped to establish the first prosthetics center in Hanoi. Although he considers himself an American, he longed to return home to promote reconciliation and help the disabled. Retaining his American citizenship, in 2002, he moved to Hanoi to start a new life. He married a girl from Ninh Binh province.

Soon he was working with several bilateral funding agencies to open an information technology resource center—on a university scale—for the disabled. To the extent he can, he also pulls money from his own pockets.

Du doesn't have room in his life for dwelling on negative feelings, and is still in touch with several of his old friends, the Green Berets. As he told me one night back in Hanoi over drinks, "The wounds heal, but the scars are always there."

Mau and I left shortly after daybreak on the short but slow road to Kontum. In the early going, the road dwindled and highway became a euphemism for buffalo trail. Mau said there was a Five-Year Plan in place to repair the road—the socialist prescription for everything that needs to be fixed. The road was flanked on the west side by a steep ridgeline, forming a natural border between Vietnam and Laos. Easterly it was verdant rain forest and the wilds of the Dak Po Ko River valley.

Rivulets poured down the cliff-sides in frothy cascades. The forest was thick with old teak trees, dew-laden ferns, palms, and flowering lianas. A fog hung over the valley and a heavy hush pervaded, cracked only by the faint warble of birds. Until recently, the valley was home to herds of wild elephants and an abundance of tigers, who are now almost extinct.

The valley widened, and the old-growth jungle disappeared as we passed through a short stretch of pine forest. After that, a succession of scalped mountains, brush-stroked in vertical swaths of washed brown, receded into the misty skies. The barren-earth landscape was probably the result of Agent Orange, the carcinogenic chemical defoliant used by the Americans to expose much of the Ho Chi Minh Trail and other VC forest hideouts.

Near the village of Ngoc Hoi, the borders of Laos, Cambodia and Vietnam imperceptibly came together. Deemed a high-security zone because of cross-border hill tribe activities, there is no chance of a foreigner legally going to the eye of the triangle. As the day grew long, fields of coffee trees wilted in the punishing sun. We stopped at a battle site near Dak To where a white monument served as a tally sheet—1,500 Americans and ARVN killed and no NVA or VC, a typical presentation of war statistics at memorials across Vietnam.

Those stats didn't exactly wash with Tuck Freeman, who engaged in several battles near Dak To as a member of the 1st Air Cav's reactionary force. In April of 1968, he even took a shrapnel hit to the face in a battle near Dak To.

Although he was uncomfortable discussing enemy body counts, his silence implied many. He did, however, tell me about cleaning enemy corpses around Dak To of their money, marijuana and opium.

As we approached Kontum the rolling hills were mantled with thousands of acres of neatly lined rubber trees on state-owned plantations. The ancient *montagnard* enclave of Kontum is crossed with a couple of boulevard-like streets, with modern streetlights and the pulse of a commercial center. The French missionaries apparently enjoyed great successes in the Central Highlands with the hill tribes.

On Nyugen Hue Street, in the town's otherwise dusty environs, was the Tan Huong Church, built by the French in the early part of the 20th century. On a landscape of palm trees, the stucco church was washed in peach and trimmed in white, evoking South Florida. The arched tile roof was crested with a bell tower bookended in the embossed images of St. George and the Dragon on one side and on the other, a traveling mendicant and horse.

On the same road was the Wooden Church, an expansive, mauve-colored chapel elevated on stilts. It was fronted by a couple of flagpole-sized totems, ornamented in colorful stylized carvings and strung with red streamers. At celebrations when there are buffalo stabbings, the animals are hitched to the base of the totem pole for slaughter.

A typical *Ba-na* communal house, or *rung* house, stood to the right of the church, a wooden A-frame on stilts scored in the tribe's signature carvings. The *rung* house is the cultural center for the *Ba-na*. Traditionally it was used for single men to gather prior to a big hunt or major battle. Now it hosts village meetings, weddings and judicial proceedings.

The next morning, I hired a local guide named Huynh to accompany me and Mau to a *Ba-na* village, Plei Chot. Once there, we walked directly to a stilted home near the perimeter, beyond which a holy mountain stood in hazy relief. We were at the home of an important village elder who had died two days before. Preparations were underway for the funeral later in the day. The ceremony was an expensive undertaking for an impoverished family and village, yet it would be sacrilege to do anything less for an ancestor. Two notched tree trunks leaned against the stilted porch as ladders. Blank stares came from the many destitute faces packing the porch. The corpse lay just inside the door.

On the earthen front yard, a flowered pavilion of bamboo was being raised to house the coffin. Nearby, two woodcutters with machetes chipped away at a tree trunk, hulling it out for a pirogue-styled coffin. The tree trunk appeared to be too narrow a fit for the flattened corpse. When asked by Huynh about the dimensions, the coffin makers explained that they couldn't find a bigger tree. The corpse would have to begin his pirogue journey to the afterlife by squeezing in sidelong. With that disclosure, the mood was lightened as a ripple of laughter flowed around us. Most of the village had gathered by then.

Meanwhile, two guys with wooden clubs had a scrawny cow tethered to a 10-foot mast. After several glancing shots, one of the two scored a direct head shot. The legs buckled, and the cow fell listlessly to the ground. It wasn't dead. That would take a while. As in a traditional buffalo stabbing, it is customary and respectful to let the creature die slowly—to awaken the friendly animist spirits of *yang* with the animal's moaning death cries.

Another man arrived with two pigs, clubbed them unconscious and kicked them into the flames. The fire cracked and popped as it slowly singed the pigs black, and they quit moving. Someone threw two chickens on.

Two women armed with long pestles pulverized banana stalks in a half-barrel-sized wooden mortar. The banana mush would be mixed with the fresh-cooked pork. Hyena-like dogs scoured the parched ground in packs of two and three, following some scent as they darted about. Men sat on a porch across the way consuming fermented cassava out of a shared clay vessel, drinking through long bamboo straws, like a communal hookah.

After a period of seven years, or an otherwise suitable interval, a much grander celebration will occur—an abandoning ceremony, giving up the tomb. The festive ritual may last three days, with dancing, music and a buffalo stabbing. Friends and families carve wooden statues and a wooden hedge is built around the burial site. The statues are placed around the tomb to watch over the deceased in the afterlife, akin to the mortuary traditions of kings and commoners alike in ancient China.

Once the abandoning celebration has ended, the spirit of the deceased travels to an Elysian Field in back of the nearby holy mountain, Chu Mo Ray, in Cambodia. The tomb is then abandoned and never visited again. The spirit and its guardians have departed.

We crossed the hot and dusty barnyard-like common to a copse of trees that shaded the cemetery. Strangled by weeds and vines, the graveyard had many abandoned tombs. They were all adorned with wooden tutelary statues—a pregnant woman, a disconsolate man squatting and crying, elephant tusks to keep evil spirits in abeyance. Statues of French and American soldiers found their way into the odd mix of afterlife guardians, the most striking of which was Charles de Gaulle dressed in full military regalia. Many of the family tombs were bestrewn with survival kits for the afterlife—lit cigarettes, trays of cassava, fresh water, and mortars and pestles.

The village chief was a hip-looking older man who wore a canary-yellow shirt, puffed on a pipe and sported wrap-around shades. He took us to a long house where several families lived. The notched tree trunk that served as a ladder was facing outward. That meant it was okay to enter. Some 20 cubicles, none larger than three to four feet in width and five feet long, were separated by shallow bamboo partitions. Each living space had an earthen hearth, a bamboo mat, one or two extra garments and a couple of calabashes of water. A husband and wife and their two or three children lived in each cubicle. If there were more children, they might have an extra compartment. The rickety floors were cracked with gaping holes, and below stood tethered buffalo and cattle. The smells of wood smoke and manure clung to everything. When we left, Huynh gave the chief a few packets of medicine for malaria.

On the way back to Kontum, we spotted a man near the road with a metal detector. He was scanning a parched hillside for unexploded ordnance around what was once a forested branch of the Ho Chi Minh Trail. We stopped in a weaving village of the *Y'long*, a sub-tribe of the *Ba-na*, overlooking the wild Dak Bla River. The muddy waterway is known locally as the "fighting river" because of its annual floods and many drownings.

As we walked out of earshot of Mau and the Russian jeep, our guide Huynh began talking in whispers about the *Kinh* who have moved from Hanoi and taken over their land. As we talked on about the tribe's impoverished conditions, I threw a curve at him when I suggested that there might be more money and goods available for barter if the *Ba-na* had fewer children. Two or three instead of five to eight didn't compute. "Where would the workforce come from?" he sputtered. Communism is a redundancy in this ancient agrarian land. Hill tribes have always practiced communal agriculture, beginning with large families.

We drove down to the river and walked through another *Ba-na* village. The stilted huts were framed in bamboo and bedaubed in mud and straw wattle. Nimble-handed fishermen carefully unfurled their nets and hung them on porches to dry. Partly naked women gathered by the river and bathed *en masse*, each with a newborn baby slung on the back. Scattered bevies of pot-bellied kids played, often chewing on stalks of sugar cane. The hyena-like dogs marauded in packs. Kapok and flamboyant trees adorned the riverfront—their boughs tangled boa-like in dragon fruit, like little shrines of plenty.

Farther upriver, along an almost impassable road, was a village home to *Gio-long*, another sub-tribe of the *Ba-na*. Rounding a sweeping parabola of white sand, bamboo rafts—five or six poles slashed together—coursed the water heavily loaded with bundles of rattan. Further downriver, a curvy grid of miniature dikes formed shallow pools in the water's margins. The pools were baited with millet or cassava, which attracted spawning catfish for capture.

The *Gio-long* village was luxuriantly cloaked in banana fronds, buzzing white apricot trees, scarlet poinsettias, papaya trees and coconut palms. A bedraggled army of 50 or 60 men gathered mostly in the shade to raise a new communal house. Waving and caterwauling like drunken steeplejacks, six men hung precariously on its 40-feet-high frame securing the bamboo lattice with straps of rattan. Several men hewed logs into rafters or beams. One man proudly showed me his machete and olive drab sheath stamped "U.S. Army, 1966."

Hemmed in bucolic pathways, their stilted huts each had a granary to one side. Normally they were filled with rice. But now they were half empty, with only small rations of cassava, a less desirable food source. Times were tough.

We returned to Kontum and dropped Huynh at his office, before driving south to Pleiku. Mau quickly apologized for not talking. He didn't trust Huynh and was reluctant to discuss the hill tribes in his presence. Huynh felt the same way about Mau, and they both thought I was in the CIA or military. The endemic paranoia in Vietnam is not surprising in a system that once encouraged children to betray their nonconformist parents. The secret police have long been the hammer used by communist governments to silence dissidents and to sustain power.

Recent protests by local tribes, believed to be incited by guerilla elements of the United Front for the Struggle of Oppressed Races (FULRO), also contributed to the paranoia. FULRO, an old militant group now shrunken in number, was a former ally of the Americans and French. There are many observers who think the U.S. government—or at minimum American-based religious organizations—have a hidden hand in FULRO and the episodic social unrest around Kontum or Pleiku. The area has recently been closed to foreigners.

As far as the eye could see, the highway north of Pleiku was corridored with piles of tarmac-dried cassava. But for the tropical milieu, it looked like the fresh trail of a snowplow. Women chopped and sliced the freshly harvested tubers beneath a motley parasol of shifting peasant hats. Others bagged the dried product while a rapid procession of trucks loaded and hauled it to a district factory. Mau said much of the product would be exported to Japan for tapioca.

Since being torched in 1975, Pleiku has been rebuilt into a nondescript center of commerce for the Central Highlands. It boasts several spacious traffic circles, the usual complement of war monuments, and three or four prominent churches. It was on February 7, 1965 in Pleiku that VC attacked a U.S. base and killed eight Americans, providing the excuse needed for a marine landing at Danang and the formal beginning of the war.

As a tourist destination, if permitted to go there, Pleiku specializes in war tours for American veterans at nearby An Khe. If a tourist fancies the life of a circus stooge, he can lumber through rice fields on the back of an elephant. I took a rain check on all the above and instead toasted an old friend. From a used water bottle filled with rice whiskey, Mau and I hoisted a couple of shots.

The last time I saw Carl Bates—the friend who co-signed my army enlistment papers and advised me to become a clerk like him—was in August 1969. I had gone home on a three-day pass to attend my brother John's wedding. Carl arrived the day of the event. He was wearing his dress greens, and his chest was heavy with medals: the Combat Infantry Badge, the wings of a door gunner, two rows of meritorious ribbons on one side and unit citations on the other. His forehead was bandaged and topped with his peaked dress hat. He was a soldier's soldier.

The undertaker had done the best job possible. The top of Carl's head had been blown off. After receiving a "Dear John" letter, Carl gave up being a clerk and a part-time lifeguard at Cam Ranh Bay. His was a Pavlovian response not of purpose or patriotism, but of wounded pride. He volunteered to be a door gunner with the 57th Assault Helicopter Company, the macho thing to do under the circumstances. It happened northwest of Pleiku—across the border in Laos, the secret war—on August 17th during the annual monsoons. He had only been on a few missions. The crippled chopper he had protected returned from Laos with his corpse to its base near Kontum riddled with over 30 bullet holes. He was dead before he hit the deck.

Mau and I crossed An Khe Pass on Highway 19—classic mountaintop vistas of misty coastal plains, with a serenity and grandeur surpassing any painted landscape. It is true what they say, "Vietnam is a country, not a war." Now.

May 5, 1968

Simon spent the morning in Hoi An retrieving a painting he had previously made a down payment on. Although he has produced thousands of works of art in his life, this was the first time he had actually bought one. In the late afternoon we took a taxi to Danang and visited the Museum of Cham Culture, arguably the finest collection of artifacts in all of Vietnam. With its idyllic views of an estuary of the Han River, the museum's open-air, colonial architecture is as impressive as the collection of Hindu stone carvings.

Known to the French as Tourane, Danang took on an American complexion on March 8, 1965 when two battalions of the 9th Marine Expeditionary Brigade landed on its shores. There were already 23,000 American "advisors" in Vietnam. The addition of 3,500 marines should have seemed insignificant at the time. Their stated purpose was to provide security, not to fight. But instead the landing marked the beginning of direct engagement between American combat units and the VC and NVA. This soon opened the floodgates of war and in three years, over half a million American soldiers were stationed in Indochina. By the end of the war, 10 years later, a total of some 2.5 million GIs had served in Indochina.

Simon and I found rooms in the center of town, loaded up on beer, and went to the airport to pick up John Lancaster, a close friend and former marine now living in Hanoi. It was drizzling. The crowd outside the baggage claim area had disappeared. Through the glass I could see there was no luggage on the conveyor belt but for a wheelchair. John couldn't be far. Soon, from the back of a Ryder-style truck, he was hydraulically lowered to the ground.

He rolled to the exit doors, working his long healthy arms with the easy rhythm of a competition rower. His handsome face was tanned, and he was wearing a baseball cap and olive drab T-shirt, the sporty look that mirrors his off-hours enthusiasms.

"Good to see you Phil… Simon… You all are gentlemen and scholars, and your good looks are exceeded only by your intelligence," he greeted us in his folksy voice and easy-going manner.

"Enough of the bullshit." High-fiving, I gave him a Tiger beer and we loaded into a taxi.

He arrived with a story. The night before in Hanoi he had been watching *Apocalypse Now* on cable television, an unprecedented screening in Vietnam. An hour into the movie, the culture police realized what was happening and scrambled the signal. The *Vietnam News* reported that after the movie was scuttled, many Vietnamese had simply gone to the video store, bought a copy and returned home to finish watching the movie.

"I don't blame the Vietnamese for not wanting to see all their people get killed," John screamed from the back seat, "It's a disturbing movie with Brando sitting there over human waste and splashing water on his face. He tells the story of the Special Ops unit vaccinating children, and then the communists come through and cut their arms off. *That* is the will to win—and *there* is the horror of war."

 John first arrived in Danang to the sound and light show of flares, mortars, and rockets a couple of weeks into the Tet Offensive of 1968. He was one of the first arrivals of the 1st Battalion of the 27th Marines, better known in the aftermath as the Young Bloods for their youthful makeup and heavy casualty rate. Recently commissioned as a second lieutenant, John had been trained to command an infantry platoon and was in Vietnam to have his mettle tested.

John was raised in Hamburg, New York, the first of three children. His father was a lawyer, a loyal Democrat, a good British Catholic and a better gin drinker. On one occasion when his father arrived home on a Friday afternoon, John and his brother were playing basketball on their new asphalt driveway. Dad jumped from the car, happy to see his boys and anxious to get into his weekend martinis, and splattered the bottle of gin on the asphalt. Without hesitation, he said to his boys, "I'd rather see a church burn than lose a good bottle of gin," wheeled back into the car and went for a replacement. John is his father's son.

John was president of the student body at Hamburg High School and a shooting guard on the basketball team. Upon graduation in 1963, John, like his father and one uncle before him, chose to go to Notre Dame—an all-male school then. He was awarded a Naval ROTC scholarship. He was a gifted small-town athlete who worked hard. Once at Notre Dame, he was the last walk-on eliminated for the school's basketball team. So he became a founding member of Notre Dame's first soccer team. A sports enthusiast, but more importantly in the family tradition, a dyed-in-the-wool Notre Dame football fan, he attended all 10 games his senior year.

In 1967, upon graduation from Notre Dame, John went to the Marine Corps' Quantico, Virginia school for basic training of infantry second lieutenants. There he learned everything he needed to know to command an infantry platoon—map reading, orientating, first-aid (making sure his men had healthy feet for walking), radio protocol, weaponry, demolitions, coordinating air attacks, hand-to-hand combat, K-bar maneuvers, and on up the technological ladder to calling in napalm and 500-pound bombs. His infantry training was shortened by a month due to troop demands in Vietnam. After six weeks of language training at Quantico, he shipped out to Vietnam with vague orders to join the 1st Battalion of the 27th Marines.

While stationed at Quantico John met Anne Steuart, a resident of nearby Alexandria, Virginia studying at a women's college in New York. They fell in love and talked about getting married. Anne wanted John to go to Canada, and she would follow him there.

Like most of our generation, John came of age driven by President Kennedy's idealism: "ask what you can do for your country."

Over dinner one night John recounted to me the choices confronting him then at the age of 22. "I was too chicken for Canada. I couldn't face my friends and family. On an emotional level I had Anne, and like most combatants headed for Vietnam, I had fears of being killed. I also had four years and seven months of testosterone-sated training. I wanted to see if I was any good at what I had been trained to do."

"On an intellectual level I believed in the principle of a democratically elected government that controlled the Defense Department—the military. Since I had chosen the Marine Corps as a career, it wasn't up to me to question the institutionalized proxy of the people. I wasn't drafted. I joined."

"Also, on the same intellectual level I was not a rabid anti-communist nor did I think the war in Vietnam was right. I saw it as an internal conflict. I did what my country asked me to do."

I kept his words in mind as we began a week of travel that would take us back into John's past. After dropping off his bag, we crossed the Han River and went south to My Khe Beach, formerly known as China Beach, the marine R&R strip and namesake of an American TV serial shown during the 1980s and 1990s. John loves the seaside vibrancy of Danang, a port city with ancient roots in commerce, and wanted to introduce us to its scenery and cuisine. But for the drizzling rain, kite flyers would have dotted the beach, taking advantage of the serenity and sea breeze in the twilight hours.

We slotted into one of many seafood restaurants lined cheek by jowl down the beach. Speaking in relic snatches of Vietnamese learned at Quantico during the war, and upgraded from two years of living in Hanoi, John ordered a bucket of iced *Larue* beer and a smorgasbord of marine fauna. Two young girls mixed a variety of sauces and served us whitefish soup, grilled squid, peeled jumbo prawns, and a massive plate of barbecued grouper, its head and tail flopped over the ends of the platter.

We talked about the war, and a few of John's lighter experiences on search-and-destroy and ambush missions. Like every foot soldier I have ever known, he talked about the insane vulnerability of a bunch of oversized Americans playing king of the mountain, walking aimlessly around paddies where 80 percent of the people you saw everyday were conspiring in one way or another to kill you at night. Americans were the sore thumbs sticking out. One veteran described it as the war of the flea:

"The flea bites, hops and bites again, nimbly avoiding the foot that would crush him. He does not seek to kill his enemy at a blow, but to bleed him and feed on him, to plague and bedevil him... All this requires time. Still more time is required to breed more fleas... the military enemy suffers the dog's disadvantages: too much to defend; too small and agile an enemy to come to grips with."

On one of John's first trips back to Vietnam in 1996, during a reception at the house of the American Charge de Affairs, John was circled up with General Vinh, the former North Vietnamese commander of troops in I Corps, the northern quadrant of South Vietnam where John had foot-soldiered. It was the site of the heaviest fighting during the war. After lots of wine, speaking through a translator, John talked as one old soldier to another, "We put a lot of firepower on you guys and you won."

For the first time all night, the general spoke in English, "If that had been our army outside of Philadelphia would you have lost?"

"I understand your point," John nodded.

As we discussed over dinner, Philadelphia, Buffalo, Baghdad, or wherever, it all works the same. Clinging to some atavistic memory, people will have their independence.

Only because we were touring through his old stomping grounds was John talking about the war. Otherwise, unless asked, he keeps all that to himself. He told another story which occurred one clear, starlit evening around midnight. John's second platoon of Delta Company was hunkered down for an ambush in the reedy elephant grasses along a narrow river. They had received intelligence reports that a platoon of VC would be crossing the waterway during the night. Sure enough this time just after midnight silhouettes of VC began hitting the water. John whispered down the line for everyone to get ready, but to let the enemy all get out of the water first. Suddenly, out of nowhere a blast from a radio shattered the stillness, "I'm a soul man..." It was Sam and Dave of 1960s' fame, of course. One of John's riflemen had turned the volume switch the wrong way on his hand-held Sony, unleashing the solid gold tunes of Hanoi Hannah, as American GIs used to call the propagandizing deejay at *Radio Hanoi*.

"All hell broke loose. Those VC out there that night owe their lives to Hanoi Hannah. And good for her and better for them," John chuckled and continued. "After a few months in country, I realized all they wanted was a better life for their wives and children and to reunify their country. It made it harder to fight them."

228

Back in Merry Old England around that time, Simon was getting his first taste of the war over "baked beans on toast" as he watched the news on the telly. British kids, like Americans, were glued to the set, learning geography from the war.

"Of course my predominant images of the war were of M-16s cracking through the jungle and shredding trees, helicopter landings and visual aid maps branded with names like Danang, Hue, Saigon and the 17th Parallel."

We departed and Simon directed us to the Bamboo Bar—one in every Asian city—for more Larue beer and Gordon's Gin. Conceived in a city of sailors, soldiers, and fishermen, the riverside Bamboo Bar hosted a rowdy array of expatriates and local hipsters. Loud music wafted through the flimsy walls of bamboo, and the musky scent of marijuana competed with the fishy smell of the Han River lapping beneath the loosely planked flooring. John was feeling the mood, "the tattoo parlors must be nearby; let's have some fun."

After almost closing the place down, we found a couple of *cyclos* for a ride to the hotel. Like bees to honey, half-a-dozen motorcycles surrounded us trying to hive off a piece of our wallets, then followed us to the hotel, where we escaped their sting and said goodnight to Simon. He found the perfect tour guides to explore Danang's buzzing world of prostitutes and late night decadence. A city of over a million people, it was often referred to during the war as the "Saigon of the North." Its reputation was deserved.

The next morning, at the hotel, we hired a driver and his old Mercedes. We wasted no time hitting the pavement toward Hue, forging through the morning crush of Danang traffic. Rumbling up the first ascent of the switchback road to Hai Van Pass, we crossed the Nam O River with a lagoon of hoisted fishnets to the west and an arc of sandy beaches and crashing tides opposite. A convoy of Day-Glo French Renault buses groaned up the mountainside. A similar number of trucks gearing down—honeycombed in bamboo baskets of pigs going to market—screeched their brakes on the steep descent. On the shoulder of the road at each hairpin turn, enterprising truck washers manned gravity-flow hoses that spewed to the sky like geysers.

It was raining and the summit was smothered in clouds. Normally Hai Van Pass provided a view of distant islands and rocky headlands plummeting to the aquamarine sea. Probably because of the rain, the unrelenting hawkers who work the pass had disappeared. French and American bunkers, however, still stood vigil.

John had not been over the pass since March 1968, when his platoon rode shotgun for a supply convoy. They were greeted at the summit with hawkers, too—selling Wonder Bread and Velveeta Cheese sandwiches, compliments of the backdoor trade from the base commissary. The convoy duty was brief. Otherwise John's second platoon operated out of an artillery base camp near Hue. Like true foot soldiers, they pounded the earth by day on search-and-destroy missions, and by night on ambush sorties.

"Except for medical evacuations, marines walked everywhere. The army guys had all the helicopters," he groused.

We rumbled down the mountain, the road intertwining once again with the Reunification Express tracks that had re-appeared from the tunneled innards of Hai Van. At the foot of the mountain, Phu Gia fishing village, one of the most picturesque in Vietnam, looked like it was under flood alert. The village lies at the southern end of the Cau Hai Lagoon, its fertile waters stirred on the edges by angry, breaking waves. Raised on shallow earthen foundations, the homes along the road were all encircled by water, each an island unto itself with pirogues parked on the porches. It was just another day in the life of a rainy season fishing village in Vietnam.

Before entering Hue we passed through Phu Bai and the airport there. Once an American base, concrete bunkers are still scattered through the rice fields. I thought of my childhood friend Tuck Freeman, who took a second shrapnel hit near Phu Bai during Tet Offensive of 1968.

Situated along the banks of the Perfume River, Hue became the capital of Vietnam in 1802 after the Nguyen Dynasty took power and consolidated Vietnam. On the south side of the Perfume, Le Loi Street traces the river. Several elegant French colonial buildings back up like palaces to the water. The National School, attended by Ho Chi Minh, sweetened with the architectural confection of a pagoda, recedes campus-like into a bower of trees. Green lawns pad the riverbanks here and there, peppered with palm trees and carved stone dragons.

Traffic was busy on the waterway: sampans hauled pyramids of sand from a dredging operation upriver; dragon-headed boats carried tourists and locals alike; fishing smacks came upriver from the estuary; and gray, steel-hulled police boats stopped and fished from all vessels that passed.

On the north side of the river was the Dong Ba Market. To the west of the market stood the famous Citadel and the Imperial City, originally built by Gia Long, the first Nguyen emperor. As it loomed next to the river, its solitary flag tower punctured the sky at 130 feet, the highest structure on the north side of the river. Due to the prominent television coverage during Tet of 1968, I stared at the flag flapping in the breeze with the euphoria of spotting a vaguely familiar bird.

During the Tet Offensive, VC kamikazes attempted to raise their flag up the Citadel pole, becoming easy targets for American snipers across the river. But they succeeded in their obsessive mission, and the flag flew for over three weeks before the north side of the river and the Citadel were retaken. After the VC and NVA were driven out of Hue—the scene of the heaviest street fighting during Tet—residents found mass graves where an estimated 3,000 people had been buried, mostly innocents pulled from their homes out of suspicion. No memorials stand for them, but the flag tower remains as a symbol of Viet Cong invincibility.

In a restaurant overlooking Con Hen or Oyster Island, we enjoyed a lunch of Hue's fine imperial cuisine: steamed rice flour cakes with ground shrimp, crab paste noodle soup and beef rolled in *lot* leaves, a nice base for a misty afternoon of drinking and looking at more of Hue's imperial and war-time history.

In 1771, the Tay Son Rebellion, a peasant uprising against the ruling Nguyen clan, caught fire near Quinhon. Like Asian Robin Hoods, the Tay Son brothers led the land-hungry peasants in a bloody free-for-all to rob from the rich and give to the poor. Usually such revolts were a flash in the pan, but this time change swept the country, toppling the Nguyen lords in the south and their Trinh counterparts in the north.

In the heat of the uprising, Prince Nguyen Anh, one of the few surviving Nguyen lords, fled to Thailand where he obtained military assistance from French mercenaries. In 1792, the Tay Son leader who had himself crowned Emperor Quang Trang, suddenly died, leaving a power vacuum.

Nguyen Anh and the French mercenaries quickly capitalized on this and regained control while at the same time ousting an army of Chinese invaders. Nguyen Anh went on to conquer the Khmer Empire of the Mekong Delta. In 1802, as Emperor Gia Long, he unified Vietnam after two centuries of strife and Hue was chosen as the new imperial capital.

To appease the feudal overlords, shaken by their loss of power during the Tay Son uprising, Gia Long returned to a strict Confucian system of mandarinism, even adopting Chinese as the language of the royal court. Thus, Hue took on imperial trappings in a subservient imitation of the Han and Ming Dynasties in China.

A stone's throw across the river from where we were enjoying our imperial rice cakes and *lot* leaves, behind the Citadel, is the palace moat at the South Gate. In 1925, Bao Dai, Vietnam's last emperor, was crowned in the palace at the age of 12.

Over two decades later, in sympathy with the nationalist movement and at the request of Ho Chi Minh, Bao Dai used the palace to abdicate the throne, signaling the official end to the Nguyen Dynasty.

On my first trip to the palace, in 1997, I entered the main gate on the south end of the imperial enclosure, a square of roughly 600 yards of fortified brick wall. To get my bearings, I mounted the stairs above the royal entrance to the airy belvedere, which housed an impressive ceremonial bell and drum on opposite sides. In the binary pull and push cosmology of Taoism, twisted dragons crowned the roof, signifying the power of the king (*yang*), balanced by the irrepressible phoenix, representing the majesty of the queen (*yin*).

The belvedere overlooked the esplanade, artfully landscaped with square ponds of purple and white lily pads. The sacred frangipanis wore their spare coats of winter like hoary antlers of coral. *Kylins*, mythical dew-drinking animals, stood as sentinels of peace on the central corridor, the king's route.

The stone path led to the Thai Hoa Palace, or the Palace of Supreme Harmony, where the emperor's throne was flanked by two bronzed statues of cranes—symbols of wisdom and nobility—standing on the backs of turtles, the image of longevity.

The palace roof was tiled in yellow and paneled in a mural of Robin-egg blue, shell-pink, and swirls of red, that depicted classical Chinese scenes of nature. Every other panel was scored with poems composed by the Nguyen royals in *nom,* the former ideogramic script of the Vietnamese. Bracketed by fire-breathing dragons, the holy calabash, the symbolic source of all sustenance in an agrarian culture, sat center stage on the roofline.

The imperial palace had come full circle—it had undergone a complete makeover since the war, restored to its former grandeur in the mid-1990s for Vietnam's promising tourist industry. Michael Herr, in *Dispatches* describes the ravaged scene from ground zero in March of 1968:

"The Palace grounds had been covered with dozens of dead NVA and the burned-over leavings of three weeks' siege and defense... The large bronze urns were dented beyond restoring, and the rain poured through a hole in the roof of the throne room, soaking the two small thrones where the old Annamese royalty had sat. In the great hall the red lacquer work on the upper walls was badly chipped, and a heavy dust covered everything. The crown of the main gate had collapsed, and in the garden the broken branches of the old cay-dai [frangipani] trees lay like the forms of giant insects seared in a fire, wispy, delicate, dead... once the walls had been taken and the grounds entered, there was no one left inside but the dead. They bobbed in the moat and littered all the approaches. The marines moved in then, and empty ration cans and muddied sheets from the Stars and Stripes were added to the litter. A fat marine had been photographed pissing into the locked-jawed open mouth of a decomposing North Vietnamese soldier."

This history duly discussed, after finishing our imperial cuisine and several beers, we hired a car and driver and struck east from Hue on Highway 552, taking with us a 35-year-old military quadrant map. We were searching for the nearby battle site of May 5, 1968, the beginning of the second wave of the Tet Offensive, where John had been wounded and many other marines and NVA were wounded or killed. On one other occasion, without the aid of maps, John had tried unsuccessfully to find the unmarked battlefield. No other marines of Delta Company, second platoon have returned there since the war.

On the south side of the erstwhile dirt track we crossed a tree-lined canal, which John recognized as a place they had bivouacked and bathed the day before the battle. Motoring along a timeless sweep of sodden paddy field, only three miles out of Hue, we came to a necropolis of mounded burial sites. The tombs were ornate like small pagodas, and gothic like Transylvania in a shroud of mist and white air.

The cemetery was marked on the old military map. We had gone too far, and so turned around and puttered west a few hundred yards. On the left, southward, was a well-trodden dike road—a T-junction—just as the map delineated. We were in the heart of the command post of Delta Company, second platoon's bivouac site on May 5, 1968.

The blink-in-the-road intersection might be called a small hamlet—even a ville in the old days—with a cluster of huts on the north side, fronted by a prominent yellow spirit house, not aligned directly with any of the homes, yet central to the hamlet and battle site. We unloaded across the road from the spirit house, in front of a *bia hoi*, a fresh beer bar, where a snarl of men played pool beneath a makeshift roof in the cold and rain.

We got in under the cover of the *bia hoi*, the rain clinking on its tin roof—it was the monsoon season. As our guidebook, we carried a coffee-table-sized book by Gary Jarvis, *Young Blood, A History of the 1st Battalion, 27th Marines*. John ordered a round of beers for the bar and opened the book to the map section to verify our location. He didn't appear maudlin in the least, only excited, talking rapidly about the details of their encampment that fateful night. And uncharacteristically, he threw cash around like a young marine on R&R at China Beach.

The pool players quit their game and huddled around us. Together we perused the maps. A man in his 50s, wearing an olive drab field jacket and Cossack hat with earflaps, hovered over John and the book. The soldierly-dressed man ran his finger along the map, reading the place names. He then spun and pointed like a weathercock in the directions of two hamlets, Thon An Ha and Ap Su Lo.

As the map read, the two hamlets bookended the battle site to the northeast and southwest, respectively. A bundled old woman in her 70s, the proprietoress, sitting away from us, smiled and nodded in agreement. John gave her 200,000 dong ($14) for that smile and for a passing moment wanted to donate the war history book to her *bia hoi*. He even started to take off his commemorative t-shirt from a Marine Corps reunion and give it to her. Instead, Simon suggested endowing the spirit house across the road with dragon fruit and rice whiskey for the next 10 years.

After toasting the fallen ones—compatriots and comrades alike—with several Huda beers, John trundled out the dike road. Two water buffalo parted a clump of flooded bamboo, their musk trailing them like an invisible cloud. Alone, wearing his blue rain jacket and beige baseball cap etched with the logo Disability Forum, he surveyed the puddled paddy fields to the west, where he had taken his last steps, and friends and foes had perished.

Thirty-five years before, Delta Company's second platoon had spent weeks sweeping the area, setting up a defensive perimeter many times at the dike-road intersection of Highway 552. Fighting in the area was so intense that most of the villages were abandoned. Ominously only a few old ladies remained behind, refusing to pack up and run. Other than rice paddies, there was nothing strategic about the place. In 1968, it was just an arbitrary patch of parched earth, to be abandoned when the fight was over.

May 4th had been another sweltering day, and everyone was dehydrated, hungry and slack with fatigue. Long bleary-eyed days had been spent staring at the ground in fear of mines or booby traps, and into the bush for the twitch of a branch, the glimmer of a sniper. The NVA had been pinging at them for days. Intelligence reports, however, foretold not the bite of a flea but a major offensive. Americans may have ruled the day, but the dark of night belonged to the VC-NVA.

That day, as the punishing sun stole away and darkness scattered across the bleak landscape, the second platoon along with two battalion mortar and ONTOS teams, dug into the parched earth. Captain Kahler, the Delta Company commander, presciently prearranged coordinates for artillery fire.

John worked the perimeter, coordinating fields of fire, defensive positions and spreading word to the marines to sleep in shifts.

Two hundred yards beyond the northeast quadrant of the perimeter, near the necropolis, three 18-year-olds —PFCs Davis, Carattini and Jarvis— manned the listening post. It was after midnight, and the temperature had dropped as the day's heat rose into the starlit sky. Out of the dim glow, Davis spotted several crouched silhouettes moving in and around the mounded burial sites. His pulse quickening, he alerted Jarvis and Carattini and then shouted back to the perimeter for Gunnery Sergeant Dobson, who bid him to call out for a password to the ever-amassing collection of crouched figures. Mute silence followed his call. The gun-wagging shadows drew closer and more numerous by the second, the kind of tension that locks the throat. Praying for their lives, the three PFCs frantically called back to the perimeter for illumination.

Two-way radios crackled with instructions, which spread through the encampment like the harsh warning calls of awakened birds. John meanwhile had been radioed about the enemy movement. He woke the marines along the southern and eastern perimeter, getting them into position. Everyone hastily limbered their nerves in an exercise of clinking metal... magazines inserted, rounds chambered and safeties off. Fear begets discipline. Once illumination occurred, all hell would break loose.

Also apprised was Captain Kahler, who had ordered the 81mm mortars directed at the area of enemy movement. Captain Kahler wore the commanding rank, but more importantly he exuded the silent, physical courage of someone who knew how to hold ground, if indeed it could be held.

Hearing the distressed cries for help from the listening post of the three PFCs, Corporal Greer, their squad leader and second-combat tour veteran, braved the open field and joined them. Having failed to dig foxholes, they all positioned themselves up against a shallow paddy berm. Greer, carrying an M-79 grenade launcher, let go of a star cluster illumination round. It turned the metallic sky into a bright orange glow. While exposing the enemy position, the thump of the grenade launcher and the muzzle flash had also revealed Greer's location.

Showered by a hail of mortars, rockets, automatic weapons and small-arms fire, he took an AK-47 round in the neck. Greer's last words were to request his dog tags be removed so the enemy wouldn't take them. PFC Jarvis wrote of Greer's ending, "...the dark red warm blood that was spurting out from the brave young corporal's neck slowed to a small gurgle." Greer was the night's first casualty.

Amid a sound and light show unlike anything he had experienced before, John made his way to the western perimeter. "I heard whistles blow and saw in the flashing light NVA running through our fields of fire into our perimeter," John recalled.

Out of that swirl of battle, Captain Kahler summoned John to the area of the 81mm mortars, and briefed him on the loss of machine guns and one ONTOS (a lightly armored, tracked anti-tank vehicle armed with six co-axially mounted 106mm recoilless rifles). He also instructed him to take a couple of marines and shore up the eastern perimeter. Before parting Captain Kahler grabbed John firmly by the shoulder and informed him, among other things, that if the situation deteriorated further, he would have to call artillery fire inside the perimeter.

"At that point fear had left me. It was about winning the battle. Kill or be killed. No one was backing up. Backing up would have been it. Some had to be restrained. They were angry. If you are going to play the game—the killing game—you do it well," John described his fellow marines' raw defiance that night.

But for brief lulls, the surreal spectacle of exploding grenades, rockets, mortars, satchel charges and automatic weapons fire went unabated, as the Local C-117 Force NVA Company advanced in a human wave. There were as many as 300 NVA against 48 marines. After just one hour, all four of Delta Company's machine gun emplacements were knocked out, the machine gunners either wounded or dead. The cries for "corpsman, corpsman," grew louder as the casualties mounted.

Friendly artillery pounded the perimeter and partly stanched the flow of NVA breaching the defensive positions. At the same time, the night air had quickly thickened into a hot gumbo of smoke, the stench of cordite, and at times, burning flesh. A C-130 gunship arrived and provided flare illumination for several hours.

John received word that the last M-60 machine gun had been knocked out. The two machine gunners, PFCs Ingram and Douglas, had been wounded. He knew there was no way to carry the night without the M-60s. Plus two marines were down and desperately needed help. Accompanied by his radioman, John sprinted with schoolboy speed through a fusillade of automatic weapons fire. In his words, "As I approached their position, I saw some 10 yards to my left an NVA soldier firing an automatic burst of fire from his AK-47, and then I was in the air like a projectile sent there by the force of a well-swung sledge hammer to my back. A single round had traversed laterally through my chest cavity puncturing both lungs and clipping the inside of my spinal column at the speed of 2,500 feet per second. I laid on my back, breathless and unable to move."

Out at the listening post, as the enemy tightened the noose around the three 18-year old PFCs—Davis, Carattini and Jarvis—they had no choice but to make a run for the perimeter. Scrambling through a whistling and whirring rain of hot metal, shell bursts blossomed around them in clouds of smoke, leaving a mixed scent of fresh-turned dirt and scorched earth. Returning fire as they retreated, Jarvis was sent careening in the air from a rocket or grenade blast and Carattini's flak jacket got shredded with shrapnel. Davis took a bullet in the chest and collapsed to the ground on the spot. Realizing the improbability of a timely rescue, Davis sealed the hole in his chest with hand pressure and staggered through the raging field of fire to a friendly foxhole on the perimeter, where a corpsman triaged his wound and saved his life.

All of this transpired in just a few minutes. Meanwhile Carattini and Jarvis were on the western flank, maneuvering toward the disabled machine gun emplacement when they saw John hurled to the ground. John was still under heavy fire, dazed and confused yet aware of his condition. He instructed his radioman to "tell Sergeant Ballinger it's all his show."

Carattini and medic Woody Larkin acted swiftly, dragging John into a bomb crater temporarily, before tugging him by inches to the triage hooch at the command post. Once there, corpsman "Doc" Whistler admonished

him, "Don't go into shock. You've got a chance of making it lieutenant. Stay
with it."

Touch and go for the next four hours, John fought the fight of his life to
breathe and remain conscious. As he lay on the paddy ground gasping for
air, he had an out-of-body interlude, levitating above the fray into an infinite
field of light, looking down on the absurdity of it all. "I had valid choices to
make: going down to the triage hooch, seeing my family and friends again
or fading into the light and peace. Once I made the decision to return, I was
back gasping for air."

In the throes of a second assault, Jarvis took over the disabled M-60
machine gun on the western flank. By wounding or killing so many marines,
the NVA had breached the perimeter in several places, charging through
the Americans' wall of fire. Like the valorous marines, the NVA too were
possessed, seized by the transcending imperative to kill or be killed.

Jarvis almost melted the barrel on the M-60 trying to stave the onslaught,
as the NVA attacked from distances more suitable to hand-to-hand combat.
Running short of ammunition, Jarvis was forced to use a 45-caliber pistol
to dispatch an NVA soldier attacking with a satchel charge. According to
Jarvis, "Death was believed to be an inevitable consequence. It seemed to
be only a matter of time."

Captain Kahler, ever the composed and determined field marshal, came
through the triage hooch looking for anyone among the growing number
of wounded who could still fire a weapon. Unaware that John's condition
was critical, he kicked him and said, "John get up, we need you out there."
When Captain Kahler realized the extent of John's wounds, he told him to
hold on, and assured him of a victory.

Reinforcements from Charlie Company arrived on the southern perimeter
in the fury of the second wave of assault. Captain Kahler directed them to
fill the gaps on the west and northwest perimeter near a treeline heavily
infested with NVA.

Jarvis continued to blaze away with the M-60 machine gun. At one point
in the twilight of gunship illumination, he counted as many as 25 NVA

bodies scattered in his field of fire.

In the early light of dawn, Jarvis and Carattini observed the NVA gathering their dead and wounded and pulling out. Jarvis barraged them with M-60 fire until their vague silhouettes vanished on the horizon. The leathernecks had held their positions in spite of withered numbers.

The attack came right out of Mao's textbook: arriving by surprise under the cloak of darkness, rarely engaging a numerically superior force, striking hard and fast and then retreating. They chose to fight up close: minimizing the effectiveness of American artillery and air power. It was a good strategy for an enemy with far less firepower, and willing to accept a disproportionate number of casualties.

The able-bodied marines, those still standing, celebrated the end to their longest night, cleaning the NVA corpses of money, weapons and valuables. The nameless commander of the NVA's C-117 Force Company was left dead on the battlefield. John and 18 other critically wounded leathernecks were loaded aboard marine helicopters.

"I only remember I had trouble breathing on the chopper. It was an uncomfortable ride. When we got to the MASH unit at Phu Bai, I remember the blurred image of green scrubs worn by the doctors and nurses. I said to myself, 'they are going to save me,' and then I went into shock and didn't wake up for two days."

The truth and consequences of the war were stark: up to six million Indochinese killed and 58,000 Americans. We won the numbers game, and lost the moral high ground. The Pentagon boys wanted more, but politically the massive occupation force would prove an unsustainable drain on American resources and morale.

No length of prose can detail all the hellish events of May 5, 1968. On a parched piece of paddy two miles out of Hue, it was the last day of earthbound life for four of the 48 leathernecks—Greer, Roberts, Chimeri, and Smith—and at least 60 nameless, yet similarly valorous Vietnamese warriors. It was also the first day of a new and sharply different life for John Lancaster.

Two days after he was shot, John regained consciousness in a MASH unit, plugged helplessly into a fragile web of over 10 life-support tubes. A harried doctor paused at his bed, "I am very busy but here's the news. You have two punctured lungs, numbers five and six thoracic vertebrate are damaged, muscle loss from the abdomen down, no bowel or bladder function and a five percent chance of that improving. Don't worry. Get on with life. You'll make it."

John was soon flown to the USS Repose, a hospital ship circling the waters of the South China Sea, and from there to a naval hospital in Guam, where the truth of his disability seemed like something from a nightmare. A nurse gave him James Clavell's book *Tai-Pan*, saying, "Read this, and take your mind off it."

John was awarded the bronze star for valor. Four months later in August of 1968 he was promoted to first lieutenant and simultaneously received a medical discharge from the Marine Corps—no parades or fanfare, the fate of all Vietnam veterans. John's patriotism had been unswerving; his country's loyalty to him had not been nearly as true. Surviving had been his highest award.

In September, the month after John was discharged, the Young Bloods of the 1st Battalion, 27th Marines, were withdrawn from Vietnam after only seven months in country—a consequence of overall troop withdrawals and a high casualty rate. They had taken a beating, but by no means were they beaten—*semper fi* to the end. Using the statistics that transform young men into arithmetic matrixes, in their brief but bloody time in country, their thousand-man fighting force had received 666 Purple Hearts, 110 of those awarded to young men killed in action. Almost half of those fatalities were 18-year-olds. In 1968 alone, 5,048 marines were killed in Vietnam, more than in the entire Korean War. The first week of May 1968 there had been more Americans killed in Vietnam than in any other week. All those valorous souls were tagged, bagged and flagged for home by the KIA (Killed in Action) Travel Bureau. Their planes home were often ordered to arrive at night, out of sight of the cameras.

Youth has always been expendable. In the same moment that young men are feeling immortal, yet blindly obedient, they were lured into a war of attrition by those who are wiser and far more wicked. The war merchants understood this timeless phenomenon. A veteran sergeant in author Philip Caputo's platoon eloquently schooled him on the subject, "Before you leave here, sir, you're going to learn that one of the most brutal things in the world is your average 19-year-old American boy."

Not mentioned in the situation reports and body counts, were the lost innocence of those who survived, their tumultuous futures, and the vanquished dreams of the critically wounded. Some would rise above the ashes of war, above their nightmares, testing their mettle once again. It was not their heroics in war that drew me to these people—John, Dany, Mado, Do Van Du or Gary Jarvis, who went on to get his doctorate and became a rehabilitation therapist—but instead it was their dedication to goals higher than themselves, their compassion and capacity to draw constructive lessons from the war. Others would fail and falter, their last drop of valor spilled on some shit hole paddy ground in Vietnam. Tuck Freeman survived, but only as a shell of his former self; for him the war rages on.

Once discharged, John was sent to the Spinal Cord Injury Center at the VA Hospital in Cleveland, the treatment center closest to his home of record. Like tens of thousands of paralyzed Vietnam veterans, after months of rehabilitation in the asylum-like starkness of 1960s veterans' hospitals, John learned to live in a wheelchair and cope with life as a paraplegic. He also dealt a mean hand of poker to fellow veterans in the rehab center. Washington's duplicity and the harsh realities of his own experiences led him to join the Vietnam Veterans Against the War. He had healed and grown in many ways. But it would be years before John would allow his thoughts to be drawn back to the six hours of carnage that occurred in the early morning hours of May 5, 1968. He blanked it out.

The marriage to Anne Steuart was not to be. He returned to Notre Dame in the fall of 1969 and began work on a doctorate in philosophy, switching after a year to law school, as his father Leon had done. In his last year of law school one of his professors encouraged him to get involved in disability legal issues.

He has advocated for people with disabilities ever since. As legislative director for the Paralyzed Veterans of America, he often appeared in front of congressional committees waving the bloody shirt, "I'm looking at your voting record Mr. Senator. You voted for the war in Vietnam at every turn, and now you don't want to help the veterans."

During the 1980s, he worked for seven years as Director of the Office of Individuals with Disabilities for Governor Hughes of Maryland. He was present in 1990 at the Rose Garden signing by President Bush of the ADA (Americans with Disabilities Act). In 1995, he was appointed by President Bill Clinton to be executive director of The President's Committee on Employment of People with Disabilities, a position he held for six years. While there he was instrumental in the implementation of the ADA, the first significant civil rights legislation for the benefit of the disabled.

For John as for so many other combat veterans, Vietnam would always be a part of himself. Having visited Vietnam on six occasions since the war, in October of 2000 as the Clinton presidency drew to a close, he decided to return as a resident and advocate for people with disabilities. In the spirit of reconciliation and friendship, working closely with disabled Vietnamese veterans, his former foes, he hopes to be a part of fostering the same cultural shift in Vietnam that he helped implement in America—civil rights for people with disabilities.

Although government officials claim there are five million people with disabilities in Vietnam—blind, deaf or having other physical or mental limitations—John thinks the number is closer to 10 million. The United Nation's Asia-Pacific Economic and Social Committee recently reported that 97 percent of people with disabilities in Vietnam have had no job training, and 35 percent are illiterate.

Already John has been instrumental helping Vietnam pass an Ordinance on Disabled Persons, modeled after the Americans with Disabilities Act. John enlisted bilateral donors to help on implementation issues: organizing the disabled to create a political force; calling out for inclusive education and job training in an integrated classroom setting; and demanding access to transportation, buildings, telecommunications and information technology.

"Employers and builders aren't going to do anything until they are forced to by the law," John assures me, admitting that even with the new Ordinance, progress in Vietnam comes at a glacial pace.

Before setting up residence in Vietnam almost three years ago, on October 27, 2000, John returned to Notre Dame as he often does for football games, to receive the Reverend William Corby Award, given to an outstanding Notre Dame graduate who has achieved distinction in the military and life. At halftime during a game between Notre Dame and its arch-rival, Air Force, John wheeled onto the grassy pitch of Notre Dame Stadium accompanied by his beautiful wife and counsel of 20 years, Christine. In front of a spirited crowd of 83,000, he accepted the prestigious award. The Corby Award mattered less to John than the progress of the game: Notre Dame miraculously tied with three seconds remaining, then went on to beat Air Force in overtime, 33-30.

Over dinner one night I asked John, "What happened to the NVA soldier who shot you—the kid whose face you saw in the blanched light?"

Shrugging expansively, he said flatly, "I feel certain he got wasted. They [marines] blasted the whole area once he showed himself. But maybe not. I hope like hell he made it."

A DMZ Tour

John, Simon and I, pimped out in a Toyota van complete with guide, swung over the Phu Xuan Bridge, waking up to Arlo Guthrie and *Alice's Restaurant*, the famous American anti-war tune. We were soon tooling up National Highway 1, during imperial times known as the Mandarin Road, and after the French Indochina War as the *Street Without Joy*. (Bernard Fall coined the name for the title of his book on the subject.)

An hour up the road, we stopped outside Quang Tri, a former citadel town and ground zero for scorched-earth fighting during the Easter Offensive of 1972. The abandoned La Vang Cathedral, its façade jaundiced and riddled with bullet holes, bore testament to the fighting.

We turned east on an alternate road to Highway 9 which mated with the Quang Tri River. The river's jade waters suggested its jungled origins in the Truong Son Mountains, which rise in all directions in steep and rugged ramparts.

The Bru hill people populate the banks of the Quang Tri River, living in small villages of stilted huts, covered in thatch with curved wooden pikes on the gables. The Bru fought for the NVA and VC during the war. Since then, many families have taken the patriotic surname, Ho.

Men, who tend to idle more, were less apparent than women, who are known throughout Indochina to work 18-hour days, all year-round. Working with post-sized pestles—worn skinny and slick in the middle from years of hand-gripping—the women pounded away making flour in the hollowed-out tree trunks used for mortars. Many dressed traditionally in embroidered black tunics, colorfully woven sarongs. They wore their hair knotted on top or in the back. The occasional T-shirt or watch were all that exposed their 21st century roots.

The Brus are patriarchal and devoted to ancestor worship. Thuy, our guide for the day, said that the women often marry between 13 and 15 years of age, and receive a water buffalo for a dowry. Before marriage, Bru women are free to choose their lovers. Once married, they are slavishly monogamous, while the men switch roles and become free lovers. If the husband dies first, which is often the case, the wife marries a brother of the deceased.

Still in the Bru homelands, we turned off the alternate road onto Highway 9, built by the French to link the coast of Vietnam with the market towns of the Mekong. As we followed the turgid Dakrong River, the clouds drifted in and out of the hills and hollows in a skyborne shell game. Through the mists jabbed stacks of karst, many now known by American wartime names like Razorback or Rock Pile.

As we approached the border with Laos, we reached an intersection of several branches of the Ho Chi Minh Trail. Many of the hilltops and mountain slopes are permanently scalped from the toxic effects of Agent Orange. The bald mountains stood in stark relief to the unspoiled luxuriance of surrounding ridge tops—like a crimson boil in need of lancing, as some have said.

From 1962 to 1971, in a campaign of destruction known as Operation Ranch Hand, the U.S. Air Force sprayed over 12 million gallons of the Dow Chemical defoliant in Indochina, mostly in the Mekong Delta and along the Ho Chi Minh Trail. "Only we can prevent forests," was the Air Force cowboys' morbidly ironic motto. In 1984, American veterans exposed to Agent Orange, a potent carcinogen, received a $180 million settlement from the U.S. government. It is now illegal to use the defoliant in the United States. But the U.S. has not sent one thin dime of remediation for such Vietnamese innocents as the Bru children, and their children's children, who were contaminated then and continue to be exposed every day to the carcinogenic defoliant.

Many studies have proven that Agent Orange spreads from the soil into the local food chain and ends up poisoning the bodies of people. Mother's milk shows high levels of deadly dioxin, and there are inordinate rates of birth defects, respiratory cancers and adult-onset diabetes. The evidence is preponderant. It doesn't take many introductions to children with unformed limbs, grotesquely enlarged heads, and Spinal Bifada-withered bodies before you understand the human consequences of America's effort to "prevent forests."

In April of 2000, only weeks before the press converged on Vietnam for the 25th anniversary of the fall of Saigon, my wife, several friends and colleagues attended a breakfast meeting at American Ambassador Pete Peterson's residence. That morning, the embassy health officer staged a Power Point presentation on Agent Orange. Performing to a visibly incredulous audience, his well-orchestrated denial was that Agent Orange has no hazardous consequences, but needs further study. To prove his point, he cited studies conducted on Operation Ranch Hand cowboys, many of whom had drunk the defoliant as part of an initiation ritual! He attributed their high incidence of diabetes to rampant alcoholism. I noticed, however, that he did not conclude his talk by inviting his wife and children on stage to demonstrate the safety of drinking Agent Orange.

Admiral Elmo Zumwalt, Jr. had ordered the use of Agent Orange from 1968 to 1970 in the Mekong Delta. Exposing VC jungle hideouts, he cleared the mangrove forests for over a thousand patrol boats. He saved many American lives in doing so, but not that of his own son, Lieutenant Elmo Zumwalt, III, who commanded a Mekong Delta patrol boat then. In an epitaph to Elmo III's battle with cancer, the admiral and lieutenant together wrote a book *My Father, My Son*, in which they both blame his unusual malignancies on Agent Orange. Elmo III died of Hodgkin's disease and a rare form of lymphoma at the age of 42.

Thus chastened, the admiral devoted his life to the health care of veterans. Upon retirement from the navy, he served on many boards, studying diseases potentially linked to military service. He was also the Chairman of the Board of Vietnam Assistance for the Handicapped, the company John Lancaster first worked for when he returned to Vietnam. John knew the admiral and attended his funeral in January of 2000.

Puttering on, John, Simon and I traversed a string of denuded mountains on the way to the Free Economic Zone, the border area of Lao Bao, designated tax-free to promote trade with Laos and Thailand. It is home to Vietnam's largest liquor store, a giant modernist building architecturally suited to an LA strip mall. Not surprisingly it is a key smuggling outpost.

Thuy pointed out several wide-eyed women skulking along the roadside, stuffed like fat scarecrows. Beneath their oversized clothes, they concealed bootleg cartons of cigarettes originating in Thailand. The women can make $10 to $20 a day smuggling, versus a subsistence living of maybe $1. They evade border police by taking a jungle path and fording a fast-flowing river. Conspicuous as a pair of 800-pound gorillas, they boarded a bus a few miles from the checkpoint.

We turned north off Highway 9 onto a branch of the Ho Chi Minh Trail, six miles from Laos and 15 miles from the former DMZ. Once the domain of French plantations until they were abandoned in 1945, the road was surrounded by fields of coffee. The Bru people used to earn cash working as safari guides for Westerners on tiger hunts but now they grow coffee. The Bru call the bucolic rolling hills *Ta Con*, meaning beautiful valley. More widely known as Khe Sanh, the American Special Forces troops garrisoned a firebase there in 1966.

We stopped at the remains of the base, now a museum, straining to find our way through a fog with 10 feet of visibility—not unlike the rains of the northeast monsoon during the Battle of Khe Sanh. John sorted through the few curious artifacts that remained: a rusted carcass of a 155 howitzer, a museum of captured and decaying M-16s, an M-79 grenade launcher, an M-60 machine gun, various sniper rifles, and black and white photos of haggard-faced Americans. The decaying symbols of a defeated imperialist America stood in stark contrast to an arsenal of shiny AK-47s and a gallery of smiling soldiers of the NVA's 325C Division, Hanoi's finest.

The truth of Khe Sanh could not have been portrayed with less accuracy. The NVA and VC certainly were clever and worthy fighters, but Khe Sanh was not a place of Vietnamese military triumph.

In 1967, the remote runway at Khe Sanh was built up to accommodate landings of C-130s. Matted in aluminum, the runway was blitzed with traffic during the troop and materiel buildup. As events progressed, American intelligence sources revealed the NVA and VC had amassed about 20,000 troops. US General Westmoreland responded with 6,000 marines, and argued for tactical nuclear weapons.

The battle of Khe Sanh began on January 21, 1968 and waged on for nine weeks. As marines slugged it out on the ground, the worldwide media covered the battle as a siege the likes of which had not been seen since Dien Bien Phu. According to Stanley Karnow's account in *Vietnam, A History*, President Johnson spent sleepless nights in his bathrobe glowering over the sand-table model of Khe Sanh in the White House Situation Room. He ordered the Joint Chiefs of Staff to sign a declaration of faith that Westmoreland would hold Khe Sanh.

Back on the ground at Khe Sanh, American fighters and bombers relentlessly showered ordnance on the valley, 75,000 tons worth in all, "...the deadliest deluge of firepower ever unloaded on a tactical target in the history of warfare," wrote Karnow. It was quite unlike Dien Bien Phu, where air support had been minimal.

Every day of the battle, American fighters and bombers were stacked to 36,000 feet in holding patterns, waiting their turns to drop bombs. The battle was fought hard on the ground. Westmoreland got a reverse Dien Bien Phu: as many as 15,000 NVA and VC perished at Khe Sanh. US marines killed were fewer than 500, and approximately 1,000 South Vietnamese died.

These lopsided results were shrugged off the following year by General Giap, the commander who prevailed at Dien Bien Phu and later against the Americans: "The life or death of a hundred, a thousand, tens of thousands of human beings, even our compatriots, means little."

By all later accounts, Khe Sanh had been a ruse to draw human and materiel resources away from the cities of the South to pave the way for the Tet Offensive, a tactic that would be consistent with General Giap's stated strategy to sacrifice troops.

Like a dying star unleashing high-energy gamma ray bursts, the battle of Khe Sanh and the Tet Offensive of 1968 gave unprecedented political support to the beginning of peace talks, and ultimately helped end the war.

General Tran Do, a co-architect of the Tet Offensive, told Karnow in an interview after the war, "In all honesty, we didn't achieve our main objective, which was to spur uprisings throughout the south... As for making an impact in the United States, it had not been our intention—but it turned out to be a fortunate result."

The fog over Khe Sanh remained thick, making it impossible to explore or even to see the valley. Thus, we decided to return up Highway 9 and spend the night at Dong Ha. During the war, the 3rd Marine division garrisoned 13,000 troops in Dong Ha, then a town of 3,000 people. Now a town of six stoplights and a surplus of amputee beggars, Dong Ha is home to many who fought alongside the Americans. It still has a war-ravaged mood about it. Not surprisingly, since the war ended, over 40,000 Vietnamese have been killed by unexploded ordnance, and another 60,000 seriously injured, the brunt of the carnage occurring around Dong Ha. John had spent the night in Dong Ha a few months before while supervising the distribution of 30 new wheelchairs.

Settling in at the DMZ Café, facing Bernard Fall's *Street Without Joy*, we cracked open a bottle of *lua moi*, labeled as vodka but no more than a Vietnamese brand of rice whiskey. John had met the pudgy, graying Café owner, Mr. Tinh, on a prior visit. A former Kit Carson scout, and translator for the marines, Mr. Tinh rambled on about his six years in re-education camps, cursing like a marine with an accent mixing African-American speech and southern drawl: "goddammmm muttafukker, asshoo son a beech."

After being released from the camps, Mr. Tinh spent four frustrating years being double-crossed by boat captains on several attempts to flee the country. His son finally made it to the Hong Kong refugee camps in the late 1980s, and periodically sends him money from his new home in Ohio.

Twisting his face in feigned anger, he bemoaned the fate of soldiers who fought for the South and don't get a pension. Worse still, many of their cemeteries have been destroyed. "We built very nice tombs for our dead soldiers. After 1975 they came and tore them down."

"I've heard that from more than one vet," John remarked.

Nostalgic for the marine camaraderie of the good old war days, Mr. Tinh asked John, "Where is the 3rd Division now. I miss those guys. Are they in the Middle East?"

"Good question. I don't know. Maybe," John stammered.

Mr. Tinh bid his wife to prepare us a meal. She arrived shortly with corn and crab soup, fried morning glory and white rice. Afterwards we drifted down the *Street Without Joy* to a karaoke bar. Although one stands on every corner in Vietnam, in five years of living in Hanoi I had never darkened the doors for "choir practice." But here, in a dim room with the ambiance of a 1940s schoolhouse auditorium, shadowed by two local divas, John grabbed the mike, and selected a song from the menu. He chuckled through the verses of *The Most Beautiful Girl* by the late Charlie Rich. One girl fought for space on my lap, signaling fellatio. Another had already straddled Simon. Delighted as I may have been by John's crooning, I led a hasty retreat to the DMZ Café, unable to stop laughing, as we splashed in the rain down the *Street Without Joy*.

Next morning, after a breakfast of baguettes spread with Laughing Cow cheese, we started on our trip to Vinh, about 200 miles to the north. It was Sunday, and as we passed a National Cemetery, hundreds of flag-carrying school kids flooded the somber grounds, picking up trash on a school outing.

"There were 70 war-related cemeteries in Dong Ha," our guide Thuy noted. "We were hit every night. They are gone today, but at that time everyone had a bunker in their house."

At the village of Cam Lo on Highway 15, we joined the main artery of the newly constructed Ho Chi Minh Highway, which upon completion, will once again connect Saigon and Hanoi. After we crossed a new bridge spanning the Cam Lo River, the rubber plantations gave way to the pride of Quang Tri province, limbless tree trunks choked with the vines of black pepper plants.

Leaving the highway, we circled a small lake and twined up a forested hillside to the Truong Son Cemetery, the largest of the hundreds of war hero cemeteries in Vietnam. Over 20,000 NVA and VC are buried in the cemetery—young individuals transformed into a monotonous blur of stone markers.

We got out of the car and found we had the cemetery to ourselves. All was still except for butterflies—black, yellow and white—swirling about fresh-laid bouquets of flowers. The dead here were killed fighting along the Ho Chi Minh Trail, each headstone bearing the fallen soldier's name and the relevant dates: birth, enlistment and death. Ceramic censors of incense adorned each slab of granite. Branded with the five-point star of the Fatherland at the top of each headstone, the words *liet si*, literally meaning martyr, were inscribed below. There were no epitaphs.

We tallied up some quick statistics: Almost all had been killed between the ages of 17 and 35; equal numbers had fought for over 10 years or been killed within months of their enlistment; and a plurality of those laid to rest were killed in 1968.

Few dry eyes could be seen among the many Sunday visitors who later arrived to pay homage. We watched a group of two men and several older women dressed in *ao dais* burn incense in a ceremonial pagoda-style pavilion. The men and women alike wore medals on their chests. I am sure many of the women fought, but the medals they were wearing were just as likely to be for sacrificing their husbands and their young. One of the men, dressed in a suit, asked John if he had been in the army. John nodded yes.

John is a magnet to veterans from both sides. As the group in their Sunday dress finished praying and making offerings to the dead, they each in turn approached him and shook his hand. One septuagenarian woman, heavily bedizened with medals, her lips stained purple from years of betel chewing, grasped John's hand and held on, staring fraternally into his empathetic blue eyes. Silently, intensely, their facial expressions flashed from pleasantries to sorrows and back.

"You look at a person long enough, you might recognize their humanity," John told me later.

Approximately three million Vietnamese were killed from both sides during the war. Among the VC and NVA alone, there are over 300,000 MIAs and fallen soldiers who have not made it into the national cemeteries. Although some of their names are inscribed on the tombs, their remains have never been found.

In Vietnamese religion, the definitive, most sacred observance is ancestor worship. Without a proper funeral, the soul of the deceased lingers, wandering, unable to be reborn. Surviving family members remain in a state of flux—extended bereavement—until they have dutifully disposed of the bones and put an altar for the deceased in their home. This traditional altar occupies a high shelf in most homes, and on it stands a photograph of the deceased, two candlesticks, and an incense burner. On important days, such as during the Tet holiday or on the anniversary of the death, incense is burned and food is offered. It is believed that the presence of an ancestor's altar in each house and the periodic acts of worship cause the spirits of the dead to remain present in the lives of the living and to urge people to preserve the honor of the family.

In 1995, as part of establishing formal diplomatic relations with the United States, Vietnamese officials reluctantly agreed to cooperate in America's endless and expensive search for MIAs. A political hot potato in the United States, politicians, veterans and recruiters alike claim they can't get young boys to join the services when the dead get left behind. Almost 50 years later the United States is willing to spend millions of dollars to uncover even a single set of remains, like Earthquake Magoon, who was bumped up on the priority list thanks to political connections. The only solace the Vietnamese get out of helping find American MIAs is making a fortune renting helicopters to search teams—$1,000 an hour.

We left the cemetery and soon headed into an infinite sweep of paddy field, punctuated with bomb craters. Herded around by shepherds with bamboo prods, flocks of clipped ducks waddled in tight formations. They shifted faithfully at each command like forward-moving shadows. Mounted by boys in conical sun hats, water buffalo fed on paddy straw. Men wearing olive drab pith helmets, the sartorial signature of the communist army, appeared more frequently. Meandering through the placid terrain was the unremarkable muddy waters of the Ben Hai River—the 17th parallel and the DMZ. Chosen by the Geneva negotiators after the fall of Dien Bien Phu, the arbitrary line that separated North and South was memorialized on a nearby obelisk: divided on July 20, 1954 and reunified on Liberation Day, April 30, 1975.

The former iron bridge, with wooden slats for flooring, built during the French era, had been dismantled in the previous two years and replaced by a modern concrete span, matching the nearby bunker.

It was impossible to dam the flow of Cold War memories, an era that brought us many similar flashpoints. I have been to the North Korean frontier of the 38th parallel where even today a million North Koreans face off across a vast minefield against 600,000 South Koreans. On another occasion, my son and I drank rum with the Brigada Fronteriza while looking out over the forested minefield and beyond to the American base at Guantanamo Bay. In each case, the tendency for apocalyptic warfare was there.

Here, on the 17th parallel, once the tension turned to fire, when all systems had failed, the primal conflagration would not come under control until as many as six million people were dead throughout Vietnam, Cambodia and Laos, over 12 percent of Indochina's population at the time.

Unarmed, without tanks, helicopters, escorts or even a passport check, we left the bridge and unremarkable paddy behind us. Only a few miles away was the turnoff for the Vinh Moc tunnels.

The oceanfront fishing village of Vinh Moc was a transshipment point for supplies and armaments going south, and came under intensive American bombing, or Operation Rolling Thunder, as the air offensive was known. Now the museum walls there are papered with black and white pictures of the rubbled aftermath of non-stop bombardment. The photos depicted the smoldering remains of an Armageddon—every home and above-ground hovel obliterated.

Instead of giving up the fight and leaving, the residents of Vinh Moc burrowed underground. Armed with shovels, hoes and bamboo baskets, they carved a maze of tunnels and rooms into a small underground village. There were 140 tunnels constructed at the time in the Vinh Moc district. If linked together, they would have stretched a distance of 60 miles.

Minh, our tour guide with the local People's Committee, was already drunk at eight in the morning when Simon and I took a walk through the tunnels. It was the rainy season, and the tunnels were dank and muddy, "A good time for snake repellent," Minh taunted, reeking of whiskey in the dark confines. Crouching through the narrow timber-reinforced shafts, we catacombed down three levels, descending to a depth of 75 feet. In rooms no bigger than a bear's den, 17 babies had been born and lived with their families. There was a radio room, three wells, showers, four ventilation shafts, very primitive toilets and a large meeting hall where movies were shown. Beaconed by a shaft of sunlight, we exited the subterranean fortress on a cliff side into a garish ground cover of wildflowers, overlooking the palm-lined beach and ocean blue.

Standing drenched in sunlight along the rocky beach, I was struck both by the tenacity of the cave dwellers, and by the notion that "bombing them into the Stone Age" had been no idle threat.

We arrived in Vinh, the capital of Nghe An province, late in the afternoon and found a room in the tallest building in town, important only because the skyline had in our generation been at sea level. Although an ancient port city, and supply terminus for the Ho Chi Minh Trail, as a city Vinh didn't exist at the end of the war. Vanquished by American bombing, but for a guesthouse and two college dormitories left standing and a battery of anti-aircraft gunners, there were no buildings or inhabitants. After the war, well-intentioned, East German engineers and architects oversaw the rebuilding of Vinh. Rebuilt in the Soviet utilitarian style, Vinh deserves the widely accepted moniker of being Vietnam's "Ugliest City."

Squeezed into a narrow band of hardscrabble land between the South China Sea and the Annamite cordillera, the fighting spirit of Nghe An was born out of a long history of poverty and overpopulation. The soil is poor in nutrients and to make matters worse, Nghe An province is plagued by seasonal typhoons as well as torrential flooding during the autumn monsoons.

A hardened lot, Nghe An peasants led the resistance against the French, and as a result of their sacrifice in blood, the area is often considered the cradle of the Vietnamese communist revolution. Organized by the freshly-inaugurated communist party, anti-tax demonstrations in Nghe An and Ha Tinh provinces in 1931 were answered by French bombs, which killed 217 peasants. Stubborn and rebellious, the people of Vinh and its locale are known by fellow Vietnamese as "the buffalos of Nghe An."

Early the next morning, we set out for the short drive to Kim Lien village, Vietnam's Bethlehem, the ancestral home of Nghe An's most famous buffalo, Ho Chi Minh (HCM). We pressed through the town's morning bustle and beep. Road crews worked out of vats of boiling tar—flaming and spitting black plumes. They added sealant to what will one day be a grand boulevard approach to the Great Patriot's ancestral home. Billboards flashed by—one on AIDS and another with Uncle Ho and a flock of children—inscribed in Vietnamese, "Nothing is more precious than independence and freedom."

As we weaved through gray fields of rice, bicycles topped in haystacks rolled down the country lane like runaway balls of tumbleweed. A few men harrowed the otherwise empty fields, others hoisted the heavy plows on their backs and walked the road. Fishponds, bamboo stands and palm trees framed homes and hamlets, with the occasional karst formation spiking up in the background.

Shaded by the lissome branches of casuarinas, Kim Lien village is approached by a sealed dike road, evoking the genteel feel of a country squire's driveway. Embracing capitalism with the zeal of new converts, the heart of the village center is a plaza of theme shops and *petite bourgeoisie* hawking HCM kitsch to visiting comrades—pith helmets and hats, alabaster and golden busts, peanut brittle, and a portfolio of photos.

Across the plaza, though simple and pastoral, the ancestral homestead has the fabricated feel of a Potemkin Village. No doubt rebuilt and refurbished many times—there are three airy huts of plaited bamboo and thatch, affixed on concrete pads. Indulging HCM's love for the simple pleasures of peasant life, the grounds of his ancestral home, set among fresh trimmed hedgerows, abound in palms trees, a fruit orchard, bamboos, a frangipani, and a neatly scored vegetable garden.

HCM's father, Nguyen Sinh Sac, was born in the village of Kim Lien in 1863 to a peasant mother and a father who was a well-to-do farmer. Within four years, both parents were dead and Sac was put in the care of relatives. The family had a history of successfully completing the civil service examinations, so as a young adolescent, Sac was put in the custody of a Confucian scholar, Master Duong, in the nearby village of Hoang Tru.

Showing promise as a scholar, Sac married Master Duong's daughter, the beautiful and literate Hoang Thi Loan. Sac and Loan were given a three-room hut on her father's property. They soon had three children: a daughter, son and then, in 1890, another son, Nguyen Sinh Cung, later known as Ho Chi Minh.

When HCM was only five, the family moved to Hue, where Sac earned a living by teaching at the Imperial Academy, and passed his civil service doctorate exam by the end of the year. He was honored in the traditional way by the village of his father, Kim Lien, in turn bestowing upon it the honor of being a "civilized spot, a literary location." The village built him a three-room house, and for the first time HCM lived in Kim Lien village, his father's ancestral home.

Sac turned down an imperial assignment, believing the whole mandarin system to be oppressive, and instead opened a Confucian school in Kim Lien. Sac followed the tradition of weaning his son from his "milk name" and dubbed him, Nguyen Thi Thanh, meaning "He will Succeed." Often dawdling at the blacksmith shop, HCM learned how to forge steel, listened to tales of local heroism against invading barbarians, and took pride in his own family history of resistance.

Phan Boi Chau, a leading turn-of-the-century nationalist and intellectual, used to drop in from his nearby village to see his friend and former classmate, Sac. With little HCM on hand, they often aired their patriotic ideas and shared a mutual contempt for feudalism, the French and the monarchy.

In June 1906, Sac could no longer turn down the imperial court's offers of employment. In spite of his growing disaffection with the mandarin system, Sac went to work at the Imperial Academy in Hue.

HCM and his brother later passed the entrance exams for the National Academy, Hue's best school. Belying his rustic visage—long hair, wooden shoes, conical hat and country clothes—HCM advanced rapidly in French and Chinese studies and took courses in history, geography, literature and science. Regarded by many as a hayseed, HCM sat in the back of the class and in his countrified accent, always asked a lot of questions. After studying under several dissident teachers, his criticism of the imperial and colonial authorities grew increasingly harsh.

By 1907, discontent among peasants over heavy taxation, corvee labor, and feudalistic land policies had swept the country. HCM volunteered as a translator of French for a mob of peasants who besieged Hue demanding tax reform. After talks broke down, a garrison of French troops arrived and opened fire at the demonstrators on the Trang Tien Bridge, killing several. The next day HCM was expelled from the prestigious National Academy.

Riots continued over the ensuing months. The French arrested, jailed and executed dissidents, even demoting HCM's father to a district-level position away from Hue. His brother was arrested and jailed in 1914 for anti-French activities. His sister was interrogated back in Kim Lien for complicity, and eventually imprisoned, too.

HCM fled south to Quinhon, on to Phan Tiet, and then embarked on a 30-year odyssey abroad. Cloaked in the mystery that marked his life, HCM would, according to his own accounts, venture aboard ship as a cook's helper to India, Saudi Arabia, Senegal, Tunisia, Madagascar and Brazil, then jump ship in the United States.

Soon he re-crossed the Atlantic, staying in London through World War I. At its end he turned up in Paris, where he immediately joined the socialist party and worked variously as a photo-retoucher, candle-maker, gardener, and domestic servant. There, in 1919 he would pen an anti-colonial petition to American President Woodrow Wilson and the allied meeting at Versailles. In 1924, he fled to the Soviet Union, where within days of his arrival, he attended Lenin's funeral.

After years of studying communist doctrine in the Soviet Union, HCM left for China, Thailand and Hong Kong as an employee of the Comintern—the

Moscow-run fraternity of international communist organizations. After founding the Indochinese Communist Party, HCM was imprisoned twice in Hong Kong and China in the 1930s and early 1940s. He returned to Vietnam in 1941, living as a guerilla leader in the rugged mountains along the Chinese border.

Absent any contact with his family, HCM assumed an estimated 200 aliases over those 30 years, always one step ahead of French authorities. During much of that period, had the diminutive, Chaplinesque revolutionary been detained by the French, they would have executed him.

Aside from HCM, his most famous pen name was Nguyen Ai Quoc, meaning Nguyen the Patriot. As Nguyen Ai Quoc, he would stir the nationalist, and later the communist revolt in Vietnam, through his smuggled Marxist-Leninist writings. He would use the pseudonym Ho Chi Minh—meaning He who Enlightens—at the August Revolution in 1945.

At that time, few Vietnamese realized that the newly-anointed President Ho Chi Minh was the Comintern agent Nguyen Ai Quoc. After 34 years of not knowing the whereabouts of her brother, his sister recognized him from newspaper pictures and visited him in Hanoi. His brother followed for a brief visit, before dying in Kim Lien village in 1950. His father Sac had died in 1929, a broken and besotted man wandering the Mekong Delta selling medicinal herbs. His body was returned to Kim Lien for burial.

Most of what the Vietnamese and the larger world knew about HCM came from two autobiographies he penned in the 1940s and 1950s. Ever the master at burnishing his own image, he even tagged himself *Bac Ho*, or Uncle Ho, a title of respect reserved for designation by friends and family. At last, in 1957 he admitted to being the Comintern agent Nguyen Ai Quoc, and in the same year paid a ceremonial visit to his ancestral home in Kim Lien village, his first in 50 years and his last.

There on our visit to HCM's childhood home, John Lancaster seemed to exude an avuncularity rather like Ho himself once did, attracting a following of 12 polite and curious kids. Together we all looked over the baby's manger in HCM's house, and a hammock and spinning wheel in the grandparent's hut next door, pages taken from the life of Jesus and Gandhi. We moseyed around back to the family altar house, furnished with a dragon chair, a gong, a ceremonial drum and an altar originally built for HCM's mother. In an air of church-like reverence, well-dressed peasants on a day's pilgrimage placed offerings on the simple altar. Because Uncle Ho left no immediate descendants to tend the family altar, all Vietnamese now play the role of his children.

We stepped over the raised entrance barrier, a Chinese architectural feature found in temples and pagodas to keep evil spirits out, and burned incense, placing yellow and white mums on the altar.

John gave an imaginary toast, "The man and myth who defeated the United States. Russia couldn't, and China didn't dare."

Emerging from HCM's homestead for some retail therapy, we were easily the most popular visitors in Kim Lien village. John promptly morphed into a shopaholic, buying two HCM busts, several mason jars of locally grown peppers, and for Christmas gifts, two hefty sacks of HCM's favorite candy, peanut brittle. Simon, too, embraced the holiday spirit, singing "Yo, Ho, Ho," as he sifted through the kitsch.

After loading our HCM acquisitions, we turned toward Hanoi and embarked on the 200-mile drive into the frontier reaches of Tonkin. The road traced the tracks of the Reunification Express, through a succession of joyless villages. The beeping of horns ratcheted up like the frenetic honking of geese.

In due course, we came upon a fresh accident in the provincial capital of Thanh Hoa. Two bicycles were crushed beneath the front wheels of a lorry. Incense was already burning at the impact site. The victims were apparently killed in an instant.

Traffic is a metaphor for Vietnamese life: "A continuous charade of posturing, bluffing, fast moves, tenacity, and surrenders," wrote Andrew Pham in *Catfish and Mandala*. Traffic flows are regulated more by the brute law of tonnage than police-enforced statutes, and stop lights a mere suggestion. The rapid motorization of Vietnam, a phenomenon of the last decade, has put 10 million motorbikes on Vietnam's roads, accruing at the rate of 20 percent a year. It is a formula for disaster—fewer than half of the operators have a license, not many drivers or passengers have helmets, and virtually no one wears eyeglasses. There are over 30,000 reported accidents a year, killing a minimum of 10,000 people and maiming and injuring untold numbers. The good news is that cars, although on the rise at about 700,000, bear an import tax of 200 percent, a disincentive designed to curb this lethal chaos.

We stopped near the accident site for some truck-stop food—tofu, fried morning glory, rice, chicken parts, and green tea. Breaking our jaws on a dessert of HCM peanut brittle, we returned to the highway and steamed past the famous karst pedestals of Ninh Binh, springing abruptly from the paddy fields. The porous limestone, stitched verdantly in vegetation, has its origins over 300 million years ago when the sea stretched inland. Chinese poets called these pinnacles of natural beauty, "the silken scroll in stone."

Farther along, many abandoned mustard-hued cathedrals of the French pierced the sky, standing in dramatic relief to the toils of peasants earthbound in the paddies. The ancient capital of Hoa Lu lay hidden in a rampart of karst formations to the west. Soon, entering the slipstream of Hanoi traffic, we were tooling around Hoan Kiem Lake, where in the year 1010 A.D. Ly Thai To beheld a dragon lifting to the skies. Inspired by the propitious spectacle, he named the riverine city Thang Long—Ascending Dragon—and made it the capital of the Ly Dynasty.

Hanoi Vignettes

The Bosom of
the Former Beast

Through a series of connecting journeys, we had come full circle to Hanoi. To understand communist Indochina, one must comprehend Hanoi, a bellwether for events that shaped my youth and now the early 21st century of Vietnam and Indochina.

I was living in Nairobi, Kenya in 1998 when my wife was asked to head a reproductive health program in Vietnam. Once the decision was made and we settled in Hanoi, I became fascinated with the ironies of living in the bosom of the former beast. Inevitably I became good friends with a few American veterans doing humanitarian work in Vietnam.

It was an interesting juncture: the end of the 20th century and Vietnam had been the only crack in the invincibility of the U.S. military. So it was fascinating to watch firsthand as one of the last bastions of communism—our Cold War domino—wobbled toward free markets under peaceful circumstances. It was perceptible every day in the streets, a passage of eras, the last days of a long and arduous epic.

Yet in many ways, Vietnam's present and future are entombed in the past. Over two and a half millennia ago, before the appearance of three historical luminaries of the East—Confucius, Lao Tse and Siddhartha Gautama Buddha—the Red River Basin provided the fertile ground for the origin myth of Vietnam. Percolating down through China, the precepts of the three prophets would trickle into local spirit and ancestor worship, and over centuries distill into Vietnam's potent cosmology.

As described by historian Keith Taylor in his book *The Birth of Vietnam*, Lac Long Quan, a dragon lord residing in the sea, came to the Red River Basin on a prehistoric *mission civilisatrice*. After the dragon lord dispersed the resident demons, he taught the *indigenes* to wear clothes, to cultivate rice, and to call upon him in times of trouble, once he returned to his sea abode. When a Chinese monarch came south and claimed the Red River Basin for his kingdom, Quan avoided a pitched battle and absconded with the monarch's wife, Au Co, taking her to the top of Mt.Tan-vien, overlooking the Red River. Absent his wife, the disappointed Chinese monarch returned home. The mythical union of Au Co, the princess of the mountains, and Lac Long Quan, the prince of the sea, produced the first of the Hung kings, out of which came the bronze-age culture of Dong Son and the historical beginnings of Vietnam and the Vietnamese.

The poetic marriage of land and sea and the seminal conflict with the Chinese would foreshadow Vietnam's complex weave of myth and history. In 1428, over four centuries after Ly Thai To founded Thang Long—the city of the Ascending Dragon (later named Hanoi)—Emperor Le Loi, aided by a magic sword, liberated the Vietnamese yet again from the Chinese yoke.

In a tale redolent of a Loch Ness monster meeting King Arthur's Excalibur, a golden tortoise rose out of a Hanoi lake while Le Loi was boating. It snatched the prize sword from the emperor's sheath. Before retreating to the bottom of the lake, the tortoise returned the sword to its divine keeper. Le Loi thus named the oxbow lake Hoan Kiem, the Lake of the Restored Sword.

Carved by the meanderings of the Red River, the 17 lakes of Hanoi endow the urban clutter with open space and a graceful magic. The last of the region's big cities oozing old Asian charm, Hanoi's confluence of lakes and street scenes provide its burnish. The mosaic of Hanoi's Sino-Viet traditions, colonial architecture, and vibrant people is undergoing a cultural renaissance, as the heavy hand of communism slowly but steadily relaxes its grip.

Walking Hanoi's streets, with names of ancient Vietnamese heroes who defeated the Chinese, the women cover their arms in stockings to keep their skin pale like their northern neighbors—perhaps shallow as an aesthetic but bone deep as a cultural trait. As Vietnam unfolds from its communist cocoon, it is their former occupiers and enemies—China, Japan, France and America—who hold the carrot of globalization. Perhaps this accounts for Vietnam's stubborn xenophobia.

Yet more important to Vietnam than outside opinion, is what their people think: in a recent global survey conducted by the Pew Foundation, Vietnam was ranked number one in the world in terms of its citizens' satisfaction with the direction in which the country is headed. Progress comes in baby steps and can't be imposed from outside, sometimes overlooked by zealots of democracy and human rights.

Vietnam sees the mistakes Russia made in exiting socialism: their headlong embrace of globalization and the mafia's usurpation of national wealth. The reformists are winning the battle, but remain wary of a plunge into free marketism.

In 1954, when France left Vietnam, 10 percent of the population was literate; today over 90 percent of Vietnamese can read and write. They are ever curious. As Nabokov wrote of Russian totalitarianism, "Curiosity is insubordination in its purest form." Coupled with the universal guarantee that every new generation is born innocent, the dark days of indoctrination are slowly being diffused. By dint of a youthful population—60 percent of Vietnam's population is under 30 years old—the Internet firewalls are slowly falling, international television is becoming the norm and parents are hocking the farm for their children to have a first rate international education.

Even today, the ruling class, the Politburo, an 18-member committee that runs Vietnam, comprises only college graduates. Just a few years ago, the committee had only a single college graduate during its 50-year history among some 100 members. They were all conservative military types who won their positions through military service, not through any ability to govern. Vietnam's National Assembly is diverse in gender terms—one in four members is a woman, the highest ratio in Asia. One in 10 members is from an ethnic minority, in proportion to their share of the populace. By degrees they are finding an equilibrium between their autocratic past—their ancient traditions—and the present era of modernization.

Today, there are still occasional sea turtle sightings around the sacred lake of Hoan Kiem. Every dawn, women in baggy garments do *tai chi* beside the mystical waters. Some move with the grace of swans, most flail and thrash as if they'd woken up on an anthill. Men in undershirts and shorts swat shuttlecocks across imaginary nets amid a steady stream of joggers. Beneath shade trees, stooped crones charge a pittance to weigh in on a set of old scales. It's a fitness center with ambiance.

Later in the morning, Hoan Kiem fills with old timers, many sprouting wisps of long gray hair from facial moles, an auspicious mark by Sino-Viet tradition. They circle for card games and *co tuong*, Chinese chess. Once in a while an optimistic angler might wet a hook, sitting in idle reverie on a park bench. Students approach foreigners to practice their English while moneychangers chase them for dollars. When darkness descends and the lake twinkles like a pool of stars, lovers and those looking-for-lovers fill the park benches, the shadowed nooks behind trees, or circle the lake on motorcycles in frozen embraces. Always working the fringes are boys hawking postcards, spotting tourists with falcon-like acuity.

The jade lake mirrors the seasons with a garden of plants and trees from around the world, rooted in the bomb shelters that once rimmed the lake. Brightening the spring in an Impressionist tapestry are red-orange flame trees from South America, the violet crowns of Queen's Crepe Myrtles from the south of Vietnam, and the golden yellow Batai, a Chinese tree. Willows from old Babylonia drape the lake like women's hair. Tamarinds from India grow tall next to a medicinal tree brought by the French from Senegal. The Buddhist holy tree, an ancient banyan, buttressed in a gnarl of its own roots, bathes a sidewalk coffee shop in year-round shade. In spring, it bears a yellow fruit that birds enjoy.

During the Mid-Autumn Festival, the first full moon of the eighth lunar month, the lake is traced in silver and tempered by a fall breeze. The lonesome Tortoise Pagoda, perched on a solitary islet in the middle, is shrouded in a melting light. In the shadow of a couple of modernist buildings, the modest Jade Mountain Temple, reached by the low arc of a candy-apple red bridge—known as the Rising Sun—is situated in a copse of trees on an islet at the north end of the waters.

Children pour into the streets around the lake, wearing paper-mâché masks of auspicious mythical beasts—unicorns, dragons, phoenixes, frogs-on-the-moon. It's not unlike Halloween. During the festival—originating in China as a celebration for a bountiful harvest—Hang Ma Street vibrates in a cicada chorus of clickers and whistles. The street is lined with a dazzling array of shops and stands selling the masks, pinwheels, five-star Chinese lanterns, tins of traditional moon cakes, and less traditional high-tech toys arriving from China.

Branching out into the pulsing labyrinth of the Old Quarter, each of the 36 historical streets is named for its main industry or craft—Hang Bac (Silver Street), Hang Bong (Cotton Street), Hang Dieu (Pipe Street) and more. Bedrocked on a millennium of family toil, the Old Quarter's century-old buildings and medieval rhythms are the living history of Hanoi.

Sprinkled into the Old Quarter's past are several modern art galleries. The most popular and progressive—Art Vietnam—exhibits the best of Vietnam's established and up-and-coming artists. It was there that Simon launched his folio of *The Ten Courts of the Kings of Hell*. He took five years to complete the collector's series of Bosch-like depictions of the Sino-Viet belief system that determines one's fate and next incarnation. He collaborated with Nguyen Manh Duc, a noteworthy local sculptor, who provided statues of Chinese mandarins to go with each court of hell. Prior to becoming a famous sculptor, Duc was an NVA sniper along the DMZ. Attended by the American and British ambassadors, and a host of scholarly Vietnamese, the opening included Russian champagne and clashing gongs as background music.

South of the Old Quarter and two blocks east of the lake, at the end of historic Trang Tien Street, is the majestic Hanoi Opera House. The crown jewel of colonial edifices in Hanoi, the Opera House was built by the French in 1911 as a replica of the Palais Garnier in Paris.

After World War II, circumstances heavily favored a popular uprising: Japan had occupied Vietnam during the war and had just surrendered to the United States; the Vichy French colonials had been imprisoned or contained by the Japanese; a war-related famine had taken the lives of a million people in the North; the literacy rate was between five and ten percent; industrial production was low and inflation high.

On August 17, 1945, on the balcony steps of the Municipal Theater, as the Opera House was then known, Ho Chi Minh's army of communist Vietminh took command. In front of 20,000 people, the Vietminh tore down the tired old imperial flag and for the first time, raised the newly-conceived communist red flag with the yellow, five-pointed star—symbolizing laborers, farmers, intellectuals, soldiers and traders. The August Revolution had begun, galvanized by Ho Chi Minh's Independence speech two weeks later.

My wife and I soon fell under the spell of living in Hoan Kiem District, encompassing the French and Old Quarters. In our brief residence there, many events happening in front of the Opera House have both mirrored and signaled the rapid and larger changes sweeping Vietnam.

Bizarrely, the State Department classifies Hanoi as a hardship tour for embassy staff and donees of aid money. Those people no longer receive the war-era hazardous duty pay of $65 a month, but instead take home an extra 15 percent of their base salary as a post-differential for enduring the rigors of Hanoi. Our hardships fall along the lines of cheap prices, having house staff, and living next to Hanoi's Opera House.

In 1998, on New Year's Eve, Joellen, our son Wes and I watched President Luong rally a legion of faithful as he stood on a stage before the Opera House. Dressed in red, the crowd sang patriotic music and waved miniature Vietminh flags.

Two years later, Simon, Joellen and I drank beer and wine across the square at the Paris Deli as the government of Vietnam hosted President Clinton at the Opera House on his historic trip. Hanoians lined the neighborhood streets to get a passing glimpse of my fellow Arkansan. He was so well received in Saigon that the communes cranked up the loudspeakers for two hours to remind everyone that Vietnam was still a communist country. In a vain attempt to outdo the public outpouring for Clinton, the next year the government feted President Putin, and we took the same seats at the Paris Deli.

For Christmas in 2001, in the first official Hanoi celebration of the religious holiday (at least that I have witnessed), the outdoor stage in front of the

Opera House was forested in Christmas trees and flocked with a troupe of 100-pound dancing Santa Clauses. In a swirl of circling Santas backed up by an English-singing chorus, the Elvis of Vietnam belted out *We Wish You a Merry Christmas* in Vietnamese. High on the same stage, whipping in the winds, were two huge banners, Nokia and Nescafe, the foreign sponsors.

Today, the Paris Deli has moved down the street, and the whole block of buildings facing the Opera House will soon open as the Hanoi Stock Exchange. Simon's streetside barber—who arrives by bicycle each day, hangs his mirror on a tree near the Opera House, and unfolds a stool below—now wears an earring, Sun Silk-brand hennaed hair, and Capri pants. Like time travel with fashion as sign posts, the older men wear berets of the French, their soldierly sons in olive drab pith helmets, and grandchildren in Gucci accessories.

In the heart of the French Quarter, our neighborhood is fairly typical of central Hanoi. During the day, the sidewalks were blazed colorfully with market ladies and choked with white-shirted students coming to and from a nearby school. All corners are occupied by *pho* stands, portable cauldrons set on charcoal fires, bubbling over with translucent noodles. Each night, to one side of our house, the popular Jungle Bar came to life, on the other side was the Smiling Karaoke Bar, an undisguised brothel, and across the street was a massage parlor. In addition to a motorcycle mechanic shop, our closest neighbors made incense; their second-story roof was lined in racks of saffron and deep pink joss sticks.

Around the corner, abutting the trade ministry building—where the U.S.-Vietnam Bilateral Trade Agreement was hatched—was the most popular CD-DVD store in Hanoi. It was guaranteed to have pirated copies of American movies out within two weeks of the U.S. premiere. In the opposite direction was the Western Store, next door to the American club. There I bought Kroger's salsa and American-grown pistachios—I know because I routinely saw employees of the store filling retail packages with the salty nuts and then placing labels on them that said "Made in America."

Our street is changing though. The Jungle Bar is now an Italian restaurant, and the Smiling Karaoke Bar is an upscale art gallery catering to foreign tourists. In an aggressive campaign intended to beautify Hanoi for the SEA

(Southeast Asia) Games, even the market ladies have been swept from the streets.

Every morning, no later than seven, we are entertained by the crackle of the antiquated Tannoy loudspeakers hung on the utility pole across the street. It's a racket that could suck the sleep from the ancestral dead. Whether shouting commands like a drill sergeant, reading public service announcements, playing a classical arrangement of Schubert or a sappy, operatic Vietnamese love song, the loudspeaker ensures everyone is awake and often out in the street in their pajamas.

Although Hanoi's population is a mere three million people, it is one of the most densely populated cities in the world, and yet the safest. Property taxes are assessed on street frontage, so homes are constructed skinny and tall. They are built Chinese-shopkeeper style with room for trading at the street level and a residence above. People live on top of each other, and even if they could afford privacy, Vietnamese prefer not to be alone.

By regulation, everyone in Hanoi is entitled to 21.5 square feet, a meager space of roughly three by seven feet. The population concentration in the Hoan Kiem District of Hanoi—my neighborhood—is reported to be over 100,000 people per square mile, said to be the highest density of people in the world. The streets are just an extension of the home—there is nowhere else to go. That's why in the early mornings and late evenings people stroll around neighborhood streets in pajamas as if in the privacy of their own living rooms. It's a big tropical pajama party!

There is, however, a street side chauvinism that goes unnoticed by most Westerners. A friend of mine, Nate Pullin, was walking through his Hanoi neighborhood one afternoon with his pregnant Vietnamese wife, Nga. A motorcycle came out of nowhere and knocked her to the pavement. As Nate tended to his wife, the assailant appeared to be trying to take off. So Nate cuffed him and told him to stay put. In seconds, a mob of a few hundred people led by an English-speaking university professor converged, stepping over Nga—calling her a "fucking American whore"—to get to Nate. Their anger subsided mildly only when she wisely lied and told them that her husband was Canadian.

Then they locked themselves into a taxi until the police came, while the crowd beat on the windows and continued shouting foul epithets. The police were unconcerned with her lacerated abdomen, and detained them for another 30 minutes before allowing her to go to the hospital. The neighborhood fix was on; the police spent months to no avail trying to extort a bribe from Nate. Nga recovered and had a healthy baby boy.

As well-funded expatriates do, we lived in a very spacious home—a tropical peach chock-a-block of four stories with two balconies and a verandah on top. As on most Hanoi streets, hidden behind the fancy French-Vietnamese facades are a maze of swarming and shabby extended dwellings. The passageways are concretized tunnels, crawling with life and reeking of ammonia. Our neighbors always seize unused space, often rattling our walls with hammers and drills. From our rear verandah, we had a view of a ramshackle of makeshift roofs, ragged pennons of drying clothes, and as many rats moving as people. Yet when looked at as a whole, all the scrofulous disarray came together with the cohesive logic of a jigsaw puzzle.

Simon lived on the ground floor. We shared the kitchen and an elaborately decorated dining room. The humidity in Hanoi is so thick the paint on the walls peeled like burnt skin, requiring a new layer of color each year. The dining room hosted a nice collection of inexpensive antiques and two wall-size paintings by Nguyen Cong Tru, a friend and arguably Vietnam's finest artist. One of the paintings, *Anthem*, had won many accolades in the art world outside Vietnam. It is a modernist vision of a symphony orchestra of tortured characters, taunting the ugliness of totalitarianism. The conductor is a multi-armed bodhisattva, bronzed in gold like some kind of robot, looming and imperious. Perched above this figure atop a cross is an apelike face, a composite of Ho Chi Minh and Lenin. How the painting made it past the culture police to win all its accolades and then into my house was fodder for many happy-hour conversations.

Three or four nights a week Ms. Quy, Simon's Hanoi girlfriend of four years' standing, stayed over. Ms. Quy has been in the army for almost 24 years, and often wears her uniform to the house. Daring and romantic, Ms. Quy and Simon first consummated their affair in the cracker-box confines of her army barracks. Routinely appearing on VTV (Vietnam Television), she is an army actress, and in the Bob Hope, USO vein, has performed for troops across Vietnam, Cambodia and Laos. She is also a member of the Communist Party, a privilege only 3 percent of the Vietnamese enjoy. Often, when we saw her in uniform, she was on her way to or from a study session on Lenin and Marx.

On Christmas Day 2001, we had several friends over for all the yuletide fixings—ham, turkey, dressing, yams, potatoes, apple and cherry pies—and many bottles of holiday spirits. Ms. Quy and Simon were there. The new district commune policeman paid us a visit midway through the bacchanal. His timing was deliberate—Viet officials often choose to negotiate with Americans on Tet or Christmas. This year his holiday greeting was to tell my wife and me that Ms. Quy could no longer sleep over.

Beautiful if not still in fresh bloom, Ms. Quy is in her mid-40s with a child in her early 20s. Yet it is against the law for a Vietnamese woman to spend the night with a foreign man. At the time, she had openly been staying at our house for over two years. The cop was shaking us down.

We paid a healthy expatriate rent so I complained to the landlord. She assured me that the meddling cop would be paid tea money the next day. He returned twice over the next two days, and each time I put the two of them back together. They finally settled the tea money. He continued to pass our house almost daily, paying us no notice as he walked his beat.

The police were usually not a problem. During all the time we lived in Hanoi, almost every week I sent Nhuong, our house girl, around the corner to have banned books copied for friends, much like in the days of the *samizdat* in the Soviet Union. No one ever said anything.

One day as I worked at home in my office on the third floor, writing a chapter on Vietnam, with maps and books spread about the floor and my desk covered in notes and diaries, I looked up and a man was standing at the door. Dressed in a suit, he said, in impeccable English, "I am Mr. Huong with the Ministry of Culture and Information. I am here to find out what you do."

Nhuong had let Mr. Huong in the house without telling me. He was part of the secret police apparatus, now much less feared by foreigners and locals alike than in the old days.

Nonplussed, I pushed the maps aside, stood and said, "Well, I have investments. I was just checking them on the computer. Why don't we go downstairs and talk?"

Once settled into the living room, Mr. Huong asked questions, took notes on my answers, and then wanted to know more about my wife. He said he needed to visit her, too. As he was asking me for her work address and phone number, I was looking at his notes; he already had her coordinates. He was probably playing me for money. He told me he was going straight to her office. He never showed up.

As expatriates, our freedoms were almost limitless. Standing on a street corner and denouncing the communist party or Ho Chi Minh would be a problem, otherwise damn near anything goes. Expats, after all, bring benefits to Vietnam—often dollars but sometimes just as important is a kindred way of thinking on important humanitarian issues that can have an influence in Washington.

During the war, the police and army shared common cause. Today they are committed to nothing. Like the masses they police, the police ignore the existing laws if they don't benefit from them.

Hanoi is a drinking town; the gutters are wide and welcoming. If you arrive in Hanoi with bad habits, they probably aren't going to get any better. Until the recent campaign to clear the sidewalks, every block in Hanoi had at least one outdoor drinking space, usually called a *bia hoi*, or "fresh beer" place. Going to *bia hois* in Hanoi is one of my favorite pastimes: sitting beneath shade trees, circled around plastic tables with steins of beer, smoke wafting in the air from the spicy chicken barbecuing nearby.

I watched people and marveled at the cosmic circulation of Hanoi's constantly beeping traffic. It is an incomparable procession of monks coming and going from a nearby temple; of well-dressed businesswomen in miniskirts driving or riding pillion on Honda Dreams; families of five piled on motorbikes with dad talking on his cell phone while a farmer blasts by with three pigs trussed on back. Or a decrepit old man pushing a rusted bicycle to schlepp a new refrigerator, who doesn't bother even to glance as his passage brings a 50-ton bus to a screeching halt.

Lottery ticket vendors roost on every street corner, pecking away at the Vietnamese vulnerability for games of chance. As dark approaches, peasant ladies in conical hats weave through the sidewalk *bia hoi* stools. Swaying to the rhythm of their step, their shoulder poles hoist empty woks, infant children or the last of their fruits and vegetables, as they vanish into the recesses of Hanoi.

When I arrived in Hanoi, I fell in with a mixed crowd of expatriates and locals at a *bia hoi* next to the Relax Bar on Ly Thuong Kiet. Joellen warned me, "Expatriates are here today and gone tomorrow. More likely than not, you will never know who they really are." She was right.

Since the beers were three for a dollar, the *bia hoi* attracted a crowd of frugal Australians overflowing from the Relax Bar. UNICEFers were regulars, officing up the block. Also such nefarious characters as Richard Petit and Phil Mulvey, editors across the street at the government-run, English newspaper, the *Vietnam News*, who came every day.

Our group was diverse, and the *bia hoi* was usually the only time I saw these people. For many of them, life was flipflopped: their work by day was surreal, debauching at night brought them back to a kind of reality.

Most of us arrived a bit past five o'clock. Editor Phil Mulvey, a Scotsman, and former golden boy in news circles back in England, would already be beet-red with drink. His fellow newspaperman Richard Petit would arrive by bicycle but never joined any of us at the *bia hoi*. He would sit by himself, lean against a wall about 20 feet away, chain smoke, drink coffee, get pumped up for the paper's night shift. Always in sunglasses, hair slicked back, he reminded us all of a broken-down Jack Nicholson.

Ricky from San Francisco was a font of street wisdom and amusing stories, including tales from his Black Panther days. Ricky taught Korean kids how to speak English, especially black American vernacular, which they loved.

He drove a chopped-up Bonus motorcycle, and was always showing up with exhaust burns and flesh-torn knees. He was in Vietnam to take a break from the obligations associated with supporting a bunch of kids and ex-wives back in the States.

Hans, a hydrologist at UNICEF, was there almost every day. Stocky, pudgy, rounded like a cannonball, Hans is a family man, married to a Burmese woman with two children. They have a farm across the Mekong in Thailand that some day Hans hopes to retire on. During some of the worst guerrilla violence perpetrated by the ousted Khmer Rouge, he spent seven years digging wells for impoverished villages in Cambodia.

I once asked Hans, an educated person who grew up in communist East Germany, "Weren't you frustrated with being told what you could read?"

His reply had a familiar ring, "I had many sex books, that's all I need," giving a menacing chuckle, skin tags framing his squinty eyes. Hans knows every brothel in Indochina, and while living in Hanoi, frequented the ones used nightly by high-level Party members.

Paul Copeland was a high-flying kid from Seattle, who had squandered a few hundred thousand dollars of his stepdad's money in a start-up computer business in Vietnam. One night he created a minor diplomatic incident when he clocked a high-ranking officer from the British High Commission. Other times he was peaceable, spending most of his time at the Buddha Belly hangout, The Spotted Cow, playing darts and talking up local investment opportunities.

Then there were the usual suspects whom I routinely saw in other places as well as the *bia hoi*: a local Kung Fu master, two Australians teaching English, an Australian publisher of a private business newsletter, an American couple from Boston, both working for NGOs, Jason Rush of UNICEF, John Lancaster, Simon, Chuck Searcy, and a few others.

Phil Mulvey, known for telling outlandish tales, joined us later than usual one evening at the miniature plastic stools. He began carrying on about having sex with prostitutes at the old Hanoi Hilton, officially known as Hoa Lo, or Fiery Furnace. "You know, blow jobs in the guillotine room, an orgy in the John McCain suite, shackled on death row," he gushed in Scottish glory. We had heard it before but Jason and I didn't believe him.

Still early but after dark, I gave Jason a ride home on my motorcycle. With no great effort, we detoured around the corner, making an innocent pass by Hoa Lo Prison. As we pulled up to the main gate, four prostitutes materialized from the shadows. I began bantering with the ladies. It became apparent that $20, no further negotiation needed, would provide just the sort of follies in the Hanoi Hilton that Phil had been reminiscing about.

Then, from behind the sliphole in the massive iron-reinforced wooden doors, the night watchman's eyes appeared. Encouraged by the sight of foreigners, he slung open the door and waved us in, girls and all.

I had taken the charade as far as good sense and my marital vows would allow. I assured all the players we would return later. Phil Mulvey's credibility soared. It all made sense, I later realized. The prison is a big empty building at night—a non-performing asset—and the ladies need a place to take their clients.

The next day I had lunch with Mark McDonald, the Asian correspondent for the *San Jose Mercury News*, and told him about the events of the night before. He pounced on the story, asking me to accompany him on another nighttime trip to Hoa Lo. Feeling like a snitch, two weeks later I agreed to go. We had a few beers around the corner at the *bia hoi* with John, waiting for darkness. The scene unfolded in front of the prison almost identically to the night with Jason, except as I was flashing cash at the girls and talking to the night watchman, John came rolling by and gave a crisp salute. "As you were, boys," he commanded.

Mark got his story that night. The next morning he interviewed the prison's curator, Nguyen Van Tu, who denied such escapades ever happened at Hoa Lo, "This is a spiritual place as well as a historical site that is important to the whole country. This could not have happened. We are closed at night. No one could come in."

Mark would later rate the prison story one of the best exposes he had done during his four years in Hanoi. And what a great story: sex and corruption in the Hanoi Hilton. When I passed by the prison late at night a few months ago, it looked like business as usual, with johns, hookers, and Party guys on the take.

One evening shortly after moving to Hanoi, I met Everett Alvarez briefly at the upscale Hanoi Towers, adjacent to Hoa Lo and built on the grounds where the bulk of the prison once sprawled. Alvarez had been the first American POW to check into the Hanoi Hilton, and stayed there the longest. He had ejected from his A4 Skyhawk after taking a hit on August 5, 1964. His bombing sortie was a response to the alleged North Vietnamese naval attacks on American ships that would become the pretext for going to war in Vietnam, the Gulf of Tonkin Incident.

I addressed him as "Lieutenant Alvarez," the rank he had when shot down. Soft-spoken, handsome, ageing with grace, he corrected me, "Lieutenant Commander, please."

He was in Hanoi as a consultant with the Department of Defense. I asked him what it's like to stay in the plush residential tower at the same address where he'd spent eight and a half years in prison.

"It feels creepy, very creepy." As he walked away, he jokingly said, "I'm getting out of this place once and for all."

No doubt it did feel creepy. Yet depending on how you look at it, Hanoi's myriad ironies can't help but evoke varying degrees of tragedy and comedy. The site of its notorious war prison now hosts a plush residential property renting to ex-POWs, with a golf store selling Callaways and Pings, while the remainder of the prison complex has become a museum with a sideline trade in pleasures of the night. Over his eight and a half years as a POW, Alvarez probably dreamed a thousand times of clean sheets and someone to cuddle up with, and now all is available plus more at Hoa Lo.

The Ly Thuong Kiet *bia hoi* gang gradually dissolved however. The UNICEF offices relocated, and several members moved abroad. Hans was transferred to a new posting in Burma, where he is skulking his way through fresh government brothels. In a four-month period in 2002, three of our tippling assembly died.

Phil Mulvey was only in his mid-40s, and was last seen on a Sunday afternoon by his friend John Peat. That evening his neighbors heard a blood-curdling scream coming from his apartment. He was found dead the next morning. Some said his heart blew out from too much Ecstasy, others said it was pure methamphetamine. John seemed to think he had a degenerative heart condition. The police kept it all hushed. He apparently had a digital camera full of girly pictures. Not necessarily related to the pictures, two hookers stood vigil waiting to scavenge what they could from their old friend Phil.

After five days, with no notice of a funeral, John Peat went to check on Phil at the hospital morgue. Phil was sprawled on a slab in a hot, deserted room. Starting to putrefy, he was still dressed in the pair of black pants he was wearing when he died. John raised enough hell that hospital officials moved the body into an air-conditioned room. A couple of days later, a few close friends and no family honored Phil at a cremation ceremony. His ashes and beloved kilt—but no digital camera—were sent to Scotland to his ageing mother.

Approaching the precipice of 60 years, Richard Petit apparently fell down a flight of stairs and broke his neck. As with Phil the details were sketchy— drunk, on heroin, no one seemed to know. Many people were familiar with the after-hours persona of Richard Petit, but few knew much about him. The American embassy couldn't find Richard's next of kin. They authorized, however, a cremation ceremony and agreed to hold his ashes for six months. I attended a wake of 20 or 30 people at a *bia hoi* on Hai Ba Trung. Not one person there seemed to know Richard's last name.

Paul Copeland was rowdy and reckless but too young to die. He wasn't much older than 30, and had only recently returned to the States. Paul's Aussie friends at the Spotted Cow said he'd careened off an icy road into a tree. It was late at night and his blood-alcohol level was in the stratosphere. At the Spotted Cow, his pithy graffiti lives on: "If you have tried everything in life and failed, try Hanoi." The Buddha Bellies remembered him with a succession of wakes.

About the time the *bia hoi* scene on Ly Thuong Kiet was breaking up, my house started to become a scene for Friday evening happy hours. Thanks partly to my central location John and others would come by. It felt like the beginning of a new season in Hanoi.

John gets around Hanoi by holding onto the back of a *cyclo*, pedaled by his full time driver Mr. Lai. "Cyclo drivers are the last of the real working stiffs," John says. He trusts Mr. Lai as an uncle would a favorite nephew. Mr. Lai was only three months old when his father, fighting for the NVA, was shot and killed by American marines near Danang.

Always before dark on those guys' nights out, I hop into Mr. Lai's *cyclo* with John, while others grab their own for a trip back in time up to the Old Quarter. Over the course of an evening, we do a barhopping loop around Hoan Kiem Lake, our Friday night Stations of the Cross.

One Friday evening, we carried road drinks and followed the designated *cyclo* route, swinging out onto Trang Tien Street, where we were greeted by the raucous gallery of familiar *xe om* drivers (motorcycle taxis), shouting, waving to let us know they were available. Stopping at the light briefly, we rounded the corner onto Ngo Quyen.

Stoplights are becoming more than just a suggestion. In 1998, when I moved to Hanoi, I was told there were only 17 stoplights in the whole city of 3 million people. Better than the year before when there were only five.

On Ngo Quyen Street stands the tropical white Metropole Hotel. Returning to the habits of the *colons*, every few months on a Sunday we would splurge at the Metropole's Le Beaulieu Restaurant. At a long table with a streetside window, we indulged in a lingering brunch of France's finest—an open flow of Champagne, caviar, pates, oysters from Brittany, entrecote of beef, clams in white wine, beef tartare, cheeses, pastries, and Cuban cigars. A Vietnamese string quartet leavened the mood. As much as the Vietnamese wanted the French out, they do like the many "Bs" of French colonialism— Burgundy, baguettes, berets, brothels, bars, boulevards and buildings in the Romantic Franco-Viet style.

Across from the Metropole, an ornate former French palace is now

Government House, used for visiting VIPs. Simon and a wide-eyed Ms. Quy once spent an evening on the street there, watching the klieg lights wash over Michael Caine during the filming of the second version of Graham Greene's *The Quiet American*, the first major Hollywood movie filmed in Vietnam.

Well-kept parks, forested in mature banyans and tamarinds, border the road on either side. The arrestingly ugly State Bank and the Hanoi People's Committee buildings engulf the stylish low-rises in a spate of Soviet realism. Into the maelstrom of traffic, John rolled—chatting, having a gin and tonic and hanging on to Mr. Lai's *cyclo*. Heads turned—foreigners and locals alike—agog at the sight.

We turned towards the lake at Lo Su Street, before whipping back onto Hang Dau, an extension of Shoe Street, with nothing but polished leather shoes arrayed along the sidewalks and in storefronts beneath a low-hanging trestle of leafy branches.

Coming to a stop on the edge of the traffic circle at the north end of Hoan Kiem, Mr. Lai and Simon assisted John up a small stairway to the elevator in a post-Soviet mid-rise, the Turtle Building. Outside of a few upscale tourist hotels, there are only a couple of restaurants and bars in Hanoi that are completely wheelchair accessible. Even UNICEF, where John has consulted on children's disability issues, is not accessible.

Leaving the elevator, we made our way through Legends, a beer hall owned by a German brewmeister. The place was packed with a crowd of middle-class Vietnamese pressed around a chain of long wooden tables. We claimed a table out on the balcony, and ordered quart-sized tankards of dark, porter-like lagers.

The day had been braising hot. The fading sun enveloped the Old Quarter, tinging the moist sky in peach and violet. Soon, the air began to move, the Lao winds of late spring blew across Hoan Kiem Lake. Below, the traffic circle dinned as the Konica and Fuji electronic billboards flashed ads like screen-savers. Cops in green and brown uniforms abandoned their traffic stations—some would say personal toll gates—for the evening. Young girls stood in the eddy of traffic, hoisting trees of balloons and pinwheels in a rainbow of colors. Postcard boys latched onto tourists one last time before vanishing for the night. An old couple in their skivvies inched through the traffic like sleepwalkers. The traffic heaved and swirled into a white blur of light, like the slow-shutter exposure of a comet.

"Action" Jackson, a gold-mining geologist joined us. Jason Rush and Simon were laughing about a new ordinance outlawing tank tops, short shorts, and pajamas in public; foreigners were generally exempt.

I eased into the fun with my "anti-Pajama Law" two cents, "The Chinese outlawed pajamas in public two years ago. They were targeting the rural folks, out in the provinces. They called the behavior 'uncivilized'."

John followed, "The problem is China is not in the tropics. It's hot and crowded in Hanoi, and people need to spread out and be comfortable."

Action chimed in, "This is one of the things I love about Vietnam. How old do you have to be to wear pajamas in public? Fifty? Sixty? I want to wear pajamas in public but I'm only forty-five."

"Don't forget it's the decade of the navel. These up and coming pop culture girls around here aren't going for the *ao dais* on Friday night," Simon added with a raffish smile.

"The cops have already quit trying to enforce it. They gave up after a week. It's still a law but it doesn't mean a damn thing," John concluded.

"Cheers, cheers," as we clanked glasses to the failure of the "Pajama Laws."

Not long after, we were in our *cyclos* on Le Thai To Street, heading towards Restaurant Bobby Chinn. Singles and young lovers cruised by, circling the lake in a Friday night ritual. The breeze kept up, and as street lights flickered on, the sacred Hoan Kiem's waters became an elliptical black sapphire, glinting in a thousand directions. Dark stencils of willow trees hung on the lake's verges, luring junkies and hookers and boy hustlers to come out and play. The beeping, the honking, the shrill voices, the whining of sirens, all banged in the air with ghosts of ascending dragons, of sacred turtles, of bygone days and nights of devilry.

Most Friday nights we stop by the Polite Pub or the nearby New Zealand-owned Puku. There, a band of younger expatriates, mostly Australians, wear berets and carry shoulder-slung monk bags, pining for the next poetry reading. As fresh members of this avant-garde tribe arrive, they all bounce up and down like jack-in-the-boxes in a competitive game of cheek kissing. The old hands—here before the Roxy Theatre was torched in 1998—get misty-eyed as they mention their former Old Quarter hangout. Those were the good old days.

Skipping the Polite Pub and Puku, we arrived at Restaurant Bobby Chinn's in a flourish. The bar was crowded with young hip Vietnamese. Sandra, a sexy blonde career diplomat at the Czech embassy who drives a "Willy" (a wartime American Army jeep), was perched at the bar with her cocker spaniel strapped to the metallic bar stool. Across the room, Marci Friedman, director of the International Red Cross in Hanoi, sat at a two-person table with her friend, Larry Holzman, a social marketer of condoms.

Lolling on the cushions, out of sight, was a thirtysomething Mizbah Sheikh, nuzzled up against her twenty-year old beau, Smurf. This unlikely union transcended all cultural cliches: she a Yale graduate of Muslim faith from Kashmir, working for UNICEF, and he a marine guard at the American embassy, hailing from southern Louisiana. Smurf's stated ambition in life was to return to his hometown in Cajun country and become a deputy sheriff; meanwhile this metaphorical summit played out in the live-and-let-live Western enclaves of Hanoi.

Rick of Rick's Café, Bobby, was working the hip in-crowd. Old Minh was playing his sax, as he had at the conservatory 40 years ago, riffing like a poltergeist. Jazzbos—artists, students, a movie director, the new Beats of Hanoi—flopped around on floor cushions near Smurf and Mizbah like fresh-hatched moths around a bright light.

Streamers of white roses and long swatches of silk hung from the ceiling. Simon, John and I joined some other friends on the low couches in back. We ordered up a communal hookah of sweet apple tobacco, a slice of Bobby's Egyptian heritage. Not even during the SARS epidemic—when many were wearing masks around Hanoi—did we give up the group hookah. We clung to it like a talisman against the more insidious ill of freedom threatened.

Food begins with grapes covered in goat cheese, embedded with chunks of pistachios. I pick up the pace with a Karber's Fizzy, which I invented using medication my doctor gave me for my back problem. It's Bombay Sapphire premium gin, tonic, two tabs of "seltzerized" codeine (sold at the corner drug store) and lime. "When you are feeling a little too much, it's for the sensitive man," Bobby's drink menu reads.

Bobby was finessing the crowd like a magician, aided by Jeff behind the bar who kept three or four conversations whizzing in the air at once, while landing exotic potions upright on the bar. A coterie of expats and local gays made a grand entrance, filling Bobby's place with drama. Party officials have only recently (and reluctantly) admitted that local homosexuality exists. Thus acknowledged, this group of gays are like caged birds finally singing.

Bobby's lakefront retreat is a revolving door of tourists who have studied the food columns, Party boys, foreign journalists, ambassadors, international school teachers, embassy functionaries, UN and World Bank folks, and the unending flow of NGO, humanitarian aid workers. Or as Bobby says, "It's a bunch of poor people from rich countries giving rich people in poor countries money."

He has some serious art on his yellow-silked walls, thanks to a consignment arrangement with a Hanoi art dealer. Not only do the life-size paintings add ambiance and bring in the art crowd, they frequently offer social and political commentary. Writers do not enjoy freedom of expression in Vietnam, but painters and musicians work in the abstract and thus can push the envelope—caricaturing communism the way the performers in the musical "Cabaret" spoof the unwitting Brown Shirts.

One painting that hung in Bobby's place nearly a year was an earthen-silver, lacquer image of Ho Chi Minh presiding over a gallery of what appeared to be wine bottles. On closer inspection, the bottles wore the faces of people. A representative from the Ministry of Culture and Information picked up on the imagery and asked that the lacquer masterpiece be removed. Bobby, who had paid a hefty price for the painting, reluctantly followed their wishes and removed it to his home. Four months later, the culture police visited the famous artist responsible for the work, told him to retrieve it from Bobby and turn it over to them. The artist gave Bobby his choice of a replacement painting, and for the sake of self-preservation, complied with the government's wishes.

Over the years, Joellen and I have entertained many visitors at Bobby's, usually from a window table looking out onto Hoan Kiem Lake. Always seductive, lady-lake changes her complexion by day, by night, and by season— trembling in the rains, glowing in spring's bath of color, or somber in winter austerity.

One early winter evening at Bobby's, sitting by the window looking out on the lake, we met Bill Schaap and Ellen Ray from New York. A civil and ideological marriage of four decades, they are a couple of leftist legends. Bill is a New York attorney, author, and publisher of *Covert Action*, a CIA watchdog magazine. Ellen is a documentary filmmaker, a political journalist and self-styled communist. Her aunt, Willa Cather, is the groundbreaking author of the early-to-mid 20th century who wrote about heroic women, and the spiritual decay of modern America caused by materialism.

Bill and Ellen spent two years working a "GI coffee house" in Okinawa as anti-Vietnam war activists. A couple of decades later, they were both consultants to Oliver Stone in the movie, *JFK*. They published the book on which the screenplay was based, and Ellen played a cameo role in a restaurant scene. Recently, Ellen co-authored the book, *Guantanamo*, about prisoner abuse at the American base in Cuba.

Bill and Ellen had been involved with Vietnam Communist Party members since their anti-war days in the 1960s, but this was their first visit to Vietnam. Ellen had been in Paris during the Peace Talks in 1972, when one of the negotiators, Madame Binh, gave her footage of the human and environmental ravages caused by Agent Orange. She smuggled the black and white film into the States, and made the first documentary on the subject. (Madame Binh recently retired as Vice President of Vietnam.)

At the same time in Paris they met Xuan Oanh, the official spokesman for the Vietnamese delegation at the Peace Talks. With the prospect of peace just over the horizon, Xuan Oanh waxed philosophical, quoting a song written by Kris Kristofferson, performed by Janis Joplin, "Freedom is just another word for nothing left to lose."

When the lunar new year holiday of Tet rolls around each January and February, and I mention the festive season to contemporaries back in the States, they usually think I mean "the Offensive" of 1968. Tet and "offensive" are two words fused in their minds like New and York. But for Vietnamese, Tet is a deeply spiritual 24 hours that ends the old year and brings in the new. It is time to wipe the slate clean, to renew hopes, welcome the spring. But most of all it is a time of gift-bearing and pilgrimages to hereditary homes and villages, to be with family, and to seek the protection of ancestors at the family altar. The same goes for Vietnamese living abroad —some 250,000 make the journey home each year, leaving tens of millions of dollars behind in Vietnam each time.

Expatriates, on the other hand, find the week of Tet a time of almost unbearable hardship: housekeepers, cooks, waiters, bartenders, secretaries and co-workers abandon us. Rather than endure this suffering, many of us flee to Thailand or Burma for a week. Those of us left behind find the streets eerily quiet—stores, restaurants and bars disappear behind steel accordion grates. The streets are empty.

Already a month before Tet, the holiday atmosphere begins gathering steam. Streets and shops are hung with sparkling red banners screaming *Chuc Mung Nam Moi*, New Year's Greetings. Storefronts from the Old Quarter and throughout Hanoi pour merchandise onto the pavement: boxed sweets, vivid decorations, calendars, votive offerings, fat Buddhas with gaping smiles to place at the family altar. Flower markets appear on the streets and along the main roads leading in from the country, which are forested in peach trees, their branches mostly spare and leafless but for pink blossoms. Mandarin orange trees, pyramidal like Christmas trees, hang with the seasonal ornament of saffron fruit. There is an ancient art to coaxing these trees into bloom precisely during the Tet season. A modern embellishment is the pragmatic custom of bungee-cording the orange trees upright on backs of motorcycles and bicycles, to deliver throughout Hanoi's streets and neighborhoods.

Joellen and I decided to stay for the full Tet festivities during our last year in Hanoi. We steeled ourselves for the rigors of washing our own dishes, taking out trash, making sandwiches, and changing the sheets.

The Tet of 2003—passing from the Year of the Horse to the Year of the Goat—began with some of the coldest temperatures ever recorded in Hanoi. It even snowed in the Tonkin Alps near Sapa. Many Hanoians boarded the train to go see snow for the first time in their lives.

Tet begins on the 23rd day of the 12th lunar month, as houses are primped and painted, old debts are settled and new clothes are purchased. Traditionalists commune with the Kitchen God, or *Ong Tao*. Journeying on the back of a carp, the Kitchen God travels that day to the Heavenly King to give an annual report on each household. Families go to lakes like Hoan Kiem and release carp, imprinted of course with the spirit of the Kitchen God, destined for heaven.

Nguyen Cong Tru, the artist of great renown, and close friend of Simon, stopped by on Kitchen God day bearing a gift of French wine. Wearing a scarf and looking dapper, he had been cleaning his house since dawn and was thirsty and hungry. He was headed for a bar in the Old Quarter on Hang Voi Street, so I jumped on the back of his motorbike. Simon and Ms. Quy followed. Ms. Quy doesn't trust her Merry Old beau out at night with Nguyen Cong Tru.

Parking the bikes curbside, we tunneled through a narrow corridor of concrete before deadending at the bar's doorway. It had the smoky ambience of a speakeasy set in the bowels of some Arab medina. Artsy patrons were squeezed snugly on cushions around low-set tables, their conversation generating a steady hum.

Someone pitched up a plastic table and four stools for us in the tiny alley. We were almost in darkness but for a fluorescent light on a balcony glowing somberly, and the alluring glare of fairy lights framing the bar's red door. Ten feet away, beneath a bird's nest of electrical wires draped in drying laundry, smoke billowed from the charcoal fires of two stoop-bodied crones. All around were sour seeps of water, reeking of ammonia. Tru began pouring bumble-bee flavored rice whiskey, mellifluous to the taste as honey but with a fiery sting going down. Tru complained about the decline of the true Tet: "In the old days when no one had money, the women prepared food all day. Now they just go to the market and buy."

He and Quy ordered a carnivore's smorgasbord of dried beef, grilled chicken, roast goat, and dog—dog sausages, dog McNuggets and dog-on-the-bone. "Dog is very good to eat at the end of the lunar year. It cleans out last year's problems and sins," Tru chirped by way of a toast. Draining our thimbles of whiskey, Simon and I timidly dipped the dog-on-a-bone in the purple, fermented shrimp paste.

Tru was wolfing down dog sausage like peanuts, and asking for the *thuoc lao*, the bamboo water pipe. In keeping with local maxim—by the virtue of the desire it must be legitimate—we filled the pipe with a pleasant mix of hashish and tobacco. Soon we got on the motorbikes to Hoan Kiem Lake and a new disco, a submarine-capsule of a place. Glistening with exposed pipes and silver railing, the club felt like the sub's engine room, half-shrouded in real and artificial smoke. Young girls in split-pea colored sailor outfits competed for our drink orders. Divas and dancing men performed on the revolving, translucent stage, circling in and out of an electrical storm of flashing lights and fake fog. It all seemed to be in slow motion, like being underwater. The deafening sound became muted and the tutu-ed dancers a faceless blur of pink coral.

On the following day, after the departure of the Kitchen Gods, Joellen and I took a Tet basket—Australian wine, chocolate-coated macadamia nuts, Lipton tea and gourmet cookies—to the house of Mr. Vu Xuan Hong, chairman of the Vietnam Union of Friendship Organizations and member of the National Assembly. After introducing us to his son Kanh, who goes to university in Australia, Mr. Hong served us candied fruits and rice whiskey out of a half-gallon Smirnoff bottle. The fiery concoction was the pride of his father's province of Nam Dinh, where he would travel in a few days to his ancestral home and cemetery. Mr. Hong toasted our visit as a good omen, the first foreigners to have entered his home during the Tet season. We again raised our porcelain thimbles to World Peace, as he pointed out that Vietnam had had 89 years of episodic war and civil strife in the last century.

Next evening we went to the seven-story townhouse of Dr Tran Nhon, former Vice Minister of Water Resources, and his wife, Le Ngoc Hue, a Senior Program Officer in Joellen's office.

After the defeat of the French in 1954, hundreds of thousands of families, most of them Catholic, went south. Dr Nhon's family was among the much smaller counter-migration that moved north, to embrace the prevailing winds of Ho Chi Minh. Although Dr. Nhon never fought in the war, he was trained in Moscow and Hanoi to return to the South upon victory and assist with the takeover. Working as a functionary in the South for 15 years, he returned to Hanoi, where he climbed to success in water management, a vitally important field in a country like Vietnam.

Having recently retired as Vice Minister of Water Resources, Dr. Nhon is also a composer. He rushed to show us his sheets of his latest works, including some in English. Then he sang a playful ditty he'd composed for the 1998 World Cup, aired on Vietnam Radio during every match.

Over the course of the evening, we ate, drank, talked politics and listened to Tchaikovsky's ballet *Swan Lake* on a phonograph. At some point, Dr Nhon raised his glass to World Peace and to the New Year, *Chuc Mung Nam Moi*. Not so interested in the upcoming Year of the Goat, he pointed out that the year the French had taken over Hanoi was in 1885, the Year of the Golden Rooster. Sixty years later in 1945, the zodiacal cycle spun around to the next Year of the Golden Rooster. Propitiously, that was the year Ho Chi Minh declared the North's independence from France. And now, his country rid of colonialism and Cold War aggression, Dr Nhon anxiously awaits the next Year of the Golden Rooster, 2005, crossing his fingers that Vietnam will join the World Trade Organization that year.

On the evening before the lunar New Year, in a drizzling rain, Joellen and I went to dinner at the home of friends Le Ngoc Bao and his wife Ha. Bao was educated in Singapore and is a policy analyst in the Deputy Prime Minister's office. Ha, a modern career woman, received a master's degree in the States and is now employed by the National Committee on Population, Families and Children.

In the heart of the Old Quarter, hidden from the street and tucked behind layers of concrete walls, Bao's family home was built in 1924 in the French-Vietnamese, chock-a-block style. Without elaborating on the reasons, which probably involved accusations of landlordism, Bao told us the house was expropriated from his family during the land reform debacle in 1956. For the equivalent of $3,000 in gold, they bought it back in 1974.

He gave us a brief tour, showing us a crawlspace beneath the stairway where his family hid from French soldiers, and then in 1972 when he and his family took shelter from American bombings at Christmas.

After the tour, we convened in a family room dominated by a large Chinese mandarin tree and a smaller peach tree. Adorning the dinner table was a branch of sweet smelling forsythia, surrounded by sugared apricots, marinated cherries, tangelos, sweet grapefruit, pumpkin seeds and a bottle of white wine.

"Like snow at Christmas in America, during Tet in Hanoi we prefer the weather to be cold and misty. It brings out the smells and tastes," Bao said, beckoning us toward the vittles.

Bao's mother, tiny like a child, crept in to greet us. When she smiled her face crinkled in kindly folds. Her hair was tied in a bun and framed in a holiday scarf. She spoke no English, but greeted us in warm bows with the quiet self-possession of her age.

Bao's father is deceased, leaving Bao in the Confucian role of being the oldest male in the ancestral house. Neil Jamieson in his book, *Understanding Vietnam,* described each Vietnamese family as a nation, "The husband is nominal head of state and in charge of foreign relations; the wife is minister of the interior and controls the treasury." Bao would preside over Tet festivities at the house the next day, with the extended family on hand. Bao's mother and other female relatives were busy preparing traditional foods for the family altar and holiday feast. As a traditional Vietnamese woman, Bao's mother is now at the end of her three submissions: first to her father, then to her husband and finally, to her son Bao.

Bao and Ha's niece and two children joined us briefly. They confessed that their favorite part of Tet would come on the second day when they would visit their maternal grandmother and receive red envelopes of money. Fourteen years old, the niece spoke perfect English and had a thing for the music of the Backstreet Boys. She also likes to "chat" with fellow Vietnamese on the Internet.

Ha stepped in to mention the temptations facing too many Hanoi teenagers: drugs, drinking and motorcycles. Their oldest daughter was 13, and was worried about her weight. She was small and thin like most young Vietnamese. Bao shook his head, "When I was young we worried about having enough to eat, now they have plenty and won't eat enough."

Dinner was served: many vegetables, pressed chicken and goat. Bao told us the upcoming Year of the Goat was a good year for boys to be born. "Many strong, intelligent, compassionate-for-the-less-fortunate leaders were born in the Year of the Goat," Bao explained. We discussed the Year of the Golden Dragon, also considered good for boys, which came three years before. Almost every woman of childbearing age in Vietnam was pregnant that year.

Still gathered around in awe at the sight of foreigners in their house, when the girls saw me penning my email address with my left hand, they lowered their heads in a tandem fit of tittering. Almost in chorus, Bao and Ha shed some light, "No child in Vietnam can pass the first grade of school unless they write with their right hand."

Such conformism! Back in America, in 1957 when I began the first grade, I was put in the back of the classroom with the other left-handers and made to write with the other hand. In the school lunchroom left-handers were made to sit at the end of the cafeteria-sized tables to avoid dueling arms. In an American age that championed uniformity, we were treated as if we had learning disabilities. Out of the classroom, coaches made me bat right-handed, play tennis right-handed, golf right- handed. Today I write and throw with my left hand, eat with my right hand, fire a shotgun from the left and fly-fish with my right. I am not ambidextrous. I am confused, yet still trying not to conform.

The next evening, after our visit with Bao's family, I met up with a few fellow nonconformists at John Lancaster's seventh floor apartment on Bui Thi Xuan Street, overlooking the three lakes where fireworks would erupt at midnight. Simon, Ms. Quy and others joined us there, on an evening when most Vietnamese are at home or somewhere celebrating with their families.

Among us was David Holdridge—a former second-lieutenant in the Americal Division who lost several feet of his intestines when gut-shot in Quang Ngai Province the summer of 1969. He was today in a buoyant mood and the subject of several toasts. David ran the Vietnam office of an NGO that owned a share of the 1997 Nobel Peace Prize for their work in banning and clearing anti-personnel landmines. On behalf of the NGO, he had just signed the first bilateral agreement with the Ministry of Defense to do a comprehensive survey of the remaining unexploded ordnance in Vietnam.

Among other appetizers and drinks, John served the traditional Tet staple, *banh chung*, cold fatty pork and bean paste tucked in the middle of lime-green layers of glutinous rice. In the old days before the relative prosperity of the 1990s, Hanoi women and children used to work slavishly for 12 hours and more, over charcoal fires preparing the traditional *chung* cakes. The cakes would be placed on the family altar on Tet Eve and eaten on the days following.

Most expatriate men living in Hanoi who are married to Vietnamese women loathe the day they have to visit their in-laws during the Tet season and eat *banh chung*. This is understandable. When unwrapped and served from its banana-leaf-like packaging, the *chung* cake resembles a radioactive blob of green and tastes like cold blubber. John and I made futile attempts at slicing the *chung* with a knife, like trying to scoop up a ball of Jell-O with chopsticks. Ms. Quy calmly brought the situation under control, grabbing the bamboo twine the *banh chung* had been bound in, and garroting the green glob into perfectly cut squares.

We washed down the cakes with gin and went gaga at midnight as we gathered on the balcony watching skies illuminated by fireworks in three directions—over West Lake, to the south at Lenin Park and to the north on Hoan Kiem. The glass facades of Hanoi's few high rises glittered with mirror images of the display. Candles and lanterns flickered below at a pagoda as devotees streamed in for Tet prayers.

With the fireworks over, we departed John's *en masse* and weaved through festive streets lit up by small bonfires of paper offerings to the dead—tiny inflammable models of televisions, bicycles, motorbikes, money and more. The money is used to bribe the Kings of Hell to lighten the suffering of their ancestors. Defying local ordnances, firecrackers crackled around us anarchically. Like a human dam breaking in all directions, waves of people flowed by, rushing from the fireworks event toward their ancestral homes.

Out of sight, on the upper floors of every home, families gathered in front of their ancestral altars to burn joss sticks, to offer food and drink and to invite their antecedents to confer happiness on the family. At the precise moment of the New Year, upon the arrival of the new *Ong Cong*—the god who oversees the family land—heaven and earth become one, and *yin and yang* shift into perfect balance. Each home is then ready for the first visitor of the New Year, whose presence and zodiacal harmony with the coming year will bestow good tidings.

The first morning of the lunar New Year, Joellen and I took a taxi with Simon to Ms. Quy's home on Le Ngoc Han Street. The roads were mostly empty, with red flags drooping in the misty tranquility; all businesses were grated shut. A few men in fedoras and suits, and a similar number of well-dressed women wearing trilby hats, motored between homes.

Ms. Quy, as well as being an entertainer and military officer, runs a coffee shop on the ground floor of her family home. With the accordion doors open to the street and the misty weather, we gathered around one of the tables there and presented her family with a Tet basket.

Ms. Quy's mother was dressed in all her finery: golden ear studs and a glinting chain around her neck weighted with a jade amulet; her hair was chignoned on top with a yellow silk scarf, and she wore a black velvet coat. She was spry as a bird, her owl-like eyes panning to and fro, full of intelligence. Ms. Quy's daughter, Phu Ang, and niece Minh, wore blue jeans and platform shoes. Red envelopes littered the table, packages of Tet gift money for friends and family. Ms. Quy and her mother served us Heineken, rice whiskey and more *chung* cake. Fortunately, Ms. Quy's mother also served a plate of pickled scallions, which helped cut the taste and fatty smell and gave a crunch to the texture.

That afternoon, our expatriate friends came over for ham-and-turkey sandwiches. With almost all Vietnamese staying at their homes, Ms. Quy was our only local visitor that day.

The next day, a time for getting out and visiting maternal relatives and friends, Joellen went to see a friend and colleague, Tu Ha, whose father had died only a few days before. Tu Ha could not leave her house to visit other family or friends for another month. That would bring bad luck to anyone her presence touched.

On the third night of Tet, the Opera House square around the corner from our residence featured singers and dancers waltzing in and out of a MTV *mise-en-scene* of stage smoke and lights.

The fourth day of Tet, a Tuesday and an even-numbered day, was selected by Thuy, our cook and new house girl, as an auspicious time to return to work. The long anticipated morning arrived with relief. Although my marriage to Joellen had not yet collapsed, our nerves were sorely tattered. Neither of us knew where to take the garbage, so it had piled up in the kitchen. I had been in charge of making the bed, now a cyclone of twisted sheets. Clothes littered the bedroom. Joellen was to act as lead dishwasher, but in the end was upstaged by Ms. Quy. Simon was charged with filling the ice trays, now filled only with cold air. With the arrival of Thuy, our home's expatriate life could revert from the offenses of Tet to a peacetime footing.

Harnessing the Masses

O ne fall day beneath the jackfruit trees of the Au Lac Café, I sat waiting at a streetside table, enjoying an unrivalled view of the backdoor of the colonial Metropole Hotel. The beggar lady Thuy, who has cerebral palsy and works the popular beat, came by and sold me the gum she hawks daily. As usual, she tried to walk off without giving me change. "Stop, stop," I shouted, as she turned around laughing and handed me my change. "No more this week," I told her. A few months later, she turned up pregnant with twins by one of the hard-bitten motorcycle taxi drivers around the corner. Her fundraising drive had only just begun.

The Au Lac and the restaurant next door, the Diva, both spill out of two old villas that are owned by a friend, Tran Tien Duc, and his family. He is the son of the former mayor of Hanoi, who held that position for 20 years beginning in the mid-1950s. Duc and his wife, Ngoc, were married next to the fireplace in the Diva villa in February 1968. Their wedding was interrupted when American bombs began pummeling the city. In their formal wedding attire, they fled to the bomb shelter in the basement.

Duc stopped by and chatted with me a bit, then went inside to see his mother, now a widow in her 80s. Simon arrived along with a mutual friend, Marie, proprietor of the only foreign-owned bookstore in Hanoi. Marie was excited about the arrival of a new shipment of books.

I asked how the Ministry of Culture and Information censored her wares.

She laughed. "I am not supposed to encourage the patronage of Vietnamese customers. There can be no foreign-published books imported or sold with 'Vietnam' as part of the title. Any book with 'Atlas' in the title is forbidden. It's hopeless trying to convince them that Ayn Rand's *magnum opus* on capitalism, *Atlas Shrugged*, does not contain sensitive maps of Vietnam."

In the shipment just received were two copies of a fascinating book, *Lenin's Embalmers*, written by Ilya Zbarsky, a scientist charged with preserving Lenin's corpse, who was preceded by his father before him as one of the original embalmers. The books made it through customs on the strength of Lenin's name. It's the story of how Lenin, and eventually Ho Chi Minh and others, were embalmed.

Few secrets in communist Vietnam are better protected than the mysterious periodic maintenance of the corpse of Ho Chi Minh. It all started back in wintry Moscow on January 20, 1924, the day Vladimir Ilich Lenin died.

Racing against the clock, as his body decomposed, Lenin's disciples—Trotsky, Stalin, Kamenev, Dzerzhinsky and other politburo members—began the debate on whether to bury, cremate or preserve the corpse for posterity.

While the corpse lay at the Trade Union House, drawing pilgrims such as Nguyen Ai Quoc (young Ho Chi Minh), Stalin foresaw a struggle for political succession. He thought the corpse could serve as a tool for "harnessing the religious sentiment of the ignorant masses in order to ensure the survival of the regime," as Zbarsky wrote.

After the pomp and circumstance of the funeral, Petrograd (née St. Petersburg) was renamed Leningrad, and Stalin won a vote of the politburo to preserve Lenin. Over a month after Lenin's death, Professor Vorobiov, a bio-chemist and expert in preserving anatomical specimens—organs, arms and legs so far— was summoned to Moscow.

At the end of March, Vorobiov, the elder Zbarsky and several assistants, all of whom had been under relentless pressure, agreed to preserve the corpse of the leader of the world's proletariat. Their task was formidable, to recreate the semblance of recent death, or better yet the illusion of napping. There was one small factor in favor of their unlikely success: just the hands and head would be exposed for viewing.

After weeks of work, the scientists came up with a successful process, and gave Lenin's family a viewing. Lenin's brother delivered the verdict: "He looks as he did when we saw him a few hours after he died, perhaps even better." Patented like a cryogenic tonic, Professor Vorobiov's formula, with only minor refinements, has been used on Lenin's body every 18 months since. Stalin got the same treatment when he died in 1953. As a favor to the Soviets and for political legitimacy—harnessing the masses—the "balsamic baths" became *de riguer* among satellite communist regimes—Dimitrov in Bulgaria, Gottwald in Czechoslavakia, Neto in Angola, Burham in Guyana, Kim IL Sung in North Korea and of course, Ho Chi Minh in Vietnam.

In his last will and testament, Ho Chi Minh requested that he be cremated. He also proposed that building schools would be a more productive use of the state's money than erecting a monument or museum in his honor. He died on September 2, 1969, Independence Day, yet the Party inner-sanctum decided not to spoil the holiday, announcing his death date as September 3.

Russian embalmers flew to Hanoi to help. By the end of November 1969, North Vietnam's Politboro had voted to build a mausoleum, and to subject the Great Patriot to "balsamic baths" every 18 months for eternity, or the unforeseeable future, anyway.

Because of the American bombing taking place then, HCM's corpse was removed from Hanoi to a field laboratory near Son Tay, 30 miles to the west on the Red River. There, in the bowels of a karst mountain, Russian scientists assisted with the deification of HCM.

In 1972, a flock of American helicopters swooped down along the Red River on a rescue mission in search of a POW camp. While having tea, the NVA officer in charge of the laboratory redoubt where HCM's corpse was being kept, looked up in astonishment at the choppers. The aircraft alighted briefly on the opposite riverbank, but took wing after they determined the camp had been abandoned only days before. The NVA strengthened security after that incident. According to an NVA general, "If the Yankees ever did get hold of it [Ho's corpse], we'd be prepared to hand over all our American prisoners in exchange for it!"

On August 29, 1975, only months after reunification, the Vietnamese government opened a permanent mausoleum on the holy ground of Ba Dinh Square. It had been there in front of a throng of thousands that the

Great Patriot delivered the Declaration of Independence on September 2, 1945, beginning with the familiar words: "All *people* are created equal. They are endowed by their creator with certain unalienable rights; among these are life, liberty, and the pursuit of happiness." Since the mausoleum's opening, 15,000 Vietnamese a week have paid homage.

In the five years I have lived in Hanoi, I have been to HCM's mausoleum nine times, possible grounds for suspicion of necrophilia. Since September 11, the mausoleum caretakers have installed a metal detector through which foreigners must pass. I recently escorted friends from Arkansas there who were visiting Hanoi. Simon refused to come along, "If Ho didn't want to be there, neither do I."

After surrendering our cameras, we solemnly fell into in a long line behind a group of older peasant women, diminutive in size and each dressed the same in her best velvet jacket, matching black trousers, with hair in a knot and wrapped in a cloth disk. We followed a single guard in dress whites and billed cap along the grassy common of Ba Dinh Square. A platoon of similarly dressed soldiers followed us with rifles resting on their shoulders in marching position. Traffic circled one end of the square in a distant cacophony. In the same direction, clusters of women clipped the grassy common by hand, moving crabwise on their haunches in the foreground of the stately and colonial Prime Minister's offices.

The squat marble walls fronting the mausoleum are as cold and gray as the Hanoi *crachin* skies. With bayonets drawn, two guards flanked the doors, their eyes scanning our body language, zero tolerance for anything but military rigidity and mortuary reverence. Twisting up a marble tunnel of three flights of stairs, the visitors' line slackened to a bottleneck, trickling ponderously through the holy of holies.

In the vaulted chamber, a black catafalque with a glass sarcophagus was set in a sunken space near the middle of the room. A guard nudged me forward as I stalled, fixated on the aquarium-like bedchamber just as I had been on previous visits. An old familiar face, the Great Patriot lay somnolently in a black tunic, his fleshy mug illuminated by recessed lighting. Accented by his wispy beard, his skin tone was immortally pink—the good results of his last "balsamic bath" six months prior.

The grave silence of the devotees was deafening. The air was icy, prompting a whisper from an English-speaking local, "Best air conditioning in Hanoi." Another guard nudged me and pointed to the exit. More guards were positioned below with bayonets fixed at the cardinal points of the sunken shrine. A third guard prodded me out the door. Herded downstairs through a tunnel of oppressive shadows and out into a garden, the mood of the peasants we had arrived with remained hushed, somber but composed.

Once outside everyone's spirits rose, along with the temperature. We talked, strolling beneath tall trees in the shadow of the Presidential Palace, the former French Governor General's residence constructed in 1906. Next to an elliptical pond, rattling with the percussive beat of golden carp breaking the water for food, was a polished wooden home on stilts where HCM lived, simple and spare in the Japanese way. He exercised around the pond in the morning, planted much of the lush garden that surrounds the house, and often in the twilight of day, enjoyed feeding the carp.

The fad for preserving the remains of communist leaders did not take long to fade. The infighting of Cold War politics, the breakup of the Soviet Union and a lack of cultural acceptance prompted its demise.

In 1961, only eight years after being preserved for posterity, Stalin was denounced by Khrushchev for genocidal crimes. Khrushchev had his corpse removed from the mausoleum and buried under the walls of the Kremlin. In July 1990, having laid in state for 40 years, Dimitrov of Bulgaria was removed from his mausoleum and buried alongside his parents. Gottwald, head of the Czech Communist Party, was displayed for three years before his body was cremated. "Embalming is not part of our national tradition," stated Czech party members. Nito in Angola spent 13 years in his mausoleum, before in 1992, the government, heeding his wife's wishes, allowed him to be buried.

Leningrad has returned to its original name, St. Petersburg. The corpse of Lenin still occupies the Moscow mausoleum, but not without considerable debate about removing him for burial. Nowadays the Russian scientists at the mausoleum no longer embalm comrades, but instead make money fixing up the bullet-riddled bodies of the *nouveau riche*—the Russian mafia—many of whom are former members of the *nomenklatura*, the ruling communist elite. About four per month are placed on the same marble slab used to prepare Lenin for embalming in 1924, and are restored at fees ranging from $1,500 to $10,000.

"It seems, therefore, that no matter what the political regime, embalming and the building of mausoleums is... both a homage paid to the dead and a demonstration of power addressed to the living," concluded the 90-year-old author and Lenin embalmer, Ilya Zbarsky.

As Stalin had done with Lenin's remains, the revolutionary disciples of HCM were "harnessing the masses," molding a martyr to evoke patriotic emotions from a peasant population. And it's never an easy task to transform a diehard atheist into a demigod.

But today in Vietnam, Ho Chi Minh's repute has decayed no more than his body, still the icon of immense national pride. Across the Pacific, the debate will never be resolved as to whether HCM was pushed into communism because the West supported colonialism. And long after HCM's corpse is finally laid to rest—or cremated according to his wishes—he will be remembered as the Great Patriot who led Vietnam's liberation from foreign control.

I am not a club member of any sort. I belong to no guilds, unions, leagues, associations or any other alliance of like-minded people, having even been dropped from the dues-paying rolls of the Arkansas and American societies of Certified Public Accountants. As for the Army and other military groups, I had almost nothing to do with them after I left the service in August 1971, other than keeping in touch with a handful of friends who were veterans. I was a veteran against the war, but never joined the organization of the same name.

In the early 1970s, following my return to the States and discharge from the army, my father and I would on occasion go to Fort Chaffee, where he played golf and liked to have a drink at the Officer's Club. During one of those Sunday afternoon sojourns, a brouhaha erupted from across the bar room. My beard and ponytail had offended a drunk colonel, who recruited several of his fellow red-faced warhorses to get the sergeant-at-arms to ask me to leave. These men had dedicated their lives to serving their country. Their bitterness was just as strong as the outrage emerging from the anti-war movement at the time.

My father came to my defense, pointing out that I had served the better part of two years overseas in the army. At the time I carried a copy of my discharge papers for student loan and GI Bill purposes. Rather than attempting to clear the bar, which did cross my mind, I reluctantly produced the papers as Exhibit A, revealing that I had received the perfunctory Vietnam Campaign and Service Medals. They deliberated as a jury in private, and then one at a time bought me a drink. I was acquitted of wearing an unpatriotic hairstyle, I guess. After draining the free whiskey, we left and I never returned to the exclusivity of their drinking club.

I never much thought about veterans or veterans' organizations until I moved from Nairobi to Hanoi. Through random circumstances—a few of those chance encounters worth a thousand appointments—I met John Lancaster, whose office was across the street from my house; Chuck Searcy, who was part of the NGO network; Eric Herter, who hung out at the R&R Tavern which I also frequented; and Suel Jones, who I met at the R&R on his first trip back to Vietnam since the war. All had been in Vietnam during the Tet Offensive of 1968.

In April 2002, Chuck shared the bones of a groundbreaking conversation he had a few months before with a representative of the VFW (Veterans of Foreign Wars) headquarters in Kansas City, "They have several million dollars in their foundation they would like to funnel into humanitarian work in Vietnam—landmines, unexploded ordnance, wheelchairs and maybe Agent Orange. All we have to do is open a VFW Post in Hanoi."

The VFW has a heavily conservative membership of 2.6 million men and women. They began over a century ago as independent, local patriotic organizations to help wounded and sick veterans returning from the Spanish-American War and the Philippine Insurrection. A few years later, the disparate organizations were consolidated under a federal charter as the Veterans of Foreign Wars of America. They boast an impressive roster of past and present members: Audie Murphy, Carl Sandburg and eight U.S. Presidents—Franklin Roosevelt, John Kennedy, big George Bush and so on. They finance war memorials, lobby for veterans' benefits such as health care and education, and in the case of Agent Orange, were instrumental in getting remediation for American veterans. On the other hand, they also support all wars on the premise that if Americans are fighting, the cause is just—blind patriotism you could say. My only encounter with the VFW had been to pass their beer halls throughout Arkansas.

The idea of opening a VFW in Hanoi seemed as counterintuitive as doing the same thing in Baghdad in a couple of decades. John, Chuck and I were intrigued, however, and became convinced that it was worth pursuing. Eric, skittish from the start, attended a few preliminary meetings, but once he saw the application—a patriotic oath to God, Country and War—he opted out.

All of us were not only drinking buddies, we were birds of a feather in our dovish politics, and sensitized to how the U.S. is perceived internationally. As for biting our cheeks to deal with the VFW, we reasoned that the worthy causes we were pursuing justified our hypocrisy.

Late in the same year, Mike Meyer, Administrator of Corporate and Foundation Development for the VFW, visited Hanoi with a group of veterans. John, Chuck and I met them in the Hilton lobby for drinks and a testing of the waters.

John, as the Post Commander-elect, gave a measured speech making clear that he favored a simple humanitarian aid agenda, and that partisan politics had no place in a Hanoi VFW Post. Nobody disagreed, and Mike Meyer said, "We welcome all political persuasions."

Soon, all the wheels were in motion for an official visit from the VFW brass. Our organizing committee came with impeccable credentials: John and Chuck are both former presidential appointees. Eric is an accomplished documentary film maker and former magazine editor, with a first-rate Eastern education. His grandfather, Secretary of State Christian Herter, sat next to Eisenhower when he shocked Kennedy the day before his inauguration by telling him Laos was the wobbly domino keeping Southeast Asia from going communist. Suel Jones has made his life mission raising money for the Friendship Village, which houses disabled Vietnamese veterans and children with disabilities. He relishes veteran-to-veteran work—hugging fat 60-year-old men who return to Vietnam to make their peace. And every serious organization needs a deskbound paper pusher. After a stint with Ernst and Ernst, I spent 16 years as chief financial officer of an independent oil and gas company, a profession and industry unsurpassed in conservatism. So, all in all, we thought we were a Dream Team for a VFW Post, with qualifications in no need of patriotic embellishments.

Only weeks before the boys back in Kansas City at VFW headquarters were to arrive, they began floating the suggestion that Pete Peterson, the former American ambassador to Vietnam, might be a candidate for our Post Commander. I doubt that Peterson would have been interested, but we roundly objected. Aside from the fact that Peterson wasn't living in Vietnam, we felt John was more qualified, and free from the baggage of embassy politics.

The day before the Kansas City delegation was to leave for Vietnam, VFW headquarters issued a press release stating that the Hanoi Post's primary goals would be veteran-to-veteran work, community outreach, widening humanitarian support, and "expanding the presence of American patriotism …" They hadn't bothered to consult, however, with us, their "comrades" in Hanoi.

It was starting to seem all too familiar. During the war, I had seen the dismal results of military brass failing to heed the views of soldiers on the ground. And more recently, I had had my fill of patriotism. My wife and I had just attended the 990th anniversary of the founding of Hanoi. At Hanoi Stadium, in a jazzed-up crowd of 40,000 Vietnamese, we were among the fewer than ten foreigners in attendance. The military pageantry there presented a reenactment of Vietnam and Hanoi's resistance against China, France, Japan and America. A meticulous choreography of patriotic songs, chants, and foot stomping reached fever pitch.

In the main event, air raid sirens screamed and the sky filled with smoke, as mock B-52s were launched on guy wires from each corner of the stadium. With the stadium plunged into darkness, we heard Ho Chi Minh's recorded voice calling for the nation to stand up and fight against American air raids. The B-52s burst in the sky, as toy Russian surface-to-air missiles plucked them down one by one. The roar of the crowd grew louder and the foot stomping literally shook the concrete stadium for 10 minutes. I leaned over to Joellen: "If anyone ask, we're Canadian. This is scary stuff!"

The VFW folks seemed naive about diplomacy. Vietnam's relationship with the United States thrives on mutual self-advantage, and not on admiration for American patriotism. Any program for "expanding" U.S. patriotism in Vietnam, whatever that might be, seemed absurd to those of us on the ground there.

On a Sunday afternoon in late February, Chuck arranged for an informal meeting at the R&R Tavern with the prospective membership in Hanoi—several of whom I had never met—and with the Kansas City boys: Ron Browning, Assistant Adjutant General for Development, Bob Frank, a fellow bean counter with the Vietnam Veterans Memorial Fund, and Alan Greilsamer, the public relations person for the Vietnam Veterans Memorial Fund.

Inconveniently, the R&R Tavern's owner, Jay Ellis, was a hard-core 60s throwback and happened to have told a local rock band they could practice their covers of Grateful Dead songs there the same afternoon we were meeting the VFW brass. "I'm sorry man. I know I said today was okay, but I made a mistake. I told the band they could use the place," Jay shrugged, clearly more eager to host the Dead than us.

So we piled into several cars, jumped on motorcycles and rode in *cyclos* around the lake to Restaurant Bobby Chinn's. Once there, we barely got through opening pleasantries when someone brought up the looming war with Iraq, a lightning rod for lively discussion. Colonel Steve Ball, the military attaché at the American Embassy, soft spoken, yet towing the military line, was sitting next to John and me. In the way you might brief Martians fresh off a flying saucer about planet Earth, he patiently explained how the United States had to move beyond the inertia of the U.N. Needless to say, "Saddam is training Al Qaeda terrorists and he possesses and is producing weapons of mass destruction." Ball was clear: "We have to get there sooner rather than later."

John cautioned, "We are in too big a hurry to get to the future. We are going so fast that if we hit a bump we are liable to spin out of control."

Colonel Ball seemed indifferent to our concerns: Was this another quagmire? Had terrorism replaced communism as an excuse to suspend civil liberties, to question patriotism, to build a massive military and to wage war using fear to garner support? To him, the answers were plain and simple: My country, right or wrong.

Soon, Ron Browning, the go-to-guy in the VFW delegation, brought the meeting to order and gave a Chamber of Commerce overview of the VFW's mission in Vietnam. He apologized for the snafu in the press release and promised to collaborate better in the future. Ron then repeated some of the optimistic wisdom he had shared in a recent letter to Chuck and John,

"You have helped me realize a personal dream [a VFW Post in Hanoi]... All of us who served in Vietnam are entering a life-stage where the legacy and the lessons we leave to the generations that follow are becoming more and more important. The nature of that legacy is in our hands. It may be that only our generation, the men and women who served in Vietnam, can make sense of this message. Perhaps it is our obligation... it [a VFW Post] has the potential to be a sounding board for a new generational message..."

Ron then opened the floor for questions, when a marine colonel of 39 years in service and temporarily attached to the embassy, dropped a grenade, "We should all support our commander-in-chief in times of war."

Post Commander-elect Lancaster responded first, laughing and banging a Heineken bottle on his wheelchair for emphasis. "I support the troops on the ground but I am also the son of Leon Lancaster, a dyed-in-the-wool Democrat, and that makes me a Democrat. Besides, I don't wear the uniform anymore. I don't have a commander-in-chief." John thus gave the conservative membership, about half of the group of 20 on hand, a piece of his mind.

In the ensuing stillness, Suel overheard the colonel harrumph, "He's not going to be my Post Commander."

Before the first Hanoi VFW meeting broke up in disarray, Suel and I got the floor a time or two to rail about the embassy position on Agent Orange. We Hanoi VFWs were divided in too many ways, with no faction to lead. And Eric Herter was missing all the fun; he was in New York City helping organize the anti-war march.

Chuck, a Georgia politician at heart, anxious to pull us all together, was so frustrated at the hostile byplay, he bolted to the nearest *thuoc lao* stand for a corrective dose of waterpipe nicotine.

Saying farewell, Colonel Ball assured me that embassy staff like himself could say what they thought, even against the official position. I assume he was being defensive, as I had mocked him earlier about being a diplomat and having to wear that State Department muzzle. On the way out, I shook hands with Bob Frank and Ron Browning, reminding them that I would see them in the morning.

The next day struck early for me. I had to find my musty, black pin-stripe wedding suit of seven years before, then organize the accessories for an important meeting with Vu Xuan Hong, chairman of the Vietnam Union of Friendship Organizations, and a National Assembly member. Mr. Hong can make things happen with new NGOs wanting to do business in Vietnam. I had met Mr. Hong a few weeks before, when Joellen and I had delivered a Tet basket—wine and food for the holidays—to his home. The three-man VFW delegation was slated to attend the meeting, along with me, Chuck and John.

Just as I was working through the third attempt to get my tie over my middle-age paunch, John rang and said we were to "stand down." It was 8:15 a.m., and our meeting was to start at 8:30. The VFW delegation wanted an exclusive meeting between officials, contending John and I weren't on the list. I later found out that the Americans judged John and I to be risky partners based on our comments at the meeting.

I called Mr. Hong's office number, pressing the numbers expressively as if I were punching Ron Browning's chest. Mr. Hong's secretary answered, and read me the official meeting list, "John Lancaster, Chuck Searcy, Phil Karber and some veteran from America."

I had him read it again, and then he asked, "Is there a problem? You will be here?"

"No, please tell everyone when they arrive that I called and that John and I won't be there. Thanks. Goodbye." Our countryman's dissembling had been confirmed.

John and I were all dressed up with nowhere to go. More than anger, disappointment set in. We saw our vision of a Hanoi VFW Post being dried up by a fly-by-night, fancy-suit crowd.

By pleasant surprise, in the early afternoon, Bob Frank called and invited me and my wife to dinner at the Press Club, an upscale favorite of ours located just around the corner from our house. Chuck and John were also invited. Bob sounded as though they would backpedal, and try to be collaborative. He laughed about the meeting glitch, as close as he or the others would come to a *mea culpa*.

At dinner Bob, a connoisseur of the grapes and the man with the Visa card, studiously worked over the wine list. John and I drained gin-and-tonics, while I called on my wife to enlighten us all on doing business in Vietnam. They hadn't asked but it seemed relevant. We talked about organizational structures, bank accounts, NGO licensing issues, and all the tools necessary to run a high-profile NGO in Vietnam.

Ron, however, changed the subject—to himself. For the third time in two nights, with whispered digressions on North Korea, he recounted having been a policeman for 10 years, how his dad had worked the loading docks for 42 years, and how his star had risen from those humble beginnings. He never asked one member of the organizing committee about themselves or Hanoi.

Chuck, who had vast political and media experience, was talking to Alan, the press relations guy who had come up with the "expanding American patriotism" blurb. Chuck struggled in vain to pass on a few nuggets of his experience, finally barking at Alan, "If you would slow down and listen for a minute, you might learn something." Alan got up in a boil and disappeared like hot vapors. The heat had been turned up.

Ron went back to his clandestine guise, telling us that in addition to the stated VFW mission objectives, the powers had formulated "a proprietary agenda."

"Well since we are helping to organize the Post can you tell us anything about it?" John inquired.

"It's proprietary, sorry," Ron snapped.

"You mean as a membership organization even the dues-paying members don't get to know about the proprietary agenda," John pressed him.

"That's right."

"Well I can't be a part of something so mysterious."

"Come on, are you guys planning a lollipop airlift for the benefit of the poor folks in Vietnam?" I mocked.

Ron ignored me and turned to John, "And you may not be the right guy to be the Post Commander," casting doubt on our best-laid plans.

"I may not be, that's right," John agreed.

It was then that we knew failure of the VFW Post was a *fait accompli*. Yet in the interest of closure, we agreed to attend one more meeting the next night at the American Club.

Located on Hai Ba Trung Street, one of the main arteries and most historical streets in Hanoi, the American Club occupies two acres that the United States owned when ties were severed with Communist North Vietnam in 1954. As part of Hanoi's efforts to normalize relations with Washington, the prime real estate was returned to the U.S. in 1995. It is now used by expatriates of all stripes for various functions, including a big blowout every Fourth of July. A few blocks to the west is the old Hanoi Hilton.

Colonel Steve Ball had organized the informal food-and-beer affair to welcome Ed Banas, Commander-in-Chief-elect of the American VFW, and a small contingent of veterans who accompanied him. Other attendees included Ambassador Ray Burghardt, who officed next door to Ollie North at the NSC in the 1980s. The scent of grilling hamburgers and the rabble of American veterans filled the Hanoi night air.

Making a surprise appearance was Andre Sauvageot, in a mismatched suit ensemble, complimented by his signature red baseball cap with the five-pointed yellow star, the flag insignia of Vietnam. Of French descent transplanted to Ohio, Andre speaks Vietnamese as well as any non-Vietnamese possibly can. He has been the manager of General Electric Vietnam for five years. A former colonel in the army, Andre was in Vietnam continuously from 1964 until the Peace Agreement in 1973.

Andre can be entertaining but is prone to manic, namedropping filibusters. He often invokes the names of famous former superiors: William Colby, once the head of the CIA and now deceased; Richard Armitage, the current Deputy Secretary of State; and a host of military luminaries. In many ways Andre is a postwar paradox: one who tears up when he talks about the carnage he witnessed during the war, and in the same breath dismisses anti-war activists as "gooey peaceniks."

Still yet, I felt he wanted to do what was fair for Vietnam and Indochina. He had been seconded by the military to the refugee camps after the war, and spoke with compassion of the human suffering he had witnessed. I had given him the application for the VFW and encouraged him to be at the meeting. In short, Andre, like many expats I had met in Hanoi, was an enigma.

Larry Flannagan, pushing 70, arrived in cowboy boots and a relic of a brown tailored suit. Larry had retired from the army while in Vietnam, and returned three weeks later as an economic advisor. Like Andre, he, too, had spent nine years in Vietnam during the war and married a Vietnamese woman.

When Larry found out I was from Fort Smith, he told the story of opening the Oklahoma City paper one Sunday morning back in 1975, to find his sister-in-law featured on the front page as a newly arrived refugee at Fort Chaffee. He and his wife drove there that day and picked her up.

Larry huddled around where John, Suel Jones and I were holding court. When Andre walked up, Larry greeted him as "Jean." We all laughed and I asked, "Why are you calling him Jean?"

"That was the name he went by back then. Everyone knew Jean. He spoke fluent Vietnamese. He wore black pajamas and trained the irregulars."

Pumping Larry's arm as an old friend would do, Andre nodded that it was true, saying only, "Jean is my first name, but my family always called me Andre. When I joined the army they started calling me Jean."

Ambassador Burghardt, an even-handed career diplomat, walked over to say hello to John and introduced himself to me. John was in the throes of a career transition, exiting his job as manager of an NGO to become a full-time consultant. The ambassador was interested in how it was coming along.

Soon, Ed Banas and his entourage of veterans just in from the States arrived. Ambassador Burghardt, Andre and Larry moved to a nearby table where they could talk old times. The group of freshly-arrived veterans had lost their luggage and were wearing the same clothes they had left the States in. Even still, with all the protective coloration of patriotic lapel pins, hats and T-shirts, they looked like the fresh-faced greeting committee at a Fourth of July picnic. They bantered about the latest MIA finds in excited voices. Not a single veteran out of Banas' entourage spoke to our organizing group.

Banas, Commander-in-Chief-elect of the whole enchilada, did, however, stumble up to our table. John saw his tall, healthy frame hulking towards us and greeted him, "Hey, Commander, just in time. We were talking about Iraq."

Banas's eyes were bloodshot, and without measuring the crowd, he spoke in the voice of a historian, "You know the Ottoman Empire ended in the

16th century, and a lot of Muslims migrated to Europe then. And now they can vote."

We weren't sure what he meant, and by the way the Ottomans lasted to the 20th century. But before he could say more, Chuck engaged him in an extended game of pool. Staggering with experience, neither one of them sank a ball, and finally gave up. (I was later told that Ed Banas had a severe allergy condition, and was not drunk.)

Ron Browning had no doubt brought everyone with a need-to-know within the VFW up to speed on our lively meetings. Thus, at the American Club there was no discussion, no question-and-answer session, and no speech by Ed Banas. Only after Chuck goaded him, did Banas blurt out, "We have a lot of work to do to make this thing happen."

Ambassador Burghardt took the floor to make a few welcoming remarks and then attempted to shame Andre into taking off his communist flag hat, "If Andre would only remove his cap so we can see his face." Andre chuckled and left his hat in place. I am sure he said under his breath, "You're in Hanoi boss, the rules are different."

By the time we reached the last bites of our hamburgers, Colonel Ball thanked all for coming and dismissed the gathering. Andre rushed up to me, and in front of Ron Browning and several others, recounted how I had persuaded him into the fold of Vets. Then he leaned over and imparted conspiratorially, "What do you think the ambassador would have thought had I had time to go home and put on my normal evening attire—a red sleeveless T-shirt with a yellow star in the middle, matching red boxer shorts and red pith helmet with another star in the middle?"

I had seen him in the outfit many times, and almost fell out of my chair laughing. John joined in, "Some things never change, Andre's been wearing the sleeping garments from the North for 40 years now."

John was Post Commander-elect as far as I was concerned, so I handed him the $20 and application Andre had given me. Seizing the moment, John hollered out to a humorless Ron Browning, "Ron wait, don't leave, here is your newest Hanoi Post member. Andre, you know Ron." Shaking hands stoically with Andre, Ron took the money and application, spun around and departed without saying a word or offering so much as a last handshake to John and me. Donald Duck steam poured from his ears. That was the last we saw of the VFW boys.

So much for harnessing these masses; we resembled more a Hatfield and McCoy reunion, held on disputed property. As for making history—drawing constructive lessons from the war and closing the circle of quarrelsome veterans—we had all failed. Old comrades, who once might have shared a foxhole in Vietnam, today, could hardly stand to be in the same room.

Epilogue

O ne of Hanoi's little-known distinctions is its Minsk Club, a loose association of thrill-seekers who have bought into the cult of two-stroke, Russian dirt bikes. Unless there is a counterpart club in Afghanistan, the only other country outside the former Soviet Union where the bikes survive in significant numbers, Hanoi's club is unique.

Yet no self-respecting Hanoian would be seen on a Minsk, a metallic water buffalo ridden mostly by *nha que*, the rural peasants who can't afford anything better. The bikes cost less than the change of clothes I would wear to walk to the post office. The club members are all wayward foreigners, like the moonshining owners of Highway 4, a restaurant and bar in Hanoi's Old Quarter. They specialize in brewing a variety of popular rice whiskies. The club members sport around on their bikes as a Pancaker might spruce up in a favorite tattered T-shirt.

Head of the club is Digby Greenhalgh, an Aussie law school dropout who runs Minsk tours around Vietnam's mountainous reaches and goat paths. His other distinction is being author of the *Minsk Repair Manual*, a 50-page self-help book for fellow English-speaking gear heads who want to motor Vietnam on their own. Digby claims that the bike's numerous mechanical shortcomings are of little real concern, "It's survival of the fittest. They molt the weaker, cheaper parts, and the stronger ones that count always pull through."

During the months leading up to the U.S. war with Iraq, Digby and I assembled an improbable Wild Bunch for a pilgrimage to Pac Bo, a cave redoubt on the Chinese border where Ho Chi Minh waited out World War II while preparing to assert the nationalist (and communist) cause when the war ended.

Among our company was Jerry Whitlock, a former rodeo cowboy from Oklahoma who is now riding high as the largest non-carbonated drink bottler in North America. Jerry likes riding Harleys and BMW bikes, and had done at least one trans-Asian trip by motorcycle.

Joining us at the last minute was Richard Moore, a good friend and world-class marketing communication executive. He and his two partners cashed out of their successful New York City agency a decade ago. Fascinated by the business opportunities here as a result of *doi moi*, he now divides his time between New York and Hanoi. His entrepreneurial endeavors are various: Working as a card-carrying capitalist teaching the Vietnamese how to brand and sell their products to America, he has also recently produced a first-of-its-kind book with a Saigon publisher entitled *Branding for Leaders*. Richard is also no stranger to adventure, having ascended peaks in Western China and Nepal as a member of various mountaineering expeditions.

Then there was Kok Hon Wong, an incurably courteous and teetotaling whippet from Singapore. A recent university graduate and budding businessman, Kok still lived at home in Singapore with his traditional Confucian parents. Against their wishes, he had saved up money and vacation time for a motorcycle trip in Vietnam. Although he had ridden in several endurance bicycle races, he had only been on a motorcycle once.

Adding color and depth to the capitalist contingent was Simon. Until the week before the trip, he had never driven a motorcycle. At Digby's insistence, he finally took a lesson. He prefers getting around Hanoi as a passenger with his personal *xe om* motorcycle taxi driver, Ms. Quy, who of course doubles as his girlfriend. After two hours of instruction, he felt prepared to take on the hinterland track along the Chinese border.

Skittish about our group's inexperience, Digby brought along an apprentice guide and motorcycle mechanic, a Boy Scout-ish Londoner named Danny Pearce. Like Digby and the rest of the Highway 4 crew, Danny speaks conversational Vietnamese and bandoleers himself in an embroidered monk pouch.

We met around eight one evening at a Thai restaurant on Ly Thoung Kiet Street, only a few blocks from *Ga Hanoi*. Digby had arranged for the bikes to be shuttled to the restaurant. Jerry, accustomed to touring around Boca Raton on his $20,000-plus, 1300cc BMW, took one look at the Minsks and guffawed, "Are you serious? These bikes ain't nothing but a piece of shit."

Jerry's verdict had some merit: the bikes were in fact bent, badly bruised, and partly bandaged. Loose wires sprouted in all directions like a cannibalized circuit board; mirrorless shivs spiked from the handlebars; the brakes were loose and the paint jobs lousy. Digby's repair manual describes them best, "The bikes are made of steel and not chrome, and prefer to be greased not polished." Before week's end, we would all come to appreciate the durability and practicality of the steel horses, however, and to some degree share in Digby's passion.

Raring to go, we strapped on our olive drab saddlebags while Digby gave a quick user's briefing—prime the carburetor, kick three times before switching the ignition on, and then one more kick for the start. That done, our bikes simulating the sounds of popcorn makers gone amok, we blasted off for the train station, leaving in our wake an atomic cloud of exhaust smoke. After only a short distance, in an eye-catching procession reminiscent of a motorized arrival of *The Good, the Bad, and the Ugly*, we edged through a crowd of passengers and turned into the backside of the train station for a de-fueling stop. The carnival buzz of arrivals and departures, the attendant hawkers, was all highly charged. Before we could board the bikes on the train, a concessionaire had to drain our almost empty tanks, starting the siphon using his mouth. This security procedure netted the man a couple of free gallons—and twice as many mouthfuls of petrol.

After the bikes got loaded and we were situated in the four-person cabins, the train snaked north out of *Ga Hanoi*, curling around the second floor flats along Phung Hung Street in the Old Quarter. We geckoed the aisle windows, peeping into the residences of pajama-clad families. Soon we crossed the Red River on the Long Bien Bridge—in its umpteenth and most enduring resurrection from American bombing three decades ago.

Richard Moore had been standing in the hallway watching the Hanoi pajama-party. When he returned to the cabin I handed him the current *New York Review of Books* for bedtime reading. He took one look at the cover, handed it back to me and said, "No thanks. I believe I'll do without that for a week."

Joellen had given the magazine to me on my way out—compliments of our weekly mail pouch. I had not had time to scan the cover. It was succinct: "War."

The next morning we refueled the bikes a block away from the train station in Lao Cai. We then turned east, traveling the breadth of the Viet Bac region, a border frontier area that has historically been a geo-political powder keg. In 1949, with the neighborly military assistance of the Communist Chinese and Mao Zedong, the Vietminh and Ho Chi Minh pushed the French south from this rugged mountainous terrain, gaining the space and time to build an army formidable enough to eventually defeat the French and later the Americans. In 1979, 30 years after that alliance of neighborly communists, the Chinese razed every border city in the region, including Lao Cai, in retaliation for Vietnam's invasion of Cambodia. The Vietnamese army replied, inflicting heavy casualties on an overconfident and under-reinforced Chinese military in retreat. Until only recently the borders were garrisoned with hundreds of thousands of troops in one more hair-triggered standoff.

After a fusion breakfast of *pho*, baguettes, green tea and Coca Cola, we traced a succession of rivers for a couple of hours as we crossed over the Bac Ha Pass to a village of the same name. On Sundays, Bac Ha hosts the most colorful hill tribe market in Vietnam, with a dozen ethnic groups converging from all points of the compass, mostly arriving on foot and by horseback. It was the middle of the week, however, and the town seemed deserted. We paused there briefly while Digby performed surgery on Kok's bike, a peerless performance of rapid diagnostics and tool-wielding repair work we would witness many times on the trip.

On the outskirts of Bac Ha, we stopped at the Hmong Palace, an architectural extravaganza of pompous majesty built by the French. In a vain attempt to fashion the *indigenes* in the image of imperial Europe, they randomly anointed one of the tribal elders as "King of the Hmongs." But the Hmong people prefer living as they always have in a diffused clan structure, and not as autocratic proxies for European occupiers. Such cultural misfires would eventually arm Ho Chi Minh and the fledgling Vietminh with a ready-made fighting force.

An hour beyond the Hmong Palace, we stopped for a picnic on a panoramic point a mile high on the rugged mountains. As quick as we dismounted and began making sandwiches, posies of Flower Hmong women and young men sprang out from the seemingly uninhabited landscape. They stared at us curiously as we ate, before we offered them candies. They responded by giving us what looked and tasted like miniature sour apples.

After our petite Thanksgiving, we pilgrims donned slickers and charged off into an afternoon salvo of spring monsoons. Instead of our Minsks, we ought to have had an ark. As always Jerry set the pace, but not before nipping Digby's bike and toppling it over. Near the back of the pack, Kok went down on the slick tarmac, trapping his leg between the pavement and his bike in a painful baseball-like slide.

Minutes later, as we turned off the pavement onto a dirt track, Simon careened into an embankment and flew over his handlebars. As he lay on the ground, several Flower Hmong appeared above his prostrate body, laughing at his helplessness before helping him and the bike upright.

Suspecting the laggards had run into trouble, Jerry, Richard and I cleared the worst of the muddy track and stopped to wait. Kok soon arrived with his ankle swelling to the size of a grapefruit, followed by Simon with grass growing from his headlight and his handlebars shifted cattywampus. It would be a long week for Kok without the use of that ankle trying to balance his bike on the many washed-out roads we were sure to come upon. But no one considered, nor did Kok suggest, that he turn back.

Simon gave me a cockeyed glare and groaned, "Is this what they call an adventure?"

Taking a deep breath, Digby cautioned everyone to keep the rubber down and metal up. He took care as well to draw our attention to the resilience of the wrecked bikes: "They are still completely functional. You have only lost or damaged the parts that were disposable or unnecessary anyway." He was right. "Long live the Minsk," I was ready to cheer.

Soon, we climbed up into high country along the muddy track, slowing the pace down, until we temporarily met an old best friend—a macadam road. A short piece later, we were overlooking the incomparable beauty of the Xin Man Gorge, wowed by the surreal sensation of having fallen out of the clouds into a secluded realm of the Flower Hmong. Foamy spigots of long narrow waterfalls bleached the dusky river valley. Hmong women in their pleated batiks ascended the steep-backed mountains they farmed in defiance of gravity. Waves of green-topped ridges sighed into an infinite mist. As we corkscrewed down to the Chay River and the village of Xin Man, children fled like scattering chickens in the road, wary of the long noses they were seeing for the first time.

We arrived at the guesthouse just as the skies burst open in a four-hour deluge. The locals rarely feel bothered by the monsoons, though. It's their sustenance, washing over them like drops of silver.

After scraping the mud off, we walked around the corner from Auberge Xin Man to one of the few public eating establishments. The open-air hovel was adorned with fresh-plucked chickens hanging from the ceiling, which Digby included in the dinner order. Next to us was a table full of boisterous, red-faced policemen, soldiers and other government officials. Their fiery faces belied their playfulness as they engaged Danny and Simon in some competitive drinking, *tram phan tram*.

The mid-fiftyish owner had just taken a 26-year-old wife. She ran the kitchen and waited on us. He envisioned an expansion to his modest restaurant: more tables, a couple of guest rooms and a Karaoke Bar, the first in town. Jerry, who is rarely without a business plan, toured the kitchen and offered the voice of capitalist experience. He suggested improving sanitary conditions and agreed with the proprietor's plan for a Karaoke monopoly.

The next morning, we returned for breakfast. The same local officials were back drinking rice whiskey and slurping down bowls of *pho*. A mobile butcher pulled up on his bicycle and sold the young wife a flank of red meat.

After a quick bowl of *pho*, we departed *en masse* and refueled at a nearby petrol station—that is a man with several jars of fuel and a hand pump standing on the side of the road. We rode along the course of the Chay River for the next 30 miles, seeing dozens of waterfalls on the way. Traffic was sparse: two motorcycles, no cars or trucks, a few tribal pedestrians.

They were Red Dao people, and they cut exotic figures. The men wore baggy trousers, Mao caps and went barefooted. The women dressed in bright batiks, shaved their eyebrows and the foreparts of their heads, and tucked the remaining hair under a pile of red-tasseled cloth. They resembled a colony of chemotherapy patients, but cheerful all the way.

In the market town of Huang Su Phi, Digby re-provisioned with fresh vegetables, mystery meat and baguettes. While waiting, we were benignly mobbed by curious tribals.

Not far beyond Huang Su Phi, the French-laid macadam turned to crumble, leaving 100 miles of mostly slop to plow through each day. Upon arriving in Ha Giang, a once small market town that has grown into a bustling commercial center, we spent an hour at a street-side car wash cleaning the mud from our bikes and bodies.

We spent the night in Ha Giang, and attempted to stir up some late night rowdiness, but the locals seemed wary of our harmless intentions. The next morning, we proceeded upward and westward, before dropping down into picture-perfect valleys and hamlets of the Red Dao. Prim vegetable gardens were surrounded by banana fronds and a glistening splay of fan palms; the whole of it flourished around longhouses and fences constructed of plaited bamboo.

Split-bamboo gutters crossed the road like goal posts, diverting the fresh mountain streams into the fields and villages. Men and women alike slogged ankle-deep behind their water buffaloes harrowing the fields. Pooled in a glassy sheen of earthen brown, and inlaid in emerald tufts of transplanted shoots, the valley smelled of its own fresh-turned essence. Women were stooped over planting, knee-high in mud, their voices ringing across the valley with a crisp, song-like call.

Road construction became commonplace, a blessing for the local economy perhaps but it foretold the modern world's arrival in Viet Bac. Jerry envisioned cheap labor and factories, better commercial distribution systems and other ingredients of business success. Pink tour buses were inevitable too.

As we plowed through Bac Me village, a wash of rutted roads, I was ahead of Digby when a construction foreman ran toward him hollering, "Stop, stop,

stop!" Because there was a high-security prison nearby, Digby was keen to avoid encounters with xenophobic cons on work release, if any. He goosed it ahead. Seconds later, dynamite cracked all around as if we had infiltrated a minefield. The man had been trying to warn him off.

Only a few miles on, we waited patiently as several peace-time sappers scurried up ropes on a hundred-foot cliffside, drilled holes for dynamite, disappeared over the brow, and blew away the earthen ramparts. The stench of cordite hung in the air as we fled past the impact area.

We passed three avalanches that day on a 40-mile track of muddy slop, before rimming a showcase river valley of farmed beauty on the outskirts of Bao Lac, an isolated market town that nuzzles the China-Vietnam border. We encamped next to the market in a walled compound that resembled a former Silk Road caravansari, with a small courtyard and four bunkhouse rooms. Indeed we deserved no more, with the smelly layers of grit we had accumulated, and the price was right: a buck a day.

Every evening around seven, the generator would be turned on for a couple of hours. When Bao Lac became dimly illuminated, the whole village would clap and cheer. Moments before the happy surge, we had settled into a makeshift bar next to the market, and tasted the local brew of grain whiskies.

We had drained several glass thimbles of Bao Lac's special—a foul-tasting corn whiskey—when a knot of people huddled around one of the village's few televisions to watch an hour of news on Vietnam TV. It was March 21st, only hours after the beginning of the bombardment of Baghdad. The lead story was 10 minutes of the light show over Baghdad. Providing the action were some of the same B-52s that three decades earlier had rained terror over Indochina. The crowd was hushed; but above the uneasy silence, we could hear the tribal men muttering "American" and "B-52," as coupled to them as search-and-destroy. It was an uncomfortable place to be just then.

The next morning, the fifth day of the third lunar month, was market day in Bao Lac. It was also the day that Digby assured us we would have good road, the EU Highway he called it. The streets were a watery gumbo of showy hill tribes, many of whom I had never seen before.

The young women of a sub-tribe of the Red Dao wore crimson pom-poms and braided their hair in a birdnested bonnet of yarn. The pile of yarn was looped around two chopstick-like hairpins protruding from the right side of the head. Young Hmong girls wrapped twists of yarn around their waists with fanciful buckles of silver coins and key rings dangling to their loins like chastity belts. The Lo Lo women wore indigo tunics that showed their midriffs, exposed to a mountain chill that turned their cheeks red. They all glistened with beads, wide silver neck-loops, studs, bracelets, and rings, many worn as amulets against evil spirits. Not exactly a "love market," the tribal tradition of meeting in market towns for purposes of courtship and marriage, but the younger ones were definitely posturing, while others bought and sold textiles, food and cheap Chinese plastics and tins.

After finding Richard and Simon up the main market street, sheltered from the downpour and finishing a cup of coffee, we set off in slickers and mingled in the crowd taking pictures. The hill folks were generally wary, turning their heads away or walking off, until Richard showed them the simultaneous replay on his digital camera. Suddenly they all wanted to model. The images were now for them, too, not just for us to take home unseen.

Giving up on the weather improving, we left Bao Lac in mid-morning, but this time with extra luggage: two itinerant schoolteachers from a nearby village had asked Richard and Jerry for rides. The road was muckier than ever, mostly resembling a giant mudslide. Richard, more so than Jerry, was having a terrible time staying upright with the extra weight. It wasn't long before we came upon our first avalanche of the day, and as Jerry attempted to Evil Knevil the fallen debris in the road, his passenger very wisely had him stop to let her off.

I pulled up seconds after Jerry attempted the leap. He was temporarily pinned beneath the bike, which landed on top of him a hair's breadth away from a 50-foot sheer drop to the river below.

It seemed important to get across the barrier of rocky debris before more fell, which would delay us for days. Two young Vietnamese men who had seen Jerry crash helped us both drag our motorcycles across the unsteady mound of avalanche debris. Ten minutes later the rest of our group arrived and began surveying the crossing. Seconds later, a bulldozer and jeep full of policemen pulled up to save the day. In light of the logistical demands of maintaining the Ho Chi Minh Trail for 15 years during the war, their prompt arrival shouldn't have been a surprise.

Leaving my bike down the hill, I walked up to watch the dozer work, when I heard the pinging of rocks above in an aftershock of the avalanche. I bolted in the nick of time, before big chunks of rocky earth fell where I had been standing. Digby and the others across the mounded field of debris had a good laugh at the burst of speed shown by this old water buffalo.

Once the way was cleared, we felt certain we had seen it all in terms of bad road and weather conditions, until we came upon what was supposed to be the EU Highway. It was a potholed track of dirt alternating with macadam, built by the French in the first half of the 20th century.

Only 50 miles out of Cao Bang, we zigzagged up several peaked ridges into a dense swell of clouds. With visibility of less than 20 feet, we twisted through what felt like a massif of cotton candy. Costumed tribal people popped out of the foggy swirl like spooks on Halloween night, many leading or riding horses. Upon seeing me, their faces went from surprise to laughter, then dissolved into the mists as in a dream, voices trailing from a shroud of white.

Jerry began racing so far ahead that he got bored and would randomly pull up to solitary villagers, give them a piece of candy and offer a ride. Most scurried away, frightened by his extraterrestrial countenance: a Billy Idol haircut, rosy sunglasses, a Hmong scarf imperiously draping his shoulders and a royal blue poncho that resembled a cape. But on two occasions, once with an older Hmong woman and later with a young tribal boy on back, he blasted off, leaned into the curves and gave them the ride of a lifetime.

"Balls to the wall," Jerry said, his adrenaline soaring when his passenger's grip tightened. Simon dubbed him, "Captain Midnight, he who swoops down, saves those in need, and then disappears with a smile and a salute."

In a gold-mining town built by the French and later managed by Russians, we took a break, poured the water from our boots and changed socks. Slightly warmed, we hit the home stretch to Cao Bang.

Everyone was beat up on our staggered arrival in Cao Bang that evening: Kok limped in with his ankle still badly swollen, Richard had a flat and was the last in after a 12-hour day, Simon had tumbled over several times in the mud, and the only bottle of gin in a four-province radius had fallen from my saddle bag.

Fortunately, Cao Bang had all the other amenities of a Vietnamese city, and we had plenty of time to rejuvenate. We stayed on the historic banks of the Bang Chiang River, an ancient population center that was razed in 1979 by the Chinese, who killed 4,000 people in their wake. The Vietnamese, in keeping with their indomitable spirit, rebuilt the town almost overnight.

In 1941, upon the return of Ho Chi Minh after 30 years of exile, Cao Bang became the Viet Bac region's epicenter—the mustering grounds for the Vietminh army. Over the course of World War II, Ho Chi Minh and a youthful General Giap patiently organized the "March to the South," or *Nam tien,* the phrase used in the 10th century when the Vietnamese migrated south of the Red River after gaining independence from a thousand years of Chinese rule. The command center for the modern-day struggle was Pac Bo Cave, nestled in the bosom of Karl Marx Peak, so named by Ho Chi Minh.

The morning broke clear and promising, but soon the monsoon spigot flowed. We put on our slickers and grudgingly left for Pac Bo in the familiar torrent, weaving through a nostalgic river valley churned by antique water wheels. Stacked-rock fences redolent of those seen in the Cotswolds of England lined Nung villages and fields in the shadow of karst mountainettes. Nung farmers harrowed the paddies while flowing stands of corn grew up to the river's edge.

The Nung, still favoring traditional dress, had inspired the incipient revolutionaries of Ho Chi Minh to accept the tribal ways and learn their language and rituals. Thus, in return for the respect the Vietminh showed for them and their culture, the Nung became willing combatants and arguably the reason the revolution succeeded.

We crossed a bridge over the turquoise waters of a stream, named Lenin Stream by Ho Chi Minh, before arriving at the park entrance in front of a kitsch stand. There, we gathered beneath the gaze of Karl Marx Peak, emblazoned in yellow with the Vietnamese name, "Nui Cac Mac."

Here Simon and I were at our destination, and yet it had been our journey that inspired and fascinated us. What a trail it had been through Indochina, in part our Asian Via Dolorosa. As for Pac Bo, it is sacred to the Vietnamese, similar to the holy places where Buddha once walked. In Vietnam's evolution toward independence, this place represented the chrysalis.

Retreating from the distant echo of water buffalo clanking their bells, we followed the limpid headwaters of Lenin Stream under a forest canopy. Signs designated the unique spot where Ho Chi Minh used to fish, and where General Giap had planted a tree in 1975 to commemorate Ho Chi Minh and the successful end to the revolution. We peeled off the paved trail up rock steps to the cave where Ho Chi Minh first encamped at Pac Bo before he had a cabin built by the stream.

Hidden behind a tumble of boulders and dense forest were two openings: one where a censer was placed for burning joss in front of a 15-foot dropoff into the cave; the other with natural steps leading down into the small, dank hideout. In the central chamber, several planks of wood were balanced on boulders, once used as a bed and for meetings of the inner sanctum. It was here that General Giap would remember the revolutionary teachings of the Great Patriot, "Like children listening to a legend."

Except for its history the cave was unremarkable. The sunlight reflected off the chandeliers of stalactites, furrowed from dampness like pickled limestone. A gnarly lump of gray, pitted rock rose from the earthen floor, once the pedestal for a famous carving Ho Chi Minh sculpted of Karl Marx, and which was long since destroyed in one of the Chinese incursions.

We stepped cautiously down the rocky hillside to the slippery banks of Lenin Stream, bubbling from the mountain in clear beginnings. Fingerlings darted underwater among the rocks over a pure white bed of sandy sediment. Beneath the commemorative tree planted by General Giap, we uncorked a bottle of French wine and picnicked on cheese, salami and baguettes. Two Nung kids sent by the concessionaires at the entry gate stalked us with cheap baubles for sale. Simon uncased his pad and pens and sketched scenes of the Arcadian communist beachhead.

I sat on a boulder positioned next to a natural rock table, feeling captive to the journey's emotions. While waiting out World War II, hiding from the French and Japanese, Ho Chi Minh used the same rock table to write about the revolution, often in Chinese quatrains:

Mountains and rivers as far as the eye can see,
What need for more space can there be,
Here's Lenin Stream, there Mount Marx,
With bare hands we are building a country.

As we picnicked at Pac Bo—the Arcadian petri dish for Ho Chi Minh's revolutionary ideas—the Communist Party back in Saigon was eating its young, voting to expel Mado and Dany for speaking out against Party corruption. At the same time in Laos, dead men were floating down the Mekong, felled in Golden Triangle skirmishes over opium and the region's new drug of choice, methamphetamine. In a forensic lab in Hawaii, Earthquake Magoon's bones were being analyzed, but still could not be pinned to an identity. After 29 years of nation-less limbo, 15,000 Laotian Hmong are preparing to leave the last of the refugee camps in Thailand for the United States. The deepening poverty in the lower Mekong Delta still supplies labor for Cambodia's prostitution industry, and the blind rage of the Pol Pot Time simmers like an untreated fever. Tons of landmines and unexploded ordnance lurks throughout the region to destroy the meager lives of peasants.

I couldn't help but ponder the fate of my old friend Tuck Freeman. After over three decades of domestic violence, failed school and work opportunities, he was recently diagnosed with PTSD, post-traumatic stress disorder. Unemployed, he now survives on his meager VA disability pay. In a recent conversation, I asked him what it was about his war-related condition that resonated with the VA psychiatrist who diagnosed him. In a voice that quavered, he said, "Thirty-six years of haunting dreams with a piece of shrapnel in the side of my face to stir them."

Still dancing with ghosts after all these years, at age 54, Tuck almost died recently from chronic pancreatitis. Though he is on the mend—playing his drums, reading and writing poetry—he lives alone in a trailer park in Oklahoma, divorced for 20 years, no children, his parents are dead; but for a few old army buddies, his friends are few and he is estranged from his only living sibling. Dispatched to Vietnam by trusted public servants, in 1968 Tuck marched valiantly into a war where so often the means are the ends: what you do becomes what you are.

In Hanoi and across Indochina, many locals, vets and expats are working towards peaceful development and lasting reconciliation. John Lancaster was a shining example among that group until recently when a freak car wreck in Hanoi left him with four leg fractures. Once again he was medivaced from Vietnam; first to a hospital in Bangkok for two months and from there to the Spinal Cord Injury Center at the Bronx VA Hospital. There he was joined by fellow vets—this time from Iraq.

Meanwhile, Indochina remains an important strategic outpost on the geopolitical map. The U.S. and Vietnam now have a bilateral trade agreement, which has led to a quadrupling of commerce between the former enemies—a two-way flow of prosperity. While we picnicked at Pac Bo the Communist Party was busy making plans to allow the first U.S. warship to cruise up the Saigon River since the end of the war. When the warship arrived in late 2003, all those Saigon taxi girls once again entertained a city full of American sailors, who departed two days later to enthusiastic, cheering crowds. John Lancaster concluded, "If you ask me, that was the end to the Vietnam war."

Before we adjourned at Pac Bo, sitting at Ho Chi Minh's rock table, I delivered an impromptu soliloquy as the Great Patriot himself:

"Dear Harry, now goddammit you haven't answered any of my letters and this shit with the French is getting damn serious. We're tired of smelling French shit. Right here at Pac Bo we rescued your goddamn pilots from the Japs during the Big One. Hell, I even got General Chennault's autographed picture up in my cave. Now we need your help. Are you for us or against us?"

Bibliography

Booth, Martin, *Opium, A History*, New York, St. Martin's Griffin, 1996

Caputo, Philip, *A Rumor of War*, New York, Henry Holt, 1977

Carne, Louis de, *Travels on the Mekong*, Bangkok, White Lotus reprint, 2000

Chandler, David, *A History of Cambodia*, Westview Press, Boulder, Co, 2000

Chandler, David, *Brother Number One, A Political Biography of Pol Pot*, Westview Press, Boulder, Co, 1999

Chandler, David, *Voices from S-21*, University of California Press, Los Angeles, 1999

Cox, Christopher, *Patterns of Hope*, Reader's Digest,

Duiker, William, *Ho Chi Minh*, New York, Hyperion, 2000

Fadiman, Anne, *The Spirit Catches You and You Fall Down*, New York, Noonday, 1997

Fall, Bernard, *Hell in a Very Small Place*, Cambridge, Ma, Da Capo Press, 1966

Fall, Bernard, *Street Without Joy*, Mechanicsburg, Pa, Stackpole Books, 1961

Fox, Martin Stuart, *The Lao Kingdom of Lan Xang: Rise and Decline*, Bangkok, White Lotus, 1998

Gargan, Edward A., *The River's Tale, A Year on the Mekong*, New York, Alfred A. Knopf, 2002

Garnier, Francis, *Travels in Cambodia and Part of Laos*, Bangkok, White Lotus reprint, 1996

Greene, Graham, *The Quiet American*, New York, Penguin, 1955

Halberstam, David, *War in a Time of Peace*, New York, Touchstone, 2001

Halberstam, David, *The Best and the Brightest*, New York, Ballantine, 1972

Herr, Michael, *Dispatches*, New York, Alfred Knopf, 1977

Iyer, Pico, *Video Nights in Kathmandu*, New York, Vintage Books, 1989

Jamieson, Neil, *Understanding Vietnam*, Los Angeles, University of California Press, 1993

Jarvis, Gary, *Young Blood*, Jacksonville, Fla, Jarvis Publishing, 1999

London, Athena Publishing, 2001

Karnow, Stanley, *Vietnam, A History*, New York, Penguin Books, 1983

Lamb, David, *Vietnam, Now*, New York, PublicAffairs, 2002

Lewis, Norman, *A Dragon Apparent, Travels in Cambodia, Laos, and Vietnam*, London, Eland, 1951

Livingston, Carol, *Gecko Tales, a Journey through Cambodia*, London, Phoenix, 1996

Mahout, Henry, *Travels in Siam, Cambodia, Laos, and Annam*, Bangkok, White Lotus reprint, 2000

McDonald, Mark, *Cambodian Underground Enslaves Girls, Women in Sex Trade*, San Jose Mercury News, December 22, 1999

Miller, Fiona, *Environmental threats to the Mekong*, World Bank document, February 17, 2000

Murphy, Dervla, *One Foot in Laos*, London, John Murray, 1999

Ngoc, Huu, *Vietnamese Culture*, Hanoi, Vietnam, Gioi Publishers, 1998

Osborne, Milton, *The Mekong, Turbulent Past, Uncertain Future*, New York, Grove Press, 2000

Page, Tim, *Derailed in Uncle Ho's Victory Garden,* London, Touchstone, 1995

Pham, Andrew, *Catfish and Mandala*, New York, Farrar, Straus and Giroux, 1999

Pipes, Richard, *Communism*, New York, The Modern Library, 2001

Poncins, Gontran de, *From a Chinese City in the Heart of Peacetime Vietnam*, Palo Alto, Trackless Sands Press, 1957

Prados, John, *The Blood Road*, New York, John Wiley and Sons, 1999

Richardson, Michael, *Illegal Logging Topples Cambodia's Forests*, International Herald Tribune, June 21, 2002

Robbins, Christopher, *The Ravens*, New York, Crown Publishers, 1995

Shapiro, Michael, *A Sense of Place*, San Francisco, Travelers' Tales, 2004

Sheehan, Neil, *A Bright Shining Lie*, New York, Vintage Books, 1988

Sheehan, Neil, *Two Cities: Hanoi and Saigon*, London, Jonathan Cape, 1992

Sophai, Chhay, *Mermaid Myths, Travelers Help Rare Mekong Dolphin*, Reuters, May 24, 2002

Stewart, Lucretia, *Tiger Balm, Travels in Laos, Vietnam, & Cambodia*, London, Chatto & Windus, 1998

Swain, Jon, *River of Time*, London, Minerva, 1996

Ta-Kuan, Chou, *The Customs of Cambodia, Bangkok*, The Siam Society, 1992

Taylor, Keith, *The Birth of Vietnam*, Los Angeles, University of California Press, 1983

Terzani, Tiziano, *A Fortune-Teller Told Me*, New York, Flamingo, 1998

Templer, Robert, *Shadows and Wind*, London, Little Brown and Company, 1998

Theroux, Paul, *The Great Railway Bazaar*, New York, Penguin, 1977

Tin, Bui, *Following Ho Chi Minh*, Honolulu, University of Hawaii Press, 1995

Warner, Roger, *Shooting at the Moon*, South Royalton, Vermont, Steerforth Press, 1996

Williams, Louise, *Wives, Mistresses & Matriarchs*, London, Phoenix, 1999

Wintle, Justin, *Romancing Vietnam*, London, Penguin Books, London, 1991

Zbarsky, Ilya, *Lenin's Embalmers*, London, The Harvill Press, 1997

Acknowledgements

My profuse thanks go to editors Brian Mertens and Crystal Ouyang, who recognized the worth of my overwritten manuscript, and laboriously whittled it into shape. Also I express my particular gratitude for the editorial feedback given by my wife, Joellen Lambiotte, by a host of informed readers and fact checkers, and to the generous people who appear in the book and have shared their stories and experiences with me. Among those, I am most indebted to Simon Redington, for his many contributions including the book's cover design, and to John Lancaster, for giving his voice and counsel to me from beginning to end. Though I have chosen to limit the names mentioned here, all these contributors know who they are, and as we are in contact, I will continue to acknowledge them personally.

There are a handful of characters in the book whose names I chose to change. The reasons for this vary, but mostly had to do with their residency in communist Indochina, where freedom of expression is often denied.

I have also used the compound spelling for some Indochina place names, which may not be consistent with the monosyllabic preferences of local languages, but are most commonly used outside the region. For example, *Hanoi* for *Ha Noi*, in Vietnam.

The book was written in a linear, narrative form, leaving the impression that the journey occurred in sequence. And for the most part it did. There are, however, discrete events embedded in the narrative that make it a composite of travel stories. Further, the bibliography was an invaluable resource for many ideas, facts and events found in the book. But in the end, I vouch for the accuracy of all details behind this personal journey.

Index

About the Author

Phil Karber was born in the Ozark Mountains of Arkansas on Halloween, 1951. He is married to Joellen Lambiotte, who works in international reproductive health, has two grown children, Maggie and Wes, and a grandchild, Parker.

Following a successful career in business, and after sending the children off to university, he joined Joellen in Nairobi, Kenya in the mid-nineties. While living there he began writing his first book, *Yak Pizza to Go!* By late 1998 he was residing in Hanoi,Vietnam, where he finished *Yak Pizza*, and over the next five years, wrote *The Indochina Chronicles*. He now divides his time between his residence in Bangkok, Thailand, and the developing world destinations to which he frequently travels.